Scholarly assessment of Jewish communities in the Hellenistic and Graeco-Roman Diaspora has generally been dominated by our knowledge of the large and influential communities in Rome and Alexandria. This is the first study to draw together evidence for significant Jewish communities in another part of the Diaspora, namely Asia Minor. By collating archaeological, epigraphic, classical, New Testament and patristic sources, the book provides an invaluable and coherent description of the life of Jewish communities in Asia Minor, and so gives a more complete picture than has been available hitherto of Jewish life at the time.

SOCIETY FOR NEW TESTAMENT STUDIES

MONOGRAPH SERIES

General Editor: G. N. Stanton

69

JEWISH COMMUNITIES IN ASIA MINOR

Jewish Communities
in Asia Minor

PAUL R. TREBILCO

Professor of New Testament Studies
Knox Theological Hall
University of Otago, Dunedin, New Zealand

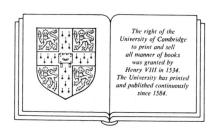

The right of the
University of Cambridge
to print and sell
all manner of books
was granted by
Henry VIII in 1534.
The University has printed
and published continuously
since 1584.

CAMBRIDGE UNIVERSITY PRESS

CAMBRIDGE
NEW YORK   PORT CHESTER
MELBOURNE   SYDNEY

Published by the Press Syndicate of the University of Cambridge
The Pitt Building, Trumpington Street, Cambridge CB2 1RP
40 West 20th Street, New York, NY 10011, USA
10 Stamford Road, Oakleigh, Melbourne 3166, Australia

© Cambridge University Press 1991

First published 1991

Printed in Great Britain at the University Press, Cambridge

British Library cataloguing in publication data
Trebilco, Paul R. (Paul Raymond) *1958–*
Jewish communities in Asia Minor – (Society for New
Testament Studies Monograph Series: 69)
1. Turkey. Jewish communities ancient period
I. Title   II. Series.
939.2004924

Library of Congress cataloguing in publication data
Trebilco, Paul R.
Jewish communities in Asia Minor/by Paul R. Trebilco.
        p.   cm. – (Monograph series/Society for New Testament
Studies: 69)
Rev. and abbreviated version of thesis (doctoral) – University of
Durham, 1987.
Includes bibliographical references and index.
ISBN 0 521 40120 8
1. Jews – Turkey – History.   2. Jews – Turkey – Antiquities.   3. Jews –
History – 168 B.C. – 135 A.D.   4. Turkey – History – To 1453.
I. Title.   II. Series.   III. Series: Monograph series (Society for
New Testament Studies): 69.
DS 135.T8T67 1991
956.1′01 – dc20   90-2296   CIP

ISBN 0 521 40120 8 hardback

WG

CONTENTS

PREFACE

This book is a revised and abbreviated version of a doctoral thesis presented to the Faculty of Theology of the University of Durham in October 1987. The thesis was prepared under the supervision of Professor James Dunn to whom I owe an immense debt of gratitude for his wise guidance, insightful comments and not least for his warm friendship.
I have profited greatly from discussions with a number of scholars. I would particularly like to thank Professor Thomas Kraabel,.Drs Tessa Rajak and Anthony Sheppard, and the late Dr Colin Hemer. In preparing the thesis for publication I have benefited from improvements suggested by my examiners, Professor Fergus Millar and Dr Robert Hayward. Dr Judith Lieu, Dr Chris Ehrhardt and Ron Mills read the whole manuscript and made many helpful comments. I would also like to thank Professor Graham Stanton for his encouragement and for including this work in the SNTS Monograph Series.
I am very grateful for financial support received from the University Grants Committee of New Zealand, the Committee of Vice-Chancellors and Principals of the Universities and Colleges in the United Kingdom, and the University of Otago. This work would not have been possible without such generous assistance. I am also indebted to the British Institute of Archaeology at Ankara for awarding me a Travel Grant which enabled me to visit a number of the sites discussed in this book.
Finally, I would like to thank my wife Gill for her loving support, encouragement and patience during the years in which I have worked on this book.

ABBREVIATIONS

As listed in the *Journal of Biblical Literature* 95, 1976, pp. 339–44, with the following additions:

AE	*L'Année épigraphique*
AJAH	*American Journal of Ancient History*
AJPh	*American Journal of Philology*
AM	*Mitteilungen des Deutschen Archäologischen Instituts, Athenische Abteilung*
ANRW	*Aufstieg und Niedergang der römischen Welt*
APF	*Archiv für Papyrusforschung und verwandte Gebiete*
AS	*Anatolian Studies*
BAR	*Biblical Archaeology Review*
BCH	*Bulletin de Correspondance Hellénique*
BE	*Bulletin Epigraphique*
BEFAR	Bibliothèque des Ecoles Françaises d'Athènes et de Rome
BJS	Brown Judaic Studies
BN	*Biblische Notizen*
CIG	*Corpus Inscriptionum Graecarum*
CIJ	J. B. Frey, *Corpus Inscriptionum Iudaicarum* I–II, 1939, 1951
CIJ²	J. B. Frey, *Corpus of Jewish Inscriptions* I, second edition, with Prolegomenon by B. Lifshitz, 1975.
CIRB	I. Struve, *Corpus Inscriptionum Regni Bosporani*, 1965
CPh	*Classical Philology*
CPJ	V. Tcherikover, A. Fuks, M. Stern, *Corpus Papyrorum Judaicorum* I–III, 1957–64
CQ	*Classical Quarterly*

CR	*Classical Review*
DAW	Denkschriften der Kaiserlichen Akademie der Wissenschaften in Wien
EJ	*Encyclopaedia Judaica*
EPRO	Etudes préliminaires aux religions orientales dans l'Empire Romain
G & R	*Greece & Rome*
HSCPh	*Harvard Studies in Classical Philology*
IG	*Inscriptiones Graecae.*
IGR	R. Cagnat *et al., Inscriptiones Graecae ad Res Romanas Pertinentes*
IGSK	Inschriften griechischer Städte aus Kleinasien
IM	*Mitteilungen des Deutschen Archäologischen Instituts, Istanbuler Abteilung*
IOSPE	I. Latyschev, *Inscriptiones Antiquae Orae Septentrionalis Ponti Euxini Graecae et Latinae*
JE	*The Jewish Encyclopedia*
JNSL	*Journal of Northwest Semitic Languages*
JÖAI	*Jahrbuch des Österreichischen Archäologischen Instituts*
JÖB	*Jahrbuch des Österreichischen Byzantinistik*
JPh	*Journal of Philology*
JS	*Journal des Savants*
JSNT	*Journal for the Study of the New Testament*
JSNTSS	Journal for the Study of the New Testament Supplement Series
JSOT	*Journal for the Study of the Old Testament*
JSOTSS	Journal for the Study of the Old Testament Supplement Series
LBW	P. Le Bas, W.H. Waddington, *Voyage archéologique en Grèce et en Asie Mineure. Vol. III,* 1870
MAMA	*Monumenta Asiae Minoris Antiqua*
MB	*Musée Belge*
MH	*Museum Helveticum*
NC	*Numismatic Chronicle*
New Docs	G.H.R. Horsley, *New Documents Illustrating Early Christianity Vol.1 (2, 3, 4). A Review of the Greek Inscriptions and Papyri published in 1976 (1977, 1978, 1979)*

OCD	N. G. L. Hammond, H. H. Scullard, eds., *The Oxford Classical Dictionary,* second edition, 1970
OGIS	W. Dittenberger, *Orientis Graeci Inscriptiones Selectae* I–II
PCPhS	*Proceedings of the Cambridge Philological Society*
RDAC	*Rivista di Archeologia Cristiana*
RE	Pauly-Wissowa, *Realencyclopädie der classischen Altertumswissenschaft*
REA	*Revue des études anciennes*
REG	*Revue des études grecques*
REL	*Revue des études latines*
RF	*Rivista di filologia*
RhM	*Rheinisches Museum für Philologie*
RIDA	*Revue internationale des droits de l'antiquité*
RPh	*Revue de philologie*
RQH	*Revue des questions historiques*
SEG	*Supplementum Epigraphicum Graecum*
SIG	W. Dittenberger, *Sylloge Inscriptionum Graecarum*³
TAM	*Tituli Asiae Minoris*
YCS	*Yale Classical Studies*
ZPE	*Zeitschrift für Papyrologie und Epigraphik*

Map of Asia Minor

PONTUS

CAPPADOCIA

GALATIA

CILICIA

BITHYNIA

PHRYGIA

LYCAONIA

PAMPHYLIA

PISIDIA

ASIA

LYDIA

CARIA

IONIA

LYCIA

100 miles
150 kilometres

50   100

0   50

0

Mopsuestia
Mallus
Tarsus
Corycus
Nazianzus
Ankara
Lystra
Iconium
Antioch
Dokimion
Prymnessos
Synnada
Eumeneia
Celaenae
Apamea
Laodicea
Heracleia
Salbace
Sillyum
Side
Termessos
Oenoanda
Phaselis
Aizani
Dorylaion
Nicaea
Cyzicus
Parium
Adramyttium
Thyateira
Pergamum
Phocaea
Smyrna
Sardis
Hypaepa
Philadelphia
Sala
Sebaste
Acmonia
Hierapolis
Nysa
Tralles
Aphrodisias
Priene
Magnesia
Ephesus
Teos
Samos
Miletus
Iasos
Myndos
Mylasa
Hyllarima
Stratoniceia
Halicarnassus
Cos
Cnidus
Amorgos
Island
Mytilene

INTRODUCTION

It is well known that in the Hellenistic and Roman eras there were Jewish communities throughout the then civilised world. This study is devoted to the investigation of one part of the Jewish Diaspora, Asia Minor. In this area Jewish communities were established at a quite early date and seem to have flourished. The decrees given in *Jewish Antiquities* 14 and 16, which are largely from Asia Minor, were understood by Josephus as setting important precedents showing that the situation of the Jewish communities in Asia Minor was significant for Diaspora Judaism in general. From some time in the third century CE until the seventh century the community at Sardis owned the largest and most impressive synagogue yet discovered. Many other factors suggest that these communities have a significant place in the history of the Jewish Diaspora. Further, an understanding of the Jewish communities in Asia Minor is important for the study of early Christianity. Paul travelled extensively in Asia Minor, lived for a lengthy period in Ephesus, founded significant churches in the area, and engaged in debate with both Jew and Gentile there. It is therefore arguable that, in addition to the Jewish communities in Palestine, those in Asia Minor are an important context within which to view Paul's mission and theology.[1] Other documents in the New Testament can also be located in Asia Minor, and it is to be hoped that a greater understanding of Jewish communities in this area will further elucidate these works. Early Christian communities flourished in Asia Minor throughout the first three centuries CE and beyond, and our understanding of their development and the literature they produced will be enriched by a greater understanding of Jewish communities in Asia Minor.[2]

Even though the focus of scholarly attention has generally been elsewhere in the Diaspora, most notably in Rome and Egypt, there have been significant studies of Jewish communities in Asia Minor. On a number of occasions Ramsay drew together the evidence

1

available to him on this topic.[3] Although other useful studies followed,[4] it was not until 1968 that the first lengthy treatment of this area was written by Kraabel. All subsequent research has been indebted to him, although unfortunately his work has remained unpublished.[5] Further studies, either of the whole area or of particular communities, have followed.[6] However, despite the fact that a significant amount of attention has been devoted to this area, we still lack a detailed analysis of the evidence and its synthesis, as far as this is possible, into a description of Jewish life in Asia Minor. It is this task which is carried forward here.

The material available to us in this investigation is diverse. Whilst, unfortunately, we do not have a substantial literary corpus from Jews in Asia Minor, some literary sources are of help.[7] Further, a number of Jewish inscriptions from a variety of places have been found, and archaeological evidence is provided by the synagogues discovered at Sardis and Priene. Reliance on inscriptional and archaeological evidence has both advantages and disadvantages and these need to be noted here. Inscriptions provide us with direct access to people in their contexts, to the language they used and to what they did, thought and valued, which is often information we cannot gain from any other source. In addition, inscriptions continue to be discovered and so provide completely new areas of knowledge and fresh insight into old problems.

However, there are a number of difficulties which arise from the nature of inscriptional evidence.[8] Firstly, this evidence is only partial. Inscriptions tend to be formal, public documents of a limited nature, and only events or honours which were considered sufficiently important were commemorated on stone, which was not inexpensive. Thus, a limited range of human activity and experience formed the subject matter of inscriptions. Further, only some inscriptions happen to have survived, and only some of what has survived has been found and published. Many of these inscriptions are fragmentary or damaged and the problems of establishing the text can be substantial. The evidence available to us, then, is a minute sub-category of the potential evidence for ancient life. In the case of Jewish inscriptions from Asia Minor these factors limit the range of our knowledge substantially. Whole areas of life do not appear at all in the inscriptions or do so only tangentially. For example, no inscription gives a summary of a synagogue sermon and we have no record of detailed Biblical exegesis on stone nor any statement of how Jewish communities educated their children. The partial nature of what was inscribed and the accidents of survival and discovery mean that the results of epigraphic studies will always be partial.[9]

Secondly, inscriptions are often short and provide little by way of a context for interpretation. Often other evidence provided by archaeology, numismatics or literary sources must be used to provide an intelligible framework. Yet, this framework may be misleading or less suitable than another possibility. This is particularly difficult in the present case since we do not have a substantial body of documents from Jewish communities in Asia Minor. This problem means that inscriptions need to be studied in groups, generally by locality or theme, in order to gain a sufficient concentration of evidence, and this is the approach followed here. Thirdly, there is the problem of dating. Some inscriptions contain a date, given according to a known system; others can be dated approximately through letter-forms, nomenclature or from their archaeological context. However, dates are often uncertain and this makes discussions of chronology difficult. Fourthly, the Jewish inscriptions available to us are very 'local' in nature and often make no reference to the wider events of a period. This makes it difficult to determine how broader historical events and changing circumstances affected the Jewish communities. Finally, the collection of Jewish inscriptions, *Corpus Inscriptionum Iudaicarum*, edited by Frey, is both inaccurate and incomplete and must be emended and supplemented by other studies.[10]

There are obvious advantages in the use of archaeological evidence: the directness and immediacy of access to ancient life and culture, the independence of archaeological method and the fact that new evidence is constantly being discovered. However, there are also difficulties. Foremost is the problem of interpretation. Is the proposed interpretation of these 'mute stones' the only possible historical reconstruction, or has the evidence been misunderstood by, for example, forcing a connection with known historical events, imposing the wrong framework or asking the wrong questions? Other difficulties include the problem of dating and establishing a chronology, the relative weighting of conflicting evidence and the problem of incomplete excavation or of excavation done before the development of more sophisticated archaeological methods.[11] These factors have had to be borne in mind during this study.

In this work, an examination of the evidence for Jewish communities in Asia Minor provided by literary sources is followed by three studies of Jewish communities for which the concentration of evidence enables a picture of Jewish life in context to emerge. Four thematic studies of issues which were significant in a number of different communities follow.[12] The temporal parameters of this investigation correspond with those of the evidence. Thus, most attention is devoted to the period from the late third century BCE to the third and fourth centuries CE.

I have sought to describe and to understand the available evidence in its own terms and for its own sake and to let the issues addressed arise from the material itself. Thus, I have sought to avoid approaching the evidence with an agenda from research in the NT or in Rabbinic literature in mind, but have endeavoured to assess and investigate the patterns and issues which are germane and central to the evidence itself.[13] Accordingly, a number of questions raised by the evidence have been kept in view throughout. For example, what was the nature of Jewish community life in Asia Minor? What can we know of the 'Jewish identity' of these Jewish communities? What sort of relationship existed between the cities and the Jewish communities? How did they respond to the influence of the predominant culture? It is to be hoped that this will lead to the description of Jewish communities in Asia Minor on their own terms as far as this is possible within the confines of the evidence.

1

JEWISH COMMUNITIES OF ASIA MINOR IN LITERARY SOURCES

Josephus, Philo, Cicero, the New Testament and Patristic sources provide us with information concerning the foundation and developing life of Jewish communities in Asia Minor. They will be dealt with here.

1 Antiochus III and the transportation of Jews to Phrygia and Lydia

Josephus quotes three documents ascribed to Antiochus III, the third of which is a letter to Zeuxis, the governor of Lydia (Ant 12:148–53), written by Antiochus III whilst he was in the East between 212 and 205/4 BCE. He wrote to his strategos Zeuxis with instructions concerning the settlement of 2,000 Jewish families in Lydia and Phrygia in an attempt to maintain internal security in the region, which was beset by unrest.[1] The Seleucids, like other Hellenistic dynasties, founded a large number of colonies or cities throughout their Empire. These foundations began as civilian colonies, garrisons of active soldiers or settlements of retired or reserve soldiers. The particular interests which led to the founding of colonies included the need to protect lines of communication, trade routes or frontier zones and the desire to halt rebellion.[2] The transportation of the Jews to Lydia and Phrygia fits into this general pattern.

The authenticity of the letter has been both impugned and defended.[3] We can note the following points in the debate which favour authenticity. Firstly, the letter is in keeping with the conventional Hellenistic form employed by a king writing to an individual and conforms stylistically to Seleucid documents of the period. Secondly, there is nothing unusual in the arrangements which suggests a forgery; the normal procedure followed by the Seleucids when founding a colony is adhered to. Thirdly, none of the objections which have been raised against authenticity stand up to examination.[4]

Since many scholars now think that the letter is authentic, we can proceed to use it as evidence for the settlement of Jews in Asia Minor.[5]

The following details emerge from the letter. Firstly, 2,000 Jewish families were sent to Lydia and Phrygia, which means that the total number of people probably exceeded 10,000. They were distributed among an unspecified number of sites, so we cannot estimate the size of any one settlement.[6] Secondly, the choice of Jews from Mesopotamia and Babylonia was probably prompted by a number of considerations. The Jews of this region were known (at least later) for their effectiveness as soldiers. Moreover, Antiochus was in the East at the time and he knew that the Jews were loyal to his interests. Thus the Jews were to maintain a pro-Seleucid presence at or near various strategically located τόποι and φρούρια in order to establish Seleucid rule in the area and thus hopefully to guarantee the peace.[7] Thirdly, the colonists were to be allowed to use their own laws and to have a degree of separate organisation, arrangements which would have made the prospect of colonisation much more attractive to the Jews.[8] They were also granted land for homes, farming and viticulture, very favourable exemptions from tax and as much grain as was needed to ensure that the settlements flourished and became permanent. Antiochus seems to have been eager to win the colonists' good will. These favourable terms probably meant that the Jewish communities concerned began well; this would have had a decisive influence on the character of the communities. Fourthly, the letter shows that the first large settlement of Jews in Asia Minor for which we have evidence came from another part of the Diaspora, that is, from Babylonia and Mesopotamia, and this is significant. We can infer that these Jews would already have adjusted to Diaspora life and would not have found the issues which faced them in Lydia and Phrygia (such as their remoteness from Jerusalem, the need to adjust to life in a pagan land and matters of internal organisation) as difficult as new settlers from Palestine would have done. This may have led to the early establishment of strong, confident Jewish communities in Asia Minor.

Other evidence suggests that Jewish communities were established in a number of cities in Asia Minor by 139–8 BCE. In 1 Macc. 15:16–23 we have a circular letter written by the Roman Senate at this time in support of the Jews and sent to a number of places. The list of recipients is not just the names of allies but areas and cities where Jews were living and were in need of support.[9] Within Asia

Minor letters were sent to Attalus II, king of Pergamum and Ariarathes V, king of Cappadocia and to the cities of Myndos, Halicarnassus and Cnidus in Caria, Phaselis in Lycia and Side in Pamphylia, which were all independent cities at this time. Copies were also sent to the areas of Caria, Lycia and Pamphylia.[10] We can conclude that there were Jews in these kingdoms, cities and areas in 139–8 BCE. Jewish settlement seems to have continued as time went on, so that in the first century CE Philo could report in Flacc. 281–2 that there were Jewish colonies in most countries, including 'Pamphylia, Cilicia, most of Asia as far as Bithynia and the remote corners of Pontus.' We know of Jewish communities in over fifty places in Asia Minor during the Imperial period; doubtless there were many more.[11]

2 The decree of Pergamum

Josephus cites a number of documents which deal with Jewish rights and privileges. These documents present numerous technical problems relating to the state of the texts, their dating and the puzzling order in which they are arranged. Although the authenticity of the decrees to be examined here has been recently questioned by Moehring, his case against their authenticity rests on minor aberrations in the text which can be satisfactorily explained by the history of transmission of the documents. As Rajak notes, detailed investigation confirms 'that the formal features of the documents are correct for genre and period to a degree which makes it very difficult to conceive of them as forgeries'.[12] Thus, most recent investigators have accepted the authenticity of the decrees,[13] which can therefore be used here as evidence for the Jewish communities in Asia Minor.

Ant 14:247–55, a decree of the people of Pergamum to be dated in the time of Antiochus VII Sidetes (138–129 BCE) or Antiochus IX Cyzicenus (113–95 BCE), explains that Jewish envoys had arrived in the city after receiving a favourable ruling on the affairs of Hyrcanus I from the Roman Senate. The people of Pergamum stated that they would take care that the Senate's decree was fulfilled and that they would do everything possible on behalf of the Jews. A copy of Pergamum's decree was to be sent to Hyrcanus along with envoys to assure him of 'the friendly interest of our people'.[14]

It is probable that Jews were actually resident in Pergamum at this time. Two generations after this event Cicero mentions that Flaccus seized a small amount of gold destined for Jerusalem from Pergamum;

some of it almost certainly came from Jews resident in the city itself. Hence, the envoys travelling from Rome to Jerusalem probably made the detour to Pergamum, not only because it was an important city, but also in order to visit the Jewish community there.[15] The decree suggests that the city of Pergamum would have had a positive attitude towards the Jewish community living in its midst. It would be surprising for the city to be positive towards the Jews of Palestine (as the decree shows), yet hostile towards its own Jewish community.[16] Josephus preserves no later documents from Pergamum, which suggests that in the first century BCE the Jewish community's relations with the city were good.

The decree mentions one Theodorus who was not an envoy of Hyrcanus but was admitted to the council and assembly of Pergamum carrying the letter and decree of the Senate. His name appears suddenly in the text without introduction, which suggests that he was already known because he was an inhabitant of Pergamum. He spoke of the virtues and generosity of Hyrcanus, which suggests he was a Jew. Perhaps he was an important member of the Jewish community of the city, who was sufficiently respected to be allowed to speak to the council and assembly and who was able to convince them to adopt his recommendations.[17] This suggests that the Jewish community in Pergamum, at some point during the last three decades of the second century BCE, enjoyed good relations in the city.

3 Roman support for the privileges of the Jewish communities in Asia Minor

The other documents Josephus cites show that on a number of occasions the Roman authorities granted various privileges to different Jewish communities. These included the right to be organised as a community, to administer their own finances, to observe the Sabbath and to be exempt from duties such as military service that conflicted with the full observance of Jewish Law. This grant of privileges for the Jewish communities in Asia Minor and elsewhere was often made in the face of local opposition from the cities in which the Jews lived. Thus, Roman support was vital and enabled these Jewish communities to continue as self-supporting communities that observed various Jewish customs.[18]

One way of explaining the fact that the Romans supported the position of the Jews is to say that Judaism was placed in the formal category of a *religio licita*. This, of course, would include the Jewish communities in Asia Minor. Consequently, a number of scholars speak of the documents associated with Julius Caesar as a 'charter of Jewish rights' that enshrined their special privileges.[19] However, Rajak has recently shown that this model is inappropriate for the Roman world.[20] Behind the model of a charter is the concept that the Jews were an intrinsically exclusive group within the homogeneous city and hence required different treatment from other groups. However, the Jews were not completely alien, and the Hellenistic polis accommodated considerable diversity of population without demanding uniformity. Thus:

> What Jewish communities needed was not the award of a special status, but, more simply, public backing with muscle behind it ... For the most part, I would suggest, Jewish *nomoi* were not formally incompatible with city requirements, though they could become contentious if the populace or the officials wanted to make life awkward ... But it was not in the very nature of the *polis* to exclude such activities and in the normal course of events they must have proceeded without question. It is for this reason that it is unsatisfactory to talk of the permanent need for *privilegia* from Rome, while it is right to stress the repeated necessity for outside, i.e. Roman help.[21]

It has been thought that the Hellenistic kings established Jewish communities on the basis of just this sort of charter. However, apart from statements in Josephus, which do not actually prove the existence of a charter, little can be known of the status of Jews in this earlier period. The permission to live 'according to their ancestral laws' was granted by Antiochus III to Jews in Coele-Syria and in Phrygia and Lydia, but this does not amount to a charter, which would have required legal precision.[22] We cannot extrapolate from these two specific situations to formulate conclusions about the terms on which Jews lived in new or established cities. Although the Romans inherited this principle of toleration from the Seleucids, it seems that the position of Jewish communities was not clearly defined before Roman rule. At Ephesus and elsewhere in Ionia it was over two generations after the beginning of Roman rule in the area that we first hear of Roman intervention on the question of Jewish status. This is probably because formal arrangements were not at issue since there had not been any generally understood settlement of the question in the past.[23] The Romans, then, did not inherit a 'Jewish charter'.

It has often been thought that the legislation associated with Julius Caesar formed the 'Jewish Magna Carta'. However, the documents do not provide an overall definition of Jewish religious liberty.[24] It is important to consider whether, in the *Romans'* perception, the documents had a general application or any validity as a precedent beyond the specific context in which they were issued. Pliny's correspondence (admittedly somewhat later) shows that Trajan distinguished clearly between universally applicable imperial rulings and those intended for certain provinces.[25] Although Josephus at times introduces the documents as if they concerned Jewish status universally, none of the texts themselves have an entirely general reference.[26] What happened in provinces where Jews had not appealed to the authorities was undetermined; we are not able to generalise. Even when we do have evidence for the grant of privileges in a certain number of cities, there is considerable variation in the constituent elements of the grant from city to city. Rome responded to the needs of the moment according to the prevailing political situation, making ad hoc decisions with differing details rather than following the predetermined guidelines of a charter.[27]

It was Claudius who for the first time made a sweeping pronouncement in 41/42 CE applying to the whole empire.[28] Faced with Greek–Jewish crises in Palestine, Alexandria and perhaps Antioch, he formulated a general policy of toleration for Jewish observances throughout the Empire in an attempt to circumvent any planned trouble in other cities. Thus Claudius wrote: 'It is right therefore that Jews throughout the whole world under our sway should also observe the customs of their fathers without let or hindrance' (Ant 19:290). Yet, even this general grant was of a limited nature. The policy was not spelt out in detail but expressed in general phrases of intent. Indeed, Claudius seems to have stressed his goodwill towards the practice of the Jewish cult but to have left it up to the Greek cities to act in accordance with his will. This arrangement was neither systematic nor precise and falls well short of being a 'charter of Jewish rights'. We conclude, therefore, that Jewish communities in Asia Minor did not have their privileges enshrined in a 'charter'.

However, it is nonetheless clear that the Roman authorities, whether Emperors or proconsuls, were willing to support privileges for Jewish communities, including communities in Asia Minor, on an ad hoc basis even if this support was not in the form of a charter. We may suggest a number of reasons for this support. Firstly, as far as we know, the Hellenistic monarchies generally supported the Jews in their Empires.[29] The Romans usually followed the precedent of the status quo ante and so in supporting the Jews were probably following the pattern which had already been established by their predecessors.[30] Secondly, it is important to note the personal nature of many of the transactions mentioned in the documents. They are part of an exchange of *beneficia* and often result from gratitude or mutual esteem between two leaders. This is seen in the relations between Hyrcanus II and Julius Caesar through which Hyrcanus gained a clearly defined role and privileges for the Jews in return for his assistance of, and support for, Caesar. In addition, the friendship between Marcus Agrippa and Herod the Great enabled the Jews of Ionia to obtain a hearing before Agrippa. It is likely that personal factors and the diplomacy they made possible were more significant in gaining support for the Jewish communities than any real sympathy for the Jews on the part of the Roman leaders.[31] Thirdly, toleration was an important principle for the Roman administration. As long as the Jewish communities and their religion were thought to be politically innocuous and morally unobjectionable, and as long as they did not cause trouble as a group, they could be treated with tolerance.[32] Fourthly, the political fidelity and support of the Jews in strategic Palestine and beyond was important. Rome could avoid unrest by supporting Jewish privileges throughout their domain.[33]

These documents also reveal a significant degree of hostility towards Jewish communities on the part of the Greek cities in Asia Minor and elsewhere. It is most likely that there were a number of reasons for this hostility. However, we should emphasise at the outset that relations were not always and everywhere bad, nor were there no Greeks who were well-disposed towards the Jews. Josephus unwittingly highlighted the tensions that existed because the decrees he used to show that the Romans supported the Jews arose out of difficult situations. We do not hear directly of harmony between Jewish communities and the cities because no documents would result from such a situation. Yet we cannot assume that such situations did not exist.[34]

Why were the cities hostile at times to the Jewish communities? Rajak thinks that the evidence of the decrees suggests that they were necessary only because of deliberately engineered attacks on Jewish practices, the attacks themselves being founded on pagan lack of tolerance.[35] Simple dislike of non-conformity was probably the basis of the problem combined with the strangeness of Jewish religious practices. Jewish monotheism and customs were distinctive and

Jewish religion was not compatible with other religious options.[36] In addition, some of the requests of the Jews, such as their desire to send large sums of money to Jerusalem even when the province was experiencing economic problems or their refusal to serve in the army, must have been annoying in themselves. Finally, Jewish communities were dependent on Roman support in the face of hostility from Greek authorities. The privileges granted by Rome were bound to be disputed by, and the cause of annoyance to, the people of the local city, who would have seen such intervention as unwanted interference in the internal affairs of the city. This situation would no doubt create a vicious circle in which renewed appeals for Roman intervention would serve to incite further local hostility.[37] Thus, we can conclude that there were a number of reasons for the hostility of the cities in Asia Minor towards their Jewish communities.

It is very difficult to assess the reception the Roman decrees and letters received in the cities of Asia Minor. However, it is clear that Roman directives were sometimes ignored or overlooked by the cities in an attempt to evade their responsibilities. A Milesian citizen told the proconsul that, in spite of the proconsul's previous instructions, the Jews were being hindered in the observance of their own laws. The proconsul replied in favour of the Jews, but the correspondence shows that something like a continuous dispute was going on.[38] We should also note that Josephus only presents evidence which is favourable to the Jews. It is likely that some Jewish claims to rights were either rejected by the Romans or later by the Greek cities. In addition, some cities could have chosen to flout decrees that were passed.[39] Hence, from the evidence we do have and from the likelihood that this evidence is one-sided, we can deduce that the decrees were probably not followed at times.

4 Facets of Jewish identity in Asia Minor as revealed by these documents

The documents under discussion here are generally viewed solely from the perspective of the political or legal history of the Jews. However, the light the documents shed on the religious concerns of Jewish communities in Asia Minor is also invaluable.[40] They reveal a concern on the part of the communities with a number of matters that are central to Jewish identity.

The right of assembly and the synagogue

A prerequisite for Jews wanting to have a communal life was the right of assembly. This should not be taken for granted, especially when it is remembered that Julius Caesar forbade most collegia to meet in Rome. The right to assemble is mentioned several times in documents addressed to Jewish communities in Asia Minor. For example, 'Julius Gaius' wrote to the people of Parium noting that Julius Caesar had explicitly exempted Jewish synagogues in Rome from the ban on collegia. Likewise he permitted the Jews in Parium to assemble and feast in accordance with their tradition. Clearly, some Jewish communities in Asia Minor were granted the right of assembly when such a grant was necessary.[41]

We also have evidence of permission being granted to build a synagogue. The people of Halicarnassus passed a decree stating that the Jews 'may build places of prayer (προσευχάς) near the sea in accordance with their ancestral custom' (Ant 14:256–8). In a decree of the people of Sardis the Jews were granted a place for prayer and a place to live in.[42] A decree of Augustus states that Jewish buildings in the province of Asia were to be safeguarded by the ruling that theft of the Temple tax or of rolls of Scripture from the synagogue should be considered as sacrilege and punished by the confiscation of property.[43] Accordingly, we can conclude that the Jews in Asia Minor were granted permission, when it was required or had been disputed, to assemble and to build synagogues and that the sanctity of these synagogues was on occasions safeguarded by the Roman authorities.

The Temple tax

The Temple tax involved the annual payment of a half-shekel (two drachmae or denarii in Josephus' time) by every male Jew, including freed-slaves and proselytes, between the ages of twenty and fifty. The tax was transported to Jerusalem where it was intended to support public sacrifices and the city's municipal needs.[44] The earliest reference to the Temple tax in Asia Minor is found in Ant 14:112–13 where Josephus, quoting from Strabo, describes how Mithridates raided Cos shortly after 88 BCE and seized money deposited by Cleopatra III along with 800 talents belonging to the Jews. Josephus argues that the Jewish money must have been sent there by Jews in Asia Minor because of their fear of Mithridates, who was then overrunning the mainland, and that the money was the Temple tax. Josephus' explanation of the source (of at least some) of the money is more satisfactory than any of the alternatives proposed by modern interpreters.[45]

In 59 BCE Cicero defended L. Valerius Flaccus against charges of misappropriation of public funds when he was the Roman governor of Asia. Included in these funds were amounts of Jewish Temple Tax which Flaccus had seized from four cities in 62 BCE: a little less than one hundred pounds from Apamea, a little more than twenty pounds from Laodicea, an unknown amount from Adramyttium and a small amount from Pergamum. Marshall has estimated that the one hundred pounds of gold from Apamea was equivalent to about 135,000 drachmae, which would give a huge Jewish population if it was the tax for only one year. However, it is most likely that the money represents more than one year's contribution. Asian Jews had probably not sent off their annual tax for some time prior to 62 BCE because of disturbed conditions in Jerusalem, so when it was sent in 62 an unusually large amount of money would have been involved. In addition, it is likely that the gold was the sum total of the tax from a number of communities in the vicinity of each city since the four cities mentioned by Cicero were each centres of a regional conventus. We also know that additional gifts of gold to the Temple were occasionally forwarded with the tax. Thus, although it remains impossible to estimate the number of Jews in these areas, we can see that large Jewish populations were involved, particularly at Apamea.[46]

The central features of the incident, which Cicero claims to have been commonly agreed by the prosecution, are as follows. Flaccus issued an edict forbidding the export of gold from his province and then confiscated the gold collected by Asian Jews that was intended for the Jerusalem Temple. The money, duly entered in Flaccus' accounts, was deposited with the aerarium. Cicero claims that these facts reflect credit upon Flaccus instead of the discredit urged by the prosecution. Marshall has shown that Flaccus' motive in confiscation was not anti-Jewish sentiment and that his intention was not to steal the money but rather to put into effect the edictal ban. Flaccus enforced a repeatedly re-enacted ruling of the Senate, banning the export of gold and silver from the provinces, that had previously been ignored by Roman officials. The reasons that Flaccus enforced the edict in 62 BCE were probably varied but included reluctance to allow gold to go to a recently conquered city, the fact that a recent ban on collegia may have meant the synagogue attracted the adverse notice of the Roman authorities and the difficult economic situation of Asia Minor at the time, worsened by the recent charge of supporting Pompey's armies. Thus, Asia Minor could not afford the drain on gold involved in the Temple tax being transported to Jerusalem. When the Jews defied Flaccus' recently promulgated decree, he enforced the ban and confiscated the money out of economic necessity.[47]

It becomes clear, then, that the Jews of Asia had been caught in an attempt to defy Roman law in order to obey their own religious law. The money was confiscated because they deliberately disobeyed an edict that they regarded as an unacceptable interference in their religious customs. Their action must have been rooted in conviction and shows the strength of their loyalty with regard to paying the tax and thus towards Jerusalem and its worship. This was a significant facet of their Jewish identity.

We have a number of documents from Asia Minor dating to the time of Augustus which relate to the right of Jewish communities to collect money and to send it to the Temple in Jerusalem without any outside interference. In order to pay the Temple tax, various Jewish communities in Asia Minor sought either explicit permission to do so or the right to administer their own finance. Clearly this issue had become particularly controversial in Augustus' time. Perhaps now that there was a settled government in Rome concerned with long-term stability in the provinces, the Jewish communities thought it worthwhile to expend effort in order to obtain a durable privilege in this regard. The decrees which we have relate to the cities of Ephesus and Sardis and to the province of Asia.[48]

The documents note that sending the tax to Jerusalem is κατὰ τὸ πάτριον αὐτοῖς ἔθος.[49] This suggests that the Jewish communities probably explained that the tax was an established commitment. In addition, in a decree to the Ephesians, Agrippa stated that anyone who stole the Jews' ἱερὰ χρήματα would be deemed to have despoiled a sanctuary and be unable to claim asylum, a right that was generally reserved for pagan temples.[50] In another decree to the Jews of Asia, Augustus stated that the Jews' sacred money was inviolable and could be sent to Jerusalem and that anyone stealing it would be regarded as sacrilegious and subject to Roman criminal jurisdiction.[51] We observe here a willingness to grant the Jews the same safeguards for their 'holy funds' as were granted to pagan temples.

The documents show that the Jews specifically requested the authorisation granted in the decrees. Roman Emperors and other officials generally responded to requests or petitions from individuals or groups, rather than searching out potential difficulties, which they then attempted to pre-empt. Thus, for example, correspondence between the Emperor and provincial governors or cities was almost always initiated by the governors or the cities themselves.[52] The letters we have from various Emperors concerning Jews are clearly of this sort and show that the Jews were willing to approach the Emperors for privileges, which in itself indicates the extent of Jewish concern for the matters in dispute. The procedure involved is completely in keeping with what we know of Imperial communication and of the Roman style of government.

There are a number of indications in these decrees that the Jewish communities themselves approached the authorities in order to obtain the privileges associated with the tax. From a letter to Ephesus written by the proconsul Julius Antonius, we learn that the Jews had approached the proconsul asking him to ratify their privileges and, in order to convince him, had referred to permission granted to them by Augustus and Agrippa. It seems they wanted to forestall any attempt to prohibit the export of the tax and implies that the community was anticipating, rather than actually experiencing, difficulty in this regard.[53] Other examples could be cited. We see, then, that some Jewish communities in Asia Minor (and elsewhere) felt sufficiently committed to the Temple tax to take active measures to ensure that they could pay it. They approached the higher authorities in order to be able to maintain a custom which, in their eyes, was vital.

The Temple tax was connected with the notion that the daily sacrifices were to be provided by the entire community of Israel. The payment of the tax by the Jews of the Diaspora was a way for them to be a tangible part of the worship offered in Jerusalem.[54] In the concern of the Jews of Asia Minor in this period to pay the tax, we see a strong attachment to the historic land of Israel and to the centrality of the Temple and its worship.

Jewish communities and military service

Jewish communities were not able to observe all their customs unless they were exempt from activities which conflicted with their own law. One important area in which an exemption was sought was military service. In this period the normal method of legionary recruitment was by voluntary enlistment and thus any Jews who held Roman citizenship had only to refrain from coming forward to avoid the difficulties for Jews caused by being in the army.[55] However, in a crisis, conscription was used and Jews were then liable for call-up. In 49 BCE in just such a crisis the consul L. Lentulus Crus was recruiting in Asia for the senatorial cause. In response to an appeal on the Jews' behalf, he issued an edict exempting Jews who were Roman citizens in Ephesus from military service. In 43 BCE an exemption which covered all Jews in Asia was given.[56]

The reasons why the Jews requested these exemptions are explained in a letter written by Dolabella to Ephesus in 44/43 BCE. Alexander, an envoy of Hyrcanus II, had explained to Dolabella that Jews 'cannot undertake military service because they may not bear arms or march on the days of the Sabbath; nor can they obtain the native foods to which they are accustomed'.[57] These exemptions are thus evidence for the commitment of Jews in Asia to the Sabbath and food laws, to which we will now turn.[58]

The Sabbath

A number of documents preserved by Josephus relate to the Sabbath.[59] It is clear from these documents that on occasions the Roman authorities granted the Jews permission to observe the Sabbath without disturbance and were prepared to protect this privilege from violation. Perhaps this is clearest in a letter of the proconsul Publius Servilius Galba to Miletus in which he says that it was the administration's wish that the Jews be allowed to observe the Sabbath and perform their native rites.[60] The documents show that the Jews themselves had sought the authorities' permission in order to be able to keep the Sabbath. For example, from a decree of the people of Sardis we learn that the Jews of that city had appeared before the Council and People and asked that their privileges, including the right to observe the Sabbath, might be ratified.[61] This demonstrates the concern of the Jewish communities to protect their Jewish identity, of which keeping the Sabbath was an important part.

At times it is clear that Jewish leaders of Jerusalem had approached the Roman authorities to obtain privileges for the Jews in Asia Minor. For example, we read that an envoy of Hyrcanus II delivered a letter from the proconsul Gaius Rabirius to the people of Laodicea that supported Jewish privileges in Phrygia. The letter shows that people sent by Hyrcanus had visited Gaius Rabirius, with documents showing that it was lawful for them to observe the Sabbath.[62] This mediation by Hyrcanus for the Jews of Asia Minor is significant and is clearly one of the reasons the Romans granted the Jews their privileges. It also shows the links at this time between Jewish communities in Judaea and Asia Minor.

As we have noted, the Jews were granted exemptions from military service at various times so that they could observe the Sabbath as they wished.[63] In addition, an edict of Augustus about the Jews in Asia states 'they they need not give bond (to appear in court) on the Sabbath or on the day of preparation for it after the ninth hour'.[64] The period on the day before the Sabbath was probably set aside by the Jews for making arrangements for the Sabbath, such as cooking or the lighting of stoves. This exemption from summons to a law court on the Sabbath or the day of preparation ensured that the Jews could observe the Sabbath fully by making certain that they would not be faced with the difficult choice between the Sabbath and obtaining justice. Clearly, these documents show a strong concern for the proper observance of the Sabbath, an important element in Jewish identity. Although our evidence does not enable us to be specific about exactly how they observed the Sabbath, we can be certain that the Sabbath was important for Jews in Asia Minor in this period.[65]

The food laws

We have some indications that observance of the food laws was a significant part of Jewish practice in Asia Minor. We have noted that one of the factors which hindered Jews from undertaking military service was that in the army they could not obtain the 'τροφαί τῶν πατρίων' to which they were accustomed.[66] In the decree of the people of Sardis we read 'that the market-officials of the city shall be charged with the duty of having suitable food for them [the Jews] brought in'. The decree makes it clear that the provision of 'suitable food' had been requested by the Jews of Sardis, who seem to have followed ancestral custom with regard to the food laws. It is also significant that both Roman officials and a city like Sardis were prepared to take cognisance of Jewish dietary requests.[67]

'To live according to their own laws'

Often we find a more general statement of Jewish privileges accompanying a decree on a specific matter. In a decree of the people of Ephesus, it is stated that the Jews have asked 'that they might observe their Sabbaths and do all those things which are in accordance with their native customs without interference ...' and also that they have been 'permitted to do all those things which are in accordance with their own laws'. As we have found before, it is often clear that the Jewish communities have approached the Roman authorities requesting the decrees which contained the statement of these general privileges.[68] Whilst the decrees were written by non-Jews, they express the intent of the Jewish communities of Asia Minor to live in accordance with 'ancestral tradition' or 'with their own laws' and the willingness of the Roman authorities to permit this to happen.[69]

When this is combined with the observation that Jews probably requested these privileges and with our findings on the synagogue, the Temple tax, the Sabbath, and the food laws, we have sufficient evidence to be confident that the Jewish communities in Asia Minor in the period covered by these documents (between 49 BCE and 2 CE) belonged to the mainstream of Jewish life since these facets (along with others such as circumcision about which these documents are silent) were fundamental to Jewish identity at this time.[70] They were anxious that they might be able to obey the commands of the Torah and that the institutions and practices incumbent upon faithful Jewish communities might be sustained.

5 Evidence from classical authors

We have already noted the evidence provided by Cicero and Strabo. Unfortunately, other classical authors give no direct information about Jewish communities in Asia Minor in particular, although of course they knew a good deal about Jews in general.[71] However, we should note that three writers from Asia Minor are reported to have written books on the Jews. Apollonius Molon, who was born in Caria and taught in Rhodes in the first half of the first century BCE, wrote a book about the Jews, parts of which have been preserved by Josephus and Eusebius. Josephus regarded him as Apion's equal in hatred of the Jews. Alexander Polyhistor (*c.* 80–40 BCE), born in Miletus, brought to Rome as a slave and manumitted by Sulla, wrote a book 'On Jews'. It is a collection of excerpts from non-Jewish authors about the Jews and from Jewish authors themselves. Clearly, he had a very great interest in Jewish affairs. Teucer of Cyzicus, who probably wrote in the middle of the first century BCE, is said by Suidas to have written a *Historia Judaica* in six parts.[72] That three authors from Asia Minor wrote about the Jews in the first century BCE is partly explained by the general interest in the Jews created by Pompey's capture of Jerusalem. However, these three authors' interest in, or antagonism towards, the Jewish people may have been aroused by the Jewish communities in Asia Minor by this time.[73]

6 Evidence from the New Testament

Acts presents a picture of Jewish opposition to the preaching of Paul in Asia Minor. It has often been noted in recent studies that this opposition is one of Luke's theological and apologetic themes. Luke shows that Jewish synagogue communities have rejected Paul's gospel, so Paul then goes to the Gentiles. Thus it has been suggested that Luke's characterisation of the Jews grows out of his own ecclesiastical situation. This raises the question of whether or not Luke has significantly heightened the element of Jewish hostility to the gospel.[74] Is there any historical basis for the incidents Luke reports? We must first turn to Paul's letters in an attempt to answer this.

Does Paul indicate in his letters that he was persecuted by Jews? In 2 Cor 11:24 we read that on five occasions Paul received forty lashes less one at the hands of the Jews. There is no actual account of Paul being flogged by Jews in Acts, although there are several occasions prior to the writing of 2 Cor (probably in 56 CE) when this could have occurred.[75] Such flogging was a punishment administered by the synagogue for a wide range of serious transgressions. The fact that Paul endured a potentially life-threatening punishment five times shows that he did not lightly give up his Jewish connections and that he voluntarily continued to attend synagogues and submit to their discipline.[76] This suggests that in a new location Paul would go to the synagogue, even if he had been severely punished in a previous town. It certainly confirms that Paul was persecuted by Jews.[77]

Further evidence points in the same direction. In 2 Cor 11:26 Paul refers to dangers from his own people. In 1 Thess 2:15–16 Paul speaks of being driven out by the Jews, probably from Thessalonica, and of being hindered by the Jews from speaking to Gentiles.[78] He knows that he can expect fierce hostility from unbelieving Jews in Judaea (Rom 15:31). In Gal 4:29 there is a typological reference to persecution of Christians 'now' by others, designated as those 'born according to the flesh', who are almost certainly Jews. Paul also mentions a number of instances of general persecution: Rom 8:35; 1 Cor 4:12; 2 Cor 4:9, 6:4–5, 12:10; Gal 5:11. It is likely that an element within these general references is persecution at the hands of the Jews. These passages were all written before Paul returned to

Jerusalem (as is recounted in Acts 21 and suggested by Rom 15:25–31), so these Jewish persecutions must belong to the period of Paul's mission in Asia Minor, Macedonia and Achaia. Therefore, we can conclude that the picture in Acts of Paul being persecuted by Jews is credible. That some of this opposition occurred in Asia Minor is a reasonable inference.

Can we ascertain from Paul's letters his opinion of why the Jews persecuted him? It is generally agreed that Paul's opposition from Jewish Christians related to his preaching a law-free gospel to the Gentiles.[79] It might be anticipated then that Jews would object on this same point and 1 Thess 2:15–16 suggests this. Paul notes that the Jews 'drove us out [probably from Thessalonica] ... and oppose all people by hindering us from speaking to the Gentiles that they may be saved ...'. Paul thus claims that it was the offer of salvation to the Gentiles which angered these Jews. Since they presumably would not have objected if Paul required Gentiles to come under the law as proselytes, we can suggest that their complaint was that Paul preached a law-free gospel (particularly without the requirement of circumcision) to the Gentiles. In Gal 5:11 Paul underlines this point by implying that he is persecuted because he does not preach circumcision, which here represents the law. He also accused his opponents in Galatia, who were trying to compel Gentiles to be circumcised, of acting in this way precisely to avoid persecution (Gal 6:12). Thus, central to Paul's conflict with Jews was his view concerning the law and his corresponding missionary practice of bringing Gentiles into the people of God without requiring full obedience to the Torah.[80] This shows the significance of the law for the Jews who opposed Paul.

I will now survey the various references to Jewish communities in Asia Minor in Acts. In Pisidian Antioch (actually in Phrygia) Paul was invited to speak at the synagogue and many Jews and proselytes were convinced by his words. The next Sabbath many Gentiles also came to hear Paul and this made other Jews envious (ζῆλος), so they opposed the message and the messengers (Acts 13:14–47). Perhaps the basis for their ζῆλος was that Paul was much more successful than they had been at attracting Gentiles. Or perhaps they were jealous of their own privileged religious position as Jews and could not accept a message which, through disregard of the Law, was open to Gentiles on the same terms as Jews.[81] The episode also shows the division in the Jewish people which resulted from Christian preaching. Some Jews accepted Paul's message (13:43), the majority rejected it (13:45). The way Luke uses the words 'the Jews' thus changes in this passage, as it regularly does in incidents like this in Acts. In 13:43 it refers to the whole Jewish community. Subsequently, it becomes an abbreviation for 'the Jews who disbelieved' (13:45, 50). As a result of some Jews rejecting the Gospel, Paul said he would go to the Gentiles since the Jews 'judged themselves unworthy of eternal life'. Finally, in 13:50 Luke records that the Jews in Antioch 'incited devout women of high standing and the leading men of the city, and stirred up persecution against Paul and Barnabas, and drove them out of their district'. That the Jews were able to stir up opposition among Gentiles in high places suggests they had influential contacts.[82]

After the rejection of the Jews in 13:46−7 it may seem surprising that Paul continues to go to the synagogue in other cities.[83] However, as we have noted, 2 Cor 11:24 suggests Paul continued to visit synagogues even though he had been severely punished by some Jewish communities. He was very conscious of the fact that Israel was God's covenant people to whom God continued to offer salvation. Paul expresses this as 'to the Jew first and also to the Greek' (Rom 1:16; see also 2:9−10, 9:1−3, 10:1). The rejection of vv46−7 seems to apply primarily to the situation in Antioch and does not rule out subsequent missions to Jews elsewhere.[84]

Paul's activity at Iconium followed the same pattern as at Antioch. Again some Jews responded, while others, along with some Gentiles, opposed the message (14:1−7). The Jews seem again to have had some influence over Gentiles in the city (and perhaps over Gentile rulers if v5 includes them) and used this to oppose Paul (14:2, 5). That Paul and Barnabas are called apostles in 14:4 (and in 14:14), a title Luke normally reserves for the Twelve, suggests Luke is using a source here.[85] This is significant since the verse refers to Jewish opposition in the city. The Jews from Antioch and Iconium are reported in 14:19 to have travelled to Lystra where they persuaded the people against Paul and stoned him.[86] This story is almost certainly referred to in 2 Cor 11:25. It is unlikely that Luke knew the extended list of Paul's suffering in 2 Cor 11:23−33, since the list goes far beyond what Luke tells us,[87] so we have two independent traditions about the event. This suggests that Luke had information which located the incident at Lystra.

The historicity of these incidents in Acts 13−14 has been questioned.[88] However, we have already noted that, from the evidence of Paul's letters, Jewish opposition to Paul in Asia Minor is credible. In addition, 2 Tim 3:10−11 is significant here: 'Now you [sing, i.e. Timothy] have observed my teaching ... my persecutions, my sufferings, what befell me at Antioch, at Iconium, and at Lystra, what persecutions I endured.' Whilst it is possible that this account in 2 Tim may be dependent on Acts, if this was the case we would expect mention of the troubles in which, according to Acts, Timothy was actually involved, since this is the point of the recollection.[89] The passage suggests that among Pauline congregations there was a tradition that Paul had endured persecution in these three towns.[90] Since Paul tells us that he was persecuted by Jews as well as Gentiles, we can suggest that at least a part of this persecution was at the hands of Jews. Thus, even if we cannot argue more strongly for the historicity of the whole of Luke's account, we can at least suggest that Luke's description of persecution by Jews is a well-attested tradition.

In Acts 16:1–3 we learn of the Christian Timothy, who probably came from Lystra. He was the son of a Jewish Christian woman and a Greek father, who was probably already dead. Paul wanted Timothy to accompany him in his travels, but since Timothy was uncircumcised, Paul circumcised him 'because of the Jews who were in those places'. There has been much discussion of the passage with some scholars concluding that Paul would never circumcise someone like Timothy since he regarded circumcision as a matter of indifference and stated that those who were circumcised were bound to keep the whole law.[91] However, we should take careful note of the circumstances. Timothy was in an anomalous situation. He would have been regarded as a Jew since he had a Jewish mother but as an apostate Jew since he was uncircumcised. As a result, he would have been barred from any effective work amongst Jews. In addition, if Paul had refused to circumcise Timothy, he would have been seen to support apostasy and this would effectively have ended Paul's mission in the synagogue.[92] Thus, whilst Paul refused to circumcise a Gentile Christian like Titus (Gal 2:3–5), Timothy's situation was different. Some of Paul's contemporaries may have misinterpreted the incident, but it seems likely that for Paul no matter of principle was involved. He was not circumcising Timothy because this was necessary for his salvation (cf. 15:1), since he was already a disciple. He was circumcising him to remove a stigma so that as a Jew he could have a ministry among Jews. The incident is therefore compatible with what we know of Paul and with such passages as 1 Cor 9:19–23 and 10:32.[93]

According to a whole range of Jewish literature, Jews were not to marry Gentiles. That Timothy's mother had done so suggests that she was not a practising Jew. If a Jewish woman did marry a Gentile, the children were regarded as Jewish and therefore liable to be circumcised.[94] That Timothy's mother did not do so suggests that she had not taken her Jewish responsibilities seriously or that her husband had prevented Timothy from being circumcised. Luke records that Paul circumcised Timothy 'because of the Jews who were in those places, for they all knew that his father was a Greek' (16:3). They seem to have assumed that, since his father was Greek, he was uncircumcised; Luke implies that this would have made his contact with other Jews difficult. This suggests that these Jews perhaps in Iconium and Antioch, did follow the custom of circumcision. More than this we cannot say.

In Ephesus Paul visited the synagogue where he argued for a short time before leaving (18:19). Later he returned to the synagogue where he spoke regularly over a period of three months before he withdrew to the hall of Tyrannus because of Jewish opposition (19:8–9). In 19:11–17 Luke records that seven wandering exorcists, sons of a Jewish ἀρχιερεύς named Sceva, tried to perform exorcisms by pronouncing the name of Jesus. No person named Sceva was ever the Jewish ἀρχιερεύς, so either the title was used loosely and meant that he was a member of a high priestly family or Sceva may have been described as ἀρχιερεύς to authenticate the activity of his sons as genuine exorcists who had contact with the supernatural and knew magical divine names.[95] The report of wandering Jewish exorcists in Ephesus is consistent with other evidence about the involvement of Jews in exorcism and the interest in magic in Ephesus.[96] However, for these very reasons, Ephesus was also a likely place to locate a good story about magic, and Jews were likely opponents in magical arts. Hence, it has been thought that the basis of the story was a traditional pagan legend and that the incident itself is unhistorical.[97] In any case, were these seven wandering exorcists even from Asia Minor? It is difficult then to know how much we can conclude from this incident. That Jews were involved in exorcism seems certain from other evidence, and it is possible that Jews in Ephesus were part of this trend.

The success of the Christian mission in Ephesus provoked a reaction from the silversmiths which resulted in the riotous gathering in the theatre (19:23–41). The story has much local colour and reveals an accurate knowledge of the municipal institutions of Ephesus. These factors argue for its historicity. Representatives of the Jewish community were present in the theatre according to Luke (19:33–4). Perhaps, since they were also opposed to Paul's work, they had been willing to join the crowd in this public protest.[98] Alexander, a Jew, is put forward to speak by the Jews.[99] The situation seems to be that the crowd had made no distinction between Jews and Christians and this caused the Jews anxiety, lest they too be implicated. The Jews wanted Alexander to show that they also objected to the Christian mission and were in no way to be associated with the accused Christians. However, when the crowd recognised that Alexander was a Jew they did not want to listen.[100] All they were concerned about was that as a Jew he was not a worshipper of Artemis. This led them to shout their cultic cry for two hours. Two important facts emerge. Firstly, the Jews attempted to assert and preserve their distinct identity compared with the Christians and to prevent any serious hostility against themselves. This is comparable to the decrees in Josephus considered earlier in this chapter, which were obtained for just this purpose. Secondly, the incident reveals a degree of anti-Jewish feeling in Ephesus; an element in this is the fact that Jews did not worship Artemis.

In Acts Jews from Asia Minor also played a part in incidents in Jerusalem. The first of these is the report in Acts 2:9−11 that Jews from Cappadocia, Pontus, Asia, Phrygia and Pamphylia were part of the crowd at Pentecost. They were probably not pilgrims, since Luke describes them as κατοικοῦντες in Jerusalem, although they may well have originally come to Jerusalem on pilgrimage and decided to live there. The passage provides evidence that Jews were living in the areas in Asia Minor specified; we can suggest that it also provides evidence that Jews from these areas had come to Jerusalem as pilgrims at some stage.[101]

Jews from the provinces of Asia and Cilicia were amongst other Diaspora Jews who started arguing with Stephen (6:9−15). The Jews from Asia, Cilicia and elsewhere considered that Stephen was speaking blasphemy against Moses (i.e. the law) and God. Before the council they claimed (falsely in Luke's view) that he was attacking the significance and permanence of the Temple and the unalterable nature of the Torah. They are seen to be zealous defenders of their faith who were prepared to dispute with Stephen and to initiate the proceedings to take him before the Sanhedrin, where other Jews also took the case up. The Jewish Christian Hellenists including Stephen probably emerged from synagogues made up of Greek-speaking Diaspora Jews who had taken up residence in Jerusalem. It is credible, then, that the opponents of Stephen should be from these synagogues.[102] That the dispute between Hellenists like Stephen and Jews centred on the law and the Temple is in accordance with what we know about the

Hellenists and their preaching. In addition, Haenchen notes that Luke has no intrinsic reason for presenting Stephen's opponents as Diaspora rather than Palestinian Jews and so must have taken this information from a tradition.[103] Indeed, it is likely that the list of ethnic groups in 6:9 goes back to a written source. We thus have evidence for the importance of the law and the Temple for this group of Jews from Asia and Cilicia.[104]

In Acts 21 Paul is said to face the problem of the suspicions of Jewish Christians in Jerusalem about his attitude to the law. He endeavoured to disarm their suspicions by taking part in a Jewish vow which involved the presentation of an offering at the Temple. Luke goes on: 'the Jews from Asia who had seen Paul in the temple, stirred up all the crowd, and laid hands on him, crying out, "Men of Israel, help! This is the man who is teaching men everywhere against the people and the law and this place; moreover he also brought Greeks into the temple and he has defiled this holy place." For they had previously seen Trophimus the Ephesian with him in the city, and they supposed that Paul had brought him into the Temple' (21:27–9). The Asian Jews are primarily from Ephesus since they recognise Trophimus (see 20:4), who had also recently been in that city. It was probably Pentecost (see 20:16) so the Asian Jews would have come to Jerusalem as pilgrims.[105] They charge Paul with attacking the fundamentals of Jewish identity – the people, the law and the Temple. Their paramount charge was that Paul had brought Gentiles into the Temple, thus defiling it. This was against the law and might have suggested that he accepted Gentiles on the same terms as Jews. It was Asian Jews who started the protest because they evidently recognised Trophimus and probably also Paul. Perhaps they were particularly hostile to Paul because he had incurred their enmity during his ministry in Ephesus (see 20:19). They attempted to take more effective action in Jerusalem than they had been able to take in Ephesus. Once again the Asian Jews are seen to be zealous defenders of the law and the Temple.[106]

We have thus gained a good deal of information about Jews in Asia Minor in the first century CE. We have suggested that according to his letters Paul was persecuted by Jews, almost certainly in Asia Minor as elsewhere and that central to the conflict with the Jews was preaching a law-free Gospel to the Gentiles. This shows the significance of the law for these Jewish communities in Asia Minor. Acts confirms that Paul was persecuted by Jews in Asia Minor and suggests that one reason for this was the success of his mission among

Gentiles. The Jews in some places seem to have had influence with Gentiles, so that they could enlist their aid in persecuting Paul. The importance of the law, the Temple and the identity of the Jewish people is also shown in events in which Jews from Asia Minor opposed Christians in Jerusalem. On one occasion the Jews in Ephesus attempted to assert and preserve their distinctive identity. We have noted that some Jews from Asia Minor went on pilgrimage to Jerusalem, showing that there was contact between communities in Asia Minor and Palestine. Other Jews may have practised exorcism in Ephesus. In that city there seems to have been some anti-Jewish feeling caused at least in part by the fact that the Jews did not worship Artemis. Finally, we know of a Jewess in the area who married a Gentile and whose son was not circumcised, although clearly some other Jews in the area expected this to be done.

In Rev 2:9, addressed to the church at Smyrna, we read 'I know your tribulation and your poverty (but you are rich) and the slander of those who say that they are Jews and are not but are a synagogue of Satan.' Rev 3:9, to the church at Philadelphia, is similar. Some scholars have thought that those who claim to be Jews but are not are actually Gentile Christians who call themselves Jews, perhaps to avoid persecution. They are thought to belong to the group which John calls the Nicolaitans.[107] However, these 'so-called Jews' are clearly distinguished from the Nicolaitans. John praises the churches in Smyrna and Philadelphia 'for resisting the persecution of the Jews, [but] he does not criticise the other churches [in Rev 2–3] for giving in to persecution by the Nicolaitans, but for being invaded by them. Whereas the Jews endanger the churches by persecution from the outside, the Nicolaitans endanger them from within by means of "heretical" teachings'.[108] It seems most likely, then, that those who say they are Jews are precisely that. For John, these Jews have forfeited the right to be called Jews by their rejection of Jesus, and through their opposition to the Christians they deserve the title of Satan's agents. Thus we can suggest that in Smyrna and Philadelphia the Jewish communities actively opposed the Christian churches.[109]

7 Evidence from patristic sources

We now turn to patristic sources to see whether they shed any light on Jewish communities in Asia Minor.[110] Ignatius of Antioch wrote seven letters to churches in Asia Minor around the turn from the first to the second century CE whilst on his way to martyrdom in Rome.

He does not discuss the relationship between the church and the synagogue, but he does refer to the 'heresies' of the docetists and the judaisers.[111] What Ignatius says about Judaising is of interest here. He had visited the church in Philadelphia and almost certainly wrote to them in the light of his experience there. He states: 'But if anyone interpret Judaism to you do not listen to him; for it is better to hear Christianity from the circumcised than Judaism from the uncircumcised' (Phld 6:1–2). The first person may refer to someone like Paul who became a Christian, although it could also refer to Jewish Christians in Philadelphia. The second person seems to be someone presently in Philadelphia. Since the one expounding Judaism is uncircumcised, it is most likely that he is a Gentile whose teaching Ignatius could call 'Judaism'. In Phld 8:2 Ignatius reports that these people say 'If I do not find it in the archives, I do not believe it in the Gospel.' This suggests that a major feature of this 'Judaism' was an emphasis on the primary importance of the OT and exegetical expertise in its use. Schoedel sees Hellenistic Jewish views reflected in this preoccupation with Scripture and the use of the title 'archives' for the OT by these Gentile Judaisers.[112]

Whilst Ignatius did not visit the church in Magnesia ad Maeander, he spoke with their representatives in Smyrna. To the church at Magnesia he wrote: 'For if we are living until now according to Judaism, we confess that we have not received grace' (Mag 8:1).[113] That he is probably referring to Gentile Christians who have adopted Jewish customs is suggested by Mag 10:3 where Ignatius calls the church to reject Judaising and to live according to Christianity. He writes: 'It is monstrous to talk of Jesus Christ and to practise Judaism. For Christianity did not base its faith on Judaism, but Judaism on Christianity.' Ignatius seems to be recalling the first generation of Jewish Christians who came to believe in Christ; Judaism yielded to Christianity, not the other way around. Christians should therefore not yield to Judaism, nor should they adopt any other name, by which Ignatius perhaps means 'Judaism' (10:1). He also notes that the early disciples once lived as Jews who observed the Sabbath but later came to live as Christians observing the Lord's Day. Similarly, the Christians at Magnesia should not observe the Sabbath but Sunday (Mag 9:1–2). This comment was probably prompted by pressure from some Christians in favour of Sabbath observance. Whilst many details of these passages are difficult to interpret, it is clear that Ignatius is talking about Christians in Magnesia who were observing Jewish customs.[114] Ignatius does not say that they were converted Jews, and so, if we assume that the situation was comparable to the one at Philadelphia, we can suggest that again it was the uncircumcised who were also Judaising here.

If this was the case, why were these Gentiles Judaising? It may be that there were a number of Jewish Christians in the two churches, although Ignatius would surely have said so if the problems he dealt with came from this source. Alternatively, following Jewish customs could have been a part of the tradition of one group in the Church. However, another likely explanation for Gentiles following Jewish customs is the influence of Jewish communities in the area.[115] Simon and Wilken note that Judaising tendencies in the church did not appear spontaneously but were prompted by the living example of Jews who had actual contact with Christians.[116] In the case of Philadelphia and Magnesia direct contact with local Jewish communities seems the most likely explanation for Gentiles who Judaised. Accordingly, we can suggest that in these two cities there were Jewish communities which were attractive to Christians and which had an impact on the Church.

According to the *Martyrdom of Polycarp* the Jews in Smyrna played a part in Polycarp's death, which probably occurred between 156 and 167 CE. The Jews are said to have joined the pagans in the condemnation of Polycarp (12:2) and in collecting wood for the fire over which he died (13:2). Christians seem also to have believed that the Jews had persuaded leading pagans to petition the Roman governor and deter him from releasing Polycarp's body to the Christians (17:2–18:1). We cannot determine whether these statements are reliable in detail, but it does seem that the Jews played a part in Polycarp's martyrdom. Clearly the Christian author of the account thought the Jews were strongly opposed to Polycarp, that they were prepared to work with Gentiles against the Christians and that the Jews had contacts in high places in the city.[117]

Justin Martyr was clearly well acquainted with elements of the Judaism of his time, both in essentials and often in detail. However, was he aware of Judaism in Asia Minor in particular? Justin's *Dialogue with Trypho*, written around 160 CE, was set in Ephesus according to Eusebius, perhaps on the basis of a well-established tradition.[118] It is impossible to say whether or not the *Dialogue* is a supplemented record of an actual debate. However, as Remus comments, 'the extended, developed arguments in the *Dialogue* point to significant contact between Justin and Jews, with his arguments hammered out in conversation and disputes with them'.[119] Thus the

Dialogue probably reflects issues at stake between Christians and Jews in the second century CE. In some passages Justin is probably drawing on the content of Jewish anti-Christian allegations. Thus, for example, Justin reports that Jews denounce Jesus as a deceiver who led Israel astray and proclaim that Christianity was a godless and lawless 'heresy'.[120] In addition, Trypho urges that Justin be circumcised and follow the law, particularly with regard to the Sabbath, feasts and new moons.[121] That Justin probably sets the *Dialogue* in Ephesus suggests that these sorts of allegations and pleas could be expected from Jews in the area who were likely to dispute with Christians, particularly concerning Jesus and the law, and to oppose Christianity. Stanton has noted that Sardis with its vigorous Jewish community is not far from Ephesus, which reinforces the likelihood that Jews in this area were involved in polemic with Christians.[122]

According to Eusebius, Apollinaris, bishop of Hierapolis, Phrygia in the time of Marcus Aurelius (161–180 CE), wrote a two-volume work entitled 'Against the Jews', which is now lost. From inscriptional evidence we know that the Jewish community at Hierapolis was a significant one. Perhaps Apollinaris wrote this work because of the strength of the local Jewish community and the attraction it had for Christians. Another apologist from Asia Minor writing in the time of Marcus Aurelius was Miltiades. He also wrote a now-lost two-volume work 'Against the Jews'.[123]

Lane Fox has recently studied the *Martyrdom of Pionius*, which is set in Smyrna, and has shown it to be a reliable historical source concerning a martyrdom which occurred during the Decian persecution in 250.[124] In the text Pionius warned the Jews not to gloat over Christians who had lapsed, because the Jews had themselves sinned in the past of their own free will (4:2–14). In his speech in prison Pionius states 'I understand also that the Jews have been inviting some of you to their synagogues ... Do not become with them rulers of Sodom and people of Gomorrha' (13:1–2). The invitation to the synagogue was almost certainly an attempt to undermine the Christians' faith and to convert them to Judaism. In a time of persecution the Jews tried to attract those amongst the Christians who would prefer to join the synagogue rather than eat pagan meat in public. Pionius also reported that the Jews slandered Jesus and, as Lane Fox notes, said that he 'had died a criminal's violent death, and like other executed criminals, his spirit still roamed without rest. Christians, therefore, could conjure it up and had already brought it back to earth by their magical sign of the cross. The "Resurrection" appearances were caused by sorcery, said the Jews, practised on a criminal's restless soul.'[125] Pionius states that the Christians themselves have heard the Jews make these charges (13:3). We thus catch a glimpse of the Jewish community in Smyrna in 250 CE. They have a continuing interest in attracting Christians to Judaism and they are involved in polemic against the Christians about Jesus and his resurrection. There is a long refutation of their allegations in MPion 14:1–16, which suggests that the Jewish charges were of concern to Christians. Pionius' martyrdom is said to have occurred on 'a Great Sabbath' (MPion 2:1; 3:6). Polycarp's martyrdom is similarly dated on a 'Great Sabbath' years earlier (MPoly 8:1). No explanation of the term is entirely satisfactory.[126] However, the important fact for us is that this dating of the event is actually given in the Christian accounts of the martyrdoms. Clearly the Jewish community's 'Great Sabbath' was well-known by Christians and probably by pagans too. Thus the Jewish community seems to have been a significant element in the city's life. Another detail of the accounts is helpful. Lane Fox notes that both Polycarp and Pionius were clearly arrested towards the end of a major pagan festival. Thus, for example, the crowd asked Philip the Asiarch to loose a lion on Polycarp. 'But he said that he was not allowed to do this since the days of the animal games were past' (MPoly 12:2).[127] The pagan festival was probably the city's Dionysia since this was the time when the governor came to Smyrna for the assizes and therefore when he investigated charges against Christians. Consequently, the 'Great Sabbath' was a Jewish festival which occurred during the course of a longer pagan festival. When the Jews joined the Greeks and the women as spectators in the colonnade, they were all on holiday (MPion 3:6). This is significant because Abodah Zarah 1:1 states that Jews should do no business with Gentiles for three days before a pagan festival. This strongly suggests that Jews at Smyrna in this period either did not know or did not observe Rabbinic regulations and also that they had considerable contact with Gentiles. Yet, note that these Jews are observing a Jewish festival.[128]

Two other Christian sources will be dealt with in detail later but can be mentioned here. The intense attack on Israel in the *Peri Pascha* of Melito, bishop of Sardis in the latter part of the second century CE, can be seen in part as a reaction to the powerful Jewish community in Sardis. The canons of the fourth century CE Council of Laodicea in Phrygia show that a number of Christians were strongly influenced by Jews, had close contacts with Jewish communities and were involved in Jewish festivals.[129]

Thus, although the interpretation of this evidence is difficult at times, we can conclude that in some places Jews seem to have been involved in polemic against Christians on subjects such as the law, Jesus and his resurrection. This opposition may even have led Jews to be involved in the death of Christians. In some areas Jewish communities were attractive and had a significant influence on the churches. In the case of Melito this led to strong anti-Jewish views; in other situations it led to a number of Christians either importing Jewish practices into Christianity or participation by Christians in Jewish worship and festivals. The Jews may also have invited Christians to be involved in synagogue life. In Smyrna in particular, the Jewish community seems to have been a significant element in the city, to have had considerable interaction with Gentiles and to have had contacts in high places in the city. Finally, the Jews in Smyrna in the third century seem to be beyond the rabbinic sphere of influence; however, we do know that they observed a 'Great Sabbath'.

8 The Jews in Asia Minor during the Jewish revolts

An examination of the situation in Asia Minor during the three Jewish uprisings of the first and second century CE is also helpful here. The Jews of the Diaspora did not support the Jews of Palestine to any significant degree in the war of 66–70 CE. The Jews of the Diaspora probably did not see their status as Jews endangered by the Romans and thus did not want to jeopardise their own favourable position through support of the rebellion. The Diaspora had much to lose and little to gain by supporting the revolt in Palestine. Further evidence of the Diaspora's lack of involvement is the fact that the Roman government continued to support the privileged position of the Jews in the Empire after the revolt. Thus, neither Vespasian nor Titus revoked the extensive privileges enjoyed by the Jews in the Diaspora after 70 CE, despite being asked to do so by various cities. The only notable exception to the continued support of the Diaspora was the imposition by Vespasian of the didrachmon tax in favour of Jupiter Capitolinus to be paid to the fiscus Judaicus by every Jew from the age of three to sixty. Whilst this was a source of humiliation and annoyance to the Jews, it did not signify the withdrawal of Roman support, as Vespasian's confirmation of Jewish privileges at Alexandria and Antioch shows.[130] All of this is important in itself and is further evidence which suggests that the Diaspora was not involved in the war of 66—70 CE. It is clear, therefore, that the sizable Jewish communities in Asia Minor took no part in this revolt and that their position was not much altered by it.

The Diaspora revolt of 115—117 CE occurred in Egypt, Cyrenaica, Cyprus and Mesopotamia but not, to our knowledge, in Asia Minor. The Jews in the Diaspora communities involved revolted against the local authorities and against Rome, the power which had previously upheld their case against the local communities. This and the geographical spread of the uprisings show the importance of local factors, such as the presence of nationalist or messianic leadership and of local grievances or tensions, as the causes of the revolt.[131] The lack of evidence for any contemporary hostilities in Asia Minor suggests that different local factors prevailed there. Given the range of evidence for the revolt — Dio Cassius, Eusebius, Orosius, inscriptions, papyri and archaeological evidence — we can suggest that the silence about the revolt in Asia Minor is significant.

Hadrian's prohibition of castration and with it circumcision would have affected Jewish communities in Asia Minor as it did those elsewhere. His successor, Antoninus Pius, authorised circumcision of the sons of Jews, restricting the prohibition to non-Jews. We have no evidence that the events of the Bar Kokhba war (132—5 CE) had any effect on Asia Minor nor that any Jews from there were involved.[132] Subsequent history does not record any particular adverse treatment of Jewish communities in Asia Minor. Apart from the continuing prohibition of proselytism, we have no evidence for restrictions being placed on Jewish communities before Constantine. Under Christian Emperors, the existing rights of Jewish communities were upheld; repressive measures were generally limited to preventing any further expansion of Judaism.[133]

9 Conclusions

We have been able to establish a number of important details about the Jewish communities in Asia Minor. The first communities for which we have evidence were settled by Antiochus III in Lydia and Phrygia on favourable terms which would have helped them to become established. These settlers were from another part of the Diaspora and thus would already have adjusted to some extent to life outside Palestine. We know of significant links between Jews in Asia Minor and Jerusalem in the first century BCE. Jewish settlement seems to have continued as time went on and was quite extensive in Asia Minor by the first century CE.

We have also seen that Jewish communities in Asia Minor sought and obtained authorisation and support from Rome in their attempts to observe Jewish customs. This support was ad hoc rather than in the form of a universal charter. The privileges which they asked for and were granted enabled them to maintain their 'Jewishness' in the face of local hostility. If Roman support had not been forthcoming, the identity of the Jewish communities in Asia Minor would have been threatened.

We have identified and discussed a number of facets of Jewish identity in Asia Minor — a commitment to the synagogue, to the Temple tax and thus to the Temple and its worship, to the Sabbath, to food laws and to living in accordance with their tradition. That Jewish communities sought help from the Roman administration to enable them to continue practising these aspects of their faith shows the strength of their convictions. Our evidence, as far as it goes, thus places the Jewish communities of Asia Minor within the mainstream of Judaism. They were anxious that they should be able to obey the commands of the Torah and that the institutions and practices incumbent upon faithful Jewish communities might be sustained. We are not claiming that the Jewish communities in Asia Minor were 'orthodox', for this is a concept of highly dubious value in the period under discussion.[134] We are claiming that these communities belonged within the fold of Judaism (albeit a fold containing many diverse entities) at this time.

After the turn of the era Josephus and Philo inform us of no difficulties experienced by Jewish communities in Asia Minor. Indeed the contentious issues of the time of Augustus seem to be less sweeping than those of the 40s BCE and concern only the Temple tax and to a lesser extent the Sabbath, which suggests that by this time earlier difficulties had been partially solved. In a time of peace and firm Roman government the Greek cities were probably less able to challenge the privileges of the Jewish communities. The external situation would have encouraged them to be more accepting of the status quo. The edict of Claudius issued in 41/42 CE arose from hostilities in Alexandria, Palestine and perhaps in Syria, with no mention being made of Asia Minor.[135] Acts tells us that there was some anti-Jewish feeling in Ephesus in the 50s CE caused at least in part by the fact that the Jews did not worship Artemis. We can thus suggest that, after some troubles in Asia Minor in the first century BCE, relations in the first century CE between the Jewish communities and their cities improved and became reasonable, with only sporadic outbreaks of trouble, such as that in Ephesus, occurring at this time.[136] Earlier causes of tension seem to have been overcome. Perhaps some sort of *modus vivendi* was established between the Jewish communities and the cities in Asia Minor which satisfied both groups. Whilst this is an argument from silence, we can note that it seems likely that Claudius would have mentioned significant trouble in Asia Minor had it occurred. That reasonable relations probably developed is significant with regard to the character of Judaism in Asia Minor. This is particularly clear when we recall that in the same period there were two major periods of revolt in Palestine and in, for example, Alexandria, which in the latter case resulted in the drastic reduction of the size of the Jewish community there. The situation seems to have been different in Asia Minor, where stability and vitality were much more likely to become hallmarks of the Jewish communities.

Acts, Revelation and Patristic sources have also been helpful. At times in the first three centuries CE we have evidence that Jews in Asia Minor opposed Christianity and that this sometimes led to the persecution of Christians. From the NT we can suggest that Christian preaching of a law-free Gospel to the Gentiles, and the success of the Christian mission among Gentiles, were factors behind this conflict. The importance of the law, the Temple and the identity of the Jewish people is also shown by Jews from Asia Minor opposing Christians in Jerusalem. On one occasion the Jews in Ephesus attempted to assert and preserve their distinct identity. Pilgrimage by Jews from Asia Minor to Jerusalem seems to have continued. We should also note that a Jewess in Asia Minor married a Gentile and that their son was not circumcised, although clearly some other Jews in the area expected this to be done. Patristic sources provide evidence for Jewish polemic against Christians on subjects such as the law, Jesus as a deceiver and his resurrection. In the second and third century the Jewish community in Smyrna observed a 'Great Sabbath' but seem to have been beyond the rabbinic sphere of influence. Since much of this evidence involves factors which were important for Jewish identity, we can suggest that Jewish communities in Asia Minor generally remained within the diverse fold of Judaism in the first three centuries CE.

The Jews in some places seem to have had influence with Gentiles, so that they could enlist their aid in persecuting Christians. In the third century CE the Jewish community in Smyrna seems to have been a significant element in the city, and members of the Jewish community were interacting with Gentiles and had contacts in high places.

In some areas Jewish communities were attractive to outsiders and had a significant influence on the local Christians. This could lead to strong anti-Jewish views among Christians; in other situations it led to Christians adopting Jewish practices or being involved in synagogue life to some extent. Jews seem to have encouraged this involvement, at least in Smyrna.

2

THE JEWISH COMMUNITIES
AT SARDIS AND PRIENE

1 Introduction

Sardis, the capital of ancient Lydia and then the western capital of the Persian Empire, was the capital of Seleucid Asia Minor north of the Taurus between 281 and 188 BCE. Its importance as a centre of royal power and administration was in part due to its position on significant trade routes, most notably as the terminus of the Royal Road. Antiochus III refounded the city in 213 BCE after it had supported Achaeus in his attempt to seize power. Around 190 BCE the Romans defeated Antiochus III and gave Sardis to the Pergamene king. Passing to Rome in 133 BCE, Sardis became part of the province of Asia and soon after became the centre of one of the nine *conventus iuridici*. In the period between 90 BCE and 17 CE the city declined somewhat, but by the Augustan era peace and confidence had returned. In 17 CE an earthquake devastated the city; reconstruction work went on well into the second century, by which time the city probably had a population of around 100,000. The Severan period was a time of great prosperity and the completion of much building work. The second half of the third century, although troubled elsewhere, seems to have been peaceful and prosperous in Sardis. Under Diocletian the city became the capital of the new province of Lydia and a major military centre. Commercial and industrial life continued to flourish until 616 CE, although conditions in the sixth century may have deteriorated. Despite the growing strength of Christianity in Sardis, continuity outweighed change. Large parts of the city were destroyed in 616 CE by the Sassanid king Chosroes II.[1]

2 The literary evidence for Jews in Sardis

In Obadiah 20 we read of 'the exiles of Jerusalem who are in Sepharad'. Sardis was called 'Sepharad' in Aramaic, as is clear from a Lydian–Aramaic bilingual found in Sardis. The 'Sepharad' referred to in Obadiah 20 may well therefore be Sardis, but the identity of the two names is an insufficient basis for certainty, given the lack of any other evidence for Jewish settlers at this early date.[2]

There were probably permanent Jewish residents in Sardis by the end of the third century BCE. The letter written by Antiochus III around 205 BCE states that 2,000 Jewish families were brought from Babylonia and Mesopotamia 'to the fortresses and most important places' in Lydia and Phrygia. Inscriptions show that Sardis was the headquarters of Zeuxis, the satrap in Lydia who was charged with administering the transportation. It seems highly likely therefore that some Jews came to live in Sardis at this time.[3] The favourable terms granted by Antiochus suggest that the community would have become established quickly. It is significant that these Jews were not from Palestine (at least, not directly) but were from another part of the Diaspora, and thus they had already lived as a minority in a gentile world and become sensitive to the problems and opportunities this raised. It is likely that the community continued to grow throughout the succeeding years as Jews came to settle in Sardis from elsewhere.

Josephus preserves three decrees which concern the Jewish community of Sardis. In the first decree, probably to be dated in 49 BCE,[4] we read that Jews had pointed out to Lucius Antonius, the proquaestor and propraetor, that 'from the earliest times (ἀπ' ἀρχῆς) they had an association (σύνοδον) of their own in accordance with their native laws (τοὺς πατρίους νόμους) and a place (τόπον) of their own, in which they decide their affairs and controversies with one another' (Ant 14:235). These rights were confirmed by Lucius Antonius. Josephus records a decree of the people of Sardis which may be a response to the letter of Lucius Antonius or may perhaps be later. It is worth quoting in full:

> Whereas the Jewish citizens living in our city have continually received many great privileges from the people and have now come before the council and the people and have pleaded that as their laws and freedom have been restored to them by the Roman Senate and people, they may, in accordance with their accepted customs, come together and have a communal life and adjudicate suits among themselves, and that a place

(τόπος) be given them in which they may gather together with their wives and children and offer their ancestral prayers and sacrifices[5] to God, it has therefore been decreed by the council and people that permission shall be given them to come together on stated days to do those things which are in accordance with their laws, and also that a place (τόπον) shall be set apart by the magistrates for them to build and inhabit, such as they may consider suitable for this purpose, and that the market-officials of the city shall be charged with the duty of having suitable food for them brought in. (Ant 14:259–61)

The τόπος that was given to them was almost certainly for a synagogue, perhaps part of a public building rather than an individual structure.[6] The Jewish community was acknowledged by the city as being different and thus requiring special consideration. The fact that this consideration was granted suggests that the community had some autonomy and was sufficiently influential and accepted in the city to be able to defend its privileges, although the patronage of the Roman authorities was no doubt also important. The mention of a proper food supply suggests that the community followed the food laws. The final decree, which is from the early part of Augustus' reign and is addressed to the magistrates and council of Sardis, forbids interference in the collection of the tax for the Jerusalem Temple (Ant 16:171). The community was obviously faithful in observing this traditional obligation and had not cut its ties with Jerusalem.

These decrees reveal a community that was granted privileges by the Romans and by the city. It was well established, had some autonomy and its own building, and was in a secure position in the city; an important reason for this was that the Jews could point to the antiquity of their customs, which made them more acceptable to the Romans.[7] They were thus able to follow their traditions, most notably, according to these documents, the Temple tax, food laws and being able to have a communal life. In view of our discussion in chapter 1, we can therefore suggest that the community belonged to the mainstream of Jewish life in this period.

We do not hear anything of the Jewish community in Sardis in the first century CE. However, 'the place' given to the Jews by the city was probably destroyed by the major earthquake of 17 CE; subsequently the Jews were probably granted some other area.

3 The synagogue of Sardis

The synagogue of Sardis, the largest extant from antiquity, was discovered in 1962 during excavations of the city. The final publication of the excavations has not yet appeared so the following account must be regarded as preliminary. The synagogue was an integral and prominent part of the mammoth bath–gymnasium complex which occupied a central position on the major thoroughfare of the city. The complex was built as part of the civic centre of the Roman city in the reconstruction programme after the earthquake of 17 CE. A palaestra led into a multi-storied and lavishly decorated 'Marble Court', which was probably the Imperial Cult Hall, dedicated in 211/2 CE. It was the entrance to the baths and gymnasium. On the north and south sides of the palaestra were symmetrical halls, each with three large rooms, which perhaps served as dressing or exercise facilities. The south hall was Stage 1 of what became the synagogue.[8]

Building work began in the late second century CE and continued into the early third century. The south hall was extensively remodelled before it had been completed, creating a long basilican hall with two rows of columns. Three new doors were made in the east wall and an apse with two diagonal passages to the north and three niches was also added at the west end. The niches were probably for statues of the Emperor or images of deities. This was Stage 2;[9] it was probably not suitable for a synagogue because it was connected to the palaestra of the gymnasium via the northern passage in the apse. It seems fairly certain then that Stage 2 was not a synagogue but was a Roman civil basilica with the apse being used for a tribunal.[10]

By around 270 CE the building had been remodelled and had become Stage 3. Nothing in what is known of Stage 3 argues against it being a synagogue. The whole structure was 95 by 18m and was probably decorated with mosaics and revetments. It was still structurally attached to the gymnasium complex, but with access only from outside that complex. The building seems to have had no forecourt, Torah shrine or bema, and may have been little different from Stage 2. It is difficult to determine the usage of the building at this stage. It is possible that the northern passage in the apse was blocked at some time before the building was remodelled to form Stage 3. The building could then have become a synagogue between the beginning of Stage 2 in the late second century and 270 CE. Alternatively, the building at Stage 3 could have remained as a judicial basilica for some time before it was used as a synagogue.[11]

Remodelling began again around 320 CE and was completed as Stage 4 around 360. These alterations were definitely carried out by the Jewish community. A porch faced the street and behind this porch was an atrium-like forecourt, over 20m long. It was colonnaded on all four sides with elegant columns. The forecourt was open in the centre where there was a fountain in the form of a large marble urn with a vertically fluted body and large volute handles. An inscription listing public fountains at Sardis and their capacities mentions the συναγωγῆ[ς κρήνη] – 'Fountain of the Synagogue'.[12] If this was the fountain in the middle of the forecourt, then the forecourt itself was a public space, accessible to anyone wishing to use the area. Marble wall decorations found in the forecourt, including an arched frieze of urns and doves, were added in the fifth century to replace earlier plaster. There was also a basin, probably for ablutions, along one wall of the forecourt. The floor was paved with multicoloured geometrical mosaics, most of which were installed between 360 and 380 CE. The forecourt probably served as a vestibule and may also have provided space for community functions.[13]

Three doors led from the forecourt into the main hall which was 59 by 18m and could accommodate over 1,000 people. Twelve large piers about 15m high supported the wooden roof. A pair of aedicular shrines in re-use, which were fitted with curtains, flanked the central entrance. They were in place when the fourth-century mosaics were installed. Both may have been Torah shrines, or one may have been for a menorah. A marble plaque showing a menorah, lulab, shofar and two spirals interpreted as Torah scrolls was found near the southern shrine, as were all of the fragments of Hebrew inscriptions found in the building. These finds confirmed the building's identity as a synagogue.[14]

There were no benches along the walls, and no cogent evidence for a gallery has been found anywhere in the synagogue. At the opposite end from the Torah shrine(s) was a large decorated apse separated from the rest of the hall by a balustrade and lined with three rows of semi-circular benches. We would expect the Torah shrine to be in this apse, but it points west, in the opposite direction from Jerusalem. Hence the Torah shrine was added at the opposite end of the building. The apse from the earlier building was used through the addition of the benches as a place of honour for elders of the congregation and perhaps for guests. Seventy people could be comfortably seated on the benches.[15]

In front of the apse was an imposing marble table, an architectural fragment from another structure. It was 2.43 by 1.23m and weighed over two tons. It is unique in a synagogue as far as is known. Its two supports were decorated with Roman eagles clutching bundles of rods probably originally intended as the thunderbolts of Zeus. The eagles, clearly in re-use, had had their heads knocked off at some stage. The table itself seems to have been used for reading the Law. A marble slab embedded in the floor shows that the reader faced the marble shrines, Jerusalem and the congregation. The table was flanked by pairs of almost life-sized Lydian stone lions in re-use. These lions symbolically stood guard, protecting the reading table and its scrolls. Perhaps the lion as a symbol of strength also indicated the power and strength of the Torah, or of the God of the Torah. A finely carved elaborate marble menorah bearing the name 'Socrates' was found in this area. It was more than a metre wide when intact (only a fragment remains) and is of outstanding quality. Eighteen other representations of menorahs or actual menorahs were also found. In the centre of the main hall four stone slabs probably supported a canopy. A late fifth- or early sixth-century CE inscription in the midst of the slabs mentions Samoe, a 'priest and sophodidaskalos'; he probably taught from here.[16]

There were elaborate mosaic floors everywhere except around the forecourt fountain. Most of them can be dated to the middle decades of the fourth century CE by coins found beneath the floor, but some mosaics seem to have been retained from the earlier Stage 3. Each panel included an inscription giving the name of the donor. The mosaics had floral or geometric designs; a panel in the apse depicted twining vines growing from a golden urn filled with water. Two peacocks flanking the urn were destroyed in antiquity. The walls were decorated with at least six different kinds of coloured marble. These revetments took two or three generations to complete; some restoration work occurred still later. The marble formed panels of geometric, floral and animal designs including fish, lions and birds. The wall decorations included many pilaster capitals, frescos and brightly coloured glass mosaics while the wooden ceiling was painted. The overall effect of the colours, shapes, the great space, the luxurious furnishings illuminated with many lamps, must have been magnificent and very impressive. Clearly members of the community had considerable wealth which they were prepared to use for the splendid decoration of the building.[17]

Architecturally, therefore, the Sardis synagogue differed considerably from other synagogues. Although it does have features in common with other synagogues (such as the Torah shrine), it has no close parallel. Its size and location, the table, the twin shrines and the marble inlay are all notable. Clearly its style was determined by the local community, by the building's previous history and by the local architectural idiom. This building, along with other Diaspora synagogues, suggests that there were no universally established canons of synagogue architecture at this time. The emerging picture of synagogue architecture in the Diaspora and in Palestine is one of a large variety of plans.[18]

It seems likely that there were no annexe rooms associated with the synagogue and that the hall itself had multiple community uses. A row of shops facing onto the busy street was built against the south wall of the synagogue, probably some time in the second or third century CE. In their last phase these shops included paint and dye shops, a glassware shop, a hardware shop and restaurants; in such a central location they must have formed a significant centre. At this time Jews and Christians lived and worked side by side in the shops. That Jews and Christians shared this complex suggests that Jewish–Christian relations were reasonable. It also shows the degree to which the Jews were economically and socially integrated into the life of the city.[19]

The building remained in use until the abandonment of the city in 616 CE after the Sassanid attack. Craftsmanship declined in the later years of the synagogue's life, but no more rapidly in the synagogue than in other parts of the city. This decline was caused by deteriorating economic conditions in the whole of Sardis and thus is not evidence for discriminatory measures against non-Christians. Reasonably ambitious alterations indicating some degree of continuing prosperity were made in the synagogue long after Theodosius II banned the repair of synagogues apart from those buildings in imminent danger of collapse. This law, promulgated in 438 CE, apparently was not enforced at Sardis and may not often have been enforced elsewhere.[20]

4 Jewish inscriptions from Sardis

The synagogue contained over eighty inscriptions, most of which concern gifts of interior decorations and furnishings.[21] Coins discovered beneath the mosaics date most of those in the main hall to

the middle decades of the fourth century CE and those in the forecourt
to the second half of the fourth century. However, during the fourth-
century renovations it is possible that third-century inscriptions were
carefully saved and reinstalled. The inscriptions which relate to the
marble revetments range in date from the second half of the fourth
century through to the fifth and perhaps the sixth centuries.[22]

4.1

The great majority of the inscriptions are in Greek. However, a few
interesting Hebrew fragments have been found; one may have read
'Beros' i.e. 'Verus' and point to Lucius Verus, Co-Emperor with
Marcus Aurelius (161−9 CE). The wall from which the fragment
probably fell was built a century and a half after Verus' death, but
the plaque may have been cut away from a larger stone and re-used
in a second location. Hence, it is possible that an earlier inscription
was reinstalled in this later wall. We can tentatively suggest that the
Jewish community formally honoured the Co-Emperor, perhaps on
his visit to Sardis in 166 CE. We know that the city erected a statue
of Verus in the gymnasium in 166 CE; it is possible that the Jews set
up a commemorative inscription honouring Verus at the same time.
Unfortunately, this possibility remains only a tentative suggestion.[23]

4.2

The following inscription was found in the central panel of one of
the mosaics in the forecourt:

> Αὐρ. Ὀλύμπιος, φυλῆς Λεοντίων, μετὰ τῆς συμβίου κὲ
> τῶν παιδίων εὐχὴν ἐτέλεσα.[24]
>
> Aurelius Olympius, of the tribe of Leontioi, with my wife
> and my children, I have fulfilled my vow.

The mention of the 'tribe of Leontioi' is without parallel in Jewish
inscriptions in Greek. It probably refers to a tribe or association within
the Jewish community rather than a tribe within the city. The choice
of the name Λεοντίοι is also significant. The name 'Leontios' occurs
regularly in Jewish inscriptions; one example was previously found
in Sardis itself and three people who made donations to the Sardis
synagogue had this name. An unpublished Hebrew graffito from the
synagogue reads 'ben Leho' − 'son of Leo', Latin for lion. We have
noted the two pairs of lions in the Sardis synagogue; a large Lydian

lion was also found outside the synagogue forecourt. The lion is clearly a significant image for the synagogue community.[25] Robert suggested that the use of the name of 'Leontioi' for a tribe of the Jews at Sardis was an adaptation of the biblical 'tribe of Judah', the tribe described as a lion in Gen 49:9. We should also note that the tribe of Dan, all of Israel, and Judas Maccabaeus are pictured as lions.[26] In addition to this 'Jewish context' the lion was a popular image in Sardis, as is shown by the number of lion statues found in the excavations. The lion had been associated with Sardis in Greek literature since Herodotus. For example, Herodotus tells the story of the fall of Croesus' Sardis at the hands of Cyrus. Meles, an earlier king, had carried the lion borne by his mistress around the acropolis after the Telmessians had decreed that Sardis would be impregnable when the lion had been carried around the walls. However, Meles overlooked one part of the acropolis, thinking it already impregnable. It was at this point that the troops of Cyrus scaled the walls and took the acropolis.[27] We see here the mythic power of the lion as a symbol in Sardis.

The Jewish use of the lion in the synagogue, the adoption of the names 'Leontios' and 'Leo' and the naming of a tribe of the Jews as 'Leontioi' should be viewed against this dual background. It seems that the Jewish community was associating itself with a significant Jewish image – members of the people of Israel as 'lions' – but also with an image which was traditionally popular in Sardis. The lion simultaneously expressed their Jewish identity and their 'belongingness' in Sardis.[28] Consequently, it was ideally suited as an image for just such a Jewish community as is revealed by the synagogue excavations.

4.3

This inscription found in Bay 7 concerns the donation of the marble revetments which decorated the walls:

> [---]ς μετὰ τῆς συμβίου μου 'Ρηγείνης καὶ τῶν τέκνων
> ἡμῶ[ν ὑπὲρ εὐχῆς ἀπέδ]ωκα ἐκ τῶν δωρεῶν τοῦ
> παντοκράτορος Θ(εο)ῦ τὴν σκούτλωσιν πᾶσαν [τοῦ
> διαχώρο]υ καὶ τὴν ζωγραφίαν.[29]

(So and so) with my wife Regina and our children [in fulfilment of a vow] I have given out of the gifts of the Almighty God, all the revetment of the [bay?] and the paintings.

The term Παντοκράτωρ 'the Almighty', 'the ruler of all things' is not common as an attribute of the gods in paganism; however, it is regularly found in the LXX, in later Jewish writings and in some inscriptions. It expresses the supremacy of God over all things.[30]

We learn about some individuals from other inscriptions, despite their fragmentary nature. The following are representative:

4.4

[Αὐρ. Ἑ]ρμογ[ένης Σ]αρδιανὸ[ς Βουλε]υτὴς [χρυσο]χόος
vac.[ἐπλήρ]ωσα τ[ὴν εὐχήν].[31]

Aurelius Hermogenes, citizen of Sardis, member of the Council, goldsmith, I have fulfilled my vow.

4.5

The following mosaic inscription was dated to after 270 CE by coins found beneath it; it seems therefore to have been retained during the redecoration which produced Stage 4.

Αὐρ(ήλιος) Ἀλέξ[αν]δρος ὁ κα[ὶ Ἀνα]τόλιο[ς Σα]ρδ
(ιανὸς) Βουλ(ευτὴς) τ[ὸ τρί]τον διαχώρημα ἐκέντησεν.[32]

Aurelius Alexandros, also called Anatolios, citizen of Sardis, Councillor, mosaicked the third bay.

Although we know the occupations of comparatively few Jews in Sardis, it is interesting to note that three were goldsmiths, one was probably a marble sculptor, one owned a paint and dye shop (two other Jews seem to have worked for this man), another owned a glass shop, some may have been mosaic workers and others had positions in the provincial administration. Two of the Jewish goldsmiths were sufficiently wealthy to be city councillors, which suggests that they owned gold-smithing establishments and were not simply artisans. It seems likely that the occupations of the Jews were not much different from those of Gentiles.[33]

Some members of the Jewish community have the title 'citizen of Sardis'. The clear mention of citizenship is unusual and shows that possession of the citizenship of Sardis at this date was still worthy of note.[34] A total of eight Jewish men held the title of 'βουλευτής' and were thus members of the city council. One donor to the synagogue was a citizen and council member of nearby Hypaepa.

It is noteworthy how regularly the inscriptions stress the status of Jews in the city and in the local and provincial government, rather than simply their status in the Jewish community, as is usually the case elsewhere.[35]

According to the Digest of Justinian, Severus and Caracalla (some time between 198 and 211) permitted those who profess the Jewish *superstitio* to hold city offices (*honores*) but only imposed on them those obligations which would not conflict with their *superstitio*. Since the cult of the city's gods had a central place in the affairs of the city, this exemption was vital for Jews and suggests an answer to the problem of how those who are clearly identified with the synagogue as Jews can also be so involved in city life. Unfortunately, however, the law is not precise, and we have no information on how it was put into practice. Severus' and Caracalla's enactment concerning Jews was probably motivated by a desire to increase the number of people who could hold office. In the third century the holding of municipal office became a burden to be avoided because of the heavy financial cost involved. There had been some unwillingness to serve in earlier periods, but it was not until the latter part of the second century CE that it became a more widespread problem. Thus less distinguished people of only modest means were elevated to the rank of councillor.[36] That Jews held magistracies from the third century CE in Sardis can be seen against this background. However, whilst people sought to evade magistracies and liturgies because of the expenditure involved, A. H. M. Jones notes that the rank of councillor was still valued in the third century, probably because of the social prestige which continued to be associated with office and the legal privileges councillors were entitled to. Whilst holding office was more of an obligation to be fulfilled than an honour to be keenly contested, it remained a method of social advancement and a duty which bestowed prestige.[37] Thus office holders continued to receive rewards for their public spiritedness (even if it was coerced), such as inscriptions which praised their efforts.

In the Roman age, the council was the sole governing body of the city, and had considerable executive functions. It guaranteed the payment of the community's taxes to the imperial treasury, nominated people to hold magistracies and supervised the erection of monuments, tombs and public works, the granting of citizenship and honours, and the general maintenance of law and order. The size of the council varied from city to city and a councillor was generally enrolled in the council for life. There was an age limit and a property qualification for membership, with a fee generally being paid on enrolment, so that only those with substantial wealth became councillors. With the nomination of magistrates being in the hands of the council, and with only ex-magistrates generally becoming council members, the council became a self-perpetuating permanent body in which membership was virtually hereditary. The result was the formation of a wealthy ruling class which held the reins of government and enjoyed political, social and legal privileges.[38] As we have noted above, even in the third century, when city office was becoming burdensome and people of more modest means were becoming councillors, some of the value and social status of the position of councillor remained. It seems that the nine Jews who were councillors belonged to this significant social class. They probably had considerable wealth, social status and political power in the city. It is likely that their parents and children did too.

4.6

In addition, other office holders are mentioned. Aurelius Basileides was ἀπὸ ἐπιτρόπων − 'former procurator'. The procurator was an employee of the Emperor; it is most likely that Aurelius Basileides was a procurator of Imperial properties and was responsible for collecting revenues due to the Imperial treasury and for management of the Emperor's private property in the province, such as landed estates, mines and quarries. Since the procurator was a personal agent of the Emperor and not a public official he was appointed by the Imperial administration. It was clearly a position of significant rank, which would have enabled Aurelius Basileides to influence higher provincial officials.[39]

4.7

Another mosaic inscription reads 'Εὐχὴ Παύλου κόμητος' − 'Vow of Paulos, *comes*'. After the Constantinian reorganisation this title was bestowed upon leading military and civil functionaries. The holders of the title fulfilled a large variety of tasks. It could also be conferred as an additional honour on the holder of an existing office; the holder retained a privileged status for life. It is significant that a Jew could hold this elevated rank and is another indication of the high standing of some members of the Jewish community.[40]

4.8

One other member of the Jewish community was a βοηθός ταβουλάριου – an assistant in the record office or archives. This title involved a position in the Roman provincial administration. The record office was the central bureau of the procurator, and assistants in the office included clerks and accountants.[41]

Thus we see how involved members of the Jewish community in Sardis were in important positions in the wider city and in provincial administration. This, taken together with the unparalleled size and position of the synagogue and the evidence for Jews and Christians trading and living side by side, gives us a picture of a large, prosperous, highly respected and influential Jewish community of considerable social status and active in civic and political affairs. The community seems to have been integrated into the economic, social and political life of the city to an unusual degree.[42]

4.9

Eleven inscriptions to be dated in the fourth and fifth centuries CE use the term 'πρόνοια'. One inscription, which is characteristic of this group, contains the phrase ἐκ τῶν Προνοίας δομάτων. The donor attributed the ability to be able to donate the mosaic to the gifts of 'Providence'. The term seems to have been used in a quasi-liturgical fashion in the Sardis inscriptions, which suggests it was a term which was regularly used in the community. Πρόνοια was a popular term with some Jewish authors; for example in IV Macc 'Providence' or 'Divine Providence' becomes simply another name for God. It was also a popular term in pagan thought; a number of treatises 'On Providence' were produced at this time. We also know of significant philosophers who taught in Sardis from the fourth century CE onwards. The school to which they belonged could trace its philosophical origins back to Neoplatonism; since one of the central tenets of Neoplatonism was 'Divine Providence', it is likely that this was a topic discussed by pagans in Sardis.[43]

It is therefore difficult to know whether the Jewish or pagan usage of the term was the stronger influence behind its use by the Jews of Sardis. Perhaps both were equally significant and we have here a term which was shared by Jews and pagans; judging by the Jewish involvement in the city the two groups seem to have been in close contact.[44] We can suggest that the Jews recognised 'πρόνοια' as a part of their tradition that was also understood by their contemporaries and which was thus a possible vehicle for communication. The situation seems similar to the Jewish usage of the lion image and the name 'Leontios'; Providence was a term which had Jewish roots but which was also very much 'at home' in Sardis. By using it, the Jewish community could simultaneously express their Jewish identity and their 'belongingness' in Sardis.

4.10

The following inscription was found in the centre of the hall, where it replaced an earlier centrepiece, perhaps around 500 CE: Εὐχὴ [Σ]αμοῆ ἱερέος κὲ σοφοδιδασκάλου – Vow of Samoe, Priest and Sophodidaskalos. Three other priests are known from inscriptions in Asia Minor, and a number of others from inscriptions elsewhere. In this period priests may have had a minor part in synagogue worship, such as pronouncing certain benedictions, or they may have been preferred readers of the Torah.[45] It is noteworthy that in Sardis it was still regarded as a status worth possessing long after the destruction of the Temple.

The title 'sophodidaskalos' is unique in synagogue inscriptions. Perhaps it means wise teacher or teacher of wisdom? Or is it the equivalent of Rabbi? It suggests that Samoe was a teacher–scholar and thus a person of importance in the community where learning seems to have been valued. Perhaps he was head of a school of some sort which met around the platform where the inscription was found. Such a school would have been an important factor in maintaining Jewish traditions.[46] That 'sophodidaskalos' was the title used is interesting. If, as seems likely, Samoe fulfilled a similar role to a Rabbi, it is noteworthy that he was not *called* 'Rabbi', a title found in a considerable number of inscriptions.[47] This suggests that Sardis was well removed from the Rabbinic sphere of influence, which reinforces the likelihood that local factors were very important in shaping the form and nature of the Jewish community in Sardis, just as such factors had a strong influence on the style of building which the community owned.

4.11

One inscription engraved on a plaque read:

Εὑρὼν κλάσας ἀναγνῶθι φύλαξον.[48]

Having found and having broken open, read and observe.

The inscription is not a dedication but a motto in what seems to be a kind of formal liturgical language. It could have been part of the base of the Torah shrine, on a pedestal, or perhaps part of the Eagle Table. κλάσας may refer to breaking open a seal of a scroll in order to open it, or perhaps to 'breaking open a text' by discussing its meaning. The inscription seems to remind the community of the importance of studying the Torah and of observing the commandments found in it.[49] Or perhaps it was meant to be read by visitors to the synagogue and to encourage them to investigate the Torah. In any case, it certainly points to the significance of the Torah for the community.

4.12

Another inscription referred to the marble inlaying of the νομοφυλ[ά]κιον – the place which protects the Law, which was probably the Torah shrine. The name implies that the Torah scrolls were held in great respect as objects of sanctity that had to be protected. In addition, it seems likely that one reason for the modifications to the synagogue which produced Stage 4 was so that the Torah shrine(s) might be built as a permanent home for the scrolls. These two factors indicate architecturally the significance of the Torah for the community.[50]

4.13

The end of a fragmentary inscription found in the main hall reads Κύρι[ε βο]ήθι τῷ οἴκῳ τού[τ]ῳ. In the LXX the verb βοηθέω is often used with ὁ Κύριος, and similar inscriptions to this one from Sardis are found in other synagogues. The inscription seems to express, albeit in a standardised formula, a reliance on God, who is understood to be 'the helper' of the community.[51]

5 Related issues

How did this magnificent building in an unparalleled location become a Jewish synagogue, especially if it had earlier been used as a judicial tribunal? All of the inscriptions relate to the decoration and furnishing of the building rather than its construction, indicating that the community acquired the building after it had been built.[52] So how did the Jews acquire such a building? Perhaps it was replaced by another judicial tribunal, although this has not yet been found. The city could then have sold the unused building to the Jewish community. There may have been a large number of Jews living nearby, as suggested by the Jewish shops in the locality at a later time, and this might have played a part in the transfer of the building. In addition, the inscriptions reveal a politically powerful and influential group, as we noted above. This 'lobby' may have convinced the city council (which had a number of Jewish members over time) to donate the building to the Jews or to sell it at a reasonable price. Perhaps the city as a whole was favourably disposed to the Jewish community and would have applauded such generosity, or perhaps it was in return for contributions to the city by wealthy Jews. All the indications are that relations between the city and the Jews were harmonious and friendly and that Jews were socially acceptable. Certainly the prominent position of the synagogue within the city and the fact that the Jewish community continued to own the building indicate a degree of cooperation and understanding, or at the very least, tolerance, between the Jewish community and the civic authority, over a long period of time. These good relations were probably a factor in the Jews acquiring the building.[53]

We have noted that although it is difficult to know exactly when the building became a synagogue, it is likely that this occurred towards the end of the third century. It also seems likely that the community was already prominent within Sardis by this time, since it is improbable that a less influential community could acquire such a building. The decrees preserved in Josephus show that even in the first century BCE the community could claim that it had been well established for a long period; it was granted privileges and seems to have been in a strong position. We can therefore suggest that there was a significant degree of continuity from the mid first century BCE to the time the community acquired the synagogue, although the lack of evidence in the interim period is unfortunate.[54] We certainly have no evidence to the contrary.

It is significant that the building was not converted into a church in the later period. We do know of Christians in the area – the letter in Rev 3:1 –6, Melito and the Church which was called 'EA' by the excavators, probably built in the last quarter of the fourth century. In the fourth and fifth century Christianity became more prominent in the city with the destruction of some pagan temples. Clearly the synagogue would have made an excellent church; we know that at Ostia a Christian basilica was built over a functioning synagogue in the late fourth or early fifth century. This suggests that the Jews retained their influence and significance in the city right up until the seventh century, despite the growing power of Christianity. As we noted above, the shops suggest that relations between Christians and Jews were not hostile. In addition, the fact that the Jewish community was able to maintain the building until 616 also shows that it continued to prosper economically.[55] All of this suggests that there was a strong degree of continuity in the Jewish community not only from the first century BCE to the third century CE but also from the third to the seventh century.

The synagogue also provides evidence for the pride and self-confidence of the Jewish community and the desire to attract others. The forecourt opening onto a busy street was built by the community, and it seems to have been designed to be attractive and inviting.[56] The hall of the synagogue was adorned in a very beautiful way; it must have made a deep impression on visitors. There is no hint of defensiveness; in fact, the building takes maximum advantage of its prime location to put Judaism 'on display'. The message about the Jewish community communicated by the luxurious building to passers-by must have been very positive, and this seems to have been by design.[57] We thus gain a picture of a strong, confident community which was endeavouring to attract others to its faith. The community could, after all, have done many things differently, particularly regarding the remodelling of the building, but it seems to have been intent on creating a synagogue that would attract Gentiles.

The synagogue contained a number of articles in re-use from other buildings and shrines, such as the Roman monument bearing eagles carved in relief, probably from a monument of the Imperial cult, and the marble lions, perhaps originally associated with an image of Cybele.[58] Given the significance of these statues in pagan Sardis, the fact that they were made available to the Jewish community, presumably by the city authorities who were closing the temples, is another sign of the secure status of the Jewish community under

Constantine and immediately thereafter.[59] The bold use of Lydian
and Roman sculpture in such prominent places in the synagogue
means the Jews considered them 'Jewish'. They seem able to use
them to enhance the table from which the Torah was read, not
to detract from it through the use of 'pagan symbols'. This attitude
expressed in the re-use of 'pagan symbols' seems to be an extension
of the community's attitude when it took over the Roman judicial
tribunal. The building's former pagan usage and its continuing
attachment to the pagan gymnasium – bath complex did not prevent
the community converting the building into an impressive synagogue.
We see again the boldness and strength of the community's Judaism.
Note also that a relief of Artemis and Cybele was put into the
forecourt face down by the Jewish builders.[60] Re-use of pagan
symbols was carefully done.

The Church at Sardis was one of the recipients of the 'Seven
Letters' of Revelation, where it is compared unfavourably with
the Church of an earlier day (Rev 3:1–6). Melito was the bishop
of Sardis in the latter part of the second century CE. He was a
Quartodeciman and we have a complete work of his – the *Peri
Pascha* – and a number of other fragments. In a prolonged section
of the *Peri Pascha* Israel is reproached for the death of Christ;
other Quartodeciman texts and early examples of *Adversus Iudaeos*
literature do not show the same intensity in their attack on Israel
as does Melito. This is particularly clear in the way he sees the
Jews as the sole agents of the crucifixion.[61]

We have noted that the social status and influential position
of the Jewish community is evident from the synagogue and its
inscriptions. Kraabel has suggested that, faced with this powerful Jewish community, Melito felt forced to mount the prolonged
attack which we see in the *Peri Pascha*. It was an attempt on Melito's
part to establish and preserve the identity of his community over
against the powerful Jews in Sardis. Melito therefore argued that
the Jewish λαός had had its day and was now superseded by ἡ
ἐκκλησία. Consequently, the socio-political reality of the local
Jewish community goes a long way towards explaining Melito's
rhetorical polemic against the Jews.[62] The evidence from the Jewish
community certainly helps us to understand the writings of Melito
more clearly.

6 The Jewish community at Priene

Priene in Ionia was always a relatively small city, its economic growth
being hampered by the existence of Miletus just to the south and by
the gradual silting up of its own harbour. It was a planned Hellenistic
city laid out on a regular grid-pattern which was retained since the
city was never modified by the overlay of Roman buildings. Its culture
was strongly Ionian and Greek.[63]

The city was excavated by a German expedition in 1895–8. They
found the synagogue of the Jewish community but incorrectly
identified it as a 'house church'. The building, situated in the 'West
Gate Street', was a remodelled house, earlier walls being removed
when the transformation occurred. From the main street one entered
a small lane and then turned into a small forecourt beyond which was
the main room, measuring 10 by 14m and entered by a single door.
This room contained two rows of columns of which only one base
remains. These columns were a later addition; it seems that the
synagogue as originally formed was an open room. There was also
a single bench along the north wall and a square Torah niche in the
east Jerusalem-facing wall. The niche is the main feature in the
otherwise plain room. At the right of the niche there was a marble
basin, nearly a metre in diameter and probably used for ablutions.
It is likely that rooms associated with the synagogue were also used
by the community for its functions and perhaps as a hostel. Three
engravings confirm the identity of the building. They contain
depictions of the menorah, lulab, ethrog and shofar; in addition a
menorah is shown on a stone with two rolled up Torah scrolls placed
between the branches and the base of the menorah.[64]

The German excavators dated the remodelled structure no later
than the fourth or fifth centuries, but they were influenced in this by
their identification of it as a house church. The synagogue could well
be earlier, but this is uncertain because no further work has been done
at the site. Kraabel suggests that a third century CE date might be
likely.[65]

The contrast between this building and the synagogue at Sardis is
striking. The synagogue at Priene was small and probably
undecorated; no mosaics or frescos have been found. It was on a side
street and was not easily identified as a synagogue. There are none
of the signs of obvious prosperity and influence that are to be found
at Sardis, although the city itself was quite small and did not prosper
in the period to which the synagogue belongs. The two buildings show

clearly the diversity of Judaism in Asia Minor. They also reveal that the local environment had a marked effect on the Jewish communities – in large prosperous Sardis, the Jewish community flourished; in smaller Priene, the Jewish community reflected the conditions of the city.

We have noted that provision for the Torah dominated the room; this suggests that the Torah was very important to the Jewish community. All the objects engraved on stones from the building are traditional Jewish symbols. The basin for ablutions beside the Torah suggests that the reader of the Torah washed his or her hands before touching the scrolls. As at Sardis, where a wash basin and fountain were found in the forecourt, we can suggest that the Jewish community at Priene observed some form of purity rules. Thus, although we know very little about the community, there are some signs which suggest that it belonged within the 'mainstream' of Jewish faith and practice of the period.

7 A synagogue at Miletus?

That Miletus had a Jewish community is clear from Josephus (Ant 14:244–6), and from an inscription in the theatre which reads: Τόπος Εἰουδέων τῶν καὶ θεοσεβίον. Early this century von Gerkan identified a building in Miletus as the community's synagogue. It was a small room (18.5 by 11.6m), built in the late third or early fourth century CE on the plan of a basilica, with a peristyle court at the side.

It is far from certain that the building was a synagogue. No Jewish evidence was found in or near the complex, and only half of the main room and less than one-sixth of the courtyard was excavated. It was identified as a synagogue because of its general similarity to the synagogues of Palestine, which had been studied by Kohl and Watzinger just prior to von Gerkan's discovery of the Miletus building. However, the synagogues at Priene, Sardis and Ostia show that Palestinian building plans were not always reproduced in the Diaspora. The one inscription that was found in the building was on a column and concerned a Poseidon altar, erected at the command of Helios Apollo. Von Gerkan thought that the building became a synagogue by adaptation after this altar had been destroyed. However, it seems more reasonable to suggest that the building was a pagan temple throughout its history. There is no positive evidence that it was ever a synagogue.[66]

8 Conclusions

The Jewish community at Sardis seems to have been influential, prominent and 'at home' in Sardis to a striking degree from the third century CE onwards. This is shown, for example, by the impressive building, the involvement of Jews in the city, the adoption of local symbols or ideas such as the lion, and the idea of Providence, both of which were prominent in Jewish tradition and pagan thought. The community's roots went back to at least *c.* 200 BCE; the involvement of the Jewish community in the life of the city from the third century CE onwards is therefore understandable − Jews had been in Sardis for a long time and had been able to establish themselves. From the evidence of Josephus we can suggest that in the first century BCE the community was also in a secure and respected position in the city and was granted a number of privileges. There seems therefore to have been a significant degree of continuity over a long period of time.

Yet the Jews at Sardis flourished as *Jews*. The Torah shrine(s) and table dominated the synagogue; the Torah was to be observed and was also protected, showing the respect in which it was held. Ritual ablutions of some sort were carried out. A number of those who had been successful in the life of the city (and thus became city councillors) made donations in the synagogue, showing their commitment to Judaism. These people seem to have been accepted in the wider city as Jews. The community had not lost its distinctiveness, nor had it abandoned its traditions just because it was well integrated in the city. Members of the community maintained their identity while partici-pating in the wider life of the city. Indeed the impression we gain is of a strong, vibrant Jewish community; their involvement in the life of Sardis and their ownership of a building which was part of the baths − gymnasium complex attests a strong assurance and confidence in their Jewish faith.[67] Further, the Jewish community seems to have been well removed from the Rabbinic sphere of influence. This is highly significant for our view of Judaism in Asia Minor.

The Jewish community at Priene was small and undistinguished. In looking at the communities at Sardis and Priene we see how different Jewish communities could be; local history and local factors − the length of time the community had been in the city, the arrangements made at its foundation, its wealth and social position, the prosperity of the city itself − are clearly vital. Nevertheless, despite their differences, both communities are undeniably Jewish.

3

THE JEWISH COMMUNITY AT ACMONIA

1 Introduction

Acmonia, a city of native origin situated on the ancient Persian Royal Road, was a city of significant wealth and commercial importance with a considerable population. The natural strength of the site and the convergence of roads nearby meant that the city was the military centre of the area. In the first century BCE Acmonia had a local government and began issuing its own coinage. Its significance is shown by the fact that it was the seat of a high priesthood of the Imperial cult and also enjoyed the Neokorate. The city probably had a group of Roman settlers and became quite Romanised. Since it was an important city in Phrygia, it is probable that some of the Jews relocated by Zeuxis in 205 BCE settled in the city. It was in the conventus of Apamea and so it is likely that some of the Jewish gold collected by Flaccus' officials in this conventus in 62 BCE came from Acmonia.[1]

2 The Julia Severa inscription

Τὸν κατασκευασθέ[ν]τα ο[ἴ]κον ὑπὸ Ἰουλίας Σεουήρας Π. Τυρρώνιος Κλάδος ὁ διὰ βίου ἀρχισυνάγωγος καὶ Λούκιος Λουκίου ἀρχισυνάγωγος καὶ Ποπίλιος Ζωτικὸς ἄρχων ἐπεσκεύασαν ἔκ τε τῶν ἰδίων καὶ τῶν συνκαταθεμένων καὶ ἔγραψαν τοὺς τοίχους καὶ τὴν ὀροφὴν καὶ ἐποίησαν τὴν τῶν θυρίδων ἀσφάλειαν καὶ τὸν [λυ]πὸν πάντα κόσμον, οὕστινας κα[ὶ] ἡ συναγωγὴ ἐτείμησεν ὅπλῳ ἐπιχρύσῳ διά τε τὴν ἐνάρετον αὐτῶν δ[ι]άθε[ε]σιν καὶ τὴν πρὸς τὴν συναγωγὴν εὔνοιάν τε καὶ σ[που]δήν.[2]

This building was erected by Julia Severa; P(ublius) Tyrronios Klados, the head for life of the synagogue, and Lucius, son of

Lucius, head of the synagogue, and Publius Zotikos, archon, restored it with their own funds and with money which had been deposited, and they donated the (painted) murals for the walls and the ceiling, and they reinforced the windows and made all the rest of the ornamentation, and the synagogue honoured them with a gilded shield on account of their virtuous disposition, goodwill and zeal for the synagogue.

The text deals with the restoration of the synagogue which was originally built by Julia Severa. We know from coinage that she was active in the 50s and 60s of the first century CE, thus suggesting that this inscription is to be dated in the 80s or 90s, in order to allow time for the synagogue to require repairs.[3] It is therefore the earliest synagogue in Asia Minor attested by an inscription.

Julia Severa is well known from numismatic and epigraphic evidence. She was ἀρχιέρεια of the Imperial cult at Acmonia for at least three terms of office in the reign of Nero and was also an agonothete.[4] The difficult matter is to decide whether she was a Jew. She built a synagogue for the Jewish community, but Luke 7:5 records an instance of an Herodian centurion doing the same for the Jews at Capernaum. Ramsay noted that Julia Severa was a magistrate with Tyrronius Rapon, which he took to mean that they were married. In addition, he thought that the name 'Tyrronius' was only used by Jews, implying that Julia Severa was a Jew.[5] However, nothing indicates that Julia Severa and Tyrronius Rapon were married and the Latin name 'Tyrronius' is certainly not always Jewish.[6] We therefore have no positive evidence to suggest that Julia Severa was a Jew. Further, she was a priestess of a pagan cult and, although it is certain that some Jews apostasised from their faith, it is most unlikely that those who had done so would have continued to associate with the synagogue or would have made a donation to the community. In addition, in the case of an apostasised Jew it is unlikely that the community would either have accepted the gift of a synagogue or have commemorated the benefaction in an inscription marking the restoration of the synagogue. It seems therefore that Julia Severa was a 'Gentile sympathiser', a pagan who was favourably disposed towards the Jews and built a synagogue as their patroness.[7]

It is also clear, as we noted above, that Julia Severa was a very important person in Acmonia, having been priestess of the Imperial cult and an agonothete. Her first husband, Servenius Capito, belonged to a family of great distinction. Their son, L. Servenius Cornutus, entered the Senate under Nero and was legatus to the proconsul of Asia, probably in 73 CE, and also held many other offices; a kinsman, C. Iulius Severus, was a consul. Levick describes Julia Severa as being of 'aristocratic blood [with] high standing in Acmonia and wealth ... [She belonged to] a nexus of leading families'.[8] She would have been a most distinguished and powerful patroness of the Jewish community and would no doubt have looked after the community's interests. It is significant that the Jewish community was able to attract her support. The fact that she was a high priestess of the Imperial cult did not deter them from accepting her gift or from recalling it a number of years later.

This inscription also gives an unusually full description of the synagogue in Acmonia. Whilst the decorations were unlikely to have been as elaborate as those of the Sardis synagogue, nor the murals as impressive as those at Dura-Europos, the overall effect in the Acmonian synagogue may still have been very impressive.[9] Two marble capitals of Jewish origin have been found at Acmonia. They were decorated with a menorah and a Torah scroll viewed end on. The editors of MAMA concluded that the two stones must be from a synagogue, possibly the building erected by Julia Severa.[10] These capitals may then be part of the decorations mentioned in this inscription. The depiction of a Torah scroll points to the significance of the Scriptures for this community, a fact which, as we shall see, is corroborated by the prominent place given to the Scriptures in the inscriptions. The community recognised the benefaction of the three office holders by honouring them with a large shield overlaid with gold. The inscription was also written to honour these three for their generosity. Both customs were traditional forms of acknowledgement for benefactors in Greek cities.[11]

3 'The curses written in Deuteronomy'

Tombs in Phrygia and elsewhere in Asia Minor were often protected against violation by the use of a fine paid to an heir, the city authorities or a religious group and/or by a curse formula invoking the vengeance of the offended deity.[12] Jewish inscriptions in Asia Minor used both fines and curse formulae to protect graves. Whilst such curses and fines are absent from Jewish inscriptions in Beth Shearim,

Palestine, Syria and Europe, they are found in the Jewish inscriptions of Asia Minor. It seems that here, Jews have been influenced by the general concern about grave violation in the area.[13] One gravestone from Acmonia is decorated with a mirror, basket, distaff and spindle and a comb, which are representative of the labour of the two women who are buried in the tomb. These decorations are characteristic of gravestones in part of Lydia, in Phrygia and in Bithynia.[14] The principal face of the stone is decorated in the centre with a large crown and is engraved with the following epitaph:

3.1

ἔτους τλγ'. Αὐρ. Φρουγιανὸς Μηνοκρίτου καὶ Αὐρ.
Ἰουλιανὴ γυνὴ αὐτοῦ Μακαρία μητρὶ καὶ Ἀλεξανδρία
θυγατρὶ γλυκυτάτη ζῶντες κατεσκεύασαν μνήμης χάριν·
εἰ δέ τις μετὰ τὸ τεθῆναι αὐτοὺς εἴ τις θάψει ἕτερον νεκρὸν
ἢ ἀδικήσει λόγω ἀγορασίας, ἔσται αὐτῷ αἱ ἀραὶ ἡ
γεγραμμέναι ἐν τῷ Δευτερονομίῳ.
On the left side is engraved:
ἀγορανομία σειτωνεία παραφυλακεία πάσας ἀρχὰς καὶ
λειτουργίας τελέσας καὶ στρατηγήσαντα.[15]

The year 333 (= 248–249 CE). Aurelios Phrougianos, son of Menocritos, and Aurelia Juliana, his wife, have constructed this monument while still living for Makaria, (their) mother and for Alexandria, (their) sweetest daughter, in remembrance. If anyone, after their burial, if anyone inters another corpse or causes damage by way of purchase, there shall be on him the curses (or the curse) which are written in Deuteronomy.
On the left hand side:
Office of Clerk of the Market, Corn-purchaser, Commander of police, having fulfilled all magistracies and liturgies, and having held the office of Strategos.

The following inscription engraved on a quadrangular altar also comes from Acmonia:

3.2

[...]ιν [ἐξ]ἐϚται ἑτέρω ἀνῦξαι τὸ κάθετον ἢ μόνον ἐὰν
συνβῇ τοῖς παιδίοις αὐτοῦ Δόμνη κ- ᾿Αλεξανδρία· ἐὰν δὲ
γαμηθήσονται ἐξὸν οὐκ ἔσται ἀνύξαι· ὃς δὲ ἂν τολμήσει
ἕτερον ἐπισενένκαι θήσει τῶ ἱερωτάτω ταμίω ᾿Αττικὰς α
κ- οὐδὲν ἔλαττον ἔσται τῶ τῆς τυμβωρυχίας ἐνκλήματι
ὑπεύθυνος· ἔσται δὲ ἐπικατάρατος ὁ τυοῦτος κ- ὅσαι ἀραὶ
ἐν τῶ Δευτερονομίω εἰσὶν γεγραμμέναι αὐτῶ τε κ- τέκνοις
κ- ἐγγόνοις κ- παντὶ τῶ γένει αὐτοῦ γένοιντο.[16]

... It is not lawful for another (person) to open the lair, but
only (his) wife for (the burial of) his young children Domne
and Alexandria. But if they are married it is not permitted
(for the tomb) to be opened. But whoever dares to assault
it with another corpse, he will pay to the consecrated treasury
1000 Attic drachmae and nonetheless he shall be liable for
the accusation of grave robbing. And this man will be
accursed and as many curses as are written in Deuteronomy,
let them be upon him and (his) children and (his) grandchildren and all his offspring.

The references to the Book of Deuteronomy make it certain that
the people mentioned in these inscriptions are Jews. These two inscriptions also enable us to understand another inscription engraved
on a quadrangular altar.

3.3

᾿Εγένετο ἔτους τκη΄. Τ. Φλ. ᾿Αλέξανδρος ζῶν ἑαυτῶ καὶ
Γαιανῇ γυναικὶ τὸ μνημεῖον κατεσκεύασεν μνήμης χάριν,
βουλεύσας, ἄρξας, ζήσας καλῶς, μηδένα λοιπήσας·
μετὰ δὲ τεθῆναι ἐμὲ τὸν ᾿Αλέξανδρον καὶ τὴν σύνβιον
μου Γαιανήν, εἴ τις ἀνύξῃ τὸ μνημῖον, ἔσονται αὐτῶ
κατάραι ὅσε ᾿ανγεγραμμέναι ἰσιν εἰς ὅρασιν καὶ ἰς ὅλον
τὸ σῶμα αὐτῶ καὶ εἰς τέκνα καὶ εἰς βίον· εἴ τις δὲ ἐπιχιρήσῃ
ἀνῦξαι, θήσι ἰς τὸ ταμῖον προστίμου* φ΄.
On the other three faces of the same altar are inscribed:
Εἰρηναρχία. Σειτωνία. -- Βουλαρχία. ᾿Αγορανομία. --
Στρατηγία. Σειτωνία.[17]

Made in 328 (= 243–244 CE).

Titus Flavius Alexandros built this tomb in his lifetime
for himself and his wife Gaiana as a memorial; having been

a member of the Council, Archon, having lived an honourable life and grieved nobody. When we are buried, myself Alexandros and my wife Gaiana, if anyone opens the tomb, there will be on him all the curses which are written, on his sight and his whole body and his children and his life; and if anyone attempts to open (it), he will have to pay to the treasury as a fine 500 denarii.
Warden of the Peace − Corn Purchaser. President of the Council − Clerk of the Market. Chief Magistrate − Corn Purchaser.

Ramsay noted that 'the curses which are written' was an abbreviation for 'the curses which are written in Deuteronomy', thus confirming the Jewish origin of this inscription.[18] I will firstly outline what was involved in the titles held by Aurelios Phrougianos (in 3.1) and Titus Flavius Alexandros (in 3.3).[19]

The 'Αγορανόμος was the elected controller of the market who supervised the sale and purchase of commodities. His tasks could involve upkeep and construction of the market buildings, collection of rentals, regulation of the quality and price of goods and inspection of the weights and measures used. The most onerous task was probably that of solving the problems of food and oil supply by causing the merchants to sell at reasonable prices or by actually providing the goods for sale himself. Thus the agoranomos was charged with duties of some importance for the life of the city.[20]

The Σιτώνης was the public corn buyer. This elected position involved ensuring that the city had a sufficient supply of corn, which was the staple foodstuff (especially of the poor) but which was subject to violent fluctuations of price because of crop failure, transportation problems or political troubles. Corn was sometimes levied from landowners, and most cities drew some rent in corn from public lands; additional requirements had to be purchased on the open market from elsewhere and many cities had special funds for this purpose. In a shortage, richer citizens were expected to give corn or contribute money for its purchase, and a public-spirited sitones often sold corn at below cost prices. At times it could involve considerable personal expenditure and some holders of the office are commended for serving at difficult times.[21]

Παραφύλαξ was the title given to the commander of the local police. He had particular responsibility for the protection of a city's rural territory against brigands and the maintenance of law and order in the countryside and had under his command a body of 'frontier-guards'. The position was an important one which involved considerable power.[22]

The title στρατηγός came to designate a member of the governing committee of the Council and thus in many cases one of the principal civil magistrates and leading officials of a city. The various duties of the strategoi could include presiding over the Assembly, administering oaths to minor colleagues, the right to propose measures to the Council and Assembly, supervising public finances and announcing the bestowal of honours. Clearly, the title involved large responsibility and considerable power in the life of the city.[23]

βουλεύω means to be a member of the Council. In the period under consideration, the Council was the sole governing body of the city. There was a property qualification for membership so that only the wealthy became councillors. Membership was usually for life and office tended to be hereditary. Thus the Council became a powerful body made up of the wealthy ruling class who had considerable economic, social and political power.[24]

The Βούλαρχος was the presiding officer of the Council. The position involved the calling of meetings, the leadership of negotiations and supervision over the execution of the Council's decisions. When we recall the importance of the Council, it is clear that this office was near the pinnacle of civic government.[25]

The Εἰρηνάρχης or 'Warden of the Peace' was responsible for the maintenance of order and public discipline, the reforming of public morals and the suppression of serious crime in the city. The eirenarch commanded a body of mounted constables, arrested and interrogated bandits, compiled evidence and gave testimony before the magistrate at a trial. He was chosen by the governor from a list of ten leading citizens submitted by the Council. The holder evidently had a high rank, for the title usually appears among those held by important officials. Clearly Titus Flavius Alexandros was in favour with both the city and the Roman governor.[26]

A provincial with the name 'Titus Flavius Alexandros' almost certainly derived his Roman citizenship from either Vespasian or Titus.[27] His family had thus held Roman citizenship for over 150 years and at least for the first 100 years were members of the privileged small minority of those who held the citizenship. It is not surprising, then, that he held offices such as boularch and strategos. Aurelios Phrougianos or his family probably gained Roman citizenship through the Constitutio Antoniniana.[28] Both of these inscriptions are to be dated after Severus and Caracalla permitted Jews to hold civic office, though only imposing on them those duties which would not conflict with their *superstitio*. As we noted in chapter 2, by the third century CE it was becoming increasingly difficult for cities to find people who were willing and sufficiently wealthy to be able to fulfil local offices. However, although holding office was burdensome, the rank of councillor was still valued in the third century.[29] The warm tone of the many inscriptions mentioning office holders shows that much honour and prestige was still associated with fulfilling these positions. It seems clear therefore that the two Jews mentioned in these inscriptions were prominent and public-spirited citizens of Acmonia whose contribution to the city's life brought them honour and respect.

As we have seen, both Aurelios Phrougianos and Titus Flavius Alexandros held significant offices in the city of Acmonia. It is not unreasonable to suggest that the Jewish community as a whole also took an active part in the life of the city. While the inscriptions are both dated in the 240s it is likely that the influence and involvement of the two men and of the Jewish community goes back quite a number of years. In the case of Titus Flavius Alexandros' family, their involvement in the life of the city may have gone back many years indeed.

We will now turn to the phrase 'the curses which are written in Deuteronomy'. Ramsay wrote as follows about this phrase:

> The allusion ... is to the great chapters of curses, Dt 27–29. The curses there written are not specifically against violators of graves, but the same curses as are there written are here invoked against violation ... The Phrygian Jews were in the habit of adapting to the sepulchral purpose that part of the Law of Moses which they found convenient for their purpose without any regard to its force in its own context.[30]

Kraabel commented further:

> These inscriptions mention curses which accompany the giving of the covenant in Deut, but [the inscriptions] make no direct reference to the covenant itself; the Acmonian curses are not seen as incurred by breaking the covenant, since they are directed to Gentiles (outside the covenant) as well as to Jews. In these three inscriptions at least, the OT is used as a magic book whose curses have a supernatural protective power.[31]

However, an examination of the LXX of Deut 27–30 suggests that the Jewish community was acting in accord with the intent of the passage rather than disregarding the context or using the book as 'magic'.[32]

Deut 27:15–28:68 is an outline of the blessings or curses which will come upon the people as a result of their obedience or disobedience to the commands of Yahweh.[33] Deut 28 contains interesting material from the perspective of a Diaspora Jew. An expulsion from the land is implied in v32 and expressed in v36. Verses 47–57 assume that the people were indeed faithless. The evils described are no longer threats or possibilities *if* certain conditions are fulfilled; rather the people will certainly experience these woes *because* these conditions have been fulfilled. Exile is a certain future event. Verses 58–68 return to conditional statements, but again the result of infidelity to the law is exile.[34] Of interest here is how Diaspora Jews would have interpreted this passage in the Roman period. The passage explains that their present circumstances result from disobedience; Yahweh had found their ancestors guilty and had carried out the threatened curses of the law. The blessings and curses of the passage would thus perhaps produce in the Diaspora Jew the will to obey Yahweh in the present and an internal consent with the message of the book.[35]

In Deut 29–30 Moses exhorts the people to faithful obedience. It is certain that future generations will abandon the covenant and that the curses of the previous chapter will come upon the people. This passage is not, as in the standard curse lists, a mere listing of possible evils. Rather the threats have become horrible realities and the question is asked why they have come about. It is because Yahweh has brought upon the land 'all the curses written in the book of this law', and has scattered the people into other lands (v26–7). The catastrophe is assumed and the present destruction is placed in the context of the broken covenant and the realised covenantal curse. Like Deut 28, the passage would speak to people of the Diaspora as an explanation of their current situation.

Deut 30:1–10 offers hope of a return to divine favour for those in exile. Good can succeed the evil which has filled the recent past. This suggests that the passage would have been of great significance for Diaspora Jews because these verses outline what Yahweh will do *after* the implementation of the curses has resulted in their being 'cast out to other lands'. Yahweh will have compassion upon his people who will return to him in obedience and experience an inner conversion. The overall effect is hortatory. If fidelity is renewed, the activated curses will end and the blessings will be renewed.[36] One of the blessings is particularly noteworthy for our study:

> καὶ δώσει κύριος ὁ θεός σου τὰς ἀρὰς ταύτας ἐπὶ τοὺς ἐχθρούς σου καὶ ἐπὶ τοὺς μισοῦντάς σε, οἳ ἐδίωξάν σε.
> And the Lord your God will place [or hand over] these curses[37] on your enemies, and on those who hate you, those who have persecuted you. (v7)

When the people have returned to Yahweh, one of the blessings he will bestow on them is the transference of the curses of the preceding chapters from them to their enemies. Thus it seems very probable that it is this verse which lies behind the reference to 'the curses of Deuteronomy' in these Acmonian inscriptions. The Acmonian writers of our inscriptions were acting in accordance with this verse, and with the intent of Deut 30:1–10 as a whole, in applying the curses of Deut 27–29 to grave violators. They had returned to Yahweh in obedience and now they were asking Yahweh to apply the curses written in Deuteronomy to their enemies, that is, to the violators of their graves. The Scripture itself encourages this application of curses against covenant breakers to a new context.[38]

We see, therefore, that Ramsay's understanding of the Jews as completely disregarding the context of the curses and Kraabel's suggestion that they were treating Deuteronomy as a magic book are mistaken. The writers of these inscriptions were sensitive to the meaning of the passage. They were acting in accordance with its intent and interpreting it in the light of their own situation and concerns in the Diaspora. They were invoking God's curse, as the Deuteronomy text suggests they should, upon grave violators. In fact far from being 'magic', Deuteronomy, and probably the Septuagint as a whole, was functioning as Scripture for them and thus as an authority and guide in their situation.[39]

The following points also arise from these three inscriptions. The phrase 'the curses written in Deuteronomy' is a formulaic way of referring to the large passage of curses. What is significant here is that, despite this being a public inscription almost certainly set up in a public cemetery, no further details were thought to be needed to ensure that grave violators were deterred.[40] The inscriptions presume an amount of knowledge on the part of any reader and a great deal of respect for this Book, or perhaps for the God whose curses were written in the Book. The mere mention of 'Deuteronomy' is presumed to be a sufficient deterrent. In commenting on grave curses in general, Lattimore writes: 'There must have been a widespread belief that such defensive curses would work, that the religious awe of the public in general would correspond to the intense concern felt by those who built the tomb.'[41] It seems that the Book of Deuteronomy must have commanded the 'religious awe of the public' for these curses to be effective. This implies a surprising respect for Jewish tradition on the part of ordinary people in Acmonia.

The use of the title Δευτερονόμιον for the fifth book of the Pentateuch suggests the Septuagint was used in the community. The Hebrew title – אֵלֶּה הַדְּבָרִים – comes from the first two words of the book, whilst the Greek title is from Deut 17:18: γράψει ἑαυτῷ τὸ δευτερονόμιον τοῦτο εἰς βιβλίον. The use of Δευτερονόμιον in our inscription shows that the Scriptures were read in their Greek translation at Acmonia.[42]

Inscription 3.1 is one of a series of third-century CE funerary altars from Acmonia engraved on altars of the same shape and size with similar decorations.[43] Of the five engraved altars of this type from Acmonia only one is clearly Jewish (3.1), whilst the other four are almost certainly of pagan origin. It is interesting to note that here again Jews and pagans have important funerary practices in common. The Jewish stone is chronologically at the end of the series, suggesting that Aurelios Phrougianos had adopted this pagan style, rather than the reverse. He had been involved in the city's life as had (the non-Jew) Aurelios Basileus Olunpos, another of the men who used this style of gravestone, who was a city councillor and whose son Aurelios Eutuchianos was a member of the decania.[44] Perhaps this was one of the styles of gravestone favoured amongst people of social standing and wealth and so the Jew Aurelios Phrougianos adopted the funerary style appropriate to his standing in the city.

We may also note here a very interesting inscription of the second century CE from Chalkis in Euboea recently studied by Robert.[45] The epitaph was set up by the non-Jew T. Flavius Amphikles who flourished about the middle of the second century CE, was archon of the Panhellenes and claimed descent from consuls. He was a wealthy man who studied rhetoric and who was involved in the Second Sophistic and in public affairs.[46] The inscription contains the following undoubted quotations of Deut 28:22, 28:

Τοῦτόν τε θεὸς πατάξαι ἀπορίᾳ καὶ πυρετῷ καὶ ῥίγει καὶ
ἐρεθισμῷ καὶ ἀνεμοφθορίᾳ καὶ παραπληξίᾳ καὶ ἀορασίᾳ
καὶ ἐκστάσει διανοίας.[47]

God will strike (the person who interferes with the tomb) with
poverty, with fever and cold shivers, irritation, blight,
derangement, blindness and distraction of mind.

Robert has shown that the wording of the inscription reflects the
impression made on Amphikles by Jewish monotheism. Horsley has
noted that the fact that two separate verses from Deut are quoted as
if they were a continuum suggests that the LXX material has been
mediated indirectly, perhaps via a collection of suitable formulae. We
know from Philo Leg. 282 that there were 'Jewish colonies' and thus
no doubt synagogues on Euboea. However, neither Robert nor
Horsley has asked why Amphikles used this particular passage in Deut
in the epitaph. In view of the Acmonian inscriptions it seems likely
that the members of a Jewish community known to Amphikles used
this passage in Deut in a prominent way in their community life.
Perhaps one of the Jewish communities on Euboea also understood
its life in the Diaspora in the light of Deut 30:1–10 and applied the
curses of Deut 27:15–28:68 against grave violators. Amphikles
followed this example and adopted the current belief of a synagogue.
This incription adds force to our interpretation of the situation at
Acmonia by showing that another Jewish community elsewhere may
have had the same sort of theological understanding.

4 The 'children's children' curse

There are eight Jewish inscriptions from Acmonia and four nearby
places which contain the 'children's children' curse, so named because
it calls down a curse upon the τέκνα τέκνων. Four representative
inscriptions will be given here.

4.1

This inscription from Acmonia is engraved on a doorstone with six
decorated panels:

’Αμμια Εὐτύχου (Κ)αλιμάχῳ ἀνδρὶ καὶ ἑαυτῇ ἐκ τῆς ἰδίας
προικὸς τὸ μνημεῖον κατεσκεύασεν· ἀρὰ δὲ ἔσται εἰς
τέκνα τέκνων ἕτερον μὴ τεθῆναι ἢ τὸν υἱόν μο[υ] Εὐτύχην
καὶ γυναῖκα αὐ[τ]οῦ.[48]

Ammia (daughter) of Eutyches, prepared the tomb for Kalimachos her husband, and for herself, from her own dowry. The curse will be to the children's children to prevent anyone from burying anybody except my son Eutyches and his wife.

4.2

This inscription, engraved on a decorated doorstone and to be dated in the late second or early third century, is almost certainly from Acmonia:

> Τιβέριος Κλύδιος 'Ιουλιανὸς ἑαυτῷ καὶ γυναικὶ μνήμης χάριν καὶ Χελειδὼν τοῖς ἰδίοις θρέψασι μνήμης χάριν. Τὶς δὲ κακῶς ποίσει ταύτῃ τῇ γουντῃ,[49] ἕξει τέκνα τέκνων ἀράν.[50]

Tiberius Claudius Julianos (made his tomb) for himself and for his wife in remembrance, and Cheleidon for her own foster-parents in remembrance. But whoever shall do harm to this grave, he shall have the curse 'children's children'.

4.3

An inscription from nearby Eumeneia likewise contains this formula:

> Αὐρήλιος Γάϊος 'Απ[ελ]λᾶ κατεσκεύασεν τὸ μνημεῖον ἑαυτ[ῷ] καὶ τῇ γυναικὶ αὐ[τοῦ] καὶ τῇ μητρὶ καὶ χ[ρη]στῷ φίλῳ 'Ονησίμῳ καὶ τῇ γυνα[ι]κὶ αὐτοῦ· Εἰ δέ τις ἐπιχειρήσει ἀνα[σ]κευάσαι τὸν τόπον, ἔστω αὐτῷ κατ[ά]ρα τέκνων τέκ[νοις] καὶ τῷ συμβουλε[ύ]σαντι. ὁ βίος ταῦτα.[51]

Aurelios Gaios son of Apella built this tomb for himself and for his wife and for his mother and for his good friend Onesimos and his wife. If somebody attempts to demolish this plot, may a curse be on him, on his children's children and on his adviser. Such is life.

4.4

The following inscription is from Acroenus:

> Σ[τ]ερτίνιος Αἰνίας [καὶ ...] ... ΑΣ. [κ]ατ[εσ]κεύασαν τὸ ἡρῶον ἑα[υ]τοῖς καὶ τοῖς τέκνοις καὶ τοῖς [τ]εθρεμένοις·

ὃς ἂν δὲ τούτῳ υ ἡρῷω κακῶς ποιήσει, ὑποκατάρατος
ἔστω εἰς τέκνων τέκνα.⁵²

Stertinios Ainias and ... prepared the tomb for themselves
and for (their) children and for the slaves brought up in their
house. But whoever does damage to this tomb, he will be
subject to the children's children curse.

We note that the curse is regularly abbreviated, for instance to 'he shall
have the curse children's children' (ἐξεῖ τέκνα τέκνων ἀράν, 4.2).
Clearly the curse is so familiar that it may be radically abbreviated.⁵³
The children's children formula is a most unusual grave curse.
Kraabel thought that the element of magic was more obvious here
than with the curses which refer to Deuteronomy.⁵⁴ We will investigate this claim. We often find curses which affect children invoked
in inscriptions. However, there is only one definitely pagan parallel
to the children's children curse formula from nearby, and, as we will
see, this is probably an imitation of the inscriptions given above.⁵⁵
Thus, commentators have agreed that this formula is Jewish because,
as we will now show, it quotes the LXX.⁵⁶

Although phrases such as τοῖς τέκνοις τῶν τέκνων are found in
several passages in the LXX,⁵⁷ such a phrase is only found in a
context of judgement or cursing in Ex 34. This passage narrates the
renewal of the covenant and the self-revelation of Yahweh after the
incident of the Golden Calf. The narrative relates a theophany in
which Yahweh passed by before Moses. We read the following:

καὶ παρῆλθεν κύριος πρὸ προσώπου αὐτοῦ καὶ ἐκάλεσεν
Κύριος ὁ θεὸς οἰκτίρμων καὶ ἐλεήμων, μακρόθυμος καὶ
πολυέλεος καὶ ἀληθινὸς καὶ δικαιοσύνην διατηρῶν καὶ
ποιῶν ἔλεος εἰς χιλιάδας, ἀφαιρῶν ἀνομίας καὶ ἀδικίας
καὶ ἁμαρτίας, καὶ οὐ καθαριεῖ τὸν ἔνοχον ἐπάγων ἀνομίας
πατέρων ἐπὶ τέκνα καὶ ἐπὶ τέκνα τέκνων ἐπὶ τρίτην καὶ
τετάρτην γενεάν.

And the Lord passed by before his [Moses'] face and he
proclaimed, The Lord God merciful and compassionate,
patient and very merciful and truthful, and maintaining
righteousness and doing mercy for thousands, pardoning
lawlessness and offence and sin, and he will not clear the
guilty, bringing lawless conduct of the fathers upon children
and upon children's children until the third and fourth
generation. (Ex 34:6–7)

The passage strongly emphasises the mercy of God, yet without abrogating or denying God's wrath and judgement.[58] Here we have the 'children's children' expression in a context which includes judgement for sin. It seems that it was this passage in the LXX which was in the writers' minds, thus explaining the very unusual grave curse. The wording of the passage in the LXX also makes it appropriate for use in these inscriptions. ἔνοχος is quite common in burial curses; ἀνομία is a general term in the LXX and often has no direct connection to a specific injunction.[59] The agent of judgement envisaged in Ex 34:6−7 is Yahweh who acts against the guilty. Thus, the children's children curse is not magical as Kraabel suggested. Rather, the writers of these inscriptions seem to have been asking Yahweh to judge the grave violator, who has committed an act of lawlessness, and to continue the judgement as far as the grandchildren of the offender. This is in keeping with Yahweh's revelation of his character in Ex 34:6−7.

There are a number of passages in the OT which are dependent upon Ex 34:6−7. The rest of the OT has used the passage as a liturgical formula, to be extended and revised.[60] A tradition as important as Ex 32−34 for its revelation of the character of God and the nature of Israel would naturally be taken up into the worship of the people. Miller notes that the use of these verses in the Psalms 'assumes a sufficiently long history of tradition to establish it [these verses] as a fundamental liturgical formula on which Israel would draw with some frequency.'[61] Hence we can suggest that just as Biblical writers (or communities represented by them) adopted this fundamentally important narrative tradition as a part of their worship, so the Jewish community of Acmonia also adopted this passage as a part of its liturgy and thereby proclaimed the mercy and the judgement of God.[62] In other words, the Jewish community was here following Scriptural precedent in utilising this passage as part of its worship, just as many other worshipping communities had done previously. Accordingly, this means that the most adequate explanation for the fact that the 'children's children' curse was used in these inscriptions is that it was part of the liturgical usage of the synagogue and thus readily came to mind in the context of calling on God to judge the grave violators. We therefore see the Jewish community creatively using their authoritative text both in its current worship and when faced with the problem of grave violators. Furthermore, the fact that we find the curse in a number of communities raises the possibility that the use of this passage in liturgy was quite widespread. Consequently, we gain an important insight into the probable content of Jewish faith and liturgy in this area.[63]

It could be argued in investigating these inscriptions that someone 'chanced upon' the phrase in Ex 34:6–7, decided that the 'children's children curse' had the right ring to it and so used it against grave violators. Others then read the epitaph, thought it appropriate and used it without any reference to the Biblical context. If this was so, its use would tell us nothing about the faith of the Jewish community. However, we can note, firstly, that the phrase in itself means little. It does not describe retribution, it refers one to a 'curse'. This seems to presuppose the text of Ex 34:6–7, especially when it is remembered that most grave curses are very explicit.[64] Secondly, why would someone 'chance upon' this particular phrase, out of many Scriptural phrases which seem suitable, and then why should it be repeated so often in different communities? It seems much better to suggest that the phrase was part of the regular liturgy of these Jewish communities and thus that the passage was well known.

We can suggest, therefore, that Scripture functioned as a revered tradition, that is, as a source for the worship and faith of the community. It was to Scripture that the members turned for revelation of Yahweh's nature and for the direction and inspiration of their liturgical life.[65]

We mentioned above that there was one occurrence of the children's children curse which is clearly of pagan origin. This inscription was found thirty-five miles east of Sardis, an area of proved Jewish habitation, and is dated to 261/262 CE which means that it is later than the majority of inscriptions quoted above. It ends:

εἴ τις θελήσει σκυβαλλίσαι τὸ μνῆμα τοῦτο, ἕξει τὸν
Ἀπόλλωνα κεχολωμένον καὶ τὴν κυρίαν Ἀναεῖτιν διὰ
τέκνα τέκνων ἔγονα ἐγόνων.[66]

If someone desecrates this tomb, he will have to deal with the wrathful Apollo and the Lady Anaetis on account of children's children and grandchildren's grandchildren.

It seems likely that the writers of this inscription borrowed the curse formula from Jewish epitaphs known to them or from their Jewish neighbours.[67] In doing so they were showing that a traditional Jewish formula was considered by them as sufficiently potent to ward off grave violators. The use of this formula by pagans again reveals a close connection between Jews and their neighbours. It is interesting that this case is some distance west of the other instances of this formula because it suggests that either the formula was well known or that the writers of the inscription had travelled in the Acmonian region.[68]

5 Other inscriptions which refer to the Septuagint

5.1

The following inscription is from Acmonia:

A [ὁ δεῖνα ἑαυτῷ καὶ] τῇ ϛυγβίῳ Τροφίμη ἐποίησεν. Τιτέδιος Ἀμέριμνος ἐπισκε[υ]άσας τὸ τοῦ πά[π]που αὐτοῦ μνημεῖον ἔθαψεν τὴν ἑαυτοῦ γυναῖκα Αὐρ. Ὀνησίμην Εὐελπίστου· ἐξὸν δὲ ἔστε καὶ τὸν ἐπισσκευάσανταν Ἀμέριμνον τεθῆνε ἰς τὸ προγονικὸν [α]ὐτοῦ μνημεῖον· ἐὰν δέ τις ἐπιχει[ρ]ήσει με[τ]ὰ τὸ τεθῆνε τὸν Ἀμέριμ(ν)ον ἕτερόν [τι]γα θάψῃ θήϛει ἰς τ[ὸ ταμεῖον * ...]
B [εἴ τίς τι]γα θάψετο, [χειρὶ] δολί[α] λάβοιτ[ο ἀπρ]οσδόκητον ὁ[ποῖ]ον καὶ ὁ ἀδελφὸς α[ὐτ]ῶν Ἀμέριμνος· ἐὰν δέ τις αὐτῶν μὴ φοβηθῇ τούτων τῶν κ[α]ταρῶν, τὸ ἀρᾶς δρέπανον εἰσέλθοι[το] εἰς τὰς οἰκήσις αὐτῶν καὶ μηδίναν ἐνκ[α]ταλείψετο.[69]

A ... [Somebody made this tomb for himself] and for his wife Trophime. Titedios Amerimnos, having restored the tomb of his grandfather, buried his wife Aurelia Onesime (daughter) of Euelpistos. Amerimnos, who has restored the monument of his ancestors, will have an equal right to be placed here, but if somebody attempts after the burial of Amerimnos to bury somebody else he will place in the treasury ... denarii.
B [If somebody] buries somebody else may he receive the treacherous blow of the unexpected sort which their brother Amerimnos (received). And if one of them is not afraid of these curses, may the sickle of the curse come into their houses and leave no-one behind.

5.2

We find a similar curse formula in another inscription from Acmonia:

[ἐὰν δέ τις ἕτερον σῶμα εἰσενέγκῃ, ἔσ]ται αὐτῷ πρὸς τὸν θεὸν τὸν ὕψιστον, καὶ τὸ ἀρᾶς δρέπανον εἰς τὸν ὖκον αὐτοῦ [εἰσέλθοιτο καὶ μηδέναν ἐνκαταλείψαιτο.][70]

[And whoever introduces another body] he will have to reckon with the highest God and may the sickle of the curse come into his house [and leave no-one behind.]

The phrase ἀρᾶς δρέπανον is derived from Zech 5:1–5 and shows that these two inscriptions are Jewish.[71] In the LXX it reads:

And I turned and I raised my eyes and saw and behold a flying sickle (δρέπανον πετόμενον). And he spoke to me, 'What do you see?' And I said, 'I see a flying sickle, twenty cubits in length and ten cubits in width.' And he said to me, 'This is the curse (ἀρά) which is going out over the face of all the earth, for every thief will be punished with death on this side and every false swearer will be punished with death on the other side. And I will bring it about,' says the Lord Almighty. 'And it will enter into the house of the thief and into the house of the one who swears falsely by my name and it will come down in the middle of his house and it will destroy it and its timbers and its stones.'

The actual wording of the inscriptions from Acmonia – involving the sickle of the curse entering the house and leaving no survivors – is in keeping with the curse in the LXX of Zech 5:1–5 where death and destruction result from the action of the sickle which is a massive instrument of divine wrath. The curse in the LXX is against the thief or robber and the person who swore falsely, not respecting the holiness of an oath. Hence the passage is suitable for use against someone who has violated the sanctity of the grave.[72]

It has been noticed that our inscriptions follow the LXX and not the MT.[73] In the MT the prophet sees a huge flying scroll (מְגִלָּה עָפָה) upon which the curse is written. The LXX translates this as δρέπανον πετόμενον – a flying sickle. It is most likely that the LXX translators read מַגָּל -sickle and not מְגִלָּה -scroll.[74] Our inscription uses δρέπανον, thereby showing that the LXX not the MT was in common use in Acmonia.[75] According to the Hexapla, the Greek texts of Aquila and Theodotion at Zech 5:1 read διφθέρα (a piece of leather) for מְגִלָּה and not δρέπανον as found in the LXX. It is generally thought that the LXX fell into disfavour with Jews in the second century CE and was replaced by Aquila's version because of the adoption of the LXX by Christians and the backing of the Rabbis for Aquila's translation. These inscriptions which use the LXX are undated, but probably come from the third century since most of the evidence from Acmonia belongs to this period. It is noteworthy that the LXX was still in use in this Diaspora community at this time.[76] Two other inscriptions are shown to be almost certainly Jewish because of their similarity to the 'sickle of the curse' inscriptions above.

5.3

The following inscription is from Acmonia:

> Ἀμμία Γαίῳ Οὐιβίῳ Κρίσπῳ καὶ Τύχῃ θρέψασι ζῶσι μ(νήμης) χ(άριν)· μετὰ τὸ τοὺς δύο τεθῆναι ὃς ἂν ἀνορύξει σάρον σιδαροῦν τὸν [ο]ἰκῶνα[77] ξάναιτο καὶ τῷ συμβουλεύσαντι.[78]

Ammia (made this tomb) for Gaius Vibius Crispus and for Tyche, her adopted parents, in their lifetime as a remembrance. After these two have been buried, whoever breaks open (the tomb) may an iron broom mangle his house and (the same) to the one who advised him.

It is likely that the unusual phrase – σάρον σιδαροῦν – an iron broom[79] is a substitute for the sickle of 5.1 and 5.2 above and that this curse formula was inspired by Zech 5:1–5. Perhaps an iron broom was considered a more appropriate weapon of judgement than a huge sickle.[80]

5.4

Another from Acmonia reads:

> Φλ. Τευθραντὶς ζῶσα ἑαυτῆι καὶ Ἑρμογένει Ἑρμογένους τῶ ἀνδρι τὸ μνημεῖον κατεσκεύασεν, μετὰ δὲ τὸ τοὺς δύο τεθῆναι εἴ τις ἀνοίσει ἢ ἐπιβουλεύσει, σά‹ρ›ον σιδαροῦν εἴσελθον τὸν οἶκον.[81]

Flavia Teuthrantis, whilst alive, built the tomb for herself and for Hermogenes, son of Hermogenes, her husband. But after the two have been buried, if anyone shall open or cause injury (to the tomb) may the iron broom go into (his) house.

Here the use of σάρον σιδαροῦν is again an imaginative variation of Zech 5:1–5. Note also the similarity between εἰσελεύσεται εἰς τὸν οἶκον in Zech 5:4 and εἴσελθον τὸν οἶκον here.[82] Thus we see that the LXX has probably inspired the creation of another Jewish curse formula.

5.5

The following inscription also comes from Acmonia:

ἔτους τλθ΄· Αὐρήλιος ʿΡοῦφος ʿΕρμῇ ἀδελφῷ καὶ ʿΡουφίνῃ ἀνεψιᾷ ταχυμύροις μνήμης χάριν. Αὐρήλιος ʿΡοῦφος ἑαυτῷ καὶ γυναικὶ Εὐελπίστῃ καὶ ἀνεψιῷ Παρθενίῳ ἑαυτοῖς ζῶντες κατεσκεύασαν· μετὰ τὸ θεθῆναι αὐτο(ὺ)ς ὃς ἂν ἀνορύξι καὶ βαλῖ ἄλλον νεκρὸν ἢ τύνβον πρίατε ἢ γράμμα μιάνι ἐξολέσι ἐκίνου σύνπαν γένος ἡ Θεοῦ ὀργή· τύνβοις γὰρ δύο τοῦτο τὸ σῆμα ἐπίκιται.[83]

The year of 339 (255/256 CE). Aurelios Roufos, for (his) brother Hermas, and for (his) cousin Rufina, both prematurely dead, as a memorial. Aurelios Roufos for himself, and for (his) wife Euelpiste and (his) cousin Parthenios — for themselves whilst living built (the tomb). After we have been buried whoever digs up (this grave) and puts in another corpse or purchases the grave or dishonours this inscription, the anger of God will destroy him utterly with all his offspring; this sign is placed on two graves.

The significant part of the inscription for the determination of its provenance is the curse mentioning the 'anger of God'. ὀργή is used eight times in the NT with reference to God, and over 200 times in the LXX.[84] Since the LXX was much used by Christians, the inscription could be either Jewish or Christian. However, whilst we have only one pre-Constantinian inscription from Acmonia which may be Christian, we have a series of Jewish inscriptions from the city. This inscription is therefore much more likely to be Jewish than Christian.[85]

5.6

A third-century CE inscription from Eumeneia written by Aurelios Gemellcs ends with the following curse on grave violators: λήψεται παρὰ τοῦ ἀθανάτου θεοῦ μάστειγα αἰώνιον – he will receive from Immortal God an eternal scourge.[86] The expression ἀθάνατος θεός could be used by either Jews or Christians. Scourging as a form of punishment is found in the LXX; Matt 10:17, 23:34 imply that the scourge was administered in the synagogue. Much of Mishnah Tractate Makkoth is dedicated to a discussion of matters concerning scourging, which seems to shows the continuing importance of this form of punishment in Rabbinic circles.[87] On the other hand in Christian writings flogging or scourging appears rarely and then is generally an action of persecutors.[88] It seems unlikely, therefore, that Christians would write of an 'eternal scourge', although we must remember that the LXX was available to Christians as well as to Jews. Thus, we can suggest that Gemellos was a Jew familiar with the Jewish practice of scourging.

Another factor to bear in mind here is that Gemellos and his father were city councillors; his father was also a member of the Gerousia. At this early date Jews were more likely to be in these positions than were Christians since the Jewish community had long been in existence and we know of other Jews who held such positions in nearby Acmonia and Sardis.[89] Consequently, Gemellos is more likely to have been a Jew than a Christian. The case is not indisputable but it is clearly the more likely possibility.[90]

6 Other inscriptions

6.1

The following inscription, to be dated between 215 and 295 CE, is from Acmonia:

> A [Αὐρ. ʼΑ]ριστέας [ʼΑπολ]λωνίου ἠγόρασεν ἀργὸν τόπον παρὰ Μάρκου Μαθοῦ πή(χεων) ι΄ ἐπὶ ι΄. ἔτει·
> Below this was added at a later time in smaller letters:
> κατεσκεύασαν τὰ τέκνα αὐτοῦ ʼΑλέξανδρος καὶ Καλλίστρα[τ]ος μητρὶ καὶ πατρὶ μ. χ.
> Β ὑποσχόμενος τῇ γειτοσύνῃ τῶν πρ[ωτ]οπυλειτῶν ἄρμ[ε]να δικέ[λ]λα[τα] δύο κ[ατ]ὰ μῆ[να] καὶ ἁ[γωγὸ]ν ὀρυ[κ]τόν, ἔδωκεν ἐφ'ᾧ κατὰ ἔτος ῥ[ο]δίσωσιν τὴν σύμβ[ι]όν μου Αὐρηλίαν.
> C [ἐὰν δὲ μὴ ἐθέλωσιν] ῥοδίσαι κατὰ ἔτος [ἔσ]ται αὐτοῖς πρὸ[ς τὴ]ν δικαιοσύ[νην] τοῦ θεοῦ.[91]

A Aurelius Aristeas, son of Apollonius, bought fallow land from Marcus Math[i]os, ten cubits wide and ten cubits long. Below this: His children, Alexander and Callistratos built (this tomb) for their mother and father in remembrance.

B promising (it) to the Neighbourhood of the First Gate, and giving (as) implements, two two-pronged forks and a shovel and a digging spade, on the condition that each year they deck with roses (the tomb of) my wife Aurelia.

C And if they do not deck (it) with roses each year they will have to reckon with the justice of God.[92]

The expression ἡ δικαιοσύνη τοῦ θεοῦ does not help us here. There is a strong continuity of usage of the term δικαιοσύνη between the LXX and the NT, with the meaning in both cases being very much controlled by the OT usage of the צדק word group.[93] This continuity of usage means that the phrase is as likely to be used by Christians as by Jews. In addition, since the LXX was much used by Christians, even if the term was rare in the NT, our current inscription could still be Christian.

Robert argued that this inscription was Jewish.[94] Firstly, this inscription contains the 'Eumeneian Formula' – ἔσται αὐτῷ πρὸς τὸν θεόν 'he will have to reckon with God'. There is general agreement that in Phrygia this formula was only used by Jews and Christians.[95] In this chapter we have discussed a series of Jewish inscriptions from Acmonia, many of which use the LXX. However, as we have noted, in this period we have only one Christian inscription from Acmonia.[96] In this context the inscription given above is much more likely to be Jewish than Christian. Secondly, the name Μαθοῦ as published by Ramsay is difficult to accept because it does not fit into the syllabic pattern of the inscription. The name spans two lines, Μαθ on the first and οῦ on the second. There was ample room on the stone in its original shape (before being chipped) for an iota at the end of the first line. Robert thus suggested that the name was originally Μαθίου, which fits the syllabic pattern. This is a Semitic rather than an indigenous name and has been found in Jewish inscriptions.[97] It seems probable, therefore, that Mathios was a Jew. It is possible that Aristeas, who bought land from Mathios and wrote the inscription, was a Christian and bought the land from a Jew, but it is far more likely in the context of this city that the two were co-religionists. Thus we seem to have two Jews, one of whom has a Jewish name. Thirdly, the 'Neighbourhood of the First Gate',[98] who are here charged with performing the rosalia (see p. 80) and are invested with the ownership of land, were most likely a legally constituted burial society or association. Burial societies were community associations which sought to care for the memory of their members after death.[99]

In this case the people who lived near the 'First Gate' of the city had formed a society 'to which bequests could be left by a legal document, and which therefore must have been legally recognised'.[100] In the third century a society which was legally able to own and inherit land was much more likely to be Jewish than Christian. Although some societies might have been united merely on account of geography, the common bond here was also that of being Jews who worshipped the Jewish God. We can claim with a high degree of certainty that this inscription is Jewish.[101]

The unusual fact that there was a legally constituted Jewish burial society in Acmonia highlights once more the accepted position of the Jewish community in the city.[102] The Jewish community was prepared to use legal methods to enhance and to further its standing in the city through the formation of a burial society. This is a helpful example of the position of the Jews in Acmonia − neither despised nor fully integrated. They were a recognised group of some standing, but they were recognised as Jews.

In this inscription the burial society is charged with the responsibility of decking Aurelia's tomb with roses each year. This was a well-known ceremony of Roman origin particularly common in Northern Italy and usually called the 'rosalia'.[103] The ceremony took essentially the same form and character in different parts of the Greek-speaking world where it gives an indication of the extent of the romanisation of the Greek Orient.[104] There were two distinct forms of the rosalia; joyous celebrations of spring and summer and the rosalia connected with the dead. Our inscription clearly refers to the second form, which was celebrated at the grave in spring each year at a date fixed in the bequest or by the family. This rosalia consisted of decorating the tomb with roses, participating in a solemn banquet and perhaps offering a burnt sacrifice. The gathering was an expression of devotion and a renewal of the memory of the deceased.[105] It seems that in our period the rosalia was religiously indifferent. The tomb of Aurelius' wife would not have received a sacrifice because this seems to have been an optional part of the festival that was clearly specified when it was to be a part of the rosalia.[106] The ceremony seems therefore to have been one of remembrance of the deceased.

The festival of the rosalia was generally associated with workers' or tradesmens' collegia, which were often burial societies. In order to pay for the festival the deceased frequently left the collegia a bequest of a plot of land or a vineyard, the revenues from which provided the necessary funds.[107] Thus Aurelius Aristeas followed the standard practice in leaving land to the Jewish burial society in order that it might conduct a rosalia each year.

We have another rosalia inscription from Acmonia, written in 95 CE, which charged the archons of the city and the secretary of the council with providing twelve denarii worth of roses for the tomb of Praxias. Financial provision for this was made in the form of a bequest. A grave banquet was to take place, along with a distribution of money to town members and six freedmen or their descendants. Theos Sebastos, 'god of the fathers', Zeus Stodmenos, Asklepios the Saviour and Artemis of Ephesus were called upon to be overseers, witnesses and guards to ensure that the wishes of the deceased were fulfilled.[108] Hence the rosalia was known in the city and it seems likely that the Jewish community followed local custom in memorialising their dead in the rosalia.[109] The arrangements made in both cases are quite similar. Both people invoked divine assistance to ensure the rosalia was carried out, but for Aurelius Aristeas this involved calling upon the justice of God. Thus he adopted a practice which was familiar in the city, but modified the procedure to make it acceptable to his Jewish faith.

Finally, the threat that 'he will have to reckon with the justice of God' is the only sanction against a failure on the part of the Jewish association to perform the rosalia. Clearly this threat must have had some power in the community.[110] This allows us some insight into the faith of the community for clearly they respected God's justice.

6.2

The following inscription from Acmonia is unfortunately mutilated:

Ὑπὲρ εὐχῆ[ς] πάσῃ τῇ πατρίδι.[111]

Because of a vow for the whole πατρίδι.

A menorah carved underneath the text indicates that it is Jewish. The stone was probably part of an object donated to the πατρίς in fulfilment of the vow. This raises the question of the meaning of πατρίς. There are two main possibilities.[112] The πατρίς could be the Jewish community of Acmonia. However, other terms such as πατριά (a clan or people) are far more appropriate to refer to a community within a city and terms like συναγωγή or λαός would be more suitable to refer to the Jewish community itself.[113] Alternatively, the πατρίς could be the city of Acmonia. Josephus consistently uses the term to mean place of residence, or country. Philo says that while Diaspora Jews hold Jerusalem to be their μητρόπολις, they regard the places in which they were born and reared as their πατρίδες.[114] There are also a number of inscriptions from the area of Acmonia in which πατρίς clearly refers to the whole city and not just one section thereof.[115] πατρίς is a geographical and not a sociological term. Accordingly we should translate the inscription: 'For a vow for the whole home city.'[116] Indeed πᾶσα seems to emphasise that it is the whole city that benefits from this vow and not just the Jewish community.

We can see from this that at least one Jew or perhaps a group of Jews in Acmonia made a gift to the city, probably of some object or some money for construction.[117] The donor or donors were involved in the life of the city and recorded on a public monument that the city was their fatherland or home city. Both these factors show a strong degree of 'at homeness'.

6.3

The following bilingual inscription is unfortunately very fragmentary. Sukenik's suggested reading is:

[− προσευ]χὰς προ[σδέχου] − 'Undertake prayers'.

[יהי שלום על] ישראל ועל ירושלים ו[על המקום
הזה עד עת] קץ

'[May there be peace upon] Israel and upon Jerusalem and [upon this place to the time of] the end.'[118]

The use of Hebrew is significant, particularly since 5.1 and 5.2 above show that the community generally used the LXX.[119] This and the content of the inscription suggest that it was some sort of formula, perhaps a brief part of the liturgy or a benediction.[120] The stone appears to have been a building fragment from a synagogue; a formula or quotation from the liturgy seems quite in place as part of the synagogue structure itself. The retention of Hebrew, even if only in a very small way, is significant and perhaps expresses a desire to preserve the traditions of the community.[121] Sukenik's reading for the inscription would indicate that the well-being of Israel and Jerusalem was a priority for the community. We can suggest that the concern for Jerusalem as the centre of the cult, shown by the persistence in paying the Temple Tax as revealed in the Flaccus incident, was a continuing facet of the community's faith even after the Temple's destruction.[122]

7 Conclusions

Although the Jewish community in Acmonia was probably founded around 205 BCE, our first evidence comes from *c.* 60 CE when the Jewish community had its own synagogue thanks to the generosity of their powerful patroness Julia Severa. By the end of the first century we know of some synagogue leaders who were zealous for the community and its building. We do not have much evidence for the second century[123] but the large number of inscriptions from the third century along with their nature suggests that the Jewish community was a significant group in Acmonia throughout the first three centuries of this era. The three synagogue leaders of the first century were well-off. However, some of the inscriptions are of a poorer quality, suggesting that there was a broad socio-economic spread within the Jewish community.

Julia Severa shows that the community in Acmonia was able to gain an important patroness in the first century CE. Although she was a priestess of the Imperial cult, the Jewish community was willing to accept her patronage. We have a number of indicators which suggest that the Jewish community was an accepted part of the city and involved in its life to quite some extent. Two Jews held a number of significant civic offices in the third century and were clearly prominent and public-spirited citizens of Acmonia whose contribution to the city's life brought them honour and respect. Members of the family represented by one of these Jews had probably held Roman citizenship since the late first century so that for over one hundred years they had belonged to the small privileged minority who held the citizenship. Part of the Jewish community was able to establish a legally constituted burial society. A formulaic reference to the curses written in Deuteronomy was a sufficient deterrent to ward off grave violators. Thus, the Jewish tradition seems to have commanded some respect and was acknowledged to be a source of authoritative, powerful curses. Clearly, the Jewish community was not marginalised within the city.

In addition to the acceptance granted to the Jewish community, we have evidence that the Jews themselves felt at home there. Firstly, they worked for the betterment of their city. As we have noted, members of the Jewish community fulfilled important positions in the city and the use of the name 'home city' speaks for itself. The donation of some sort for the 'home city' reveals that Jews made contributions to the city. Secondly, they adopted many local practices and customs. They decorated their gravestones in the local manner, they honoured their own benefactors in the traditional way for the city, they used grave curses to deter violators and they adopted the locally known rosaliá. The reverse side of this was that pagans adopted the Jewish 'children's children' formula, which suggests there was a close connection between some Jews and their neighbours. We conclude that the Jewish community became acculturated and seems to have been both accepted and 'at home'. To a large extent the Jews had identified their interests with those of the city to which they belonged.

However, we find a number of unambiguous displays of Jewish religious conviction and of Jewish identity. Some of the Temple tax collected by Flaccus' officials in Apamea probably came from Acmonia, showing a concern for Jerusalem. Sukenik's suggested reading of inscription 6.3 points in the same direction. The community may have used Ex 34:6–7, a fundamental tradition in the OT, in its liturgy. This passage seems to have remained a primary element in the faith of the community. Members of the community also followed the precedent of Scripture in applying this passage afresh in a new context. The LXX, whose language and content was well known, was the source for many of the grave inscriptions. These inscriptions invoked God, whose power was relied on to punish violators. Thus members of the community turned to Scripture as a revered tradition, a reliable guide to the nature of their God and their faith, and a source book for their liturgical life. It is also noteworthy that the two men who held a number of civic offices referred to Deuteronomy in their grave curses. Notwithstanding their involvement in the life of the city, Scripture remained an authority for them. We can conclude, therefore, that Scripture was an important element in reinforcing the religio-ethnic identity of the Jewish community in Acmonia.

In all of this, Scripture was interpreted by the community to apply to the new situation which it faced. The community seems to have understood itself to be living in the time spoken of by Deut 30:1–10 and interpreted its life in the light of that passage. Likewise the children's children curse and the curse of the flying sickle were understood to be present realities which related to the continuing need of the community. This witnesses to an ongoing tradition of the interpretation of Scripture, which was sensitive to its meaning, yet which reactualised Scripture so that it was relevant in the present context.

4

THE JEWISH COMMUNITY AT APAMEA

The city of Apamea in Phrygia was founded by Antiochus I Soter (280–261 BCE) as part of a scheme to strengthen the Seleucid hold on Asia Minor, to facilitate trade and to protect the highways. It was one of a series of garrison-cities and was built at a point of strategic importance on the Great Southern Highway. Antiochus I Soter founded the city on a plateau on either side of the Marsyas River by moving the inhabitants of nearby Celaenae into his newly created city. Celaenae itself was a large and prosperous city with a long history. Under Persian rule, Celaenae became the principal royal seat in Phrygia and a residence of the satraps. After Alexander conquered the city, it was designated as the Greek Capital of Inner Anatolia.[1]

At the beginning of the common era, Apamea was the second most important market and distribution centre in Asia Minor owing to its geographical location. The city commanded the cut in the mountain range through which the Southern Highway climbed to the plateau of Central Anatolia, making it the commercial junction through which wealth-laden traffic passed to the East. Roads of commercial importance also led to Western Phrygia and into Pisidia.[2] Its position meant it was a strategic city with regard to defence. Antiochus III used it as a defensive refuge after the battle of Magnesia ad Sipylum in 190 BCE and it was here that he signed the treaty in 188 giving up much of Asia Minor to the Romans, who entrusted the territory to the kings of Pergamum. They allowed the city to develop as a Greek polis with both a city council and a gymnasium. In 133 the city passed to Rome, who granted it in 129 to Mithridates V along with the rest of the province of Phrygia. On the death of Mithridates Rome declared it free, but this freedom was probably only nominal. In 88 the city surrendered to Mithridates VI in return for aid to rebuild after a recent earthquake. After the defeat of Mithridates in 85, Sulla incorporated Apamea into the Roman province of Asia. Although it twice formed part of Cilicia, it became permanently part of Asia in 51 BCE.[3]

Apamea was also a regional centre having under its authority many towns and villages and was the seat of the conventus, probably from 133. Dio Chrysostom's speech at Apamea shows how much the conventus both reflected and increased the importance and prosperity of the city. In the second century CE the name Celaenae reappeared on coins during a time of reinvigorated national sentiment encouraged by the Romans. This was also a period of prosperity, that lasted until the mid third century; Apamea declined to a third-rate city in the Byzantine Period.[4]

1 The first Jewish settlers in Apamea

It is possible that Antiochus I included Jews among the original settlers of Apamea, since Seleucid kings seem on occasions to have used Jews as an element in the cities they founded. It is almost certain that Apamea was one of the cities in which Zeuxis settled Jews in around 205 BCE, at the instruction of Antiochus III, since Apamea was the most prominent city in Phrygia and the transportation involved sending Jews to Phrygia and Lydia alone.[5] The Jews were settled by Antiochus III on very favourable terms as we noted in chapter 1. Thus, it is likely that the Jewish community quickly became established in Apamea.

2 Cicero and the Jews of Apamea

In chapter 1, section 4 we discussed Cicero's report of Jewish Temple tax seized by Flaccus from Apamea and other centres in 62 BCE. We concluded that the Jewish population in the city of Apamea must have been large and that Flaccus acted out of economic necessity and not anti-Jewish sentiments. Furthermore, the incident shows that the Jews of Apamea (and elsewhere) were prepared to defy a Roman edict in order to pay their Temple tax to Jerusalem. The tax, a significant feature of Jewish identity, was clearly highly important to the Jewish community in Apamea.

3 The Noah coins of Apamea

We have a series of coins minted in Apamea from the end of the second century CE which bear the scene of Noah and the Ark. These coins are unique in that they are the only coin type known to bear a Biblical scene. That it is the Biblical scene of Noah and his wife and not, for instance, Deucalion and Pyrrha is clearly shown by the inscription ΝΩΕ on the side of the ark. The coins have often been briefly explained as the result of 'Jewish influence' in the city.[6] Can we be more precise about the involvement of the Jewish community in the minting of these coins?

The coins depict Noah and his wife inside the Ark, shown not as a boat but as a rectangular box riding on the waves. It is most likely that the engravers followed the model of Greek artists who had already used box-forms to represent boats.[7] Above the Ark are a raven and a dove holding an olive branch in its claws. They symbolise the subsidence of the waters and the end of the flood and are probably directly inspired by the Biblical account. To the left of the Ark Noah and his wife stand on dry land with their right arms raised. This is the 'orans' gesture and symbolises an attitude of grateful prayer for their salvation. Prayer is repeatedly portrayed in this fashion in classical and Hellenistic art. The Jewish community has followed this precedent, as did Christian art at a later stage.[8] The coins thus juxtapose two successive episodes – the flood and the departure from the ark. This style of representing a narrative by portraying the principal actors in successive scenes is frequent in antiquity, especially in sarcophagus art. It is, however, unusual on a coin.[9]

The coins bear the profile and inscriptions of five Emperors: Septimius Severus (193–211), Macrinus (217–8), Severus Alexander (222–35), Philippus Arabs (244–9) and Trebonianus Gallus (251–3). It seems likely that the coins formed a continuous series, with these five being the representatives of the series which have been found to date.[10] The inscriptions on the reverse in chronological order are:

   (i) ΕΠΙ ΑΓΩΝΟΘΕΤΟΥ ΑΡΤΕΜΑ. Γ. ΑΠΑΜΕΩΝ[11]
   (ii) ΑΠΑΜΕΩΝ[12]
   (iii) ΕΠΙ ΠΟ. ΑΙΛ ΤΡΥΦΩΝΟΣ ΙΠΠΙ. ΑΣΙΑΡ. ΑΠΑΜΕΩΝ[13]
   (iv) ΕΠ. Μ. ΑΥΡ. ΑΛΕΞΑΝΔΡΟΥ. Β. ΑΡΧΙ. ΑΠΑΜΕΩΝ[14]
   (v) ΠΑΡ. ΚΛ. ΑΠΟΛΙΝΑΡΙΟΥ ΑΠΑΜΕΩΝ[15]

The city of Apamea seems to have had an unusual preference for picturesque coins. A coin of Severus portrays the local legend of Athena and Marsyas; another coin portrays the legend of Zeus' birth.[16] It is also significant that our five Noah coins span a number of years, without significant change. Ramsay thought this implied that 'a permanent model existed for engravers to copy'.[17] This, together with the city's preference for picturesque coins which sometimes portray a story, led him to suggest that all were taken from models, probably a painted Stoa or a set of pictures devoted to Apamean legends on a public building. Since the earliest of these picturesque coins is from the reign of Commodus (180–192), he thought the building was erected before his reign.[18] If this is correct, then Apamea not only had a Jewish scene on its coins but also had such a scene as part of a public mural of local legends.

The local flood legends

There were a number of flood legends in the ancient world, such as the story of Deucalion and Pyrrha, the two survivors of a flood caused by Jupiter.[19] We will discuss the local Phrygian flood legends which were antecedent to, or independent of, the Jewish community in Apamea, and we will then investigate the bearing these legends have on the interpretation of the coins.

Iconium in Lycaonia was the centre of the Nannakos flood tradition. In Suidas and Zenobius we read of Nannakos the ancient king of Phrygia who foresaw the flood that is identified in these sources with Deucalion's flood. He gathered together all his people into the temple and 'made supplication with tears'. According to Stephanus of Byzantium Nannakos received an oracle that all people would perish when he died. After the resulting flood, the earth was repeopled when Prometheus and Athena fashioned images (εἰκόνες) of mud at Zeus' command. Iconium was named after these images.[20] In this story original Phrygian characters are probably identified with the Greek heroes, and the framework is provided by the connection with Deucalion's flood. The antiquity of (at least part of) the legend about Nannakos is shown by the fact that the *Mimes* of Herondas of the third century BCE include the proverb 'Though I weep like Nannakos'.[21] Thus we have a number of different versions of an ancient legend about Nannakos, King of Phrygia, who was connected with a flood, that is identified in our sources as Deucalion's flood.

It has been suggested that Nannakos, or Annakos as the name is given by Stephanus of Byzantium, was the Biblical Enoch so that this was not a Phrygian but a Jewish flood story. Apart from the similarity of name, they both lived for a long time directly before a flood, which both are said to have foretold.[22] However, this suggestion does not stand up to investigation. Firstly, that a third century BCE source knew the proverb about Nannakos' tears suggests that at least part of the tradition of a deluge predated known Jewish settlement in the area. Secondly, an inscription gives the name of a village as

Νονοκοκώμη – 'the village of Nonokos'; Nonokos for Nannakos is a common Anatolian vocalisation. This shows that 'Nannakos' was the name of a deified hero or a god in Anatolia and that the original name of the King was Nannakos not Annakos. Thus the Nannakos flood story had no connection with Enoch but is seen to be an ancient Anatolian tradition independent of any Jewish community.[23]

A second flood story comes from Ovid's *Metamorphoses*, written about the turn of the era. Jupiter and Mercury received hospitality from the Phrygian couple, Philemon and Baucis, after being turned away by all the inhabitants of the area. The gods then flooded the area because of its inhospitality, but Philemon and Baucis were saved by climbing a mountain at the instruction of the gods. Philemon and Baucis are then changed into an oak and a linden tree; added value is given to the veracity of the myth as a Phrygian tradition by the way that Ovid emphasises that his source is an eye-witness of the locality. In addition, many features such as the trees, the subterranean waters that cause the flood and the resulting lake are in keeping with Anatolian geography. The fact that Ovid pays no special attention to the flood also increases the likelihood that his story is reliable.[24] Fontenrose suggests that 'Baucis' is a native Phrygian name and 'Philemon', whilst meaning 'lover' in Greek, probably translates a native name. Thus, we can be sure that here Ovid tells us a Phrygian flood story and not a flood myth that he decided to locate there.[25] This flood story is clearly distinguished from the Biblical account. Rain plays no part in the flood, which is caused solely by subterranean waters, there is no ark and Philemon and Baucis are saved by walking up a hill at the suggestion of the gods. This tradition is then independent of the Jewish community in the area.

A third flood tradition is found in the writings of Nonnos who wrote around 500 CE but who is a rich source of earlier mythology. The hero of the story is Priasos, later described as 'the proud son of Phrygia'. Zeus caused torrential rain to fall on Phrygia so that everything was flooded including the house of Priasos, who then migrated to 'the Aonian land to escape from the fatal showers of rain' where he mourned his lost land. Zeus finally quieted the storm and drove the waters away, laying bare the cliffs. Priasos returned home and joyfully embraced Zeus who had saved him from destruction 'for his pious works'. This is then another tradition about a flood in Phrygia, here involving a hero who escaped because of his piety.[26]

Fourthly, Plutarch quotes a tale about King Midas and his son Anchouros set at Celaenae, the city which later became Apamea.

A chasm full of water opened in the earth and engulfed many people and their homes. An oracle instructed the King that if he threw his costliest possession into the chasm, it would close up. Finally, after everything else had failed, Anchouros leaped in on horseback and the chasm closed. The myth arose from local circumstances in the vicinity of Apamea where earthquakes had caused new lakes to appear and where an abundance of underground water, which here causes the flood, flowed from the ground.[27] The tradition is clearly located at Apamea and shows the existence of a flood story in the area.

Accordingly, we have four distinct local flood traditions, although only one is from Apamea itself. One of the stories is located some distance away at Iconium, although perhaps close enough to be known in Apamea. The area is geographically suitable, with a large number of lakes, hot springs and frequent earthquakes. We have seen no detailed resemblance between these traditions and the Biblical story, a fact that implies that the latter did not create the former. We can, therefore, be confident that in Phrygian legend the area claimed to be the home of a flood hero or heroes.[28]

It is difficult to date these traditions. Ovid lived from 43 BCE to 17 or 18 CE, so the story of Philemon and Baucis must be dated then or earlier. Herondas in the third century BCE shows that in his time there was a legend of Nannakos which probably involved a Phrygian flood. It is possible then that the Jews who arrived in Apamea around 205 BCE already found a flood tradition associated with the area.[29]

Apamea Kibotos

Apamea had a second name, ἡ κιβωτός, which means box, chest, coffer or ark. This name for Apamea is first mentioned by Strabo around 19 CE, and Pliny and Ptolemy also knew it.[30] In addition, the word Κιβωτοί is found on a coin issued under Hadrian that also bears a representation of five rectangular chests. The coin, which shows Marsyas (a local river here portrayed as a god) lying in a rocky cave, above which are five chests, has the inscription Ἀπαμέων Μαρσύας Κιβωτοί – Of the people of Apamea, Marsyas, Kibotoi. Two other coins are similar, but they only have one or two chests depicted on them.[31] It is important to note that κιβωτός is the Septuagint's term for the Ark of Noah.[32] Can we explain these facts?

Ramsay suggested that the name Kibotos was a Grecising of a Phrygian name, which A. Reinach suggested was Kibyza.[33] However, this Phrygian name is unattested for the city; in fact

Celaenae seems to have been the indigenous name. It is possible that the local flood traditions led the city to adopt the name Kibotos, thus claiming to be the landing place of an ark that survived the flood.[34] However, this is most unlikely. An ark is never mentioned in these local traditions because escape is made on foot in marked contrast to the Deucalion tradition. It is possible that this later tradition with its ark was known, although our only reason for thinking so is that the Nannakos tradition has been joined with it. Yet, the most likely place for this to have occurred is in our sources rather than in the Phrygian version itself. The fact that the Ark, integral to the Deucalion tradition, is never mentioned in any of our flood traditions seems to indicate that the Phrygian traditions were originally independent of the Deucalion story. In any case, the word used for 'ark' in the Deucalion story is almost always λάρναξ and not κιβωτός.[35] Consequently, the city is very unlikely to have given itself this name as a result of the local flood traditions.

Head wrote that the name Kibotos arose because the city 'became a commercial junction where goods arriving by the caravan route from the East were packed in chests to be forwarded to the various seaports, Ephesus, Pergamum etc'.[36] The earliest evidence for this name comes from the period of the city's considerable prosperity and importance. In addition, the plural 'kibotoi' on the coin of Hadrian's time can only mean 'chests', which strongly points to Head's interpretation. A city like Apamea is likely to gain some 'nickname' because there were numerous cities of that name in the ancient world. Thus, it seems probable that the name was attributed to the city in this period because 'chests' became a symbol of the city's economic activity and eventually of the city itself.

Nevertheless, Ramsay, followed by Tcherikover,[37] rejected this explanation in favour of the theory that a local legend of a flood led the Jews of Apamea to regard one of the neighbouring mountains as the resting place of the Ark and that their influence caused the name to be given to the city. However, this theory fails to explain why the coins of Hadrian's time portray five 'Kibotoi'. If 'Apamea Kibotos' was a shorthand for 'Apamea, the resting place of the Ark', how can we understand the city depicting five 'kibotoi' (which in this case would have to mean 'arks') on a coin?[38] Clearly the only satisfactory explanation of the term's origin is that which does justice to the commercial importance of the city.

A proposed hypothesis

We can now venture to suggest the following hypothesis to explain the Noah-coins of Apamea. The city gained the nickname 'Kibotos' in or before the time of Strabo because of its economic significance. 'Kibotos' at this stage only meant 'chest'. There was no ark in the local flood legends and if one had been known it would have been called a λάρναξ, in which case there would have been no reason for it to be connected with the city's name.

The coins clearly imply that the Ark's resting place was associated with Apamea. Sibylline Oracles I/II (see below) reflects the local Jewish tradition that the site was the hill of Celaenae behind the city. Were the Jews the first to identify this hill with the flood? A decisive point against this is the geography of the area, as was shown by Ramsay. The hill of Celaenae at 3660′ is dominated by Mt Ai-Doghmush, which is only six miles away and 5580′ high. Two other mountains in full view from the city are 6619′ and 8013′ high. Hence if the Jews had, *de novo*, chosen a landing site for the Ark it would almost certainly have been one of these lofty, more distant mountains.[39] We also recall that Philemon and Baucis fled up a hill to escape the flood. The fact that the hill of Celaenae was chosen on the coins and in Sibylline Oracles I/II suggests that the local legend of the flood was strongly associated with this hill from the distant past and that the Jewish community did not wish to change the location. Perhaps this was the hill up which the Apamean equivalents of Philemon and Baucis were reputed to have climbed.

The Jews connected the city's name of Kibotos with the 'kibotos' they read about in their Septuagint as the vessel in which Noah had endured the flood, and thus they interpreted the city's name to mean 'ark'.[40] This fully explains the Jewish community's action. There is no apparent reason why the Jews should have introduced the Biblical flood story into Apamea without any external cause. But with a pre-existent flood tradition in the area and with their own story using the very word that was the 'nickname' of the city, their actions are entirely understandable.[41] The Jewish community also followed the strong local flood tradition in localising the landing of the Ark on the nearby hill. The city accepted as their own this different version of the flood story, with its account of an escape being made not by fleeing up a hill but by survival in an ark that later came to rest above the city. For the first time the nickname 'Kibotos' acquired the double meaning of chest and ark in Apamea. The connection between the chest, ark and flood is uniquely a Jewish contribution. This acceptance of the tradition by the city would only have been possible if the Jewish community was already a respected element in the city's population. This gave the city's nickname a prestige it had lacked; it was now given an ancient significance. The name not only testified to the city's commercial importance but also to the fact that they had famous ancestors – Noah and his wife.[42] Cities were enthusiastic for this sort of aetiology of their names that gave them a link with antiquity, particularly cities like Apamea which were of relatively recent foundation. It achieved this notable advance through the Jewish community, which would thus be seen to add to the prestige of the city. Part of the acceptance of this tradition by the city involved the portrayal of the scene on coins of the city and probably in a public Stoa. The city also accepted a new name for the flood heroes – Noah and his wife. Many of the coins of the city portraying well-known deities such as Hermes or Artemis Ephesia do not name the figure. That Noah is named suggests that his name has suppressed a local name. Without Noah being named expressly, the scene could have been ambiguous.[43]

It is important to note that our coins depict two people – Noah and his wife. In the OT and NT mention is made either of Noah alone or of the whole group of people involved. Noah and his wife are never jointly emphasised.[44] In fact, Noah's wife is quite secondary to his three sons. The emphasis in Jewish literature of the Intertestamental Period and later is on Noah as the prime actor in the drama of the flood. Noah's wife, when she is mentioned, functions only as an illustration of an attribute of Noah himself. Thus Philo mentions her but only in the context of Noah's abstinence from sexual intercourse during the flood. In Jubilees she is named as Emzara, but in the actual story she is ignored and plays no part.[45]

This emphasis continues in the portrayal of the flood in Christian art. Here we find an exceedingly standardised depiction of Noah alone in a box-like Ark, with arms upraised and a dove flying towards him. In one scene on the Trier sarcophagus eight people are depicted; in only one other case – a Christian catacomb in Rome – do we see Noah and his wife by themselves.[46] Thus Biblical and Jewish literature and Early Christian art do not explain why our coins have two people in the Ark instead of Noah alone or a group of eight. Christian art and Lewis' analysis of the treatment of the Flood story by writers of this period suggest that we should look to influences in the local environment for an explanation.[47]

In the light of our analysis of the local flood stories, the conclusion seems clear. The Jewish community found an already existent legend involving *two* people of equivalent importance who escaped the flood, the Apamean Philemon and Baucis. The community then identified the two with the heroes from its own tradition, Noah and his wife. Noah's wife remained nameless despite ample room on the coin because there was no name for her in the local Jewish tradition.[48] Yet the influence of the antecedent tradition meant that both appeared on the coin. This seems further evidence that the Jewish community did not create the local legend but rather reinterpreted it and that its version was accepted by the city. In the process the Jewish community allowed its own tradition in which Noah's wife played a very peripheral role to be influenced by the pre-existent tradition.

It is difficult to date these developments. They certainly occurred before the end of the second century when the coins were first minted. The connection between Apamea, the Ark/Kibotos and Noah are all present in Sibylline Oracles I/II (see below), which was probably written around the turn of the era. The contribution by the Jewish community to the prestige of the city could date from then.[49]

That the city accepted the superimposition of the Jewish version of the story on their own suggests that the Jewish community was influential and respected before this time and was probably active in public life. Jews made a real contribution to the life of the city by adding a prestigious local ancestor, which shows that the Jewish community was in no sense marginalised in the city's life.[50] Yet the community was also distinctive, their flood hero having a different name. On the other hand, the Jews accepted a modified significance for Noah's wife from the position she had in their tradition, or in any other Jewish literature known to us. We see here some 'give and take'. The city accepted the Ark and Noah as part of the local flood tradition, whilst the Jewish community accepted a female flood hero who had a significant place in the city's tradition as part of its own tradition. The Jewish community re-interpreted its tradition in the light of the local story, though of course Noah is still called Noah. Thus we see that there was mutual recognition and respect between the Jewish community and the city, with reciprocal acknowledgement of each other's traditions.[51]

The style of the portrayal on the coin is also noteworthy. Although the engraving would probably have been done by the city authorities, it is likely that the Jewish community would have had some say. It is clear that the portrayal followed current artistic styles, for instance in the shape of the Ark and in the 'orans' gesture. The Jewish community seems to have accepted these current styles.

4 Sibylline Oracles I/II

Even though it is often difficult to ascertain the provenance of the Sibylline Oracles because of their very nature, there is general agreement that the Jewish substratum of Books I/II was written in Phrygia, probably in Apamea. Firstly, in I, 195–8 Phrygia is said to be the first land to emerge after the flood and the 'nurse' of a new humanity. In I, 261–7 we read:

> There is a certain tall lofty mountain on the dark mainland of Phrygia. It is called Ararat. When all were about to be saved on it, thereupon there was a great heartfelt longing. There the springs of the great river Marsyas had sprung up. In this place the Ark remained on lofty summits when the waters had subsided ...

The spring which formed the Marsyas river was situated just behind Apamea; clearly, 'Ararat' is located there in this passage. Thus the case seems strong that part of Sibylline Oracles I/II is from Phrygia, probably Apamea.[52] It is the only document to have survived from Jews in Asia Minor in this period.

The book as we have it contains both a Jewish substratum and a Christian redaction. There is general agreement that I, 1–323 and II, 6–33 are part of a Jewish oracle treating world history in ten generations. I, 324–400 is a Christian section dealing with the Incarnation and career of Christ. II, 34–347, an account of eschatological crises and the last judgement, is more difficult to assign. J.J. Collins thinks that the Christian writer modified the eschatological conclusion of the Jewish work by interpolations, although the extent of the redactor's work is difficult to determine.[53] Although the eschatological passages are probably substantially Jewish (and thus reveal a concern with the judgement of individuals after death), the difficulty of determining the Jewish sections in II, 34–347 means that we cannot use this part of the work as evidence for our study.

J.J. Collins has recently discussed the dating of the Jewish substratum. The mention of Rome in the tenth generation in II, 18 points to a period when Roman power was consolidated in the Near East and thus to a time after 30 BCE. The Jewish substratum contains no reference to the destruction of the Temple or to Nero's supposed return, a favourite Sibylline theme. The Christian section in I, 387–400, which does mention the destruction of the Temple, was probably added to bring the Jewish oracle up to date. Hence, the original oracle probably carried its review of history no later than the time of Augustus. Consequently, a date around the turn of the era is most likely with outer limits of 30 BCE and 70 CE.[54]

A conspicuous feature of Books I/II is the extent of the influence of Homer and Hesiod on the author. There are some verbal parallels that reflect direct use of Hesiod's *Works and Days* and *Theogony* by the Sibyl, and the schema of the first five generations is inspired by *Works and Days* 109–174.[55] However, the final composition is still very much the work of the Sibyl. For example, in Hesiod's *Works and Days* the first generation is a golden, blameless race whereas in the Sibyl's work this generation 'sinned, smitten with folly', and thus Adam tasted death. This disturbs Hesiod's general scheme of a progressive decline. Nevertheless we can still see how the Sibyl accepts the scheme of world history and the detailed description of one of the Greek epic poets. Clearly these traditions were for him/her a respected guide to world history. However, the Sibyl is also dependent on Jewish traditions and these predominate, for instance, in the description of the sin of the first generation in I, 38–64. There are similarities here with the process which led to the minting of the Noah coins. The use of Hesiod, and indeed of the Sibylline form itself, emphasises the common ground between Jew and Gentile in the author's context, which as we have seen was probably Apamea.

A large part of the Jewish substratum is devoted to the flood story (I, 125–282). Noah is introduced as the single upright and true man of the abominably wicked fifth generation (I, 120–6). This theme of the righteousness of Noah as unique in his time is frequently found in Biblical and Intertestamental literature.[56] As in the description of creation, the narrative follows the Biblical flood story to a large extent. It seems likely that the author, in locating the landing spot of the Ark as the hill behind Apamea, was here re-interpreting the local flood tradition(s) in accordance with his/her Jewish tradition. (S)He was identifying the story he/she has told with the local flood stories, and identifying Noah with the indigenous flood hero(es). The impetus for this re-interpretation, and thus the localisation of the flood story, was probably Apamea's nickname Kibotos. It seems then that the Sibyl was doing much the same thing as we have seen occurring in the late second century with the coins. It is possible that the Jewish community was at that time following the lead the 'Sibyl' had provided at the turn of the era. It seems likely that the Sibyl was aiming his/her work at the city, at those who knew *only* the local flood story. (S)He was identifying for them a new and ancient flood hero. Perhaps the fact that the city did accept this identification, as the coins show, is a sign of the success and acceptance which the Sibyl's work achieved among his/her intended audience.

In the book Noah is portrayed primarily as a preacher of repentance,[57] a feature which is entirely lacking in the Genesis account. In Sibylline Oracles I, 128−9 God says to Noah: Νῶε, δέμας θάρσυνον ἑὸν λαοῖσί τε πᾶσιν κήρυξον μετάνοιαν ὅπως σωθῶσιν ἅπαντες − Noah, embolden yourself and proclaim repentance to all the peoples, so that all may be saved. There follow in I, 150−170 and I, 174−198 two sermons preached by Noah. The book is not alone, however, in portraying Noah as a preacher of repentance. In Josephus' account of the flood we read that Noah urged his contemporaries 'to come to a better frame of mind and amend their ways'. Noah is not presented as a preacher of repentance in any of the Jewish Apocryphal or Pseudepigraphical literature. The theme is found, however, in Rabbinic writings. For example, in *Ecclesiastes Rabbah* ix, 15, as an example of Noah's wisdom, we read: 'For he said to the people, "Woe ye foolish ones! Tomorrow a flood will come, so repent." They answered him, "If punishments begin, they will begin with your house."'[58] The emphasis in these Jewish writings is on the wickedness of Noah's contemporaries who refuse to repent. Noah's preaching functions as a foil; their wickedness is proved by the fact that, even when urged to repent, they scorned Noah's words.

In 2 Peter 2:5 Noah is described as δικαιοσύνης κῆρυξ − a herald or preacher of righteousness. In I Clement 7:6 as part of an exhortation to repentance we read that 'Noah preached repentance and those who obeyed were saved.' Likewise, mention of Noah as a preacher of repentance is found in the *Apocalypse of Paul* and in a number of patristic writers.[59] Generally the statement is very brief or is part of a piece of extended allegorical exegesis with the emphasis on God providing an opportunity for repentance. The theme is used for homiletical purposes in order to promote certain behaviour in the listeners.

It emerges from this survey that Sibylline Oracles I/II is probably the earliest written record which portrays Noah as a preacher of repentance. It is also the only piece of writing in which a long sermon purporting to be preached by Noah is given. Against this background, our account in Sibylline Oracles I/II is seen to be unique. We will now investigate the content of Noah's sermons in more detail. In I, 150–2 and 174–80 Noah outlines both the ethical values on which judgement is based and the way to avoid destruction. The list of sins given has much in common with the lists frequently found in Jewish literature of this period. Noah, faced with the imminence of the flood, exhorts his hearers to repent. If they will repent, propitiate God, change their ways of behaviour and live a holy life (I, 170) the wrath of God will be averted. However, the people sneer at Noah, whereupon he preaches against their wickedness again, describing what will happen to them when the flood comes (I.174–98). We see, therefore, that the work is basically hortatory and attempts to discourage the sins which lead to condemnation and to encourage the behaviour of which the author approves. The sermons are concerned with ethics rather than conversion. It would seem that the Sibylline Oracle genre was not appropriate for 'conversion literature' because then the pretence of being the Sibyl would have been exposed.[60] On the other hand, it was an appropriate medium for religious propaganda that encouraged a certain type of lifestyle,[61] a lifestyle which was perhaps a precursor to regular involvement with the Jewish community. The use of the Sibylline form and the incorporation of Hesiod were designed to increase the attractiveness of the book for Gentile readers and thus to further this apologetic aim.

The whole structure of I, 1–282 was devised to give weight and urgency to the thrust of Noah's preaching. The five generations build up to the judgement, with the imminence of the flood providing the occasion for presenting these crucial ethical values.[62] Judging by the structure of the first half of the Jewish substratum, the message of Noah's preaching was a vital reason for the book's composition. Given its probable provenance in Apamea, we can suggest that preaching to the people of Apamea was important to our author.[63] Indeed, it seems reasonable to suggest that our Phrygian author put two sermons in the mouth of Noah because the Jewish community in Apamea was involved in just such preaching to its generation. Noah is a 'preacher of repentance' because the book mirrors the situation in Apamea. It is hard to see any other explanation for such long, detailed and unique sermons.[64]

We have seen that I, 261–7 makes it clear that Noah was the Apamean 'flood hero' who had probably settled in their city. Perhaps the implication of the sermons was that Noah had preached to their ancestors in the fifth generation; they had not repented and so had been judged by the flood. Therefore, the generation in Phrygia to whom the Jewish community spoke, probably around the turn of the era, should now repent, stand in awe of the Great God, propitiate him and live a holy life, avoiding the sins of their ancestors, who sneered at Noah rather than responding to his preaching. The book seems to reveal an active concern on the part of the Jewish community to communicate its message to the city. Furthermore, although Noah fully condemns the wickedness of his generation, in I, 189–94 he says that they do not respond to his preaching, he will still weep that they perished.[65] Noah clearly hoped that people would respond to his preaching and that the flood would be averted. We can suggest that this likewise reflects the attitude of the members of the Jewish community in Apamea. They actively and fervently sought to convince the city to accept the content of their message, which they placed on the lips of Noah.

We can conclude that here we have a document from around the turn of the era, behind which are shared traditions from the Jewish community, from the local environment and from Hesiod and Homer. It seeks to encourage a turning away from an unacceptable lifestyle (as far as the Jewish author was concerned) and the adoption of a holy life – a lifestyle which would perhaps be a precursor to regular involvement with the Jewish community. It therefore reflects the message of the Jewish community to its neighbours.

5 The inscriptions from Apamea

We possess a number of inscriptions which may have come from the Jewish community in Apamea. Apart from one exception, they contain, or are related to, the so-called 'Eumeneian Formula'. This formula was used by both Christians and Jews so that we cannot be certain of the origin of an inscription when no other indicator of Jewish provenance is present. This is the case for three of the inscriptions from Apamea.[66] There is one other inscription, however, about which we can be more certain.

5.1

Αὐρ. Ῥοῦφος Ἰουλιανοῦ Βʹ ἐποί[ησα τὸ ἡ]ρῷον ἐμαυτῷ
κὲ [τῇ συμβίῳ μ]ου Αὐρ. Τατιανῇ· ἰς ὃ ἕτερος οὐ τεθῇ, εἰ
δέ τις ἐπιτηδεύσι, τὸν νόμον οἶδεν [τ]ῶν Εἰουδέων.[67]

Aurelios Roufos, son and grandson of Iulianos, I have made
this grave for myself and for my wife Aurelia Tatiana. Let
no one else be buried here. If, however, someone buries
(another person) here, he knows the Law of the Jews.

This third century grave inscription reflects the common Phrygian
desire to secure one's grave against grave violators. What is unique
here is the form of the grave curse: 'he knows the Law of the Jews'.
In 1897 Ramsay wrote that 'We recognise there, not the law of Moses,
but a regulation agreed upon between the city and the Jewish
community for the protection of Jewish graves.'[68] He later explained
that since the Mosaic Law made no provision for the protection of
graves, it must be some local legal convention agreed with the city
protecting Jewish rights that is in view here.[69] However, in 1914
Ramsay changed his interpretation of this phrase due to the discovery
of the inscription from nearby Acmonia which invoked the 'curses
which are written in Deuteronomy' on grave violators. Thus, in the
Apamean inscription, the 'Law of the Jews' must refer to the Book
of Deuteronomy so that the protection of the tomb relies on the curses
written in Deut 27–9.[70] Accordingly, our findings in chapter 3,
section 3 with regard to the use of Deuteronomy by the community
at Acmonia also apply to Apamea.

A further factor to note here is what is assumed in saying 'he knows
the Law of the Jews'. The inscription is veiled and seems to presume,
at the very least, some knowledge of Deuteronomy on the part of the
reader, even if only that it contained serious curses. More than that,
however, the inscription also seems to presume that the reader will
acknowledge the *validity* of this Jewish Law. This must be the case,
or the inscription would offer no form of grave protection at all. The
writer of the inscription clearly assumed that the mere mention of the
'Law', which contains these curses, would be a sufficient deterrent.[71]
Obviously, this would only be true if the general population of
Apamea had some knowledge of the Jewish Law. This in itself appears
quite remarkable. However, when we combine this with our hypothesis regarding the Noah coins, it becomes understandable. Just as
the Jewish flood tradition was accepted by the city, so we see here
that a part of the Jewish Scriptures was also accepted as valid by the

wider community; the content of the Scriptures was also known to some extent. This shows again that the city had in large measure recognised the Jewish community and its traditions.[72]

6 The Council of Laodicea

The canons preserved from the Council of Laodicea in Phrygia, which probably met in the last half of the fourth century CE, are helpful for our study. The canons clearly concern the situation that was prevalent in the surrounding area, as is shown by the introduction which reads, 'The holy council, gathered together from various provinces of Asia at Laodicea'.[73] It was not an international council and its evidence can be taken to reflect the situation in Phrygia and its capital city, Apamea.

Of interest here is what the canons reveal about the impact of Judaism on the Church and the frequent contact between Jews and Christians. The following canons are noteworthy:

> (16) 'On the Sabbath the Gospels and other portions of the scripture shall be read aloud.'
> (29) 'Christians shall not Judaise and be idle on the Sabbath, but shall work on that day; but the Lord's day they shall especially honour, and as being Christians, shall, if possible, do no work on that day. If, however, they are found Judaising they shall be shut out from Christ.'
> (37) 'No one shall accept festal presents from Jews and heretics or keep the festivals with them.'
> (38) 'No one shall accept unleavened bread from the Jews or take part in their profanity.'[74]

Canon 16 suggests that some Christians read only the OT on the Sabbath. Canon 29 shows that some Christians observed the Sabbath, at least to some extent. In view of these facts, a realistic rather than an idealistic line was adopted by the Council. Realising that it could not remove all prestige from the Sabbath, probably because of the influence of the Jews, the Council attempted to give the Sabbath a Christian character. It was to be a normal working day, with only Sunday being a day of rest. By prescribing the reading of the Gospels on the Sabbath, the Council attempted to ensure that the members of the Christian communities went to their own service and not to the synagogue where only the Old Testament would be read.[75] Canon 29 also anathematises those who actually 'Judaise' ('Ιουδαΐζειν) by adopting Jewish customs such as the Sabbath. In addition, some attendance at the Jewish synagogue by Christians is implied by the fact that some took part in the Jewish festivals, including accepting festal presents and unleavened bread. Close contact with the synagogue community seems to have been quite normal, with some Christians even attending Jewish festivals.[76]

This attractiveness of Jewish practices to Christians was certainly not unique in this period. Perhaps our best evidence comes from the 'Homilies against the Jews' preached by John Chrysostom at Antioch in Syria.[77] The strength, vitality and attractiveness of the Jewish community is not surprising in Syria. Here daily contact between Christians and Jews was probably unavoidable. Lightstone writes of Antioch: 'at the level of common believer ... Chrysostom could neither halt the praxis of Judaism among his Gentile Christians nor impede their actual participation in ritual along with the formal Jewish community.'[78] The Council of Laodicea in effect shows us that the situation was very similar in Phrygia with Christians adopting Jewish practices and participating in Jewish festivals. The strength of the Canons from Laodicea reflect the crisis felt by the Church. It was seen by the Council to be vital to ban formal contacts completely although daily contact could probably never be legislated against.[79] This in itself testifies not only to the attraction of Judaism to outsiders, but also to the strength and vitality of the Jewish communities in the area.

If a group of Christians participated by regular custom in the praxis of the synagogue then this must have been with the full knowledge and compliance of the Jewish people. These Christians seem to have acknowledged the validity and efficacy of Jewish rituals and traditions by their very desire to be involved. In return, the Jewish community allowed and perhaps encouraged such involvement. The most likely reason for this was the hope of converting these Christians to Judaism. We have noted that in an earlier period Sibylline Oracles I/II suggests the Jewish community actively sought to convince the city to accept its message. Similarly, in the fourth century it seems likely that the Jews sought to interest Christians in their Jewish faith.

The evidence of the Council also suggests that in the fourth century the Jewish community retained its elements of 'Jewishness'. By combating Jewish practices, the Council shows that for the Jewish communities in the area the Sabbath was a holy day, the Scriptures were revered and read, and the community observed the Jewish festivals. These features, which were fundamental to Jewish identity, remained intact. The evidence is all the more reliable because it comes from a 'hostile' source.

7 Conclusions

We have thus been able to draw together from diverse pieces of evidence a picture of the Jewish community at Apamea over a number of centuries. Firstly, although the evidence does not always enable us to trace continuities we can note that the community retained its 'Jewishness'. Over a considerable time period we have evidence that the community was concerned about the Temple tax, it honoured Scripture as containing its sacred traditions, it observed the Sabbath, it encouraged Gentiles to adopt an acceptable lifestyle as a precursor to regular involvement with the community. Secondly, the community was not closed and insular but attempted, often successfully, to convince others, whether pagan or Christian, of the validity of its own traditions. We see this in the Noah coins, in Sibylline Oracles I/II, in the inscription which mentions the 'Law of the Jews' and probably also in the adoption by Christians of Jewish practices in the fourth century. But there was some give and take involved here, with the community accepting a modified significance for Noah's wife. Thirdly, the community was an influential element in the city, where it seems to have been both accepted and respected. This influence certainly extended to the Christian community in the fourth century.

5

THE PROMINENCE OF WOMEN IN ASIA MINOR

The investigation of the status of women in Early Judaism has generally begun with an examination of intertestamental and rabbinic literature. However, only Sibylline Oracles I/II comes from Asia Minor and it has no relevance to this subject. Fortunately, we do have some very helpful inscriptions from Asia Minor and these will be examined here.

1 Women leaders in Jewish communities in Asia Minor

1.1 Rufina from Smyrna, Ionia

'Ρουφεῖνα Ἰουδαία ἀρχισυνάγωγος κατεσκεύασεν τὸ ἐνσόριον τοῖς ἀπελευθέροις καὶ θρέμασιν. μηδενὸς ἄλου ἐξουσίαν ἔχοντος θάψαι τινά. εἰ δέ τις τολμήσει, δώσει τῷ ἱερωτάτῳ ταμείῳ (δηνάρια) ᾱφ καὶ τῷ ἔθνει τῶν Ἰουδαίων (δηνάρια) ᾱ. Ταύτης τῆς ἐπιγραφῆς τὸ ἀντίγραφον ἀπόκειται εἰς τὸ ἀρχεῖον.[1]

Rufina, a Jewess, head of the synagogue, built the tomb for her freed slaves and the slaves raised in her house. No one else has the right to bury anyone (here). If someone should dare to, he will pay 1,500 denarii to the sacred treasury and 1,000 denarii to the Jewish people. A copy of this inscription has been placed in the (public) archives.

This inscription is probably to be dated in the second or third century CE. The ἀρχισυνάγωγος was one of the best known titles of synagogue office. He or she was probably the leading official in the synagogue and was held in high esteem, as is shown by the fact that the title-holder was always mentioned first in lists of officials. The archisynagogos seems to have been the spiritual and intellectual leader of the synagogue and responsible for its spiritual direction and regulation, including at times teaching the community and on other occasions inviting some one else to preach. Thus the archisynagogos was a scholarly person learned in the law who supervised the worship.[2]

What did the title mean when it was given to a woman? Scholars have argued that a woman received the title from her husband who was also an archisynagogos and hence that the title was purely honorific and involved no responsibility for the woman.[3] However, in each of the three occurrences of women archisynagogoi no husband is mentioned, which is most unusual if the title is only held in connection with his office.[4] In the present case, if the title was received from her husband (and we do not know her marital status), we would have expected Rufina to be introduced as 'wife of X'. Yet in the legal matter of guaranteeing a burial place, Rufina acted in her own name, without the mention of any man. Further evidence against this interpretation is provided by the fact that in only three out of twenty-two cases in which a husband bears one of a number of titles, does his wife also bear a title.[5] In the three inscriptions in which the wife of a male archisynagogos is mentioned, the wife does not receive her husband's title.[6] In our present case in which no husband is mentioned, it seems most unlikely that Rufina received the title through a man in a purely honorary sense.[7]

Salomon and Theodore Reinach suggested that the title was honorific for both men and women in the later period from which our inscription comes although in the earlier period, when only men bore the title, it was functional.[8] The logic behind this explanation, first made in 1883, is clear. In an earlier study of the Jewish community at Rome, Schürer had concluded that the title of 'archisynagogos' designated a genuine function in the community, compared with the titles of 'mother' or 'father of the synagogue', which he thought were primarily honorific. An important factor in his argument was that up to that point 'archisynagogos' was used only of a man and hence indicated a genuine role.[9] One of Schürer's presuppositions was clearly that women could not have an active role in the synagogue. S. Reinach's dilemma when our inscription was found in 1880 is obvious and his solution ingenious. Because women could not hold active positions, this third-century CE inscription meant that by this stage the title was honorific for both men and women. However, men had earlier held the title so S. Reinach postulated a development whereby the title became purely honorific. The evidence for this theory was simply the conviction that women were never active officials.

No sources allude to this development in the title's meaning and no evidence can be given to support it.[10]

Finally, scholars have argued that whilst the title was always functional for a man, it was purely honorific when held by a woman. Often few reasons have been given for this view, apart from the conviction that the community 'could hardly have entrusted the actual charge of an office'[11] to a woman. It could be suggested that Rufina received the title in an honorary sense in recognition for some contribution to the community, but this is unlikely. Only once in the twenty-three instances in which women were donors to various synagogues does a woman bear a title, and then probably not as a result of her donation.[12] Thus there seems to be no basis for this interpretation, apart from the presupposition that women did not hold active office. In addition, the whole concept of an 'honorific title' in the ancient synagogue is questionable. In the ancient sources, there is no indication that any of the titles of synagogue leadership were honorific. Further, in the ancient world honorific titles were those like *clarissima femina* – 'distinguished woman', or πρώτη γυναικων – 'first of women', and not titles that involved an office when applied to men.[13] Interpretations which understand 'archisynagogos' as an honorary title when held by Rufina are thus untenable.

The inscription does, however, give us cause to think that Rufina actively fulfilled the functions of the office outlined above. Firstly, she seems to have been a woman of some administrative and managerial skill, with the slaves and freed men and women probably being her daily responsibility. In making the arrangements for the tomb, she has acted alone and in her own name. We can envisage that her administrative skills were used in the synagogue just as they were in her household. Secondly, Rufina was probably a woman of some education. She has dealt with the legal matters involved in the protection of the tomb and the deposition of a copy of the inscription in the public archives. It is thus not unreasonable to assume that she was capable of teaching and exhorting the community. Thirdly, Rufina was a woman of some means, having built a large tomb out of her own wealth.[14] In the ancient world wealth was important in gaining influence and office, and it is likely that this was also the case in Diaspora Judaism. Consequently, we can suggest that Rufina was an active 'head of the synagogue' in the fullest meaning of the term.[15]

1.2 Theopempte from Myndos, Caria

['Από Θ]εωπέμπτης [ἀρ]χισυν(αγώγου) κὲ τοῦ υἱοῦ αὐτῆς
Εὐσεβίου.[16]
[From Th]eopempte, head of the synagogue, and her son
Eusebios.

The inscription, to be dated in the fourth to sixth century CE, was carved into the top of a quadrangular marble post about one metre high which was probably part of a synagogue chancel screen. The inscription commemorated the donation of this structure by Theopempte and her son. Scholars have again thought that Theopempte held the title archisynagogos in 'a purely honorific sense.'[17] However, as we have seen, this interpretation does not stand up to examination. Although the inscription does not tell us much about Theopempte, we know that she was married and that her husband, if he was still alive, took no part in the donation. She had sufficient wealth to make this donation together with her son, whose age we do not know but who was probably unmarried. Theopempte was mentioned first and hence was probably primarily responsible for the donation. She was thus an independent, moderately well-to-do lady. Both these factors are positive reasons for us to suggest that, like Rufina, Theopempte was an active head of the synagogue.[18]

1.3 Jael from Aphrodisias, Caria

A long inscription discovered at Aphrodisias in 1977 is probably to be dated in the early third century CE. Of interest here are lines 9–10 of face *a* which read: Ἰαηλ προστάτης *ν*. σὺν υἱῷ Ἰωσούα ἄρχ(οντι?).[19] Both Jael and Iosoua are members of the δεκανία. The name Jael was taken to be a woman's name by scholars who discussed the inscription prior to its publication. However, Reynolds and Tannenbaum take it to be a man's name and refer to the man named Ἰιηλ or Ἰαηλ in IV Ezra 10:43 rather than to the woman named Ἰαηλ in Judges 4–5. This seems to be primarily because the lists given in the inscription 'are otherwise demonstrably and consistently masculine'.[20] However, as far as 'Jael' is concerned, we need to focus on the decany, which is a group within the Jewish community of which s/he is a member along with seventeen or eighteen others. It is further defined as 'the decany of the students/disciples/sages of the law, also known as those who fervently/continually praise God, (who) erected for the relief of suffering in the community, at their personal expense, (this) memorial (building).'[21] Is it conceivable that one of the members of this group was a woman?

The members of the decany are clearly wealthy enough to make a donation towards the building. We know of a number of wealthy Jewish women, and Rufina, Theopempte and Tation discussed here are good examples. Further, we have suggested that Rufina was a woman of some education; we also learn of Beruriah in Rabbinic literature who is said to have been skilled in rabbinical methods of interpretation and application and to have given opinions on points of law.[22] She is indeed an exceptional woman, but it is not unreasonable to suppose that there were other women like her. Thus a woman could well have been a member of a group that, along with other activities, studied the law. There is no *a priori* reason why 'Jael' could not be a woman. Given the number of women leaders elsewhere (see section 1.5), one woman in a significant position in this group is not surprising.

A further observation is that when Jews in Aphrodisias adopted a name from the LXX they generally chose a name of a significant Jewish person rather than of someone who was relatively unknown. Thus we find the names Βενιαμιν, Ζαχαρίας, Ἰακωβ (three times), Ἰούδας (ten times), Ἰωσῆς (twice), Ἰωσηφ (three times), Μανασῆς, Ῥουβην, Ῥοῦφος, Σαμουηλ (five times), and Συμεών.[23] Accordingly, we would expect Ἰαηλ to be named after the person of that name who was most significant in Jewish tradition. This is clearly the woman Jael who murdered Sisera (Judges 4:17–22) and who is praised in Deborah's song (Judges 5:24–7).[24] The man Jael in IV Ezra 10:43 to whom Reynolds refers is one insignificant name in a very long list.

There is also a difficulty concerning the text of IV Ezra. In Judges 4:17f the LXX text reads Ἰαηλ, the Hebrew text יָעֵל. In IV Ezra 10:43 the Hebrew name is given as יְעִיאֵל; there are a number of translations in the different manuscripts of the LXX. Ἰαηλ is found a number of times, but we also find Ἰεειηλ, Ἰεηλ, Ἐιηλ and Ἰειηλ.[25] However, the principle of *lectio difficilior* suggests that the original text did not read Ἰαηλ. We could understand a copyist supplying this latter name as a more familiar reading in place of a name (such as Ἐιηλ) which was otherwise unknown to him. The fact that the Hebrew Vorlage in IV Ezra is different from that in Judges 4 reinforces the likelihood that Ἰαηλ is not the original reading in IV Ezra and that we are in fact dealing with two different names in the LXX. We cannot

rule out the possibility that the *Aphrodisias* text of IV Ezra read
'Ιαηλ, but the fact that this was probably not the original reading
seems to count against Reynolds' and Tannenbaum's interpretation.
This in turn suggests that 'Ιαηλ in the inscription was named after
the prominent woman of that name in Judges 4, rather than after a
man with a (probably) different name in IV Ezra 10:43.[26] Thus we
are able to include Jael in our list of prominent women in Asia Minor,
although with the caveat that the case is not absolutely certain.[27]

We must now determine the meaning of the title προστάτης. The
word can mean either one who stands before as the front-ranking
person and is thus the leader, president or ruler, or one who stands
before and protects as a guardian, champion or patron. Although
these two meanings are not mutually exclusive, we must decide if one
or the other is more likely in the case of Jael. The title occurs in six
Jewish inscriptions in which it is impossible to decide whether 'leader'
or 'patron' is the more appropriate translation. These inscriptions
do show that there was often more than one prostates in a community,
and that it was a significant position in some synagogues. In the LXX
and in the three intertestamental texts in which the term occurs,
προστάτης means 'leader' or 'ruler' and never 'patron'. In the
writings of Josephus and Philo both meanings of the term are equally
prominent and occasionally the term also means 'champion'. The title
occurs quite widely in the ancient world. In Asia Minor Magie thinks
προστάται were the equivalent of πρυτάνεις, the chief magistrates
in the city. προστάτης was also used of the patron of a pagan religious
society, who would have defended the group's interests.[28]

Consequently, it seems that we cannot decide between the two
possibilities of leader and patron and must leave the question open.[29]
We can, however, note that in some communities the prostates was
probably the most important official (for example at Xenephyris),
whilst in others he or she was second or third in rank behind other
office-bearers (for example, at Antioch behind the archons). Nothing
indicates that the title was honorary and this has never been suggested.
The literary references all imply the προστάτης actively fulfilled a
role.[30] In addition, in the Aphrodisias inscription, Jael is the first
member of the decany to be named. There are two other title-holders
mentioned – archon (?) and archidecanos – but the order implies
that Jael is of higher social standing in the community than the other
office-bearers. She is the only prostates mentioned and although she
has a son, Iosoua (who was archon (?) of the community), no husband
is recorded. The position is thus Jael's in her own right. All these

factors suggest that Jael was a prominent leader of the Jewish community at Aphrodisias. She was either the patron of the community and represented their interests to the wider society or the president or leader who directed community affairs.[31]

1.4 Tation from Phocaea, Ionia

Τάτιον Στράτωνος τοῦ Ἐνπέδωνος τὸν οἶκον καὶ τὸν περίβολον τοῦ ὑπαίθρου κατασκευάσασα ἐκ τῶ[ν ἰδ]ίων ἐχαρίσατο τ[οῖς ᾽Ιο]υδαίοις. Ἡ συναγωγὴ ἐ[τείμη]σεν τῶν ᾽Ιουδαίων Τάτιον Σ[τράτ]ωνος τοῦ Ἐνπέδωνος χρυσῷ στεφάνῳ καὶ προεδρίᾳ.[32]

Tation, daughter of Straton,[33] son of E(m)pedon, having erected the assembly hall and the enclosure of the open courtyard with her own funds, gave them as a gift to the Jews. The synagogue of the Jews honoured Tation, daughter of Straton, son of E(m)pedon, with a golden crown and the privilege of sitting in the seat of honour.

The text, almost certainly from ancient Phocaea, is probably to be dated in the third century CE. We know of other individuals who erected a building or gave their own dwellings for use by the community as a synagogue and of women who donated decorations for a synagogue or shared in such a donation with their husbands. However, Tation is unique in being a Jewish woman who donated a whole synagogue building.[34] This is also the only evidence in our corpus of Jewish inscriptions of a woman being given the privilege of the προεδρία and of a golden crown.

The προεδρία, unique in Jewish inscriptions with this sense, means that Tation sat in the pre-eminent position in the synagogue. In the Diaspora we find such seats of honour in the synagogues at Dura-Europos, Delos and probably at Ostia. In pagan honorific decrees, whose wording is very similar, the gift of the proedria is mentioned quite frequently. Again in this matter, the synagogue at Phocaea seems to have adopted the current practice of its environment.[35] The presentation of a golden crown was a familiar celebratory honour in the ancient world which was adopted by the Jewish communities in their inscriptions and in their art. Crowning as a mark of honour is found in the OT, in intertestamental literature and in the NT.[36]

Tation was clearly a woman of independent means who had considerable wealth and was able to build a synagogue with an open courtyard. She may have been married but no husband is mentioned. Her father Straton apparently had no part in the donation and was not honoured; this testifies to Tation's independence.[37] Thus, the Jewish community at Phocaea honoured a woman who was able to act independently of any man and who had considerable wealth which she used to erect a synagogue for the community. She was given the honour of a golden crown and the seat of pre-eminence, both of which were esteemed privileges in Jewish and pagan communities. Although this was an honorific as opposed to a functional position, it clearly shows that Tation was an important and respected person in the community. We have no indication from any other Jewish community in the ancient world that such honours were bestowed on a woman on any other occasion.[38]

1.5

Women received titles in other synagogues in the ancient world. In Crete, Sophia was a πρεσβυτέρα and ἀρχισυναγώγισσα. In Thebes, Phthiotis (Thessaly), Peristeria was an ἀρχήγισσα – probably 'leader' or perhaps 'founder'. In Bizye, Thrace, Rebecca was a πρεσβυτέρα. In Venosa, Southern Italy, three women held the title of πρεσβυτέρα, one was a μήτηρ, another a 'pateressa'. At Venetia, Italy, Coelia Paterna was a 'Mater synagogae'. In Rome, three women held the title of μήτηρ συναγωγῆς, Sara Ura was a πρεσβύτις, 'elder' or 'aged woman' and Gaudentia was a ἱέρισα – 'priestess'. At Oea, Tripolitania, Makaria Mazauzala was a πρεσβετέρησα. At Tell-el-Yahudiyyeh (Leontopolis), Marin was a ἱέρισα – 'priestess'. At Beth Shearim, Maria was a ἱερεία – priestess. On Malta, Eulogia was a πρεσβυτήρα.[39] The inscriptions range in date from the second century BCE to the sixth century CE.

Thus we have a total of twenty-one women with titles in ancient synagogues. They come from a range of locations and indicate that women held significant titles in a number of communities, although the exact reconstruction of what was involved, especially with mother of the synagogue and priestess, is difficult. We note that five Jewish women held titles at Venosa in Italy. We know of fifty-six Jewish inscriptions from this city, which means that 9 per cent of the known inscriptions refer to women title-bearers. This suggests that the Jewish community in Venosa may have had a tradition of granting women official functions.[40] It is also notice-able that Asia Minor had a significant number of Jewish women leaders. Of the seven archisynagogoi known to us in Asia Minor, two were women. In addition, 2.2 per cent of the inscriptions from this region mention women title-bearers. Although this is lower than at Venosa, it is significantly higher than in Rome where the figure is 0.94 per cent.[41] We should also note that women in Asia Minor held important positions − two women were ἀρχισυνάγωγοι and one was προστάτης − titles which were held by a woman in only one other place (Crete), albeit in a small sample.

Further, donor inscriptions from synagogues are also a helpful guide. 40 per cent of women donors known to us (either by themselves or jointly with husbands) come from Asia Minor even though the region only accounts for about 8.5 per cent of inscriptions.[42] If we restrict ourselves to the donor inscriptions from Asia Minor, we find that four out of around fifty-three inscriptions are by women alone and another fifteen are by women with their husbands.[43] Hence women were involved in approximately 36 per cent of the donations to synagogue buildings in Asia Minor. This suggests a significant degree of involvement by women in the Jewish communities in Asia Minor.[44]

Although the evidence is limited, we conclude that women did have a significant degree of involvement and leadership in synagogue life in Asia Minor. At least two and probably three women held high office, with only one woman elsewhere being in a similar position.[45] Another woman was very highly honoured. A higher percentage of inscriptions from Asia Minor allude to women donors than is the case in most other areas.[46] Consequently, the situation is sufficiently different from that elsewhere for us to seek an explanation.

We cannot discuss in detail the literary sources which provide help in an attempt to determine the position of women in Early Judaism. What emerges from these sources is a variegated picture which spans a wide spectrum of views. Some prominent men − Ben Sira, Philo, Josephus, some Rabbis − clearly held strong 'anti-women' views.[47] However, it would be a serious over-simplification to compile a list of their statements and claim that this represented 'the view about women' in this period. This wrongly presupposes a monolithic picture of Judaism and ignores the more positive side of the picture represented by the Book of Judith, Pseudo-Philo, TJob and Jubilees. In these works we find a much more positive image of women who featured in the tradition. This positive picture is less well-represented, but it does reveal that there was a diverse spectrum of attitudes towards, and images of, women.[48] We need not be totally surprised, therefore, to discover that there were women leaders in various synagogue communities because one strand of the literature of the period should prepare us for such prominent women. It is also not surprising that the picture across the Jewish world of the time is not uniform — although there were a number of prominent women in some areas (Venosa, Asia Minor), there were very few in some others (Palestine). This seems to reflect the diversity of opinion which is evident in various texts.

Moreover, given this diversity, it means that, when Jewish communities in Asia Minor appointed women leaders, they were following one strand of contemporary Jewish thought (albeit the minority view) rather than going against their Jewish tradition altogether. This is a significant result. However, this observation does not explain why Jews in *Asia Minor* followed the minority view on this subject. Why should some Jewish communities adopt this particular stance? We will now present the evidence provided by inscriptions concerning prominent women in Asia Minor in an attempt to answer this question.

2 The prominence of women in Asia Minor

A number of scholars have noted the prominence of women in the social system of Asia Minor. The most thorough study of this topic was done by Braunstein — *Die politische Wirksamkeit der griechischen Frau* (Leipzig, 1911) — who built on the earlier work of Paris.[49] Following Braunstein, I will deal with the civic titles that women received in Asia Minor. These are a more helpful indication of women's position in society than is the evidence provided, for example, by praise given to women in inscriptions.[50] However, it could be argued against this approach that, since my comparison will be with women in Judaism, I should concentrate here on women's position in the cults of Asia Minor. My reasons for not doing so are twofold. Firstly, women played a valuable and essential role in cults throughout the ancient world; for example, there were numerous priestesses in Greece, and the priestess of Athena Polias in Athens was a person of great importance and some influence. Yet, this seems not to have significantly affected the social position of women in general.[51] The dignity awarded to a priestess did not lead on to a higher status for women in general. Thus, although there were priestesses in Asia Minor, and a number of the women we will discuss held important cultic offices, this did not necessarily affect the

position of women in society there. Indeed, there appears to have
been no *necessary* connection between the primacy of women
in a religious cult, or the prevalence of the worship of goddesses
and the actual political or social status of women.[52] In contrast,
a woman archisynagogos in a Jewish synagogue did have a say
in the community's activities. Consequently, it seems that we should
look elsewhere than to the cults of Asia Minor for an explanation.
Secondly, the Jewish synagogue in the Diaspora was the centre
for worship, for social and educational activities, for financial
affairs and generally for all aspects of the life of the community.[53]
The organisation of the Jewish community was to some extent
modelled on that of the Greek city or of the collegia,[54] rather than
on any form of cult. Accordingly, when we are looking for an
explanation of synagogue practice, the social system of the city
will often be a helpful guide.

I do not claim to have discovered every inscription in which
women bear the titles under consideration but I do hope to be
able to point to a significant body of evidence. We begin by noting
the predominant bias of past scholarship in this area. The work
of Chapot demonstrates the presuppositions some scholars have
had when they examined this evidence. When women bore a title
that could have involved a leadership role, such as gymnasiarch,
Chapot claimed that all that was involved was providing the necessary
finance; there was no active leadership by a woman. When women
did hold titles that could involve real power (as well as honour),
he argued that the scope of the office was restricted. For example,
when dealing with the title of hipparchos, Chapot argued that,
since women held the title, its nature was religious – the only
role Chapot seems to have been able to envisage for women.[55]
This sort of presupposition certainly complicates the treatment
of these titles. Many other scholars have been influenced by their
view of what women could and could not do in city life.[56] Magie,
after discussing a number of offices, comments:

> In numerous instances the nominal character of many
> of these offices appears in the choice of incumbents whose
> chief qualifications were the possession of wealth and a
> readiness to spend ... During the imperial period ... women
> held the office of hipparch (at Cyzicus), stephanephorus,
> prytanis and demiurge. Their duties were presumably purely
> honorary, and in those cases in which the title was borne

also by the husband it was evidently given to the wife merely as a compliment. In what was probably a more active capacity a woman served as *dekaprotos* at Sillyum in Pamphylia and perhaps as clerk at Tralles.[57]

His comment about the office of gymnasiarch is also revealing:

> Occasionally, as also in certain of the civic offices, a woman assumed the burden of expense and with it the title. In some cases, to be sure, in which her husband also appears as gymnasiarch, it is a question whether this title was not merely honorary.[58]

Magie's assumptions are clear. A woman generally bore a title in a purely honorary sense or simply provided the money required for the fulfilment of the office; when both husband and wife bore the title, the wife received it as a 'compliment'.

Brooten has recently noted that although wives of religious functionaries in the ancient world sometimes received a title because their husbands held a cultic position (for example the wife of a *flamen dialis* was called *flaminica*), the wives also fulfilled a role in the cult along with their husbands.[59] Thus, attaining a title through marriage in no way *necessarily* implied that no duties accompanied the title or that the position was not an active one. In addition, where a husband and wife bear the same or related titles, this does not *necessarily* imply that the wife is dependent on the husband for the title. The woman could serve as a title-holder quite separately from her husband.[60] Hence, Magie's view that a wife received a title 'merely as a compliment' with no active role being undertaken is questionable.

A complicating factor here has been that an Emperor, or a member of his family, occasionally held magistracies in a Greek city. Clearly the Emperor did not attend council meetings or appear in person at festivals. In these cases the title was purely honorary. Similarly, deities and deceased people sometimes held magistracies; this involved the payment of a sum of money in return for the honour of the office.[61] However, when a woman held a title, should what this entailed be deduced from the situation when an Emperor, deity or deceased person held the title or when a man did so?[62] *A priori*, the comparison should be with a man since both the man and the woman were present in the city in a way that the Emperor, deity or deceased person clearly was not.

Magie's admission that Menodora at Sillyum probably served actively as dekaprotos is significant. The inscription, which is probably to be dated in the third century CE, reads:

['Η β]ου[λὴ καὶ ὁ δῆμος] ἐτείμησεν ἀρχιέρειαν τῶν Σεβαστῶν, ἱέρειαν Δήμητρος καὶ θεῶν πάντων καὶ ἱεροφάντιν τῶν πατρίων θεῶ[ν] καὶ κτιστρίαν καὶ δημιουργ[ὸν] καὶ γυμνασίαρχον ἐλαί[ου θέσει Μ]ηνοδώραν Μεγακλέους τ[ελεσαμ]ένην δεκαπρωτίαν, θυγα[τέρα καὶ] ἐγγόνην καὶ ἀπόγονον [ἀρχιερέ]ων καὶ δημιουργῶν [καὶ γυμνασ]ιάρχων ἐλαίου θέσει καὶ δεκαπρώτων ...[63]

The Council and People honoured Menodora Megakleos, chief-priestess of the Sebastoi, priestess of Demeter and of all the gods, hierophant of the ancestral gods, founder, demiourgos, gymnasiarch paying for the oil, having completed the office of dekaprotos, daughter and grand-daughter and descendant of chief-priests, demiourgoi, gymnasiarchs paying for the oil and dekaprotoi ...

Menodora clearly belonged to an important family in Sillyum. The phrase τελεσαμένην δεκαπρωτίαν strongly suggests that Menodora actively fulfilled this office, as Magie conceded. In addition, she had been a demiourgos and a gymnasiarch, of which the most notable task, the provision of oil, is mentioned as it is for the other holders of these titles from her family. She was also the daughter and descendant of people who had carried out these three offices. However, her husband is not mentioned, although the inscription goes on to mention her children. Likewise, no indication is given that 'demiourgos' and 'gymnasiarchos' were honorary titles. They may have been hereditary, but this in no way implies that she did not fulfil the tasks involved herself. She almost certainly actively fulfilled the office of dekaprotos; the inscription suggests that she was also active as demiourgos and gymnasiarch. We will now discuss what was involved in these three offices.[64]

2.1 Dekaprotos − Δεκάπρωτος

The dekaprotoi are rare before the end of the second century CE, and may have begun as a finance committee of the Council. They became a group of (normally) ten officials chosen from the body of citizens who served for one or more years and were responsible for the collection of the taxes levied on the city by the Roman government.

The office also involved an obligation to make up any deficit at the dekaprotoi's expense and they might be assigned other duties of a financial nature in municipal affairs, such as administration of an endowment or ensuring the payment of interest. The office was an important one which was given to people of high standing.[65] The title occurs outside of Asia Minor and the coastal islands, but Menodora is the only woman known to us to have definitely fulfilled this office, and she seems to have done so actively.[66]

2.2 Demiourgos – Δημιουργός

This title was found in the Peloponnese, Asia Minor and elsewhere. We know of ten women who held this title in six cities, dating from the second century BCE to the third century CE.[67] No woman seems to have held this title outside of Asia Minor and the coastal islands, despite its popularity in other places.

It is difficult to determine the exact function of the demiourgos in Asia Minor. That it was a position of much honour is shown by it being eponymous in some cities, in which case it involved a role in the city's festivals. Women were eponymous demiourgoi, for example, on Samos.[68] Where the title was not eponymous it involved a magistracy, and although this was not the principal magistracy, it was nonetheless a significant one. At Mallus in Cilicia, for example, the title involved holding office as a magistrate and here a woman held the title.[69] In some cities there was a group of ten demiourgoi; it seems reasonable to envisage a situation in Asia Minor in which one of these at times was a woman.

2.3 Gymnasiarch – Γυμνασίαρχος

The gymnasiarchy was a position which affected the communal life of a city to a great extent, since the gymnasium was the place for both physical and mental development of citizens and became the centre of the social life of the community.[70] The gymnasiarch was responsible for the direction of the whole establishment and so had to provide for both the athletic and intellectual training of citizens. This involved maintenance of the buildings and equipment, management of the staff of public slaves, the provision of oil (often at the gymnasiarch's own considerable expense), the organisation of both athletic and intellectual contests and the giving of prizes. The gymnasiarch had general control over the intellectual training provided, although he or she was

often assisted by other magistrates in this area. In the period from
the fifth century BCE to the fourth century CE we have evidence of
either a gymnasium or a gymnasiarch in 130 cities in Asia Minor and
the coastal islands.[71] It can be assumed that every city of any importance had at least one gymnasium.

We know of forty-eight women gymnasiarchs in twenty-three cities
of Asia Minor and the coastal islands, dating from the first to the
third century CE.[72] A woman in Cyrene and another in Hermopolis,
Egypt, were also gymnasiarchs.[73] In Asia Minor we have instances
where a woman was described as a gymnasiarch whilst her husband
was not and also where a woman was a gymnasiarch but her father
was not. This suggests that in (at least) some cases women actively
fulfilled the liturgy independently of men and therefore in their own
right. In some cases husband and wife both held the title.[74] It is
possible that they shared the responsibilities jointly or that they did
not simultaneously hold the title so that in either case they would both
have been active. Further, we know that in this period women were
able to gain considerable wealth, had access to education and were
often involved in sports.[75] Thus a woman could have been well-
qualified to act as gymnasiarch. It seems most likely, therefore, that
women actively fulfilled this liturgy.[76]

Levy has argued that all that was involved in a woman being a
gymnasiarch was the donation of money.[77] However, if this was all
that was involved without any active participation in the running of
the gymnasium, then it seems strange that the title should have been
given at all. Such generosity could have been noted by the word
ἐπίδοσις (benefaction or charitable endowment) or εὐεργεσία (public
service, good deed) without the bestowal of an important title.[78] An
inscription from Rhegium near Byzantium of the first or second
century CE suggests that more than the often recorded expense was
involved. Crispina was described as γυμνασιαρχήσασαν πολυτελῶς
καὶ καλῶς. Here the addition of καλῶς (thoroughly or well) suggests
that more than lavish expenditure (πολυτελῶς) was involved.[79]
Thus, although we cannot prove that women actively fulfilled this
role (which is very difficult to prove for men in any case), the evidence
suggests that they did so.

2.4

Women held other titles in Asia Minor. The following inscription
from Phocaea is noteworthy:

Ἡ Τευθαδέων φυλὴ Φλαουίαν, Μόσχο[υ] θυγατέρα,
Ἄμμιον, τὴν καλουμένην Ἀρίστιον, ἀρχιέρειαν Ἀσίας
ναοῦ τοῦ ἐν Ἐφέσῳ, πρύτανιν, στεφανηφόρον δὶς, καὶ
ἱέρειαν τῆς Μασσαλίας, ἀγωνοθέτιν, τὴν Φλαουίου
Ἑρμοκράτου γυναῖκα, ἀρετῆς ἕνεκεν καὶ τῆς περὶ τὸν
βίον κοσμ[ιό]τητός τε καὶ ἁγνείας.[80]
The Teuthadeos tribe, Flavia Ammion, daughter of Moschos,
who is called Aristios, chief-priestess of the Temple of Asia
in Ephesus, prytanis, twice stephanephoros, priestess of the
Massalia, agonothete, wife of Flavius Hermocrates, on
account of excellence and propriety regarding conduct and
purity.

Flavia Ammion had three titles apart from her religious offices. Her
husband T. Flavius Varus Calvesianus Hermocrates is also known
from another inscription; he was ἀρχιερέα Ἀσίας ναοῦ τοῦ ἐν
Ἐφέσῳ, πρύταν[ιν], στεφανηφόρον καὶ ἱερέα τῆς Μασσαλίας δὶς,
ἀγωνοθέτην – chief-priest of the Temple of Asia in Ephesus,
prytanis, stephanephoros and twice priest of the Massalia,
agonothete.[81] It is interesting to note that he is only mentioned by
name in the inscription given above and that his titles are not listed;
one would expect the titles to be included if those of his wife were
dependent upon them. Further, Flavia Ammion was stephanephoros
twice, whilst there is no evidence that he ever repeated his term of
office. These two factors suggest that her titles were not honorary
and that she had not received them simply as a 'compliment' because
she was Flavius Hermocrates' wife. Thus, although married to a very
significant man, she was important in her own right and the titles she
carried seem to be her own. She therefore probably actively fulfilled
the roles involved. We will now discuss the titles she was given.

2.5 Prytanis – Πρύτανις

The office of πρύτανις dates back to the earliest republican period
of Greek history when the single πρύτανις was the highest magistrate
and had wide-ranging powers. As with a number of these individual
offices, there was a progressive deprivation of the power of the
position over time in favour of the Council and People, who were
led by a new group of magistrates. The real power of government and
administration was vested with these new magistrates. The πρύτανις
then became the eponymous official who retained little political

power; instead he or she was assigned more formal and sacral tasks which could include entertaining honoured guests of the city, making sacrifices on the city's behalf and fulfilling certain tasks on ceremonial occasions.[82] The office, which was held for a year, involved considerable expenditure. At times the eponymous office did, however, retain some of its former power; for example, we know of a prytanis being involved in the purchase of property, keeping records and doing restoration work. It is also clear that it remained a position of very high rank in the city. Thus, as was regularly the case, the prytanis was listed before the strategos in an inscription, despite the fact that the strategos had the actual power of government. In processions the prytanis took second place only to the priest(s) of the deity whose festival it was.[83]

We know of twenty-eight women who held the post of eponymous prytanis in eight cities in Asia Minor, dating from the first to the third century CE.[84] It is noteworthy that women were elected to this eponymous position. Although it had lost most (though probably not all) of its political power, it seems to have been a significant position in the city with a role in the leadership of the city, a 'high profile' and a considerable amount of honour.

We know of cases in which a woman held the title but her father or husband did not. In one case a woman was described as πρυτανεύσασαν καλῶς, which suggests that she actively fulfilled the role. In other cases a woman did hold the title along with her husband or other relatives, but this does not necessarily mean that she received the title from them, nor that she did not actively fulfil the position.[85] The fact that many title-holders were husband and wife is best explained by the custom of inter-marriage among wealthy and distinguished families whose members dominated office-holding in the cities and not by the wife receiving the title in an honorary way from her husband.[86]

In other cities a number of πρυτάνεις were the magistrates who formed the principal executive committee of the council. This committee was the board that actually provided the political and administrative leadership of the city and often presided over the meetings of the council and assembly. For example, in Phocaea, the home of Flavia Ammion (see above), the board of prytaneis fulfilled this executive role. As we argued above, Flavia Ammion seems to have actively fulfilled the office. At Thyateira, however, we are not able to determine if the πρύτανις was a single eponymous official or a member of the board of magistrates. Three women held this title in

Thyateira; the possibility that they were members of the board of magistrates must be left open.[87] Although the title was widely used in the ancient world, it was never given to a woman outside of Asia Minor and the coastal islands.[88]

2.6 Stephanephoros – Στεφανηφόρος

The stephanephorate, literally 'the one who has the right of wearing a crown', probably originated in Miletus where it was of great antiquity. In our period it was the general title for the eponymous official in Phrygia, Caria and Lydia and was at the top of the whole pyramid of offices in these cities. The title was generally bestowed upon someone who had already held a magistracy or a religious office. Thus the eponymous stephanephorate was a formal title of honour and prestige bestowed upon leading citizens in the community. It normally involved some public appearances, the giving of banquets and the provision of very lavish entertainments. It was not a position which involved matters of civic government, but it did give the holder a high profile and much praise and honour in the city, involving as it did presiding over civic entertainments and representing the city to the outside world. As is the case with a number of other eponymous offices dealt with here, the fact that a year should be named after a woman is noteworthy. Consequently, although the position involved more honour than power, its significance should not be underestimated.[89]

We know of thirty-seven women who held this title in seventeen cities in Asia Minor and the coastal islands, dating from the second century BCE to the third century CE.[90] In an inscription of the second century BCE from Sardis we learn that Menophila held the title of eponymous stephanephoros. She is depicted, along with two attendants, on the stele; also visible are a wreath and other objects. The inscription in her honour states: ὁ δ'αὖ περὶ κρατὶ φορηθεὶς ἀρχὰν μανύει – the wreath worn about the head signifies public office.[91] This indicates that Menophila herself wore the crown involved with the office; it seems likely that other aspects of the position, for example, presiding at banquets, were also performed by her. A woman named Phile held this title in Priene in the first century CE. She had built a reservoir and an aqueduct for the city and perhaps received the title as a reward for her donation.[92] Phile's husband is named, but he does not hold any title in the inscription; it is also clear that Phile made the donation by herself. Hence, it seems that the title Phile held was her own and that she fulfilled the role of stephanephoros herself. In a number of other cases it can be shown that a woman has not simply received this title from a man. For example, in some cases the father of a woman is known but has no title or the husband is known and similarly has no title. Even on those occasions where both husband and wife held the title, or both father and daughter,[93] it is probable that the woman held the title on her own account since we have seen that there are many cases that demonstrate that a woman could hold the title independently of any man.

Often the title was not eponymous, in which case it probably involved the bestowal of honour to a slightly lesser extent, along with considerable expense. Women held the non-eponymous title in fifteen inscriptions in nine cities.[94] In an inscription from Heracleia Salbace it is noted that Tate had held the stephanephorate λαμπρῶς – magnificently. Robert notes that she had fulfilled the functions involved herself. She also paid 2340 denarii, the *summa honoraria* associated with the position.[95] Although the title is found rarely elsewhere,[96] it was only held by women in Asia Minor.

2.7 Agonothete – Ἀγωνοθέτις

This position involved responsibility for the athletic contests and other spectacles such as competitions in music and drama which were connected with the festivals and games of the city. These contests were probably the most important feature of such occasions in the eyes of the public. When, as often happened, the money from the city was insufficient to maintain the splendour of the occasion, the agonothete had to provide the necessary amount personally. However, there was far more that a public-spirited agonothete might undertake, such as providing lavish hospitality for the competitors, serving refreshments to the audience or even distributing money and wine to all for the duration of the festival.[97]

We know of eighteen women who held this title in fourteen cities in Asia Minor, dating from the first to the third century CE.[98] Again, women held the title in their own right, though it was sometimes also held by other family members. In an inscription from Thyateira, Julia is described as – ἀγωνοθετήσασαν λαμπρῶς καὶ πολυδαπάνως – having been agonothete with magnificence and at great expense.[99] Such praise suggests that Julia did all that a man who held this office would have done. The title was widely used in the ancient world. In Sparta one woman is recorded as being an agonothete although Braunstein regards the reading as dubious.[100] We will now discuss the other titles women held in Asia Minor.

2.8 Panegyriarch – Πανηγυριάρχης

In some cities the festivals were under the supervision of a panegyriarch, who had general financial and organisational responsibility for the occasion. In an inscription from Cnidus a woman bore this title. She is described as πανηγυριαρχήσασας φιλοτειμῶς καὶ ἐπιφανῶς – 'having been panegyriarch with public spirit and distinction'.[101] This seems to indicate that she filled the position actively. No other instances of a woman holding the title are known, although the title does occur elsewhere.

2.9 Hipparchos – Ἵππαρχος

This title, which means 'master of the horse', was the title for the eponymous magistrate in Cyzicus, Phrygia, and thus was the highest civic office. It probably involved some civil authority and the provision of money for civic activities. We know of five women who held this title in Cyzicus, dating from the first to the third century CE. When a father is mentioned, he does not bear the title. In some inscriptions no man is mentioned in association with the woman hipparchos.[102] No woman held this title outside of Asia Minor.

2.10 Gerousia – Γερουσία

The gerousia was an aristocratic society of elders centred on the gymnasium. Whilst these societies enjoyed both political and religious influence, they were primarily social societies without any administrative involvement in the life of the city. An inscription from Sebaste in Phrygia, dated to 99 CE, records the admission of seventy-one people to the gerousia, three of whom are women from a prominent family. In an inscription from Heracleia Salbace, Tate, who had been gymnasiarch and stephanephoros, was described as the first woman honoured with admission to the college of the very sacred geraioi. At Thessalonica in the third century CE a woman was γερουσιάρχισσα – probably president of the Gerousia.[103] Clearly, the number of women honoured in this way was very limited; four come from Asia Minor and one from Thessalonica.

2.11 Strategos – Στρατηγός

We have previously noted that this was the most frequent name given to the magisterial board of a city and involved large responsibility and considerable power. In an inscription from Aegiale on Amorgos, the Strategoi and the Dekaprotoi together proposed a piece of legislation to the council. One of the Strategoi was a woman.[104] Although this is the only known case, it is notable that a woman could attain this leading position in a city.

2.12 Women as officials of the federations

In Asia Minor a number of federations of cities were formed which were responsible for the imperial cult and also discussed matters of general interest concerning the administration of the province. The Lyciarch was the presiding officer of the Federation of Lycia, and it was an office that was highly prized as the pinnacle of a federal career. In inscriptions we find two female Λυκιάρχισσαι and in both cases the husband does not hold the corresponding title of Lyciarch. It seems likely, therefore, that two women held this important position in the Lycian League in their own right. We also find one woman with the title of Asiarch, which was the foremost title in Asia and was probably given to benefactors. Her husband was also an Asiarch, but this does not necessarily mean that she received the title through him. In another inscription both husband and wife are Pontarchs.[105]

This brings to a close our discussion of the various titles held by women in Asia Minor.[106] We have suggested that women held these titles in their own right and actively fulfilled the tasks involved. It has been difficult to prove this point, but the evidence points strongly in this direction. Any other hypothesis must account for the evidence as well or better. We are able to conclude that, although there are a very few exceptional cases elsewhere, the prominence of women in social and political life, as shown by the titles they held, has been confined to Asia Minor and the coastal islands.[107] Some significant points emerge. Firstly, the prominence of women is not uniform across the whole of Asia Minor. The phenomenon is most noticeable on the West Coast, especially in Caria and Ionia, less noticeable on the Southern Coast, very infrequent in the north of Asia Minor (Bithynia and Pontus) and seems not to occur at all in the regions of Galatia and Cappadocia. Secondly, we should note that there are some titles which women did not receive in Asia Minor, such as ταμίας (treasurer) and ἀστυνόμος (city guardian) and others which were given only infrequently. We cannot argue for anything like the equality of men and women; there were limits to the responsibilities given to women by a city. Thirdly, many of these women leaders probably belonged to the wealthy classes because considerable wealth was required before one became, for instance, a gymnasiarch. It is clear that the rich had a virtual monopoly on the sort of offices which were likely to be recorded in inscriptions.[108] In addition, social standing was vital in gaining office. Yet, when we remember that only a small proportion of inscriptions are preserved, it seems likely that we are dealing with a significant group of wealthy and prominent women who had the freedom to use their wealth as they saw fit.[109]

We noted in section 1 that Jewish communities in Asia Minor seem to have followed the 'minority Jewish view' with regard to the position of women by accepting women in leadership positions. The evidence suggests that they did so because of the influence of the environment on the synagogue communities. The fact that women were prominent in the political and social life of the city led to the Jewish communities adopting a minority strand in their tradition and thus to the appointment of women leaders in the synagogues.[110] This interpretation is underscored by the fact that our four prominent Jewish women (including Jael) came from Ionia and Caria, the two regions in which women's leadership in the city was most noticeable and widespread. We are also able to cite parallels from the same localities as the Jewish women leaders. In Rufina's city of Smyrna we know of three women who held the eponymous stephanephoros and one woman who was an agonothete. In Phocaea, where Tation was honoured by the synagogue, we find one woman who was prytanis, twice stephanephoros and agonothete. Here we are able to recognise a great similarity between the bestowal of the stephanephorate by the city and the honouring of Tation with a golden crown and with the proedria. Both involved a position of prestige given to a leading woman of some means. It is possible that the synagogue community at Phocaea had the honour of the stephanephoros in mind when it made its award to Tation. In Aphrodisias where Jael was prostates we know of one woman who was both the eponymous stephanephoros and gymnasiarch, another who held the title of stephanephoros sixteen times in all, and six other women who were the eponymous stephanephoros.[111] These parallels make our interpretation very plausible.

3 Conclusions

We might conclude from our Jewish inscriptions that this phenomenon of women's leadership in the synagogues of Asia Minor is only an aberration found in a few communities. However, we must recall the problem of inscriptional evidence. Apamea and its environs had a Jewish population sufficient to donate one hundred pounds of gold in Temple tax; this represents a Jewish population of many thousands in the vicinity of Apamea. Yet we have only very few inscriptions from Apamean Jews.[112] Likewise, before the discovery of the inscription from Aphrodisias, we could only guess that there was a community of Jews there. Now we know there were over 120 people involved in the community. Clearly the existence of four known women leaders in Asia Minor makes it possible to postulate that there were in fact many more.

We cannot show that women in all the synagogues of Asia Minor were honoured with a respect and prominence they did not have elsewhere. What we are able to do, however, is to add another dimension to the emerging picture of the diversity of Judaism in Asia Minor. Just as some communities were prominent in their cities and others less so, just as some were prosperous compared to others, so also at least some Jewish communities in Asia Minor gave an unusually prominent place to women.

We have shown that this is an area in which the local environment influenced the practice of the synagogue. We have also mentioned the effect of the environment on the Jewish communities with regard to the bestowal of honours. It seems that local factors were a strong formative influence on the Jewish communities.[113]

6

THEOS HYPSISTOS AND SABAZIOS –
SYNCRETISM IN JUDAISM IN ASIA MINOR?

There are a number of inscriptions from Asia Minor and elsewhere in which we find ὕψιστος, 'the Highest', or Θεὸς ὕψιστος, 'the Highest God'. The word ὕψιστος is used of Yahweh in the Septuagint, in the NT, in Jewish Pseudepigrapha and by other Jewish authors. It is also used in classical literature and inscriptions of pagan divinities, most frequently of Zeus. The problem with the inscriptions is therefore to discover when the term is used by Jews to refer to Yahweh and when it is used by pagans to refer to a pagan divinity. In fact, at the hands of Cumont, the body of evidence to be examined here gave rise to a complex and influential theory of syncretism involving Judaism in Asia Minor. He argued that the title ὕψιστος, whilst being used of Yahweh, was used of Zeus because of Jewish influence. Similarly, in Asia Minor 'Theos Hypsistos' was used in inscriptions by both Jews and pagans as the name of the God of Israel. Associations of the cult of 'Theos Hypsistos' were formed by these people, associations which adopted some but not all of the practices of the synagogue.[1] Further, again under Jewish influence, 'Theos Hypsistos' was used of the deity Sabazios. This, with other evidence, led Cumont to believe that the two deities were identified in certain thiasoi. Thus, some groups which worshipped Θεὸς ὕψιστος in fact represented a fusion of the two cults – Yahweh and Sabazios. All this occurred in Asia Minor where the Sabazios cult was thought to have originated, where 'Theos Hypsistos' occurs particularly frequently as a title and where many Jews were known to have lived. Thus, it was thought that Jews in Asia Minor were highly syncretistic and that in this area a 'mixing' of Judaism with paganism was particularly prevalent. A number of others followed Cumont in adopting this opinion.[2] In this chapter we will examine the evidence which Cumont considered and assess the validity of his views.

1 The pagan use of Ὕψιστος

Ὕψιστος was used quite widely in the ancient world. It is well known that in the time of the Roman Empire there was a distinct trend towards monotheism and thus towards the worship of one god as the supreme deity. This trend was prepared for by Greek philosophy and promoted by the influence of Oriental religions, and it was widespread even where there was no Jewish influence.[3] In addition, under the Roman Empire, in parallel with the reality of Emperors with almost universal powers, some local gods were thought of as the supreme rulers of the universe. Local deities seemed insufficient; to be worth honouring they needed to have world-wide authority. It was natural, therefore, that the epithet 'the Highest' should be used by pagans to indicate that the god to whom they were referring was, in their eyes, the most important god. Thus, the epithet Hypsistos, or the name Theos Hypsistos, was used of pagan deities throughout the Roman Empire.[4]

Zeus, the most exalted god of the Olympion, was often described as Ζεὺς Ὕψιστος and the cult of 'Zeus Hypsistos' was fully recognised in some places. For example, we know of a temple of Zeus Hypsistos at Thebes, a precinct at Iasus, a priest at Mylasa and a cult association at Edessa.[5] In dedications Zeus Hypsistos is sometimes called 'Theos Hypsistos' or simply 'Hypsistos'. Nock mentions votive inscriptions from a cult at Athens in which we find Διὶ ὑψίστῳ three times, Θεῷ ὑψίστῳ twice and ὑψίστῳ eight times. Clearly the three titles are treated as equivalents in this case. Thus, 'Hypsistos' by itself or 'Theos Hypsistos' could be used for Zeus. It seems that, with the trend towards monotheism, the god Zeus Hypsistos could gradually come to be given the general, elevated but more colourless title Θεὸς ὕψιστος.[6]

However, dedications or inscriptions to 'Theos Hypsistos' are sometimes clearly to deities other than Zeus or are made to an unnamed pagan deity who was worshipped under this general name. Nock pointed out: 'A dedication was addressed to the gods and not to the public, and therefore there was not in antiquity that need, which a modern man might feel, for the avoidance of ambiguity; circumlocutions were used which were intelligible only to the dedicant ... or the god was not named at all.'[7] Hence the same title can be used for a number of different gods. For example, in Syria 'Theos Hypsistos' (and also 'Zeus Hypsistos') was used to refer to the local Baal of a region, who was often a mountain god. In Lydia, 'Thea

Hypsiste' was used for some form of the Mother goddess. In Egypt, Hypsistos was used as an epithet of Isis. Clearly, 'Theos Hypsistos' or 'Hypsistos' can designate a whole range of exalted deities.[8]

2 The Jewish use of Ὕψιστος

In the LXX, ὕψιστος occurs over 110 times, particularly in the Psalms. Apart from a few topographical references, it is always used to denote Yahweh and is generally the translation of עֶלְיוֹן or עַלִּי. Whilst there is no one standardised form of usage of ὕψιστος in the LXX, it occurs most frequently in the phrase ὁ ὕψιστος – 'the most High' – and quite often in the phrases ὁ Θεὸς ὁ ὕψιστος (on occasions without the articles) and Κύριος ὁ ὕψιστος. Hypsistos is found particularly frequently in some of the later writings of the LXX. For example, after Κύριος it is the most common divine name used in Ben Sira.[9]

The term occurs quite often in various books of the Pseudepigrapha, often simply as ὕψιστος. It appears a number of times in the Testaments of the Twelve Patriarchs in particular. For example, in the TAsh. 5:4 we read: τὰς ἐντολὰς τοῦ ὑψίστου ἐξεζήτησα κατὰ πᾶσαν ἰσχύν μου.[10] In Joseph and Aseneth, Theos Hypsistos occurs as a title for God when pagans are addressed by Jews or by the 'heavenly man'. In 17:5 the heavenly man pronounces a blessing on the seven virgins: εὐλογήσει ὑμᾶς ὁ Θεὸς ὁ ὕψιστος εἰς τὸν αἰῶνα χρόνον. The title also occurs when pagans are speaking to Jews of Yahweh, as in 8:2 where Aseneth greets Joseph: χαίροις, κύριε, εὐλογημένε τῷ Θεῷ τῷ ὑψίστῳ.[11] Thus, Hypsistos was used as a way of designating Yahweh in the Intertestamental Period and as an appropriate name for God which could be put in the mouth of pagans in Jewish literature.

Philo uses ὕψιστος, although quite rarely. Often he is simply quoting the LXX; he does not use the term much when writing freely. In Leg. 278 Agrippa writes to Gaius: 'I was born, as you know, a Jew. Jerusalem is my home where stands the holy Temple of the Most High God (ὁ τοῦ ὑψίστου θεοῦ νεώς).' Philo uses similar wording in Flacc. 46, likewise addressed to non-Jews. In reporting the orders of both Julius Caesar and Augustus with respect to Jewish sacrifices, Philo refers to the Jewish God as 'the Most High God'.[12] Thus, 'the Most High God' was also a name for Yahweh which was considered appropriate when addressing non-Jews.

In L.A. III.82, Philo seems anxious to guard against a polytheistic or syncretistic interpretation of the phrase 'the Most High' in Gen 14:18 and betrays an awareness that other gods are also called 'the Most High': 'For he [Melchizedek] is priest of the Most High (τοῦ γὰρ ὑψίστου ἐστὶν ἱερεύς)[13] not that there is any other not Most High – for God being One "is in heaven above and on earth beneath and there is none besides Him"' (Deut 4:39). Philo is therefore generally cautious about the use of the term and is anxious to avoid misunderstanding. The title was perhaps too 'loaded' with meaning for pagan readers for Philo to use it freely. Indeed, in view of the pagan usage outlined above, the term would not even imply monotheism for a pagan reader. Rather, it would simply suggest the creation of a hierarchy in their pantheon. This must have limited its usefulness for a writer like Philo. Yet, he does use it when speaking to non-Jews of the Jewish God, or when he wants to have non-Jews, whose words he purports to give, refer to Yahweh in an intelligible way.

Josephus uses the term only when quoting Augustus' decree in favour of the Jews. Augustus writes: 'the Jews may follow their own customs ... just as they followed them in the time of Hyrcanus, high priest of the Most High God (ἀρχιερέως Θεοῦ ὑψίστου) ...' (Ant 16:163). Although the evidence is very limited, we can suggest that Josephus also regarded the term as one which was prone to encourage misunderstanding and syncretism and so had too many overtones in his society for him to use it freely.

To summarise, we have seen that the term Hypsistos is found to a significant degree in some Jewish writings. We have noted that, for some authors, it was regarded as a term which would be readily understood by pagans and could be used in the mouth of pagans to refer to Yahweh. For Philo (and perhaps for Josephus) it was also a title which had to be used with care because of the danger of misunderstanding.

In the NT, Hypsistos is used as a title for God seven times by Luke, once by Mark and once in Hebrews in a quotation from Gen 14.18. It is used only in passages which have a strongly Jewish background (and hence use ὕψιστος because of its frequency in the LXX and intertestamental literature), or in a Gentile context, in the mouth of demon-possessed pagans. When the title is used in a Jewish context it occurs simply as ὕψιστος or ὁ ὕψιστος; when it occurs in a Gentile context we find ὁ θεὸς ὁ ὕψιστος.[14] This usage seem to reflect the fact that for Jews ὁ ὕψιστος – the Most High – was a name for the only true God. That the term is not found in this form in a Gentile setting in the Gospels suggests that Luke (and perhaps Mark) was aware that for Gentiles ὁ ὕψιστος was a far less specific and meaningful title than it was for Jews.[15] Consequently, ὁ θεὸς ὁ ὕψιστος – the Most High God – which is a comparative superlative of more significance for Gentiles, is the form found on Gentile lips.[16] It seems likely, therefore, that Luke distinguishes between the use of Hypsistos in a Jewish and in a Gentile setting and that he was aware of the term's Jewish and pagan backgrounds. Its limited use in a Gentile setting (and then only in the mouth of demoniacs) is in keeping with Philo's caution about using the term.

3 Yahweh and the pagan usage of "Ὕψιστος – identity or influence?

It has been claimed that 'Hypsistos' was used as the name for Yahweh by both Jews and pagans in Asia Minor. Thus Cumont, in referring to a bas-relief in which Cybele was shown along with 'Theos Hypsistos', wrote: 'Theos Hypsistos, that is to say, the god of Israel.'[17] However, we have seen that many gods received the title 'Theos Hypsistos'. Definite proof is required that Yahweh is meant, and this is highly unlikely in this case when Cybele is also shown on the relief. In a similar way, Nilsson wrote: 'That Zeus was the highest God suggests that the Jewish God was identified with him and that he (the Jewish God) was to be called Ζεὺς ὕψιστος.' This sort of custom, Nilsson argued, began principally in inland Asia Minor where Jewish influence was thought to have been considerable.[18] Thus, dedications to 'Zeus Hypsistos' would be made by Jews, who understood that they were making dedications to Yahweh. However, that Zeus was given the epithet 'Hypsistos' and that Yahweh was called 'Theos Hypsistos' does not imply a relationship between them. We can explain the parallel usage of the epithet quite satisfactorily through the popularity of belief in the 'Highest god', on the one hand, and the Biblical usage of the term, on the other, without proposing any relationship between the two gods.[19] We have no evidence that Zeus Hypsistos and Yahweh (= Theos Hypsistos) were related as Nilsson suggests.

Some scholars have claimed that, whilst in the majority of cases 'Hypsistos' was used of a pagan deity, *this particular title* was used because of 'Jewish influence'. Anderson wrote: 'The title of "the Most High God" was borrowed by the Phrygian and other native religions from Judaism, which exercised a profound influence on them. They still remained pagan, but the absorption of Biblical ideas paved the way for the rapid progress of Christianity in Asia Minor.'[20] However, this claim is highly unlikely. The trend towards monotheism meant that a number of different gods were thought of as the Supreme deity or the 'Highest god', quite independently of Jewish influence. The frequency of the title 'Theos Hypsistos' in non-Jewish contexts reflects this tendency to concentrate powers in the hands of one exalted deity. Thus, there was sufficient reason for pagans to use 'Hypsistos' of any god and sufficient usage in clearly non-Jewish circles for there to be no need to suggest that Jewish influence was involved. Further, there is also no reason to think that the use of the title by a pagan would suggest to another passer-by that the dedicator was a 'Judaiser'. 'Hypsistos' was a vague title and it would not be clear which god was being referred to. Jewish influence would not have been an explanation for the use of the epithet in the period of its use; neither is it required now to explain its popularity.[21]

However, it is important to note the particular popularity of the epithet 'Hypsistos' in Asia Minor, especially in Phrygia and Lydia. Was it popular there because of the significant Jewish population in the area and thus because of 'Jewish influence'? It has been noted by a number of scholars that in Asia Minor, particularly in Phrygia and Lydia, the trend towards monotheism with its concentration of powers in the hands of one deity appears to have been particularly prevalent. Hence, in Asia Minor in the Imperial period there is a noticeable popularity of vague, abstract and almost anonymous divine titles such as Θεὸς Ὅσιος καὶ Δίκαιος or Ὅσιον καὶ Δίκαιον or simply Θεῖον. It seems that a quasi-philosophical notion of divinity was popular. Robert claimed that this was 'a powerful, original and complex religious movement in Phrygia and its neighbouring regions'.[22] This religious movement was clearly pagan and does not seem to have itself been influenced by Judaism.[23] Another feature of pagan piety is indicated by the occurrence of the terms ἄγγελος, ἀγγελικός or Θεῖος ἀγγελικός in inscriptions which come from Stratoniceia in Caria and elsewhere in Lydia and Phrygia.[24] It seems that here the deity was considered to be so remote that a 'messenger' or intermediary, sometimes considered to be a deity himself, was required to intercede for his worshippers and thus to bridge the gap between the divine and the human. Certainly, the trend towards a more abstract notion of the deity is clear in these inscriptions. In a religious atmosphere in which dedications to such abstract deities as these are found, and in which mediation between the god and his worshippers was felt to be necessary, the dissemination and particular popularity of dedications to 'Theos Hypsistos' in Asia Minor can be explained without any recourse to 'Jewish influence'. This local trend is therefore sufficient explanation of the observed phenomenon and 'Jewish influence' is not required to explain it.[25]

4 'Theos Hypsistos' in Jewish inscriptions

Given the usage of the term outlined above, an inscription using 'Theos Hypsistos' is to be regarded as Jewish only if there are clear signs of Jewish provenance and no indications that it might be pagan. In this section we will discuss all the known 'Theos Hypsistos' inscriptions which are Jewish in order to gain a complete picture of the use of the term in both Asia Minor and the Diaspora as a whole.[26]

4.1

A proseuche built at Alexandria in the second century BCE was dedicated [Θε]ῶι ὑψίστωι. This wording was repeated in an inscription of the second or first century BCE from Athribis in Egypt and probably in another (fragmentary) inscription from Leontopolis.[27]

4.2

Two Theos Hypsistos inscriptions from the end of the second century or the beginning of the first century BCE come from the island of Rheneia, the burial place of the inhabitants of Delos. These almost identical inscriptions are prayers which call upon the Highest God to revenge the untimely murder of two girls and are shown to be Jewish by their repeated allusions to the LXX.[28] Clearly, in these two inscriptions ὁ Θεὸς ὁ ὕψιστος is derived directly from the LXX.

4.3

A number of other inscriptions from Delos use 'Theos Hypsistos'. They come from a building, first excavated in 1912–13 and constructed in the first half of the first century BCE,[29] which has been claimed to be the synagogue of Delos. However, much of the debate about the identity of the building centres on whether or not these crucial inscriptions are Jewish. The inscriptions are:

(a) Ζωσᾶς Πάριος Θεῶι 'Υψίστωι εὐχήν.
Zosas of Paros, to the Highest God, in fulfilment of a vow.

(b) Λαωδίκη Θεῶι 'Υψίστωι σωθεῖσα ταῖς ὑφ' αὐτοῦ
θαραπήαις εὐχήν.
Laodice to the Highest God, who cured her of her infirmities,
in fulfilment of a vow.

(c) Λυσίμαχος ὑπὲρ ἑαυτοῦ Θεῷ 'Υψίστῳ χαριστήριον.
Lysimachos, in his own name, to the Highest God, a thank
offering.

(d) 'Υψίστῳ εὐχὴν Μαρκία.
To the Most High, Marcia in fulfilment of a vow.

(e) 'Αγαθοκλῆς καὶ Λυσίμαχος ἐπὶ προσευχῆι.[30]
Agathocles and Lysimachos, in fulfilment of prayer.

In 1970 Bruneau, who had recently excavated part of the site, argued that these inscriptions were Jewish and that the building was a synagogue.[31] Some points from the debate are noteworthy. Firstly, whilst the dedications to 'Theos Hypsistos' could be to Zeus Hypsistos or some other deity, we know from the two inscriptions from Rheneia that Jews on Delos did call Yahweh 'Theos Hypsistos'. This is precisely the 'further evidence' which is required to suggest that any Theos Hypsistos incription is Jewish. Secondly, it is unlikely that this is a sanctuary of Zeus, because 'Zeus Hypsistos' had his own sanctuary on Mount Cynthus on Delos.[32] It seems probable, therefore, that 'Theos Hypsistos' here means Yahweh for this is a title used by Jews on Delos. Further, whilst ἐπὶ προσευχῆι without the article probably means 'in fulfilment of (a) prayer' rather than 'in (the) synagogue', as Mazur pointed out, προσευχή remains almost exclusively a Jewish term.[33] Clearly, this is also a major point against those who do not consider the building a synagogue. Bruneau claims, therefore, that the convergence of evidence allows the identification as a synagogue to be assured. We can thus be confident that the building was a synagogue[34] and that the dedications to 'Theos Hypsistos' are Jewish.

4.4

One of four Jewish inscriptions from the island of Cos reads: Θέανος Θεῷ 'Υψίστῳ εὐχήν – Theanus to the Most High God, a vow.[35] S. M. Sherwin-White notes that 'Theos Hypsistos' is unlikely to denote a pagan deity in this case since there is no evidence that the epithet

'Hypsistos' was used to denote pagan gods on Cos, despite a large number of inscriptions. In addition, we know that a Jewish community existed on the island and the dedication is precisely paralleled by the series of dedications to 'Theos Hypsistos' from the synagogue on Delos. Thus, S. M. Sherwin-White concludes that 'Theos Hypsistos' was in this case the God of the Jews and that Theanus was a Jew or a 'Judaizing Greek'.[36] We cannot decide between these two possibilities, although the first is more likely, given the Jewish population on the island.

4.5

We have previously discussed this inscription from Acmonia, Phrygia:

[ἐὰν δέ τις ἕτερον σῶμα εἰσενέγκῃ, ἔσ]ται αὐτῷ πρὸς τὸν θεὸν τὸν ὕψιστον καὶ τὸ ἀράς δρέπανον εἰς τὸν οἶκον αὐτοῦ [εἰσέλθοιτο καὶ μηδέναν ἐνκαταλείψαιτο].[37]

[And whoever introduces another body], he will have to reckon with the Highest God and may the sickle of the curse come into his house [and leave no-one behind].

The phrase ἀράς δρέπανον is an allusion to the LXX of Zech 5:1–5, and it is therefore generally agreed that the inscription is Jewish. The inscription also contains the phrase τὸν θεὸν τὸν ὕψιστον and shows that some Jews in Phrygia used this expression to refer to Yahweh.

4.6

The following inscription has been found recently near Acmonia:
Ἐβίκτητος ἐπύησεν Θεῷ Ὑψίστῳ εὐχήν – Epiktetos fulfilled his vow to the Most High God.[38]

This inscription was found in the village of Yenice where inscription 4.5 was also found. Drew-Bear's comment is cautious: 'It is thus probable that there existed a Jewish community in this portion of the territory of Acmonia and that our Epiktetos had relations with it.'[39] However, it seems likely that Epiktetos was in fact a Jew. We know of large Jewish communities in the area and also that they actually used the term 'Theos Hypsistos' for Yahweh. There is also no indication of pagan provenance in the inscription. We cannot be certain, but this seems the most reasonable explanation.

4.7

A manumission document from Gorgippia in the Bosporus Kingdom and dated to 41 CE begins θεῶι ὑψίστωι παντοκράτορι εὐλογητῷ – 'To God Most High, Almighty, Blessed' and ends with the oath formula ὑπὸ Δία, Γῆν, Ἥλιον – under Zeus, Ge, Helios. The manumission took place (ἐν) τῆι προσευχῆι.[40] The opening formula strongly suggests that this is a Jewish inscription, παντοκράτωρ and εὐλογητός being common in Jewish literature and only rarely used by pagans.[41] The oath is a common pagan formula. Schürer-Vermes-Millar note, however, that the Elephantine papyri show that observing Jews might make use of pagan oath formulae and argue that, in the present case of a manumission, its use could well have been a legal necessity. They are satisfied that it is therefore a Jewish inscription, and this is confirmed by the manumission taking place in the προσευχή.[42] There are three other inscriptions in which the same opening formula either occurs or can be confidently restored. All three are from Gorgippia and are clearly related. An inscription from nearby Panticapaeum, dated to 306 CE, is almost certainly Jewish. It is a dedication to Θεὸς ὕψιστος ἐπήκοος and records the building of a προσευχή.[43] Thus in these five inscriptions we see 'Theos Hypsistos' almost certainly used by Jews of Yahweh.

4.8

The following undated inscription was found at Sibidunda in Pisidia and published in 1960:

Θεῷ Ὑψίστῳ καὶ Ἁγείᾳ Καταφυγῇ Ἀρτίμας υἱὸς Ἀρτίμου Μομμίου καὶ [Μ]αρκίας ὁ αὐτὸς κτίστης ἀνέστησεν καὶ τὸν θυμιατίστηρον κά(λ)κεον ἐκ τῶν ἰδίων.[44]

To the Most High God (who is) also the Holy Refuge, Artemas son of Artemas Mommios and Markias, the same founder, set up also the bronze incense burner out of his own (wealth).

Robert has noted that, 'In the religious texts of antiquity, it is in the Septuagint alone that καταφυγή appears and that God is the Refuge.'[45] It seems, therefore, that this inscription has been inspired by the LXX and that 'Theos Hypsistos' here is Yahweh. The epithet Ἁγία is also consonant with it being a Jewish inscription.[46]

4.9

A newly discovered inscription, to be dated in the late second or third century CE, from Kaleciuk, north-east of Ankara, reads:

Τῷ μεγάλῳ Θεῷ ‘Υψίστῳ καὶ ’Επουρανίῳ καὶ τοῖς ‘Αγίοις αὐτοῦ ’Ανγέλοις καὶ τῇ προσκυνητῇ αὐτοῦ προσευχῇ τὰ ᾧδε ἔργα γείνεται.[47]

The works here set forth are for the Great and Most High God of Heaven and for his holy angels and for his venerable house of prayer.

Whilst there is an absence of specifically polytheistic elements in the inscription, there are a number of indications that it is Jewish. The article is unusual with Theos Hypsistos in dedications but is found in many of the occurrences of Hypsistos in the LXX and in some Jewish inscriptions. The epithet ’Επουράνιος is found in non-Jewish inscriptions but is also used in the LXX, although rarely. The expression ἅγιοι ἄγγελοι is found in Jewish sources, and προσευχή is characteristically used to describe a place of prayer in Jewish inscriptions.[48] Thus, the inscription can be included among Jewish inscriptions using Theos Hypsistos, with a high degree of certainty.[49]

4.10

This inscription, probably to be dated in the first century CE, from Kayakent in North Galatia has also been published recently: ‘δύναμις Υψιστοῦ – The power of the Most High.[50] S. Mitchell writes of this inscription: ‘The allusion to the power of the Almighty is typically Jewish. Compare the frequent allusions in the Psalms to ὁ Θεὸς ἡμῶν καταφυγὴ καὶ δύναμις.’ Although a Jewish provenance is not the only possibility, it remains the most likely one for this inscription.[51]

5 Inscriptions in which Jewish influence can be detected behind the use of ‘Theos Hypsistos’

We have seen that Jews used the title ‘Theos Hypsistos’ for Yahweh in both literary sources and inscriptions. We have rejected the view that Jewish influence was required to explain the considerable popularity of the epithet ‘Hypsistos’ in pagan inscriptions. However, we need now to consider the possibility that in at least some cases, however few they may be, the epithet ‘Hypsistos’ was used precisely

because of the influence of local Jews. Did such influence in fact
occur? It is extremely difficult to tell. If a pagan used the term because
of Jewish influence but made a dedication to a pagan deity, we will
be unable to discern the Jewish influence.[52] It is thus likely that there
will be some cases in which such influence will go undetected.

However, we will probably have more chance of detecting Jewish
influence if the dedicator of an inscription had regular contact with
the Jewish community and thus comes into the category of a 'sympathiser' or 'God-worshipper'. Hence, if we can see that the use of
a pagan term is only purely formulaic and that predominantly Jewish
terms are used, including Theos Hypsistos, and if we know that there
were Jewish communities in the area, we can at least suggest that here
the dedicator has been influenced to a significant degree by Judaism
and is perhaps a 'God-worshipper'.[53]

5.1

This inscription has recently been found near Acmonia:

Ἀγαθῇ Τύχ[ῃ]· Αὐρ. Τατις Ὀνησίμου χαλκέος σύνβιος
σὺν τῷ συμβίῳ Ὀνησίμῳ Θεῷ Ὑψίστῳ ἐκ τῶν ἰδίων
ἀνέ[θ]ησαν.[54]

With good fortune. Aurelia Tatis, spouse of Onesimos the
blacksmith, set up (this monument) along with her spouse
Onesimos, to the most high God, at their own expense.

It is unlikely that this inscription is Jewish, beginning as it does with
a common pagan formula.[55] In view of the size and influence of the
Jewish community at Acmonia and in nearby Apamea and the fact
that Jews at Acmonia did call their God 'Theos Hypsistos' (as 4.5
and 4.6 show), it seems reasonable to suggest that Aurelia Tatis and
Onesimus had some links with the Jewish community. They still repeat
a pagan formula, yet they also make a dedication using a common
Jewish name for Yahweh. It is likely, therefore, that they had had
sufficient contact with the Jewish synagogue in the area to make a
dedication to the Jewish God using current terminology. They seem
to fit the category of 'God-worshippers' although this cannot be
proved.[56]

5.2

Schürer discussed a series of inscriptions to be dated in the beginning of the third century CE from Tanais in the Bosporus Kingdom. Some of the inscriptions give lists of the εἰσποιητοὶ ἀδελφοὶ σεβόμενοι θεὸν ὕψιστον – the adopted associates worshipping the Highest God.[57] These new members of the cult are placed under the guidance of πρεσβύτεροι. Other inscriptions show that there were a number of σύνοδοι devoted to the cult of 'Theos Hypsistos', which the above ἀδελφοί joined.[58] They appear to be autonomous groups which catered for a range of the needs of their members.

Schürer thought that these groups were not Jewish, primarily because they had ἱερεῖς, which he took to imply sacrificial worship, and because some of the stones bore a representation of an eagle. However, subsequent work has shown that neither point is decisive.[59] Goodenough has also pointed to five of the inscriptions which describe the setting up of seemingly autonomous groups of 'newly received brethren'. These seem strange in a Jewish context. Newly arrived Jews would be able to join the existing σύνοδοι; it seems therefore that some sort of conversion is involved here. In addition, Goodenough pointed out that many of the inscriptions begin with 'Αγαθῆι Τύχηι. He thought that this phrase had no reference to the goddess Tyche, but was a common talismanic formula and simply meant 'luck'.[60] It is difficult to know if the formula is significant, but no Jewish use of it is known.

It seems, therefore, that unambiguous evidence of a Jewish origin for these inscriptions is lacking. Neither is a συναγωγή nor a προσευχή mentioned. However, the convergence of a number of factors which suggest that Jewish influence *could have been* involved (Θεὸς ὕψιστος, σεβόμενοι ..., personal names) is surely not fortuitous. Thus, it seems that these groups were influenced by both Judaism and paganism and were on the border between the two.[61] This is probably another instance in which pagans used the term 'Theos Hypsistos' because of the influence of Jews.[62]

5.3

Finally, we should note that patristic literature informs us about the 'Υψιστιανοί who worshipped the Highest God and observed some Jewish and some pagan customs. They were known in parts of Asia Minor and elsewhere. They will be discussed more fully in chapter 7;

suffice it to note here that they were similar to the groups from Tanais and probably called their God Θεὸς ὕψιστος because of Jewish influence.

6 Sabazios and Judaism

We need now to discuss the supposed connection between Sabazios and Judaism. Sabazios was a Phrygian-Thracian god whose syncretistic cult was widely disseminated around the Mediterranean. He was identified with Zeus and later with Jupiter, and there was also a link between Dionysus and Sabazios which was perhaps of secondary importance. In Asia Minor he was probably originally a fertility god, but subsequently he became the protector of country people and ruled over their daily lives and souls. He thus approached the character of a universal god, and it was logical that he should be thought of as a manifestation of Zeus.[63]

Cumont was the first to propose that, particularly in Asia Minor, there was widespread syncretism between the Sabazios cult and Judaism, to the extent that Sabazios was identified with Yahweh in Asia Minor, where Jewish monotheism had been strongly influenced by paganism. His opinion has been widely accepted.[64] The evidence upon which this claim is based must be examined. Firstly, Valerius Maximus was often taken to have said that Jews who worshipped Jupiter Sabazios were expelled from Rome by Cornelius Hispalus, the praetor peregrinus in 139 BCE.[65] It was understood that Hispalus had actually expelled Jewish-Sabazios sectarians whose rites had offended public order and decency and who had come to Rome from Asia Minor.[66] However, the passage in Valerius Maximus used as evidence here actually falls in the middle of a long lacuna. In a recent study of the three manuscript traditions of the two epitomists used to supply an outline of what was originally said by Valerius Maximus, Lane has shown that only one tenth-century CE manuscript actually implies Sabazios worship by the Jews. Lane suggests that the original text of Valerius Maximus mentioned three expulsions by Cornelius Hispalus − (i) of the Chaldeans, (ii) of the Sabazios worshippers and (iii) of the Jews. One manuscript tradition mentions only (i) and (ii), a second only (i) and (iii). Lane suggests that a later scribe copying a manuscript of the first tradition also had before him a representative of the second tradition and thus introduced the Jews into the first manuscript tradition in such a way as to describe them as Sabazios worshippers. The original text almost certainly did not say this but rather reported that Jews were expelled and so were Sabazios worshippers, with no connection being made between the two groups. Accordingly, this text is very insecure evidence for Jewish-Sabazios syncretism.[67] Yet, this passage was the keystone of Cumont's argument. That his text of Valerius Maximus was almost certainly incorrect greatly weakens his case.

Secondly, it was argued that the mention of Jews who worshipped Jupiter Sabazios was not based on a fortuitous assonance with 'Sabaoth' or 'Sabbath', but that *Jews* had identified their god with Sabazios. Thus, the supposed note in Valerius Maximus was not a simple error of popular etymology but was an identification made by Phrygian (or perhaps Thracian) Jews, since this was where Sabazios originated.[68] However, with the evidence of Valerius Maximus shown to be unreliable on textual grounds there is no evidence that *Jews* identified Yahweh with Sabazios simply because of the similarity with the word 'Sabaoth' or 'Sabbath'. Popular etymology is the most likely explanation for the very limited and solely *pagan* identification of the two gods.[69]

Thirdly, the third-century CE tomb of Vincentius in the Praetextatus catacomb in Rome is an example of the syncretism of the Sabazios cult. One scene portrays an *angelus bonus*, and several paintings show a banquet, one of which carries the inscription: '... manduce, bibe, lude et veni ad me – ... Eat, drink, relax and come to me.'[70] It was claimed by Cumont that the presence of the angel was due to Jewish influence and that the paintings and the inscription reflect Jewish belief in a messianic banquet. Since Vincentius was a priest of Sabazios, it was argued that the tomb shows a connection between Sabazios and Judaism.[71] However, belief in angels was not restricted to Judaism; rather than referring to a messianic banquet, the inscription quoted above is purely hedonistic, and in any case such banquets were common in religions other than Judaism.[72] The tomb provides no evidence for a connection between Judaism and Sabazios. Rather, the murals probably represent a late and sophisticated form of Sabazios worship.

Fourthly, an association of Sabazios worshippers made a dedication to Θεὸς ὕψιστος in Pirot, Macedonia. Scholars who thought that 'Theos Hypsistos' was always Yahweh have thus seen this as a link between Judaism and Sabazios.[73] However, as we have seen, a number of pagan deities were given the epithet 'Hypsistos', so it is highly likely that in this instance Sabazios is being called 'the Highest God' by some of his own worshippers. This is not at all surprising in view of his identification with Zeus and the fact that Sabazios himself was thought of in some places in terms approaching those appropriate for a universal god.[74] No Jewish influence is involved here.

Fifthly, we do know of an amulet which bears the inscription 'Ιαὼ Σαβαώθ along with the sort of figures often found on votive hands dedicated to Sabazios. Whilst it is more likely that this amulet was made by a pagan than by a Jew, we know in any case that Jews often employed symbols used in the cults of pagan gods.[75] The amulet is therefore not necessarily evidence that Jews were involved in Sabazios worship.

Consequently, it turns out that none of the arguments put forward by Cumont are convincing.[76] In addition, Kraabel has shown the complete lack of any evidence from Sardis which suggests that Jews there were connected with the Sabazios cult.[77] Melito of Sardis would surely have attacked the Jews for any syncretism with Sabazios, and yet he does not. None of the more than eighty Jewish inscriptions from Sardis show any knowledge of Sabazios. Yet, we know that Sabazios was worshipped in Sardis from the fourth century BCE through to the second century CE, and almost certainly later as well.[78] Thus, there is a lack of any firm evidence connecting Judaism and Sabazios worship in Asia Minor, and we know, moreover, of factors which strongly suggest that such a connection never in fact existed.

7 Conclusions

We have seen that scholars like Cumont and Nilsson argued that Judaism in Asia Minor was at times a strange mixture of Judaism and paganism. These arguments have been based on the supposed links between Yahweh and Zeus (or other gods who were also called 'Hypsistos') and Sabazios. We have shown that both of these connections are unfounded. No evidence has arisen from this study to suggest that Judaism in Asia Minor was syncretistic or had been compromised by paganism. This is a very important finding.[79]

We have also seen that in a very limited number of cases, two of which were in Asia Minor, pagans or pagan groups used the title 'Hypsistos' because of Jewish influence. It is likely that there were more cases like this, but it is exceedingly difficult to demonstrate that such Jewish influence did in fact occur. A. D. Nock noted that we are on a religious frontier when we examine the use of ὕψιστος.[80]

This explains the difficulty we have had identifying the religious provenance of some inscriptions and determining when 'Jewish influence' has occurred. Those who are on the frontier between the two groups will be difficult to recognise. However, perhaps the most important fact is that the frontier existed, so that in an albeit limited number of cases, Jews and pagans shared the same religious vocabulary.

Jews used Hypsistos in literature and inscriptions because it belonged to Jewish tradition. In addition, its use was in keeping with the trend of the period to exalt one's god to a supreme position. Thus the term suited both Yahweh and the religious environment in which the Jews lived and so Jewish (and to a limited extent Christian) writers used it themselves and put it in the mouths of pagans who recognised Yahweh. However, we need to recognise that only a Jew or a Judaiser would understand that 'Theos Hypsistos' referred to Yahweh.[81] There were many 'Highest gods' and a pagan hearer or reader would understand the referent of the term to be the deity he or she considered to be supreme, if in fact he or she considered any deity in this position. They would not think of Yahweh.

Some scholars have clearly misunderstood this. Burchard writes: 'In a polytheistic environment it sounded both inviting and exclusive (e.g. against *Zeus Hypsistos*).'[82] However, the primary effect of the term on pagans who were reading or hearing Jewish literature must have been to mislead them. They would recognise, not Yahweh, but the deity they thought to be the Highest god. If pagans had a good knowledge of Judaism, they would indeed understand that Yahweh was being referred to, but the 'occasional hearer' would not make this inference. The term would not even imply monotheism for a pagan but would simply suggest the creation of a hierarchy in their pantheon. The term was thus not easily understood by pagans with the meaning intended by Jews.[83] This explains the reluctance to use the term which we found in both Josephus and Philo.

Just as significant as the use of the title for Yahweh in inscriptions by Jews is the fact that its use seems to have declined during the period under investigation here. Although these inscriptions are often difficult to date, it seems that the majority of occurrences of the title are found in the second century BCE to the first century CE whereas the bulk of Jewish inscriptions come from after this period. After the first century CE, the term seems to have been used mainly in areas which had a large Jewish population (Acmonia) or in groups where its use had become traditional (Gorgippia).[84]

We can suggest, therefore, that in both Asia Minor and elsewhere the syncretistic dangers of the title were recognised and it was avoided.[85] The fact that it misled pagans meant that it ceased to be used on inscriptions which were essentially public documents. Its continued use would have involved too great a danger of pagan neighbours losing sight of the distinctive identity of the Jewish community. It is perhaps also possible that the syncretistic dangers of the title meant that its use threatened the internal identity of the Jewish communities, that is, members of the community could themselves be confused or misled by the term. We see that Jewish communities are again part of their environment, but that this has led them, not to the adoption of a certain custom, but to the avoidance of a term.

With this in mind, there are two possible explanations for the early use of the title. Firstly, the pagan use of the title may have been much greater from the second century CE onwards than it was in the second or first century BCE.[86] The possibility of pagans misunderstanding the term would therefore be less in the early period. Certainly, the trend towards monotheism intensified as time progressed. Secondly, in the early period it seems likely that the Jewish communities were often comparative new-comers in the Diaspora and perhaps were not so concerned about 'external identity' (that is, who pagans thought they were) nor involved to such an extent as they were later with their neighbours. Thus, they were not so sensitive to the religious language of Gentiles around them.

Again, this is in keeping with what we found in our investigation of the use of the term by Philo and Josephus. The dangers of misunderstanding were too great for authors who wrote with pagans in view to use the term freely; the same situation seems to have applied for Jewish communities in the Diaspora. Thus, despite the fact that the term was strongly rooted in the tradition of Biblical and inter-testamental literature, the use of the term seems to have declined markedly in Jewish communities in the Diaspora because of its use in their environment.

7

'GOD WORSHIPPERS' IN ASIA MINOR

1 Introduction

In this chapter I will examine the evidence for 'God-worshippers' in Asia Minor.[1] They are to be understood as a group of pagans who attended the synagogue regularly and adopted some Jewish customs such as Sabbath observance and food laws but who were not circumcised and so were not full members of the Jewish community in the way that proselytes were. In 1877 Bernays suggested that three expressions found in a range of literature (and in the case of the last term also in inscriptions) – σεβόμενοι τὸν θεόν, φοβούμενοι τὸν θεόν and *metuens* – were 'technical terms' denoting Gentiles on the fringe of Judaism. Other scholars adopted Bernays' view and added a fourth 'technical term' – θεοσεβής. The concept of a God-worshipper was built up as a montage of these four terms.[2] Thus, the meaning of any one term has often been regarded as the sum total of the four.

Lake and Feldman both cast doubt on this interpretation and showed that the most natural meaning of the terms was simply 'religious' or 'devout' and that they could be applied to people of any belief. Whilst they could denote Gentile God-worshippers, the terms were normally applied to Jews; the meaning of the terms in each instance was to be discovered from the context.[3] As far as θεοσεβής is concerned, this means that it cannot *a priori* be regarded as a technical term for God-worshippers; a detailed investigation of its usage in literature and in inscriptions must be undertaken. A corollary is that this one term must be examined as a distinct linguistic entity without importing into its occurrences the meanings associated with the other three terms.

The discussion of these four terms as 'technical terms' for God-worshippers has assumed that these terms were either *always* technical terms or were *never* used in this way. Hence, some scholars have argued that they always applied to Gentile God-worshippers, others that they were always applied only to Jews.[4] Underlying this is an assumption that Judaism was monolithic and that it was always and everywhere of roughly the same nature. However, we now know that Judaism in Asia Minor was a diverse entity.[5] Communities in different areas had quite different characteristics. There is therefore no *a priori* reason why the term θεοσεβής could not be used in one place to mean 'God-worshipper' and in another as an epithet of a pious Jew. Our examination will proceed with this in mind.

2 The pagan and Jewish use of θεοσεβής

θεοσεβής is found in literary sources from the time of Herodotus with the meaning of 'pious' or 'devout'. It distinguished true piety from superstition and was regarded as one of the old particularly important virtues. Thus, Herodotus wrote of the Egyptians: θεοσεβέες δὲ περισσῶς ἐόντες μάλιστα πάντων ἀνθρώπων νόμοισι τοιοῖσιδε χρέωνται – They are beyond measure religious, more than any other nation, and these are among their customs.[6] A marble stele of pagan origin depicts a man lying on a couch, a seated woman and a boy pouring a libation on an altar. An inscription on the stone begins: 'Επιθέρσῃ τῷ θεοσεβῆ κ‹α›ὶ Θεοκτίστῃ ... – For Epitherses, the pious one, and Theoktista ....[7] The occurrence of θεοσεβής in pagan sources, even if comparatively rare, makes it unlikely that it was also a Jewish technical term for God-worshippers. Further, it also means that the mere occurrence of θεοσεβής in an inscription is insufficient to prove that the person concerned was linked with the Jewish community (and thus was a Jew or a God-worshipper); the inscription could be pagan. We should note, however, that εὐσεβής is much more common in pagan inscriptions than θεοσεβής.[8] Consequently, the use of θεοσεβής in an inscription does give rise to the suspicion that the author has had some contact with a Jewish community, although its use in pagan sources means that each individual case must still be investigated on its merits before we can draw conclusions as to its religious provenance and significance.

The adjective θεοσεβής, which occurs only seven times in the LXX, is used of particular people in Israel to describe their character and has a strong ethical flavour. For example, Job is referred to as θεοσεβής three times, along with other terms which show the excellence of his faith and character.[9] Josephus uses θεοσεβής six times. In Ant 12:284 the dying Mattathias charged his sons that τοὺς δικαίους καὶ θεοσεβεῖς are to be joined to the ranks of the Maccabees. In Ant 14:308 Mark Anthony writing to Hyrcanus stated that he was aware of the latter's 'obliging and pious (θεοσεβής) nature'.[10] In Ant 20:195 Josephus states that Poppaea the imperial consort (62–5 CE) was θεοσεβής. The meaning of the term here is debated. It seems likely that Josephus means her actions showed that she was supportive of Judaism, without wanting to suggest she was a proselyte or in any way a Judaiser.[11] In CAp 2:140 we read: 'Had Apion been asked who, in his opinion, were the wisest and most θεοσεβεῖς of all the Egyptians, he would undoubtedly make the admission "the priests".' Here θεοσεβής means 'devout' or 'religious'; no connotation of adoption of Jewish practices is involved. Clearly θεοσεβής can be used by Jews of pagans to describe their general piety just as it can be used by pagans of themselves.

θεοσεβής occurs a number of times in *Joseph and Aseneth* where it distinguishes Jews who worship the only God and live rightly from others. Thus ἀνὴρ θεοσεβής is used as a designation for a Jew as opposed to a Gentile. In the rest of the Pseudepigrapha the term's use is limited and it is applied only to members of Israel.[12]

Thus, in the LXX, Philo, Josephus and the Pseudepigrapha θεοσεβής is generally used of Jews. It denotes their piety and devout faithfulness to Yahweh and distinguishes them from the uncircumcised. It was an intelligible term to non-Jews, yet one which was distinct from the more common εὐσεβής. We would thus expect Jews to use θεοσεβής of themselves in grave inscriptions. θεοσεβής can also be used of pagans like the Egyptian priests to mean that they are 'devout' or 'religious', without implying any particular interest in or involvement with Judaism. In the literary sources Jews do not seem to call Gentiles who were involved in synagogue life θεοσεβής. To some extent this is perhaps due to our lack of literature which describes synagogue life in detail.

3 'God-worshippers' in literary sources?

Our investigation of the Jewish literary usage of θεοσεβής has uncovered no evidence which suggests the term was used in these sources for the group of Gentiles whom we have called 'God-worshippers'. There are, however, indications from Jewish, classical and Christian literature which suggest that the 'God-worshippers' did in fact exist. In Ant 14:110 Josephus writes: 'But no one need wonder that there was so much wealth in our temple, πάντων τῶν κατὰ τὴν οἰκουμένην Ἰουδαίων καὶ σεβομένων τὸν Θεόν, even those from Asia and Europe have been contributing to it for a very long time.' The translation of the middle clause has been much debated. Should it be translated as 'all the Jews throughout the world and those who worshipped God' or 'all the Jews worshipping God throughout the world'?[13] Marcus has argued that the first translation is correct. It is supported by the rules of Greek grammar, which we can assume Josephus would have followed. If Josephus had intended to identify the σεβόμενοι with the Jews he should have written 'τῶν... Ἰουδαίων τῶν σεβομένων...'. However, one could argue that the omission of the τῶν before σεβομένων indicates that the participle belongs with τῶν Ἰουδαίων. But Marcus noted that 'in good Greek when two different classes are associated in some activity or state, the article is omitted before the noun which designates the second of the two classes'.[14] In addition, the first translation also makes better sense of the rest of the passage. If the second translation is accepted, the next phrase – 'even those from Asia and Europe' – would be repetitious since this group is included among those Jews who are living 'throughout the world'. However, according to the first translation this additional phrase refers to 'worshippers of God', and emphasises that these people live not only in neighbouring Syria and Egypt, but even in Asia and Europe. Hence, in this passage Josephus seems to be referring to Jews and to Gentile worshippers of God who make a contribution to the Temple. This interpretation of the passage has commanded widespread support. That Gentiles made contributions to the Temple implies that they were involved to some significant degree in the life of the synagogue.[15]

Other passages, although difficult to interpret, probably refer to Gentile God-worshippers. In BJ 7:45 Josephus writes of the Jews that 'they were constantly attracting to their religious ceremonies multitudes of Greeks, and these they had in some measure incorporated with themselves (κἀκείνους τρόπῳ τινὶ μοῖραν αὐτῶν πεποίηντο)'. Finn notes that μοῖρα is used by Josephus to denote sharing in a fate, lot or destiny. This passage implies at least 'some kind of (undisclosed) status which distinguished these synagogue adherents from other Gentiles'.[16] In CAp 2:123 Josephus writes: 'Many of them (the Greeks) have agreed to adopt our laws; of whom some have remained faithful, while others, lacking the necessary endurance, have again seceded.' It is possible that those who 'adopted Jewish laws' became proselytes, although if this was the case one could expect Josephus to make this clear as he does elsewhere. It is likely therefore that this passage refers to God-worshippers.[17]

In Quaestiones in Exodum 2.2, commenting upon Ex 22:21, Philo speaks of Gentiles who were circumcised of the passions of the soul, reject polytheism and worship the one true God. The passage makes it clear that for Philo these Gentiles 'had standing in the Jewish community, however difficult to categorize legally'.[18] It seems that they fit into the group we have called God-worshippers.

In his fourteenth Satire, Juvenal depicts a father who reveres the Sabbath (metuentem sabbata), 'worship(s) nothing but the clouds and the divinity of the heavens' and abstains from eating swine's flesh and whose son is circumcised and practises and reveres the Jewish law. The father seems to fit into the category of a 'God-worshipper'.[19] That he observes the Sabbath suggests he is a regular attender at the synagogue, as does the comment about the deity he worships. Juvenal's remarks are clearly based on observation of a person or perhaps a group that has engaged his attention. The Satire relies on the father and the son being recognisable and well-known figures; Juvenal's denunciation would have been meaningless were it not directed against a situation prevalent in his day. It seems clear that the 'God-worshipping' father was reasonably common.[20]

Epictetus writes of the person who is not a Jew but acts the part of a Jew and who is not prepared to make the decisive move of conversion and yet carries out some of the requirements of Judaism. He is also aware that such a person sometimes becomes a proselyte. The first state of this person – not being a Jew but acting the part, which perhaps includes synagogue attendance along with other things – probably corresponds to the category of God-worshipper. Again, such a person seems to be well known to Epictetus.[21]

Does Acts provide evidence for this group? The two expressions – φοβούμενοι τὸν θεόν and σεβόμενοι τὸν θεόν – have often been understood to be technical terms referring to 'God-worshippers'. However, as we have noted, Feldman and Lake have shown that these are not technical terms but expressions meaning 'pious' or 'those who were worshipping' and that they can be applied to Jews or proselytes or Gentiles as the context may decide.[22] Does Luke then refer to Gentile 'God-worshippers'?

In looking at this question, scholars have concentrated too narrowly on the use of φοβούμενοι τὸν θεόν and σεβόμενοι τὸν θεόν. The evidence for Gentiles who are involved in synagogue life goes beyond the use of these two terms. On four occasions in Acts when

Paul preached in a synagogue he encountered both 'Ιουδαῖοι and Ἕλληνες there. In 14:1 Paul and Barnabas spoke in the synagogue at Iconium, and a great company believed, 'Ιουδαίων τε καὶ Ελλήνων. The unbelieving Jews then stirred up the Gentiles (τῶν ἐθνῶν) against the missionaries (14:2). By using a different term in v2 (ἔθνη) Luke consciously distinguishes those who opposed the Christian message from those who heard it in the synagogue and accepted it.[23]

Who are the Ἕλληνες? Clearly they were present in the synagogue when Paul arrived there. Are they proselytes?[24] This is possible, but Luke distinguishes elsewhere between Jews by birth and proselytes by using the terms 'Ιουδαῖοι and προσήλυτοι. Thus, in Acts 2 the group of listeners is introduced in v5 as 'Ιουδαῖοι, which is clarified in v11 as 'Ιουδαῖοί τε καὶ προσήλυτοι.[25] Clearly in v5 the 'Ιουδαῖοι include προσήλυτοι, as Luke explains in v11 where he is being more specific. The προσήλυτοι are not regarded as true Gentiles but as part of the 'Jews' of v5 since the Gentile mission has not yet begun at this point in Acts. In 6:5 Nicolaus is singled out as the only proselyte amongst the Seven and, as befits his slightly lower status, is given last in the list. The others were clearly Jews by birth. In 13:43a, the only other occurrence of προσήλυτος, σεβομένων is not a technical term but an honorary epithet. As in 2:11, Luke distinguishes between Jews by birth and Jews through conversion, the latter group being described as 'worshipping'. This accords with 13:43b; since these Jews and proselytes already trusted in God's grace as they knew it in the OT, Paul now urges them to continue in that basic attitude by believing in Jesus. There follows the gathering of the whole city and the jealousy and rejection of the Jews, and only then does the conversion of Gentiles begin (13:48). Clearly, therefore, Luke does know the technical meaning of προσήλυτοι; he can at times include them among the 'Ιουδαῖοι, or he can at other times single them out as a specific sub-category. If he particularly wants to indicate that some of the 'Ιουδαῖοι are proselytes he does so. We can therefore be sure that in 14:1 Ἕλληνες does not mean 'proselytes'.[26] Consequently, at the Iconium synagogue there was a mixed congregation of Greeks and Jews when Paul arrived there. This suggests that the Greeks were regularly to be found there and had some sort of commitment to the Jewish community, so that they fit the category of 'God-worshippers'.[27]

In 17:4 we read that some Jews were persuaded as a result of Paul's preaching in the synagogue at Thessalonica for three sabbaths.

Luke adds: τῶν τε σεβομένων Ἑλλήνων πλῆθος πολύ, γυναικῶν τε τῶν πρώτων οὐκ ὀλίγαι. Lake notes that σεβόμενοι here is not a technical term; 'the worshipping Greeks' is a good translation.[28] Yet, the text does seem to refer to non-Jews who are involved in the synagogue's life and who thus fit the category of 'God-worshippers'. In 17:12 many Jews from the synagogue at Beroea believed καὶ τῶν Ἑλληνίδων γυναικῶν τῶν εὐσχημόνων καὶ ἀνδρῶν οὐκ ὀλίγοι. The passage suggests that the Greek men and women were part of the synagogue congregation which heard Paul preach and then responded. Luke does not call the Greeks proselytes. In 18:4 we have similar evidence from Corinth: διελέγετο δὲ ἐν τῇ συναγωγῇ κατὰ πᾶν σάββατον ἔπειθέν τε ᾿Ιουδαίους καὶ Ἕλληνας. Again the Greeks could be proselytes, but we would expect Luke to call them προσήλυτοι if this was the case. They seem to be God-worshippers.

Having seen that Luke does speak of 'Greeks' who are not proselytes but who are involved in the synagogue we can now note that this makes it more likely that Luke refers to this group elsewhere. In 17:17 we read with respect to Athens: διελέγετο μὲν οὖν ἐν τῇ συναγωγῇ τοῖς ᾿Ιουδαίοις καὶ τοῖς σεβομένοις. The use of the article with σεβομένοις argues against the possibility that there is a hendiadys here.[29] Thus, although we do not have a technical term, it seems likely that Luke does refer to 'God-worshippers'. There are other passages in which it is difficult to make a decision about whether φοβούμενοι/σεβόμενοι τὸν θεόν refers to God-worshippers or Jews.[30]

We conclude that Luke refers to a group of 'God-worshippers' in at least some passages. However, some scholars have shown that whilst this group is vitally significant for Luke's theology, they do not appear at all in Paul's writings. Is Luke here writing theology in narrative form rather than giving an historical record?[31] If Acts was our only evidence for the existence of the 'God-worshippers' then using it as an historical source at this point would be problematic. But, in view of the independent corroboration for the existence of 'God-worshippers' provided by Juvenal, Epictetus, Philo and Josephus, we can be confident that Luke's presentation is historically credible, whilst also noting the theological points he is making. Thus, Acts becomes further evidence for the existence of the 'God-worshippers'.[32]

We conclude that the evidence of Jewish and classical literature shows that there were Gentiles in a variety of places who, although they did not become proselytes, observed some Jewish practices or accepted some Jewish beliefs and were in some sort of regular relationship with the synagogue. We are justified therefore in calling these people 'God-worshippers'. That the evidence comes both from Jewish authors and from 'outside observers' reinforces the credibility of both strands of evidence. Thus, although the examination of the term θεοσεβής in Jewish literature did not reveal any God-worshippers who were given that designation, we can conclude that the group existed although often described by other terms. We can also note that there is no 'technical term' for God-worshippers in the above literature. We will now look at inscriptions to see if the God-worshippers have left any trace there.

4   θεοσεβής in Jewish inscriptions from Asia Minor and elsewhere

It has been claimed that in some inscriptions θεοσεβής is used by Jews to designate the group we have called Gentile 'God-worshippers'. However, other scholars have stated that θεοσεβής in these inscriptions is used of Jews with the meaning of 'pious', in the same way as it is in Jewish literature. We will now examine these inscriptions.[33]

4.1

The most significant piece of evidence in this regard is the stele found at Aphrodisias and published by Reynolds and Tannenbaum in 1987.[34] It is inscribed on two faces in different hands, with additions to both faces by another hand or hands. The stele is clearly Jewish, as is shown by the many Biblical names and the word προσήλυτος as a status-designation. It seems likely that the texts on faces *a* and *b* belong together and are both to be dated to the early third century. The inscription shows that the members of a group within the synagogue called the 'decany' were the initiators of, and major donors to, a memorial building, which was probably a soup-kitchen of some kind. Those named on face *b*, the first line of which is missing, seem also to have contributed to the building. Face *a* lists the members of the decany – thirteen born Jews, three people described as προσήλυτος and two as θεοσεβής.[35] Face *b* contains two lists. The upper list contains a considerable number of people with Jewish names and seems to be a list of Jews by birth who were also contributors to the project. The second list is introduced by the heading Καὶ ὅσοι θεοσεβῖς – As many as are theosebeis.[36] There are fifty-two people listed under this heading, compared with over sixty-nine Jews in the other two lists. Of the sixty-three names given in the list of θεοσεβεῖς, none are Jewish and only two have Jewish connections. One other name may be Semitic, two are Greco-Roman names popular among Jews and the rest are Gentile names. This contrasts with the other two lists, in which well over half the names are either biblical or names strongly favoured by Jews. It seems very hard to avoid the conclusion that the θεοσεβεῖς are not Jews by birth. Since nearly all have Gentile names, they are surely Gentiles. Clearly, the fifty-two θεοσεβεῖς on face *b* are involved with a project which has been instigated by a Jewish 'decany' and is strongly supported by other Jews. Two of the θεοσεβεῖς belong to the decany which is devoted (though not exclusively) to study of the law and prayer. The conclusion that they are all Gentile 'God-worshippers' seems unavoidable.[37] They are attached in some definite way to the Jewish community as a distinct, separate and formal category of people who are neither Jews nor proselytes. They have all been allowed to belong, seemingly as enrolled members of a subsection of the whole community. We now know that at least at Aphrodisias there was a group of Gentile God-worshippers involved with the Jewish community who are given the title θεοσεβεῖς.[38]

This is confirmed by the observation that the θεοσεβεῖς are inferior in status in the synagogue community to the Jews, as is shown by the fact that the two θεοσεβεῖς in the decany are found towards the end of the list, which is clearly ranked according to status. In addition, the list of θεοσεβεῖς on face *b* is given after the list of Jews. This is not because of the social standing of the θεοσεβεῖς, since the first nine are city-councillors. The θεοσεβεῖς are therefore different from, and inferior to, the Jews. This must be because they are not full members of the Jewish community in the way born Jews and proselytes are. They are a group of Gentiles who belong to the synagogue, although in an inferior way compared with proselytes.[39]

Does the inscription help us to describe what was involved in being God-worshippers at Aphrodisias? They belonged to the synagogue community, and thus they almost certainly attended the synagogue and were part of the services. From the inscription we learn that some θεοσεβεῖς made donations to projects. Two θεοσεβεῖς were part of the decany and thus studied the law, prayed and took part in initiating charitable activities. The trade designations of five θεοσεβεῖς are interesting. There is one ἰκονο(ποιός) or ἰκονο(γράφος) – sculptor or painter of pictures with images; a λατύ(πος) – stone cutter or

carver; an ἀθλη(τής?) – athlete; a πύ(κτης) – boxer; and an
ἰσικιάριος – seller/producer of mincemeat. Did the God-
worshippers' trades cause the people involved to break Jewish law?
Reynolds and Tannenbaum conclude with regard to this question:
'We can in all five cases simply observe that it is possible, and that
no such problem arises in connection with the trade-designations of
the list of Jews. This suggests that God-fearers may be in some way
free of laws that bind Jews, but it hardly proves it.'[40] Further, we
note that there were nine βουλ(ευταί) – city-councillors – among
the θεοσεβεῖς. Did they attend public pagan sacrifices? We do not
know. Thus, although the inscription is informative, it does not solve
the problem of what God-worshippers actually did and did not do.

We can also propose that the three proselytes listed among the Jews
were once God-worshippers. Given the much larger number of God-
worshippers listed on the stone, this suggests that some, though few,
God-worshippers went on to become proselytes and that the number
of God-worshippers in some ancient synagogues was often considerably greater than the number of proselytes. The scarcity of
proselytes can be explained by the fact that conversion was a risky
step to take, in view of Roman laws against circumcision beginning
at the time of Hadrian.[41]

It is interesting that nine God-worshippers are βουλ(ευταί) – city-
councillors – who are placed at the beginning of the list as befits their
importance.[42] They must have owned sufficient property to qualify
as councillors. They are men who are simultaneously able to fulfill
the role of a city councillor and to be accepted by, and involved in,
this Jewish organisation. That there appears to be no difficulty for
the councillors in identifying themselves openly with a Jewish group,
itself highly significant, suggests that no great loss of social status was
incurred through involvement with the Jewish community in this
way.[43] This implies that the Jewish community was a well-
established and accepted group with good standing in the city. It also
shows that (at least) some of those committed to the Jewish community as God-worshippers continued to be involved in the city.

This new evidence for 'God-worshippers' sheds light on the other
occurrences of θεοσεβής because here we have precisely the sense of
the term which has been disputed by those who wished to see it as a
description used to stress the piety of Jews. Although this inscription
cannot be used to dictate the meaning of θεοσεβής in other Jewish
inscriptions (since it could still be used to refer to a Jew as 'pious'), it
considerably strengthens the case for seeing θεοσεβής as a designation

for a 'God-worshipper' elsewhere. Other inscriptions will be examined with this in mind.

4.2

The following inscription from Panticapaeum on the north coast of the Black Sea was first published in 1935.[44]

--- ΚΑ --- κου ἀφίημι ἐπὶ τῆς προευχῆς 'Ελπία[ν ἐμ]α[υ]τῆς θρεπτ[ῆς?] ὅπως ἐστὶν ἀπαρενόχλητος καὶ ἀνεπίληπτος ἀπὸ παντὸς κληρονόμου χωρὶς τοῦ προσκαρτερεῖν τῇ προσευχῇ ἐπιτροπευούσης τῆς συναγωγῆς τῶν 'Ιουδαίων καὶ θεὸν σέβων.[45]

... I set free in the synagogue Elpias the son(?) of my slave bred in my house; he shall remain undisturbed and unassailable by any of my heirs except for (his duty) to visit the synagogue regularly; the protection (of his freedom) is accepted by the community of the Jews καὶ θεὸν σέβων.

The inscription, which is probably to be dated to the first century CE, is one of four very similar emancipation inscriptions from the city which all state that the ex-slave is to continue to visit the synagogue and that his or her protection against re-enslavement is provided by the synagogue. However, the other three inscriptions end with συναγωγῆς τῶν 'Ιουδαίων.[46]

How is τῆς συναγωγῆς τῶν 'Ιουδαίων καὶ θεὸν σέβων to be understood in this inscription? It has been suggested that καὶ θεὸν σέβων should be linked with χωρὶς τοῦ προσκαρτερεῖν τῇ προσευχῇ but this is grammatically unlikely considering the sentence structure. If the text is left as it stands, the only possibility seems to be that the last three words are a postscript of some sort which does not cohere with the rest of the text since, in the other three inscriptions of this series, what is required of the ex-slave is expressed in the middle section of the inscription.[47] Any extra requirement, such as 'worshipping God', is never expressed right at the end because such an injunction would not fit the sense and the synagogue itself is normally mentioned there. However, that the words form an unrelated postscript seems highly unlikely, particularly since they are not in a different hand. Consequently, the most likely explanation is that the last three words actually belong with the immediately preceding phrase. The inscription can be read in this way if we emend it to θεο‹ν›σεβῶν instead of θεὸν σέβων. The two genitives ('Ιουδαίων and θεοσεβῶν) then fit together and the end of the inscription becomes intelligible. Although the ν was definitely engraved on the stone, it is possible that the stonemason was unfamiliar with the word θεοσεβῶν, since it is comparatively rare in non-Jewish usage, and that he regarded it as two words, the first lacking ν, which he subsequently supplied.[48]

We should therefore read 'Ιουδαίων καὶ θεοσεβῶν.[49] But how should we translate θεοσεβῶν? 'The synagogue of the Jews (who are) also pious', or as 'The synagogue of the Jews and God-worshippers'? Does the Jewish community here ascribe to itself an honorary epithet, or does the synagogue contain two groups – Jews and Gentile God-worshippers? This inscription as a whole and the other three inscriptions suggest that the second interpretation is correct. Elpias and the other three ex-slaves are required by the inscriptions to attend the synagogue. A Jew or a proselyte could be expected to attend the synagogue without compulsion, or at least without the kind of powerful compulsion provided by these inscriptions, which are legal documents. It is likely, therefore, that Elpias and the other three ex-slaves were not Jews; accordingly, our inscription seems to require Elpias to become a 'God-worshipper' – a Gentile who attends the synagogue. Although such compulsion with regard to people becoming God-worshippers is unrecorded elsewhere, it seems the most convincing interpretation here. Since we know of four ex-slaves, including Elpias, who were compelled in this way, we can infer that Elpias was required to join an established group of God-worshippers, some of whom perhaps joined voluntarily. This would explain the title of the synagogue – 'of the Jews and God-worshippers'.[50]

Therefore, rather than the Jews proclaiming their own piety, the inscription shows us that 'God-worshippers' were an officially recognised and active group in this synagogue and that they were considered as part of the synagogue *by* the synagogue.[51] That the group's name formed part of the official title of the synagogue shows that they were in some sense members of the synagogue (albeit in a subsidiary sense since they are not part of the 'Ιουδαῖοι) and that this was with the full agreement of the community. The Aphrodisias inscription, which implies a very similar state of affairs in a different Jewish community, corroborates this interpretation of the Panticapaeum inscription. Clearly in Panticapaeum the two groups associated together in worship and probably also in the many other activities of the synagogue, the centre of Diaspora Jewish life.

4.3

The following inscription was found at Tralles in Caria:

Καπετωλῖνα ἡ ἀξιόλογ(ος) καὶ θεοσεβ(ἡς)[52] (π)οήσασα τὸ
πᾶμ βάθρο[ν] ἐσκούτλωσα τ[ὸν] (ἀ)ναβασμὸν ὑπ[ὲρ]
εὐχῆς ἑαυτῆς [καὶ ?] πεδίων τε καὶ ἐγγόνων. Εὐλογία.[53]

I, Capitolina, worthy and θεοσεβ(ής), have made all the
platform and the inlaying of the stairs in fulfilment of a vow
for myself and my children and my grandchildren. Blessings.

The inscription is to be dated in the third century CE. Robert
recognised that this inscription, previously published in CIG and
interpreted by Groag as a Christian inscription, concerned a Jewish
building. Firstly, θεοσεβής is found in Jewish (and some pagan)
inscriptions but not as far as we know in Christian inscriptions in this
period. Secondly, εὐλογία is very common in Jewish inscriptions, so
it seems most likely that the building structures mentioned were to
be found in the synagogue at Tralles.[54] The question is therefore
whether θεοσεβής, here applied to Capitolina, means she was a Jew
or a 'God-worshipper'.

We know of Capitolina from another inscription from Tralles
which tells us that she was part of an important family. Her full name
was Claudia Capitolina and she was the daughter (or sister) of the
consul Claudius Capitolinus Bassus who was proconsul of Asia. She
married T. Flavius Stasicles Metrophanes who had been a senator in
Rome and, like his grandfather before him, was priest for life of Zeus
Larasios in Tralles and thus permanently resident there. His grandfather was also twice Asiarch (a position also held by his uncle) and
was given the title πρῶτος Ἀσίας. His father was a consul and his
brother a senator. Capitolina and T. Flavius Stasicles Metrophanes
had two sons who both received the honourable title ὁ κράτιστος
and may well have gone on to be Senators themselves. There was
clearly considerable wealth in the family.[55]

We see therefore that Capitolina came from a distinguished
background and married into a family of similarly high standing. That
she was herself distinguished is shown by the use of ἀξιόλογος. It
is also apparent that she was not a Jew by birth. Accordingly, as a
Gentile she would not be regarded as θεοσεβής by the Jews unless
she was considerably involved in the synagogue.[56] It seems therefore
that to use the title in a Jewish synagogue inscription, Capitolina must
have been a regular attender at the synagogue; thus, we conclude

that θεοσεβής here means 'God-worshipper'. Indeed, this seems to accord well with the facts. We can understand why Capitolina would want to remain as a God-worshipper; it could have been difficult for a person of her distinguished status to become a proselyte. That she was regularly involved in the synagogue is confirmed by the use of εὐλογία at the end of the inscription, a Jewish blessing she has learnt through attendance at the synagogue.[57] We thus see that there was a 'God-worshipper' in the Jewish community at Tralles who also belonged to the highest echelons of society.[58] This illustrates once more the attraction and influence of Judaism and the Jewish community and suggests that the Jewish community at Tralles in this period was well-respected.

4.4

These two inscriptions were found in the centre panels of mosaics in the forecourt of the Sardis synagogue:

Αὐρ(ήλιος) Εὐλόγιος θεοσεβὴς εὐχὴν ἐτέλεσα.

Aurelios Eulogios, Theosebes, I have fulfilled my vow.

Αὐρ(ήλιος) Πολύιππος θεοσεβὴς εὐξάμενος ἐπλήρωσα.[59]

Aurelios Polyippos, Theosebes, having made a vow, I have fulfilled it.

θεοσεβής is also found in four other inscriptions, all of which are to be dated after 320 CE.[60] Robert argued that the epithet θεοσεβής was always applied to Jews and not to Gentile God-worshippers.[61] However, the Aphrodisias and Panticapaeum inscriptions make this claim unlikely. In addition, Robert thought that Eulogios and Polyippos (donors of the first two inscriptions) must be members of the synagogue community since the inscriptions were found in the synagogue. However, he did not support this contention and it is far from self-evident. If Julia Severa, a pagan sympathiser at Acmonia, could donate a whole synagogue and be acknowledged for her generosity in an inscription,[62] there appears to be nothing to prevent a 'God-worshipper' from making a donation for the decoration of the synagogue and being commemorated for this in an inscription. Furthermore, the Aphrodisias and Panticapaeum inscriptions show that in some sense God-worshippers were members of the Jewish community. The synagogue is therefore the natural place for them to make donations.

Other considerations relating to the Sardis synagogue suggest that θεοσεβής is used here to designate a Gentile God-worshipper. Firstly, a number of members of the Sardis synagogue community were involved in the city's life and the community commanded much respect in the city. Such a Jewish community could have attracted the interest of Gentiles who wanted to find out more about the Jews. One would not therefore be surprised if a group of Gentiles regularly visited the synagogue, adopted some of its practices and became 'God-worshippers.' Secondly, Gentiles may have visited the synagogue forecourt regularly if the fountain found there was the public fountain mentioned in an inscription. In this way Gentiles may have conversed with Jews about Judaism, ventured into the synagogue itself and gradually become involved in its life without becoming proselytes. Thirdly, the excavators emphasised that the synagogue building seemed to be designed as a 'show piece' for Judaism. The forecourt, the decorations, the mosaics and the vast space would have attracted the interest and admiration of visitors. It was a building well-suited to communicating a message about the grandeur and splendour of the Jewish faith and the Jewish community. It would not be surprising if the message was communicated effectively through this medium to at least some Gentiles, who then became involved in the synagogue's life.[63]

These considerations create a strong probability that θεοσεβής designates Gentile God-worshippers at Sardis. Nevertheless, we cannot entirely rule out the possibility that the term could simply mean 'pious', which would indicate that the donors were Jews. The name of the first donor, Eulogios, could well be that of a Jew, although this is not necessarily the case.[64] Certainty is not possible, but the former interpretation does seem much more likely particularly in view of the involvement of the Sardis community in the city and the respect it commanded there.[65]

4.5

There are a number of inscriptions on the seats of the theatre of the Roman period in Miletus. One inscription in the fifth row from the front reads: Τόπος Εἰουδέων τῶν καὶ θεοσεβίον.[66] The inscription is to be dated to the Imperial period, probably in the second century or the beginning of the third century CE. θεοσεβής is normally found in the singular or as a personal name. The form used here – θεοσεβίον – is to be understood as the name of a group, analogous to group names like 'Λεοντίοι', 'Eusebii' or 'Eutropii'.[67] There are three possible interpretations of this inscription.

Firstly, if θεοσεβής is taken as a term designating *Gentiles* who are associated with the synagogue then we have a contradiction in terms – 'Jews who are also God-worshippers (= Gentiles)'. However, we have seen that θεοσεβής can be used of a Jew to mean 'devout' or 'pious', and it could be used here as a proper name with that sense. If the text is read as it stands, therefore, this must be the meaning, and we should translate it as – 'Place of the Jews who are also called the Pious Ones'.[68]

Secondly, Schürer suggested that the stone mason made a mistake and that the text should read καὶ τῶν instead of τῶν καί. We would then translate the phrase as 'Place of the Jews and those who are called God-worshippers.' Lifshitz has noted that, according to the first interpretation, the Jewish group advertised its piety in the theatre. He regards this as strange and inappropriate in this purely pagan context. However, he thinks the inscription was probably written by the theatre management and not by the Jewish community. Since the Greeks would hardly think the Jews more devout than themselves, they would be unlikely to denote the Jews as 'pious' when no one else in the theatre was given this epithet. Thus, it is unlikely that the theatre management thought the inscription designated the Jews as pious.[69] It is likely that they thought the inscription referred to two groups – the Jews and 'The Pious' or 'God-worshipping Ones'; that is, they understood the second term as an additional name. The Jewish community would have suggested this wording (and its meaning) to the theatre authorities and so the inscription contains the normal term the Jews used for Gentile God-worshippers. The authorities agreed to write the inscription in this way, but the stone mason made a mistake in the execution of the inscription. Many scholars have objected to this line of interpretation on the grounds that it emends a text which is able to be interpreted satisfactorily as it stands.[70]

Thirdly, in 1975 Hommel proposed a new line of interpretation. He thought, on the basis of Acts, that θεοσεβίοι was a technical term designating God-worshippers. He claimed that our inscription belongs to the category of 'synthetic relative clauses' and that in this type of clause the second noun functions by delimiting the first noun in order to avoid confusion. Thus the inscription can be translated: 'Place (not of the Jews as such, but only) of those Jews, who are also called Godfearers.' It therefore refers to the group of 'Ιουδαῖοι who are further defined by calling them θεοσεβίοι. Since θεοσεβίοι means 'God-worshippers', the inscription means the seats were reserved specifically and only for a group of (Gentile) God-worshippers who could occasionally be called 'Jews'. The seats were not for Jews themselves.[71] However, three problems arise for this interpretation. Firstly, the only evidence that 'God-worshippers' were ever called 'Ιουδαῖοι comes from Cassius Dio. He states that the title 'Ιουδαῖοι applies not only to the inhabitants of Judaea 'but it applies also to all the rest of mankind, although of alien race, who affect their customs'.[72] Whilst this shows that an outsider could call God-worshippers (or sympathisers?) 'Jews', it begs the question of whether the God-worshippers would have called *themselves* 'Ιουδαῖοι, even with the qualification of θεοσεβίοι. If they were regularly involved in the synagogue they would know they could not call themselves 'Ιουδαῖοι, for God-worshippers are nowhere called 'Jews' in Jewish sources. Secondly, Hommel decided on the basis of Lucan usage of different terms that θεοσεβής meant 'God-worshipper' not 'pious'. However, we cannot rule out either meaning in advance on the basis of the usage of different terms. Thirdly, his interpretation is based on classifying this inscription as a 'synthetic relative clause'.[73] Only in this way can the second term be understood to delimit the first. In our inscription (as it stands) it seems just as likely that the second term explains the first and does not delimit it; thus it would be translated as 'Jews who are called the pious ones', i.e. our first interpretation.

Hommel's interpretation is therefore unconvincing and we are left with the first two options. Rajak has recently suggested that in the light of the Aphrodisias inscription, Schürer's emendation of the inscription gains in appeal. It is not unusual to find ungrammatical constructions, improper idioms and mistakes in word transposition in this kind of provincial notice.[74] It is significant to note that most of those who decided against the emendation were not aware of the Panticapaeum inscription nor, of course, of the new evidence from Aphrodisias, and thus they knew of no thoroughly convincing epigraphical evidence for God-worshippers. In addition, Lifshitz's argument that a reference to the 'piety' of the Jews is very strange in the context of the theatre is compelling and has not been refuted. This argues strongly against the first interpretation and suggests that the theatre management understood the term as a designation of a group of Gentile 'God-worshippers'. There is therefore the strong probability that the second interpretation is correct.[75] Two groups – Jews and God-worshippers – were probably grouped together by the theatre management and allocated the privilege of special seats. Both groups would be regular, prominent and respected (as befits those with the privilege of reserved seats, and fine fifth row seats at that) among the theatre audiences. That both groups enjoyed official recognition and respect in the city, and thus were granted this privilege, is highly significant in terms of the acceptance accorded to them within the city and their own integration into city life.[76] It further suggests that the 'God-worshippers' were involved in the synagogue since they are in a definite relationship with the Jews and are regarded as belonging with the Jewish community by the theatre management and thus presumably by the Jewish community itself.

4.6

The following third-century CE inscription was found on a rectangular column from Deliler, east of Philadelphia, Lydia:

[T]ῇ ἁγιοτ[άτῃ σ]υναγωγῇ τῶν Ἑβραίων Εὐστάθιος ὁ θεοσεβὴς ὑπὲρ μνίας τοῦ ἀδελφοῦ Ἑρμοφίλου τὸν μασκαύλην ἀνέθηκα ἅμα τῇ νύμφ(ῃ) μου Ἀθανασία.[77]

To the most holy synagogue of the Hebrews, Eustathios θεοσεβής, in remembrance of my brother Hermophilos, I have dedicated together with my bride (sister-in-law?) Athanasia, the wash-basin.

What does ὁ θεοσεβής mean as it is applied to Eustathios? Is he 'the pious one', or is he a God-worshipper? It is helpful to note the way in which the two other people mentioned are referred to. If Eustathios was a Gentile God-worshipper then his brother Hermophilos would similarly be of non-Jewish birth. One would expect him to be described as a proselyte or a God-worshipper. It is, after all, unlikely that Eustathios, if he were a God-worshipper, would make a dedication *in the synagogue* in memory of his brother if Hermophilos himself had no connection at all with the synagogue. Yet, Hermophilos receives no epithet; nor does Athanasia. It seems unlikely that one God-worshipper would make a dedication to the synagogue in memory of a Gentile who had no regular connection with the synagogue (even if he was his brother) in conjunction with another Gentile who likewise had no connection with the synagogue. It seems more probable that all three were Jews and that θεοσεβής records the noteworthy piety of Eustathios. As we have seen, this usage is in keeping with that found in Jewish literature.[78]

4.7 The altar of a God-worshipper?

This inscription does not use the term θεοσεβής but can be conveniently discussed here. A small altar, with the following inscription to be dated in the second century CE, was found at Pergamum.

At the top of the altar: Θεὸς κύριος ὁ ὢν εἰς ἀεί.
At the bottom: Ζώπυρος τῷ Κυρίωι τὸν βωμὸν καὶ τὴν φω[ι]τοφόρον μετὰ τοῦ φλογούχου.[79]

God (is the) Lord (the one) who is forever.
Zopyros (dedicated) to the Lord the bomos and the lantern-stand with the lantern.

The name of the deity is given merely as ὁ Κύριος in the second half of the inscription. This points distinctly to Judaism, where Κύριος by itself is used as a name for God, although there are some rare parallels outside of Jewish usage.[80] When the title 'Θεὸς Κύριος' is considered along with the expression ὁ ὢν εἰς ἀεί it is clear that the whole clause is hardly able to be derived from Greek religious usage. It thus seems highly likely that Zopyros made the dedication to the Jewish God.[81] The erection of a lantern is quite compatible with Judaism, although lamps were also used in connection with the Imperial cult and other pagan cults.[82] Yet, what was the bomos used for? It is possible that it designates an altar which was used for some sort of sacrifice. We know that for Jews of this period sacrificial worship was normally limited to Jerusalem, and thus Bickerman argued that a bomos at Pergamum must have been used by a 'God-fearer'. He thought that Jews encouraged Gentile 'God-fearers' to worship Yahweh in the way that was natural for them, that is, with sacrifices. However, it seems more plausible to suggest that the bomos was in fact a base (as the term can be translated) for the lantern stand.[83] Hence, it seems best to suggest that Zopyros was a Jew; we certainly do not have decisive evidence to classify him as a God-worshipper.[84]

4.8

Patristic literature informs us of two very interesting groups in this regard. Cyril of Alexandria writing at the beginning of the fifth century refers briefly to a group in Phoenicia and Palestine who called themselves Θεοσεβεῖς. He reports that they worshipped the Highest God (Ὕψιστος Θεός) who was beyond the stars, but that they also accepted the existence of other gods.[85] This group appears to be similar to a religious community which existed in Cappadocia in the fourth century and called itself the Ὑψιστιανοί. Both Gregory of Nazianzus and Gregory of Nysa tell us about them. They followed some Jewish practices, whilst adopting other customs of non-Jewish origin. Thus they rejected images and sacrifices, kept the Jewish sabbath and some food laws but dismissed circumcision. They also honoured the fire and light and called the only God Παντοκράτωρ, but they did not regard him as father of all.[86]

What is of interest to us in these groups is the mix of Jewish and non-Jewish beliefs and practices. It seems likely that some God-worshippers (who in the case of the first group continued to call themselves by the name they were known by among the Jews) from the synagogues in these areas borrowed beliefs and practices from Judaism and paganism and then formed their own autonomous groups. They can thus be included amongst the probable evidence for God-worshippers.

5 Conclusions

We have seen that God-worshippers, who are mentioned in Josephus, Philo, Juvenal, Epictetus and Acts, can be detected in inscriptions. Although θεοσεβής at times is probably an epithet given to a Jew (for example at Deliler), we do have cases where it certainly or almost certainly refers to Gentiles who were in a regular relationship with the synagogue. This is certainly the case at Aphrodisias, almost certainly at Panticapaeum and Tralles. In other cases (Sardis and Miletus) this is a strong probability.[87] In addition, that θεοσεβής was almost certainly used of *Jews* in some places in Asia Minor and of *Gentiles* in others reinforces our initial view that Judaism in Asia Minor was not a monolithic entity.

The literary sources which mention God-worshippers suggest that they were a well-known group in Rome (e.g. Juvenal), Iconium, Thessalonica, Beroea, Corinth, Athens (Acts) and elsewhere (Josephus and Philo). However, our inscriptional evidence for God-worshippers comes predominantly from Asia Minor. This may simply be a result of the nature of inscriptional evidence. However, that God-worshippers existed in some synagogues in Asia Minor suggests that these particular synagogues were attractive places, as were the Jewish communities which worshipped there. They had a significant degree of influence on local pagans and their beliefs and practices were appealing. These communities had not withdrawn into themselves but were open to Gentiles learning about Judaism. This is in keeping with our earlier findings concerning the distinctive involvement of some Jewish communities in Asia Minor in their cities, the respect granted to them and their willingness to be influenced by their environment. This suggests that the geographical spread of the inscriptional evidence is heavily weighted towards Asia Minor because here, more than elsewhere, Jewish communities were interacting with Gentiles in their cities, with the result that Gentiles were attracted to what they saw as inviting and appealing communities.

It seems clear from the inscriptions that, in at least some cases, there was a form of membership in the synagogue available to Gentiles who chose to attend regularly and to adopt some Jewish customs. The evidence from Aphrodisias and Panticapaeum suggests that for God-worshippers there was a definite sense of belonging; they were not simply observers or casual attenders but were an integral and distinct part of the synagogue whose presence could be acknowledged in the synagogue's name. Thus, it seems likely that, by giving a definite and formal place to Gentiles in synagogue life, Jewish communities were encouraging others to join the ranks of the θεοσεβεῖς. We cannot assume that this was the situation everywhere though; small Jewish communities made up of recently arrived members might not have welcomed God-worshippers or might not have welcomed them into some form of membership. However, we do know of at least some synagogues where Gentile God-worshippers were members of the community.[88]

The inscriptions have not enabled us to specify exactly what being a God-worshipper in Asia Minor entailed, beyond the general aspects of belonging to, and regular involvement in, the synagogue. In view of the diversity of Judaism in Asia Minor, it seems likely that there was a range of affiliation, involvement and practice covered by the term 'θεοσεβής'. Perhaps it meant different things in different communities, although there was probably a core of common practice, including attendance at the synagogue and observance of some Jewish customs.[89]

Our inscriptional evidence for God-worshippers is to be dated from the first to the fourth century CE.[90] In chapter 1 we suggested that Jewish communities in Asia Minor were little affected by the three revolts between 70 and 135 CE and that continuity of conditions prevailed. If this is correct, it means that later evidence is relevant for the earlier period, and we can tentatively suggest that this is the case here. We should also note that, if the events of 70 to 135 CE did have any effect in Asia Minor, it would probably have been to decrease the ranks of God-worshippers in the later period. We can therefore be moderately confident that there were a significant number of God-worshippers in at least some of the synagogues of Asia Minor in the first four centuries CE.[91]

8

JEWISH COMMUNITY AND GREEK CITY IN ASIA MINOR

In this chapter I will examine the relationship between Jewish communities in Asia Minor and the cities in which they lived. I will discuss the evidence concerning Jews being citizens of their city or Roman citizens and for Jews being actively involved in different facets of the life of their city.

1 The constitutional position of Jewish communities in Asia Minor

The investigation of the civic rights of the Jewish communities in the Diaspora in general and in Asia Minor in particular is difficult and much debated. Owing to differences in the foundation and development of the various Diaspora communities, the position of the Jews outside Asia Minor does not help us in the examination of the civic position of Jews in Asia Minor itself. Thus, other evidence will be discussed only as it is relevant to Asia Minor.

In Ant 12:119 Josephus states that Seleucus Nicator (d. 280 BCE) granted the Jews citizenship (πολιτεία) in the cities he founded in Asia, Lower Syria and Antioch and gave them equal privileges (ἰσοτίμος) with the Macedonian and Greek settlers.[1] They still possessed this citizenship in Josephus' own day. Similarly, in CAp 2:39 Josephus claims that:

> Our Jewish residents in Antioch (οἱ τὴν ᾿Αντιόχειαν κατοικοῦντες) are called Antiochenes, having been granted rights of citizenship (πολιτείαν) by its founder, Seleucus. Similarly, those at Ephesus and throughout the rest of Ionia bear the same name as the indigenous citizens (τοῖς αὐθιγενέσι πολίταις ὁμωνυμοῦσιν), a right which they received from the Diadochi.

However, as Tcherikover has pointed out, Josephus' claim regarding citizenship in Seleucid foundations is dubious. Firstly, we have no independent confirmation of the claim. Secondly, in Ant 12:120 Josephus endeavours to strengthen his argument about citizenship, but his attempt to do so — by stating that Jews in Antioch could receive money in lieu of foreign oil — is weak. It need imply no more than that Jews had permission to use municipal oil together with citizens, rather than that they were citizens themselves. Thirdly, in BJ 7:110 Josephus speaks of the δικαιώματα of the Jews in Antioch being inscribed on bronze tablets. The use of this term is surprising since it could refer simply to the privileges of an immigrant community rather than to citizenship.[2] These points clearly count against Josephus' claim.

In Ant 16:160–1 Josephus again refers to the Hellenistic kings. He states that the Jews of Asia and Cyrenaean Libya had been granted ἰσονομία by 'the kings'. After the Greeks took their sacred monies, the Jews sent envoys to Augustus who granted them ἰσοτέλεια. ἰσονομία is a political ideal, and the exact implications of the term remain unclear. ἰσοτέλεια denotes the privilege granted to metics whereby they became subject to the same taxation as citizens.[3] If Josephus is using the term in its technical sense, then it does not suggest that the Jews had citizenship rights.

Josephus gives two accounts of a dispute in 14 BCE beween the Jews of Ionia and their cities which was heard by Marcus Agrippa. The two accounts differ and so will be examined in turn. In Ant 12:125–6 we read:

> And we know that Marcus Agrippa had a similar view concerning the Jews, for when the Ionians agitated against them and petitioned Agrippa ἵνα τῆς πολιτείας ἣν αὐτοῖς ἔδωκεν 'Αντίοχος ὁ Σελεύκου υἱωνός, ὁ παρὰ τοῖς ῞Ελλησιν Θεὸς λεγόμενος, μόνοι μετέχωσιν, and claimed that, if the Jews were to be their συγγενεῖς, they should worship the Ionians' gods, the matter was brought to trial and the Jews won the right to use their own customs, their advocate being Nicolas of Damascus; for Agrippa gave his opinion that it was not lawful for him to make a new rule.

Josephus' report of the outcome of the dispute seems quite straight-forward — Agrippa decided to confirm the status quo and allowed the Jews to follow their own customs. This would suggest that the Ionians had contested the Jews' right to follow their customs and that it was these customs which were the centre of the trouble. However, the beginning of the report most naturally relates to citizenship and claims that the Jews received the citizenship from Antiochus II Theos. We note, then, the anomaly in the report; it starts by asking that the Jews should be deprived of their citizenship and ends with a confirmation of the status quo, which is said to be the privilege of following their own customs, with no mention being made of citizenship.

A solution to this difficulty is provided by examining Josephus' other account of the incident in Ant 16:27–61. In this report the Jews (not the Ionians) approach Herod and Agrippa and complain of mistreatment – having to appear in court on holy days, being deprived of the Temple tax and being forced to do military service and civic duties despite exemptions granted by the Romans. Nicolas spoke on behalf of the Jews and concentrated on the Romans' willingness to allow people to follow their own traditions and the current difficulties the Jews in Ionia were having in doing this. He made no mention of the Jews in Ionia having citizenship, nor did he ask for this. His request was that Agrippa might confirm the Jewish privilege of being able to follow their own customs.[4] Agrippa sided with the Jews and agreed to their request. We read in Ant 16:60 that:

> he was ready to grant the Jews all they might ask for ... And since they asked that the rights which they had formerly received should not be annulled, he would confirm their right to continue to observe their own customs without suffering mistreatment.

This is therefore a coherent account of the confirmation of Jewish privileges by Agrippa, with no mention of citizenship. It agrees with the end of the account in Ant 12:125–6 but not with the beginning of that passage. This means that the report in Ant 12:125 that the Jews were granted citizenship by Antiochus II Theos cannot be accepted.[5]

In Ant 14:235, to be dated in 49 BCE, we have a letter from Lucius Antonius, the proquaestor and propraetor to Sardis. The text is uncertain and it is unclear whether he refers to 'Ιουδαῖοι πολῖται ἡμέτεροι or ὑμέτεροι who had come to see him. There seems no sure way of deciding whether the passage refers to Roman citizens or citizens of Sardis, although the second reading is perhaps more likely.[6] In any case, it is only the envoys who are referred to in this way and it is likely that they would have been the most prominent members of the community.

The details of the letter suggest that the Jewish community in Sardis was organised as a πολίτευμα. The term can denote a normal Greek city or the entirety of the inhabitants of a locality or a quasi-autonomous community of aliens with the right of residence in a city and the right of managing their own judicial and religious affairs.[7] It is in this last sense that the term applies to Jewish communities. The politeuma was a form of organisation whereby a group of aliens could be incorporated into a city without making them citizens. Thus it would allow the Jewish community to have official standing in a city without losing its identity. It also means that where we have evidence for a politeuma we can conclude the Jewish community concerned did not possess the citizenship of the city as a body.

The actual term πολίτευμα is found in LetAris 310 with respect to the Alexandrian Jewish community. The civic status of the Jewish community in Alexandria is a complex matter which need not be discussed here in detail. Suffice it to note that the 'Letter of Claudius' seems to establish that the Jewish community as a whole did not possess Greek citizenship but rather lived 'in a city not their own (ἐν ἀλλοτρίᾳ πόλει)'.[8] It seems likely that LetAris is correct and that the Jewish community was organised as a politeuma. The term also occurs in two Jewish inscriptions from Berenice in Cyrenaica, one probably to be dated in the Augustan era, the other in 24 CE. Here again it seems clear that the Jews did not possess citizenship as a group.[9]

Ant 14:235 suggests that the Jewish community at Sardis was organised as a politeuma. The Jews had stated that from the earliest time they had had a σύνοδος of their own and a τόπος in which they decided their own affairs. The use of σύνοδος indicates that they had their own jurisdiction.[10] Further evidence is provided by an undated decree of the people of Sardis given in Ant 14:259−61. The Jews had approached the council and people and asked for a confirmation of their privileges. They asked that:

> in accordance with their accepted customs [they may] come together and have a communal life and adjudicate suits among themselves (συνάγωνται καὶ πολιτεύωνται καὶ διαδικάζωνται πρὸς αὐτούς), and that a place be given them in which they may gather together with their wives and children and offer their ancestral prayers and sacrifices to God ...

Their request was granted. The privileges mentioned are those which constitute a politeuma.[11] It is only the fact that the term itself is not used which casts a little doubt on the matter.

Ant 14:259 begins ἐπεὶ οἱ κατοικοῦντες ἡμῶν ἐν τῇ πόλει Ἰουδαῖοι πολῖται …. Tarn suggested that this was a contradiction in terms and that πολῖται was an interpolation. Other scholars who have thought the Jewish community in Sardis was organised as a politeuma have suggested that members of a politeuma within the polis may have been called πολῖται.[12] However, even if Jews described fellow members of a politeuma as πολῖται,[13] it seems very doubtful that the city of Sardis would use the term of the Jewish community (especially along with κατοικέω) unless all the Jews were citizens of the city, and we have no evidence which indicates this. It seems reasonable to suggest that πολῖται is an interpolation and does not provide evidence for Jewish citizenship. Thus, it seems likely that the Jewish community at Sardis was organised as a politeuma and did not possess Greek citizenship as a body.

On the basis of the likelihood that Jewish politeumata existed at Alexandria and Berenice and the probability that they also existed at Antioch and Sardis, some scholars have thought that this was the general constitutional form of organisation for Diaspora Jewish communities.[14] However, this generalisation cannot be justified. The communities where we have evidence for politeumata were long-established large communities. Smaller communities, or those with a shorter history, probably had a different organisational form. The fact that there was no 'Jewish charter' at this time as we noted in chapter 1, means that arrangements were governed by ad hoc local decisions. There are no grounds, therefore, for thinking that Jewish communities were everywhere organised as politeumata.[15]

Two other terms are found in inscriptions from Asia Minor which have some bearing on the issue of the constitutional position of the Jewish communities. In an inscription of the Roman period from Hierapolis it is stated that a fine is to be paid τῇ κατοικίᾳ τῶν ἐν Ἱεραπόλει κατοικούντων Ἰουδαίων. A κατοικία can be either a separate settlement or a group of residents within a foreign city; the latter is the sense here. The members of such a group would have the right of residence and some independence.[16] Secondly, in an inscription from Nysa we read τὸν τόπον … τῶι λαῶι καὶ τῇ συνόδωι τ[ῇ περὶ] Δωσίθεον Θεογένου. The double description of the group indicates that the 'people' formed an association which was grouped around Dositheus.[17] We can suggest that the Jewish community at Nysa formed a σύνοδος of some sort which was recognised by the city. This does not allow us however to make any statement with regard to citizenship, although it does suggest the community had a measure of autonomy. We note the different forms of internal organisation adopted by these communities at Sardis, Hierapolis and Nysa. This raises the possibility that other communities adopted different forms of settlement and organisation. In any case, we are not able to make generalisations.

We conclude that the case for the possession of citizenship rights by Jewish communities in Asia Minor is not proved.[18] The evidence does suggest that the Jewish communities at Sardis and Hierapolis were independent units of foreign people with rights of residence and some autonomy and that the community at Nysa also had a degree of autonomy. However, this does not mean that Jews were never citizens of their cities in Asia Minor. According to Acts 21:39, Paul was a citizen of Tarsus, and it is likely that the Jews involved in the gymnasium at Iasus and perhaps Hypaepa became citizens of their cities (see section 3). We know that a number of Jews in Sardis from the third century onwards were Σαρδιανοί; clearly possession of the citizenship of Sardis at this date was still worthy of note. One Jew from Corycus was also described as Κωρυκιώτης.[19] We have no direct evidence which tells us if individual Jews found a way to hold Greek citizenship without engaging in acts which most Jews would have regarded as idolatrous. This issue will be dealt with at the end of section 3.

2 Did Jews in Asia Minor possess Roman citizenship?

According to Ant 14:228, in 49 BCE the consul L. Lentulus Crus released from military service 'those Jews who are Roman citizens (πολίτας 'Ρωμαίων 'Ιουδαίους) and observe Jewish rites and practise them in Ephesus'. That the exemption applied to Jews with Roman citizenship is stated in related letters or statements in Ant 14:232, 234, 237, 240. Ant 14:231 implies that the exemption covered all Jewish Roman citizens in Asia. This number of documents strongly suggests that the restriction to Jews with Roman citizenship goes back to the Roman authorities themselves.[20] The difficult matter is to know how many Jews were able to claim this exemption. Smallwood thought that the number of Jews affected must have been 'infinitesimally small' and that the significance of Lentulus' action lay in the principle of toleration which it embodied. However, others have taken the documents to imply that a significant number of Jews possessed Roman citizenship.[21] Although the matter cannot be decided, this is certainly a possibility.

We do have some evidence that individual Jews in Asia Minor were Roman citizens. Prior to 212 CE we know of (a) Paul, (b) Π. Τυρρώνιος Κλάδος (Acmonia) and (c) Μ(ᾶρκος) 'Αρ(ήλιος) Μούσσιος (Ephesus). From Acmonia we also learn that (d) Titus Flavius Alexander's family almost certainly held Roman citizenship since the late first century CE. In an undated inscription we learn of (e) Λούκιος Λόλλιος 'Ιοῦστος, secretary of the Jewish community in Smyrna.[22] We do not know how any of these men gained Roman citizenship.

In the Constitutio Antoniniana of 212 CE Caracalla gave Roman citizenship to all (or nearly all) free inhabitants of the empire. All Jews who were free would have been included in this grant.[23] We conclude, therefore, that we know of very few Jews in Asia Minor who had local citizenship; the situation is similar as regards Roman citizenship prior to 212 CE.

3 Jewish involvement in city life

Our evidence is insufficient for us to be able to present a complete and rounded picture of Jewish involvement in city life in Asia Minor. However, we are able to bring together some material which throws light on this issue. Although our conclusions in the previous sections were predominantly negative, some Jews and some Jewish communities took an active part in their city's affairs and were integrated to quite some degree into city life.[24] We know of Jews in Asia Minor who held local offices in their cities from the third century CE. We have noted previously that eight men held the title βουλευτής at Sardis, and another was a citizen and councillor in nearby Hypaepa. In addition, we learn of a 'former procurator', a *comes* and one assistant in the record office at Sardis, all positions in the Roman provincial administration. Two men in Acmonia held a range of important positions in the city in the mid third century CE. An undated funerary inscription from Corycus, Cilicia informs us that Aurelios Eusanbatios Menandros was a member of the city council. In a fifth century CE inscription from Side, two Jews, Leontios and his father Jacob, bear the title ζυγ., which can only be an abbreviation for ζυγοστάτης. This office involved control of the weight of money and of precious metal in the city and was a modest but responsible position.[25] At Ephesus a Jew whose name was probably 'Ιουλίος held the title of ἀρχίατρος, which probably designates an official doctor. Such officially recognised public physicians were paid by the city and their principal task was to give medical attention to citizens. They were granted immunity from civic office by Vespasian, but Antoninus Pius limited the number of doctors to whom the cities might grant exemption to ten for a metropolis, seven for a conventus centre and five for ordinary towns, evidently because people had been evading office through taking up the medical profession. In an inscription such as the one under discussion from Ephesus to be dated after Antoninus Pius, it is probable that ἀρχίατρος designated one of these publicly recognised doctors, particularly since we have a series of inscriptions from Ephesus in which ἀρχιατροί almost certainly has this meaning. This strongly suggests that the Jew Ἰουλίος held this office.[26]

Thus, we can conclude that some Jews in Asia Minor held significant offices in their cities.[27] We also have evidence for a number of Jews who held significant positions in government or civic life elsewhere.[28] The situation in Asia Minor was not exceptional, although the fact that a number of office holders are known in Asia Minor after 200 CE does suggest that the members of some Jewish communities (notably in Acmonia and Sardis) were considerably involved in the life of their cities at this time.

We noted in chapter 2 that between 198 and 211 CE Severus and Caracalla permitted Jews to become office-holders in their cities but only imposed on them those obligations which would not conflict with their *superstitio*. This exemption, which probably included an exemption from pagan rites, is highly significant, although we do not know how it worked out in practice. Severus and Caracalla probably passed the law to widen the circle of those eligible to hold office since to do so had become burdensome by this time. Nevertheless, it remained a method of social advancement and a duty which bestowed prestige. That this law was enacted suggests that there were sufficient Jews in the eastern Mediterranean who could meet the property qualification and so were eligible for office. The fact that Jews did hold office shows that some individuals had gained wealth, social advancement and some standing within their city. This also suggests that by the beginning of the third century there was a significant number of Jews who had, or who might be given, local citizenship in Asia Minor (a prerequisite for holding office), a possibility which the Sardis inscriptions with their number of Σαρδιανοί has made all the more likely.[29]

We have evidence of Jews being 'good residents' of their city. In an inscription from Smyrna written in the time of Hadrian

(117–138 CE) we read of a list of people who had made donations to the city for public works. Among them is a group called οἱ ποτὲ ᾽Ιουδαῖοι who gave 10,000 drachmae, a small amount in the context. The phrase has often been translated as 'the former Jews', that is, people who had apostatised in the interests of obtaining citizenship and were now advertising their rise in the social scale. However, Kraabel has shown that the phrase should be translated as 'the former Judaeans' signifying that the donors were people who had come originally from Judaea. This seems more likely, especially since the citizens of Smyrna who set up the monument would have chosen the exact wording. By donating money the group of Jews, who were perhaps an association of some sort, were doing their civic duty as residents of Smyrna. In a time when Jews in Egypt, Cyrenaica and Cyprus had revolted against their Gentile neighbours and those in Palestine had fought a full scale war against Rome, some Jews in Smyrna showed a completely different attitude by demonstrating that they were loyal and benevolent members of their city.[30]

We have previously noted that in Acmonia, some Jews made a donation to the city and in doing so called Acmonia their πατρίς – their 'home city' or 'native town'. The donation shows the Jews' involvement in the life of the city, and the term used indicates a strong degree of 'at homeness'.[31] We have also discussed the seating inscription of the Imperial age from the theatre at Miletus which reads Τόπος Εἰουδέων τῶν καὶ Θεοσεβίον and shows that there was a group of seats in the theatre reserved for Jews and, as we have argued, probably for 'God-worshippers' as well. Clearly, some Jews regularly attended the theatre, which was a centre of the cultural life of the city where speeches, choral dances and dramatic performances could all be enjoyed. In addition, that the Jews enjoyed the privilege of reserved seats (and fine fifth row seats at that) shows that they were prominent and respected members of the theatre audiences. That the Jews enjoyed this sort of official recognition and respect in the city shows the acceptance accorded to them in Miletus and their own willing involvement in the city's cultural life.[32] In Aphrodisias Jews had reserved seats in the odeum according to two sixth-century CE (?) seating inscriptions which read: Τόπος Βενέτων ῾Εβρέων τῶν παλειῶν, and Τόπος ῾Εβρέων. The odeum was a small theatre for musical competitions, recitations and other gatherings such as philosophical disputations.[33] In the sixth century CE Jews appear to have participated in this part of the social and cultural life of the city of Aphrodisias.

In a decree of Augustus to be dated in 12 BCE and addressed to the Jews of Asia we read: 'As for the resolution which was offered by them in my honour concerning the piety which I show to all men, and on behalf of Gaius Marcius Censorinus, I order that it and the present edict be set up in the most conspicuous (part of the temple) assigned to me by the federation of Asia ...'.[34] It seems that some Jews of Asia had passed a resolution concerning Augustus and so had shown themselves to be loyal supporters of the Emperor. Augustus appropriately acknowledged their action.[35]

A Hebrew inscription discovered in the Sardis synagogue may suggest that the Jewish community formally honoured the co-Emperor Lucius Verus, perhaps during a visit to the city in 166 CE, but this is uncertain.[36] However, the evidence from Sardis as a whole suggests that the Jewish community was actively involved in the life of the city. The synagogue was an integral and prominent part of the bath–gymnasium complex. The lion symbol and the term πρόνοια, both significant in the city as a whole, were probably adopted by the Jewish community precisely because of their usage in Sardis. These facts, taken with the involvement of Jews in the city council and other inscriptional evidence that we noted above, suggest that the Jewish community was a respected and integrated element in the city, active in civic and political affairs.

At Apamea, we have suggested that the city accepted a new name for a flood 'hero' because of the influence of the Jewish community and this was portrayed on the city's coinage. In addition, the Jewish community contributed a new and prestigious significance for the city's name Κιβωτός; the Jewish community themselves accepted a new prominence for Noah's wife. We therefore see some 'give and take' between the city and the Jewish community. Clearly, the Jewish community was influential and respected within this city.[37]

Hence, a good deal of evidence suggests that members of some Jewish communities in Asia Minor were 'good residents' of their cities who actively participated in cultural and civic life.[38]

We learn from inscriptions about Jews who were ephebes or involved in the gymnasium. Ephebes were youths who were engaged for a year or more in training in the gymnasium in activities which included military and athletic exercises as well as intellectual and cultural development. The gymnasium was the centre of the social life of the city, and education in the gymnasium was a normal prerequisite for Greek citizenship. Thus, the ephebate was highly valued and there were strong incentives for parents to enter their sons in the gymnasium.[39] At Iasus an ephebe list from the beginning of the Imperial period includes a Jew named Ἰούδας Εὐόδου – Ioudas son of Euodos. Others mentioned in the list might also be Jewish.[40] An inscription probably to be dated in the late second century CE from Hypaepa, south of Sardis, reads – Ἰουδα[ί]ων νεωτέρων – Of younger Jews. The 'Neoteroi' were probably an association of young men. The ephebate of one or two years was often followed by membership of the 'young men' who formed a group primarily devoted to gymnastic exercise but who also played a role in political and public life. The inscription suggests that a group of Jews formed a Jewish 'association of young men' in the gymnasium. The inscription might have been a public marker, perhaps designating the place of the Jewish neoteroi in the local palaestra or a gift made by the group.[41] The group was called the *'Jewish* younger men', which emphasises that they retained their Jewish identity and did not become completely associated with other neoteroi.[42]

Another indication that Jewish communities in Asia Minor participated in the life of the wider city is provided by the evidence that they were influenced by the customs of their local city. In a number of areas we can see that Jews did certain things or adopted a particular practice because of the influence of their environment. By itself, this evidence would be unreliable; one could well understand if, over a period of time, a highly insular and inward-looking community adopted some local practices. However, taken with the above evidence of involvement in the city, the following points indicate that the Jewish communities were integrated into the life of their cities to a significant extent.

The clearest example of this influence is provided by the position of women in Jewish communities in Asia Minor, which was discussed in chapter 5. I suggested there that some Jewish communities in Asia Minor adopted one strand of their tradition with regard to women because of the precedent of prominent women in the cities of Asia Minor. We have previously pointed out other areas in which environmental influence is evident. In 80–90 CE three synagogue officials at Acmonia were honoured with a large golden shield; the honour of the golden crown and the proedria was given to Tation at Phocaea in the third century CE. Both these forms of honouring benefactors were common in the ancient world. The practice of using grave curses on Jewish tombstones in Asia Minor and the manner of decoration of gravestones in Phrygia were both adopted from the environment. In Acmonia in the third century CE some Jews formed a burial society and adopted the practice of the rosalia, thus following local customs. As was the case elsewhere in the Diaspora, the organisational form of the Jewish communities tended to imitate the structures of the Greek city. We should also note that, although we do know of some Jews who had Jewish names, the majority of Jews in Asia Minor had Greek or, to a lesser extent, Roman names.[43]

A very interesting inscription in this regard is the late second or third century CE inscription from Hierapolis which states that Publius Aelius Glykon had prepared a tomb for himself and for his wife and children. The inscription also states that he had bequeathed a sum of money to the most honourable president of the guild of the purple-dyers so that, from the interest of the money, the guild could decorate his grave annually with a wreath on the Festival of Passover (ἐν τῇ ἑορτῇ τῶν ἀζύμων). In addition, he left money to the guild of the carpet-weavers so that the grave might be similarly decorated on the Festival of Pentecost (ἐν τῇ ἑορτῇ πεντηκο[στῆς]).[44] Clearly Aelius Glykon was a Jew since τὰ ἄζυμα can only refer to the Passover.

There is disagreement about whether the two guilds were solely Jewish or had both Gentile and Jewish members.[45] Judeich noted that the inscription does not state that Aelius Glykon was a member of either guild; he suggested that the guilds were purely pagan. If this was the case, Aelius Glykon, a Jew, had been able to secure the services of these pagan guilds to decorate his grave.[46] On the evidence available we are unable to decide this issue. However, these possible interpretations are all interesting as regards the investigation conducted here. If the guilds were Jewish, it means that the community at Hierapolis had adopted a local form of organisation, since the trade guilds are very common in the city.[47] If the guilds contained both Jewish and Gentile members, then it shows that Jews were an accepted part of such groups. If Judeich's view is correct, it shows that Aelius Glykon was able to induce two Gentile guilds to agree to decorate his grave in perpetuity on the days he requested. These last two possibilities involve a significant degree of integration into the life of the city on the part of either one Jew or a number of Jews. All three interpretations suggest that Jews participated in the life of the wider city; it is only the degree of that involvement which is debated. Yet, note that, whichever possibility is correct, Aelius Glykon asked that the graves be decorated on two *Jewish* festivals. Jewish identity seems to have been retained. We can also note that Aelius Glykon has adopted the local custom of decorating a grave with a wreath, a practice which is attested in Hierapolis by pagan inscriptions. Similarly, the arrangement for ensuring that this is carried out – the bequest of a sum of money to a guild – is regularly encountered in pagan inscriptions in the city.[48] Accordingly, this is a further example of a Jew being influenced by the environment.

We should also note that this involvement in city life did not invariably lead to the adoption of local customs. We argued in chapter 6 that Jews recognised that 'Hypsistos' was a title that was used extensively for pagan deities. Jews seem to have perceived that their continued use of the term may have led to misunderstanding and to the dangers of syncretism. In this case being part of city life led Jews to avoid using a term. Consequently, we can suggest that the Jews were discerning and careful in their relationship with the city in which they lived. It was a nuanced relationship with the environment.

We also have evidence for important non-Jews acting as patrons or being involved in the Jewish communities in Asia Minor. Around the middle of the first century CE the Gentile Julia Severa built a synagogue for the Jewish community at Acmonia. She was a very important person in the city, having been high priestess of the Imperial cult for at least three terms. She belonged to a nexus of leading families and had connections with influential people. That she built the Jewish community a synagogue shows that she was also a patroness of this community. Clearly she was a distinguished and powerful friend in the highest circles of society. The Jewish community welcomed and accepted her friendship. Capitolina, a God-worshipper in the Jewish community at Tralles, also belonged to the highest echelons of society. She provides evidence for the attraction and influence of the Jewish community in this place. The new inscription from Aphrodisias, probably to be dated in the early third century CE, lists nine city councillors who are the first names in a list of θεοσεβῖς, which, as we have argued, almost certainly means 'God-worshippers'. Although not proselytes, they were people who were involved in the synagogue community and also held important positions in the city. They illustrate the measure of acceptance achieved by this Jewish community in the higher levels of society at Aphrodisias. That these city councillors were prepared to identify themselves openly as God-worshippers suggests that no significant loss of status was incurred by doing so and thus that the Jewish community was an accepted group with good standing in the city.[49]

We can also recall our findings in chapter 7, where we concluded that a group of 'God-worshippers' existed in at least some synagogues in Asia Minor. This suggests that the Jewish communities concerned had not withdrawn into themselves but were open to Gentiles attending the synagogue and learning about Judaism. Perhaps some Jews were on sufficiently close terms with Gentile neighbours to be able to attract their interest in the Jewish community and its faith. This is in keeping with the involvement of some Jewish communities in the life of their cities, the respect accorded to them and their openness to their environment.

We should note at this point that pagan cults were intimately connected with many of those features of civic life, in which, according to our evidence, Jews were also involved. Theatre audiences would at times have watched scenes involving pagan mythology and pagan religious ceremonies, and the theatre was, of course, dedicated to pagan gods. Gymnastic education was closely linked to the worship of the city's gods, and Hermes, Heracles and the Muses were the gymnasium's guardian deities. Being a city councillor involved attendance at pagan sacrifices, which were a regular part of the beginning of city council meetings. Large-scale pagan festivals were a vital part of the fabric of city life, and it was these festivals which created the divisions of civic time. Pagan worship was not just encountered in a temple, but athletic and musical performances, processions and pantomimes were all dedicated to the local deities, major gods or the divine emperor. Public celebrations could take over the town square and would involve sacrifices. Pagan worship would have been a particular problem for Jews who had citizenship, since citizenship involved sharing in the worship of the city's gods. Consequently, pagan cults were bound up with every aspect of the city's life and with the city's identity.[50] Since pagan cults were such an all-pervasive and enduring presence in the city, a Jew who was significantly involved in city life (as opposed to living in a self-contained group) must have encountered the problem of pagan rites. Jews who were ephebes or regularly attended the theatre would certainly have been faced with this issue, as would a Jewish community which was integrated to some extent into the life of its city. A clear example of this comes from the Martyrdom of Pionius. The narrative shows that in Smyrna in the third century Jews joined Gentiles in the town square on an occasion that was both a pagan and a Jewish festival. This suggests that the Jews in Smyrna were prepared to put themselves in a situation where they might have contact with pagan worship.[51]

Our evidence, then, raises the question of how Jewish communities in Asia Minor reacted to pagan religious activities. There are clearly a number of options. Firstly, they could completely avoid anything to do with pagan cults. This was clearly advocated in the Mishnah tractate Abodah Zarah by some Rabbis, who argued that a Jew should always keep a clear distance from any association with idolatry.[52] That some Jews in Asia Minor probably followed this option at some stage is suggested by Ant 12:125–6 where Josephus reports that the Ionians complained to Marcus Agrippa in 14 BCE that 'if the Jews were to be their fellows, they should worship the Ionians' gods'. The passage suggests that, in the Ionians' opinion, the Jews known to them completely avoided pagan worship.[53] However, this option is clearly not followed by Jews who attended the theatre. A second option might have been to be involved in pagan institutions but to seek an exemption from participation in pagan rites. Such an exemption was granted by Severus and Caracalla when they permitted Jews to hold city offices but only imposed on them those obligations which would not conflict with their *superstitio*. We can suggest that Jews sought this particular exemption from Severus and Caracalla, although we have no information on how it was put into practice in individual cities.[54] Perhaps some Jews who were citizens of their cities were tacitly excused participation in cultic acts.[55] A third option might have been to attend, for example, the theatre but to try and avoid occasions when pagan worship actually occurred, was difficult, if not impossible, as this must have been.

A fourth option was for a Jew to be present during pagan ceremonies, but 'turn a blind eye'. This sort of behaviour could be justified by saying that idols have no reality and so being present as an uninvolved spectator did not constitute idolatry. Although rabbinic rulings would probably not have been known or followed in Asia Minor, they give an indication of how Jews could deal with a problem like this. It is revealing that rabbinic rulings in Palestine from the later third and fourth century (and possibly earlier) allowed Jewish artisans to make idols for sale provided the artisans did not worship them, although there are other opinions given. This sort of leniency as regards idolatry was based on the view that the Jews concerned would not be seduced into idolatry themselves since they knew idols were worthless.[56] The purpose of the leniency, according to Urbach, was 'easing the restrictions on Jewish economic life and particularly on business relations with Gentiles.'[57] Perhaps in Asia Minor similar reasoning, taking into account the unreality of idols and the importance of relations with Gentiles, could have led Jews to 'turn a blind eye' to the manifestations of paganism they encountered. This attitude seems to be expressed by the Jews from Gorgippia who ended a manumission inscription with the oath formula 'under Zeus, Ge, Helios'.[58] They probably used the formula because it was a legal necessity and perhaps argued that such gods were 'no gods'. A fifth option with regard to pagan worship was for Jews to accept it and take part. Some Jews known to us from inscriptions followed this path. We can mention Jason the Jerusalemite, who was probably a Jew, who supported the festival of Dionysus at Iasus in the second century BCE by donating money.[59] There is little evidence that Jews in Asia Minor adopted this option.

Some hints from our evidence are helpful here. None of the occupations of the Jews at Aphrodisias seem to have involved them in pagan cults, whilst the occupations of five of the 'God-worshippers' at least raise the question of involvement. For example, amongst the 'God-worshippers' we find a sculptor (or painter of images), a stone-cutter, an athlete, a boxer and a seller and producer of mincemeat. Did the sculptor make idols? Was the athlete part of pagan cultic ceremonies in the gymnasium?[60] That none of the Jews were involved in occupations which raise these questions suggests that the Jews in Aphrodisias were aware of the problem of ever-present pagan cults and were discriminating in the occupations they followed, an attitude that they did not require of the 'God-worshippers'. But this does not answer the question of how they would react when faced with pagan worship. Another clue is provided by the Sardis synagogue. The evidence suggests that it was precisely the confidence and vitality of their Judaism which enabled them to be in such a close proximity to the pagan cult conducted in the gymnasium complex and yet to remain thoroughly Jewish. Again, this does not tell us how Jews in Sardis would have reacted when faced with pagan worship. We should also note that the Hypsistos inscriptions suggest that Jewish communities were discerning and careful in their relationship with the cities in which they lived.

Therefore, whilst our evidence suggests that Jews in Asia Minor were in situations where they were confronted with pagan cults, the evidence does not allow us to say how they actually dealt with the problem nor which of the above options was adopted in each situation. Inscriptions are a poor source within which to find an expression of personal attitudes. In different situations the possibilities of completely avoiding pagan worship, of gaining an exemption from involvement, of trying to avoid the occasions when pagan worship occurred, of 'turning a blind eye' or of accepting pagan worship and taking part all remain.

We can, however, suggest that there was a range of opinions on the matter amongst Jews in Asia Minor with some Jews or Jewish communities being more lenient than others. Some Jews, like those in Ionia in 12 BCE, may have tried to avoid the problem completely. Certainly a group of Jews (e.g. those who were ephebes) were regularly willing to be in situations where they would face the problem head on, whilst others seem to have been more reluctant. This suggests there were different basic approaches to pagan worship. The Jews at Aphrodisias were careful in this area to the extent that they did not enter occupations where pagan worship might have been a constant dilemma. The Hypsistos inscriptions point to a similar carefulness in the Jews' relationship with the city. In some places (Sardis, Smyrna) we see a boldness when facing paganism which enabled the Jews to be in close contact with pagans or pagan institutions. Yet some of those who seem potentially to have faced the problem of pagan worship head on exhibit a clear Jewish identity. The group at Hypaepa who were involved in the gymnasium and who called themselves 'the *Jewish* Neoteroi' seem to have remained as Jews. Similarly, the strength of the Jewish identity of the Sardis community seems clear. We can conclude that many Jews participated in the wider community of their cities, and, although we cannot say how they actually faced the problem of the all-pervasiveness of pagan cults, we can suggest they did so as Jews and can point to a strong Jewish identity in some cases.

4 Conclusions

In chapter 1 we noted that Jewish communities in Asia Minor and elsewhere were granted significant privileges by the Roman authorities, privileges such as being able to send the Temple tax to Jerusalem, to observe the Sabbath, and to follow their own laws. However, these Jewish privileges were also challenged or withdrawn by the local cities at various times. Although there were reasons for the actions of the local cities, there seems to have been a significant amount of hostility between the cities and the Jewish communities, at least from 49 BCE to 2 CE. Apart from one incident recorded in Acts, our sources are silent about any tensions after this date. Although this may reflect the state of our sources, we suggested that a *modus vivendi* was reached between the cities and the Jewish communities in some places in the first century CE or shortly thereafter. Other evidence which points in the same direction can now be noted. In the 60s CE the distinguished Gentile Julia Severa was a patroness of the Jewish community at Acmonia; her contribution was positively recalled in the 80s or 90s. Some time between 30 BCE and 70 CE the author of the Jewish substratum of SibOr I/II, who was probably from Apamea, reinterpreted the local flood traditions in accordance with Jewish tradition. In doing so s/he was probably building a bridge between the Jewish community and the city, which suggests (although it does no more than this) that relationships between the Jewish community and the city were good. According to Acts, Jews were able to influence Gentiles to oppose Paul and Barnabas in Pisidian Antioch, Iconium and Lystra.[61] This is perhaps a further indication that Jew–Gentile relations were reasonable in these cities in the first century CE. In the time of Hadrian when there were Jewish revolts elsewhere in the Diaspora and in Palestine, some Jews in Smyrna probably showed themselves to be loyal and benevolent residents of their city. In addition, the evidence for positive relations between various cities and their Jewish communities from the second and third century CE onwards is quite strong. These clues suggest that the paucity of references to hostility in the literary sources between the cities in Asia Minor and their Jewish communities from 2 CE onwards is significant and that some sort of peace was arrived at. Although it is quite likely that the way peace was worked out varied in different places and occurred at different times, we can suggest that at least in some cities a *modus vivendi* was reached between the city and the Jewish community, perhaps some time in the first century CE and in any case probably before the Diaspora revolt of 115–117 CE. We can thus suggest that in many cities in Asia Minor a tradition of tolerance and positive interaction was established between the city and its Jewish community.

We have also shown that we have no convincing evidence which suggests that Jewish communities in Asia Minor possessed the citizenship of their cities as a body. However, some Jews in Asia Minor did possess local citizenship, although we do not know the arrangements under which this occurred. Similarly, we have evidence that some Jews possessed Roman citizenship. The vital matter for the Jewish communities in Asia Minor in the first century BCE was not citizenship but gaining and retaining the privileges which enabled them to live according to Jewish tradition.

The evidence discussed in this chapter shows that some Jewish communities in Asia Minor were involved in the life of their city and were influenced by that society to a large degree. We have noted the problem of contact with pagan cults which this raises and suggested some possible options for how Jews reacted to these cults.

CONCLUSIONS

It is not my intention to reiterate here the conclusions reached at the end of each chapter. However, some more general comments are appropriate. Many scholars have thought that Jewish communities in the Diaspora formed tightly-knit, introverted groups. Faced with a hostile environment, the Jews formed exclusive communities in order to retain their Jewish identity.[1] However, this view is questionable with regard to Jewish communities in Asia Minor. Despite the fact that the evidence is often fragmentary and spans a wide period of time, we can suggest that, although Jewish communities did not have local citizenship as a body, many members of the communities interacted regularly with Gentiles and were involved to a significant degree in city life. Moreover, some Jewish communities were influential and respected in their cities. Gentiles were also involved in some Jewish communities, most notably as 'God-worshippers' or as patrons, which suggests that the communities concerned had not withdrawn into themselves. There is evidence from Apamea and Smyrna that Jewish communities encouraged non-Jews to be involved in synagogue life; the existence of God-worshippers also suggests this. In addition, the extent to which some Jewish communities were influenced by the customs and practices of their environment indicates a degree of integration within the city. We conclude that the Jewish communities we have studied belonged in the cities in which they lived. They were a part of the social networks of the city and shared in many of the characteristics of everyday life.

Jews who were significantly involved in city life must have encountered the problem posed for Jews by the all-pervasive presence of pagan cults in a city. We have suggested that there were a number of different options Jews could have adopted in this regard, although our evidence does not enable us to say which option was followed in different situations. We have also suggested that there was a range of opinion on this matter. However, some of those who potentially faced the problem of pagan worship most severely exhibit a clear Jewish identity and we have evidence which suggests that the Jews were discerning and careful in their relationship with the city in which they lived. In fact, much evidence points to the strong retention of Jewish identity by communities in Asia Minor, despite close relations with the pagan environment.[2] We have noted that the Jewish community in Acmonia turned to the LXX as an authoritative guide for the community's life and faith and perhaps for the direction and inspiration of their liturgy. An inscription in the Sardis synagogue probably reminded the community of the importance of studying the Torah. In both the Sardis and Priene synagogues provision for the Torah dominated the room. There was a group within the Jewish community at Aphrodisias which was dedicated to the study of the Law and to prayer. At Apamea the 'hero' of the Jewish community, who was accepted by the city, was a figure drawn from Jewish tradition. Thus, we get some indication of the importance of the Scriptures in these communities.

We also have evidence that in the first century BCE Jewish communities in Asia Minor were committed to paying the Temple tax, and this shows that Jerusalem and its worship remained the geographical focus of their faith. Decrees in Josephus also show a strong concern on the part of various Jewish communities to be able to observe the Sabbath, to live according to their native customs, to follow the food laws and to be exempt from any requirements, such as military service, which would conflict with following their customs. NT and patristic sources show the importance of the law (including circumcision), the Temple and Jewish identity to these communities in Asia Minor. On the other hand, Acts also provides us with a counter-example of a Jewess from Asia Minor who, contrary to much Jewish teaching, married a Gentile; their son was not circumcised. Overall, however, we have noted the lack of evidence for syncretism on the part of these Jewish communities. Hence, we can suggest that the 'Jewishness' of these communities was generally maintained. A degree of integration did not mean the abandonment of an active attention to Jewish tradition or of Jewish distinctiveness. It was as *Jews* that they were involved in, and a part of, the life of the cities in which they lived.

We should note that the evidence for what may be called 'Jewish identity' begins in the first century BCE with the Temple tax and continues through to the fourth century CE and later with the Sardis material. The evidence for 'integration' begins most clearly in the mid first century CE with Julia Severa at Acmonia and continues throughout the period under consideration. Although there were regional variations, we can suggest that these communities remained *Jewish* (for which the evidence is earlier) whilst becoming more integrated into city life as the first and second century CE proceeded. From the second century CE onwards we have clear evidence for both integration in the city and retention of Jewish identity.

It is noticeable that modern authors who see Jewish communities as aloof and exclusive base their view to a significant degree on the evidence of a number of classical authors who accuse the Jews of exclusiveness and of living in self-imposed segregation.[3] However, we must ask how well these classical authors knew Jewish communities not only in Rome and Judaea, but also in Asia Minor, Syria and Egypt.[4] Further, some of these classical authors had their own presuppositions, such as an antipathy to Oriental religions and a general prejudice against 'barbarians'.[5] The evidence of classical authors must therefore be used with great care when speaking of the Diaspora as a whole or when discussing a specific geographical area such as Asia Minor. This study suggests that the epigraphical, archaeological and literary evidence presented here adds another important dimension to the total picture of Diaspora Judaism. I am not claiming that the evidence of classical authors is incorrect; rather we must recognise that it is tendentious and incomplete.

We should note the significant extent of diversity in Jewish communities in Asia Minor, perhaps most clearly illustrated by the differences between the communities at Sardis and Priene.[6] It seems that local factors – the date at which communities were founded, the circumstances under which they developed, the attitude of the local city, the size of the community – provided a strong formative influence on Jewish communities in Asia Minor. Distinct local and regional Jewish traditions seem to have developed. However, despite this diversity, the evidence studied here suggests that significant features of Jewish identity were retained in the various communities, as we noted above. In comparison with Palestinian Jewish communities, these Diaspora communities can therefore be seen as equally worthy and legitimate but distinctive heirs of Old Testament faith.

We lack evidence which clearly shows that Jewish communities in Asia Minor knew or followed rabbinic teaching.[7] There is no evidence that the Jewish community at Sardis was at any time within the rabbinic sphere of influence; they also called their teacher a 'sophodidaskalos'. In Smyrna Jews seem to have had contact with Gentiles during a pagan festival, contrary to rulings in the Mishnah. The leadership of women in some communities was at odds with rabbinic teaching. Thus, in accordance with much recent work, we can note that after 70 CE rabbinic Judaism was not the 'normative' form of Judaism which everywhere held sway; rather it was only one of a number of different forms of Judaism, at least until it became standard among Jews some time after the fourth century. Jewish communities in Asia Minor, whilst remaining Jewish in their own eyes, probably had different religious institutions, did different things and emphasised different aspects of Judaism from the rabbis.

The strength and vitality of Jewish communities in Asia Minor are clear from our sources. Dating is often difficult, but we know that this was often the case in the third century CE and beyond, and we can suggest that in some cities it was also the case much earlier. Patristic sources show us that Christian communities in Asia Minor were very aware of the presence of Jewish communities, which were attractive and had a significant influence on the churches. This could lead to the adoption of Jewish practices by Christians or to anti-Jewish views. The evidence leads us to suggest that in Asia Minor in the patristic period Jewish communities were very much part of the 'foreground'[8] for the local Christian churches. Consequently, Christians would often be forming and preserving their identity in a context in which significant Jewish communities were visible and attractive. These Christians would be confronted with Jews in their own cities who would be rival interpreters of the Jewish tradition which Christians now claimed as their own. The fact that much of our material is later than the first century CE means that we cannot say whether this would have been the situation for Christian communities in the NT period, but this is certainly likely. In interpreting the NT and patristic sources, the likely presence of Jewish communities in the 'foreground' of the Christian communities must certainly be taken more seriously than has been normal hitherto.

This study also raises a number of issues and questions in relation to New Testament interpretation which I hope to pursue further in subsequent work. We may note the issues of the significance of the 'God-worshippers' in early Christianity, the position of women in early Christian communities, the relationship between Jew and Gentile, particularly in Pauline theology, and the 'loyalty' motif in Rom 13:1−7 and 1 Peter 2:13−17.[9] In addition, it is to be hoped that further light can be shed on Paul's mission and theology by seeing him in relation to Jewish communities in Asia Minor and that further understanding of other NT books and early Christian writers can be gained by seeing them against this background. I hope that this study will stimulate further research into both early Judaism and early Christianity.

NOTES

Introduction

1 See in general Meeks 1983, p. 34.
2 See Johnson 1975, pp. 77–145.
3 Ramsay 1897, pp. 647–51, 667–76; 1902a, pp. 19–33, 92–109; 1904b, pp. 130–3, 142–57, 420–2; 1907, pp. 169–86, 255–9; 1914b, pp. 353–69. The first study was by Graetz 1886, pp. 329–46.
4 Levy 1900, pp. 183–8; Pilcher 1903, pp. 225–33, 250–8; Schürer 1909, 3, pp. 12–23; Juster 1914, 1, pp. 188–94; Krauss 1922, pp. 229–39; Leclercq 1928 in *DACL* 8, i, cols. 76–81; Kittel 1944, cols. 10–20. Other studies dealt with a more specialised area; for example one particular community.
5 Further studies by Kraabel are also very helpful. Note in particular: Kraabel 1969, pp. 81–93; 1978, pp. 13–33; 1979a, pp. 477–510; 1981a, pp. 79–91; 1982, pp. 445–64; 1983, pp. 178–90.
6 Studies of the whole area in N. G. Cohen 1969, Hebrew with English summary; Saltman 1971; Roth-Gerson 1972, Hebrew with English summary; Blanchetière 1974, pp. 367–82; 1984, pp. 41–59; Safrai and Stern 1974, pp. 143–57; Ovadiah 1978, pp. 857–66; Schürer, Vermes and Millar 1986, 3.1, pp. 17–36. The most notable studies of particular communities have been by Robert; see Robert 1955, pp. 249–53; 1958b, pp. 36–47; 1960b, pp. 381–439; 1964, pp. 37–58; note also Reynolds and Tannenbaum 1987.
7 We argue in chapter 4, section 4 that SibOr I/II is from Asia Minor. SibOr IV is probably from Syria (see J. J. Collins 1983a, p. 382), although some scholars locate it in Asia Minor and this is possible; see Johnson 1975, pp. 91–2. Other literary sources are used in chapter 1.
8 On the advantages and liabilities of epigraphy see Millar 1983b, pp. 80–136; Levick 1971, pp. 371–6; Daux 1971, pp. 1–8; Woodhead 1981, pp. 1–5; Gordon 1983, pp. 34–42.
9 Because of the nature of the evidence I concentrate here on Jewish praxis and such areas as relationships with non-Jews rather than on topics such as election, obedience and atonement, which are inaccessible given the evidence available.
10 For a review of *CIJ*, vol. 2 see J. and L. Robert *BE* 1954, pp. 101–4, no 24. On *CIJ*, vol. 1 see Robert 1937a, pp. 73–86 and see now

CIJ^2, vol. 1 by Lifshitz. Other epigraphical collections such as *MAMA*, *TAM* and IGSK are also helpful.
11 See Snodgrass 1983, pp. 137–84; Wright 1971, pp. 70–6; see also Trigger 1978, pp. 19–36.
12 I do not present and discuss every inscription or piece of evidence for the Jewish communities in Asia Minor. This is unnecessary since it has already been done by Kraabel 1968 and Schürer, Vermes and Millar 1986, vol. 3.1, pp. 17–36. Some features which Jewish communities in Asia Minor shared with other Diaspora communities, but for which we have little evidence from Asia Minor itself, will also not be dealt with specifically. Comparative evidence from other Jewish communities will be presented only when this serves to sharpen our picture of Jewish communities in Asia Minor.
13 The debate between E. P. Sanders and Neusner is instructive here; see Neusner 1978, pp. 177–91; 1984, pp. 195–203; E. P. Sanders 1980, pp. 65–79; see also J. Z. Smith 1980, pp. 1–25.

1 Jewish communities of Asia Minor in literary sources

1 On the date see G. M. Cohen 1978, p. 5. Translations of Josephus are from the Loeb Classical Library edition. Zeuxis is known from several inscriptions and from passages in Polybius; see Robert 1964; pp. 9–14; Gauger 1977, pp. 108–14. On the unrest see Schalit 1960, p. 289. The claim in Ant 12:119 that Seleucus I settled Jews in Asia is not supported by any documentary evidence; see Tcherikover 1961, p. 328; chapter 8, section 1, where CAp 2:39 and Ant 12:125 are also discussed.
2 Rostovtzeff 1941, pp. 491f; Tarn and Griffiths 1952, p. 126; G. M. Cohen 1978, pp. 4–7, 87–9.
3 Reviews of the debate about the letter in Schalit 1960, pp. 290–2; Marcus in Josephus, vol. 7, pp. 744–51, 764–6; Gauger 1977, pp. 33–52.
4 For evidence that the letter is in keeping with the conventions see Schalit 1960, pp. 292–304, 317–18; he discusses structure, style, general contents, the appeal to ancestral authority, and the vocabulary; see also Welles 1934, pp. xxxvii–l; Bickerman 1947, pp. 137–41; cf. Gauger 1977, pp. 88–133, 143–5. On there being nothing unusual in the arrangements see G. M. Cohen 1978, pp. 6, 30–2, 63–4, 66–9; Wilhelm 1974, p. 49; Schalit 1960, pp. 304–10. With regard to objections to authenticity see, for example, Gauger (1977, pp. 23–151), who places too much weight on the letter's silence and does not allow sufficiently for the incompleteness of our knowledge. Other arguments against authenticity have been refuted by Tcherikover 1961, pp. 287–8; Marcus in Josephus, vol. 7, p. 766; see also Holleaux 1920, p. 23; Meyer 1925, p. 25 n2.
5 The authenticity of the letter has been impugned by Schubart 1920, p. 343; Willrich 1924, pp. 21–3; Niese 1914, pp. 574–5; Gauger 1977, pp. 23–151. Its authenticity is supported by a number of scholars; see e.g. Kittel 1944, col. 11; Schalit 1960, pp. 289f;

Tcherikover 1961, pp. 287–8; Robert 1964, p. 12; Safrai and Stern 1974, pp. 468–70; Hengel 1974, 1, pp. 16, 263; Bickerman 1980a, pp. 17f; Smallwood 1981, p. 121; Kraabel 1983, p. 179; Schürer, Vermes and Millar 1986, 3.1, p. 17 n33.

6 Bar-Kochva 1976, p. 43 estimates a manpower of slightly more than 100 soldiers per Seleucid military settlement. The Jews may then have settled at about twenty sites, although it is not clear if the two forms of settlement are comparable.

7 On Babylonian Jews as soldiers see Ant 17:23–31; Schalit 1960, pp. 297–8, 309–10. It is difficult to know whether the Jews were military settlers because this is not made explicit by Antiochus. Zeuxis is instructed to ensure they were free from harassment, which does not seem appropriate for soldiers. Yet Antiochus urges Zeuxis to be especially generous 'to those (Jews) engaged in χρεία', which probably means some sort of military service. However, we cannot be certain that they formed military colonies of their own; see G. M. Cohen 1978, pp. 8–9. Those who see the settlements as military colonies include Schalit 1960, pp. 297–8; Broughton 1938a, 4, p. 633; cf. Bickerman 1980b, p. 84; Gauger 1977, pp. 41–2.

8 On the variant readings at this point, which do not affect the general sense, see Gauger 1977, pp. 50–1; G. M. Cohen 1978, p. 7. Rostovtzeff 1941, p. 1067 notes that Hellenistic rulers found well-established civil law, which they generally accepted in its entirety, in the territories they conquered. Thus Antiochus III's attitude to the Jews on this point is in keeping with the general tolerance of the Hellenistic authorities.

9 Whilst there is some doubt about the authenticity of the letter as it stands, the list of states in vv22–3 corresponds exactly to the prevailing circumstances in the period concerned; see Goldstein 1976, pp. 496–500; Schürer, Vermes and Millar 1973, 1, pp. 194–7.

10 Note that the areas were distinct from the Greek cities mentioned above, which were enclaves within the areas.

11 See Schürer, Vermes and Millar 1986, 3.1, pp. 17–36; on the extent of the Diaspora see also Philo, Leg. 214; Strabo in Josephus, Ant 14:115; SibOr 3:271; BJ 2:398, 7:43. Van der Horst (1989, pp. 106–7) estimates that about one million Jews lived in Asia Minor in the first century CE.

12 Rajak 1984, p. 109; see also Smallwood 1981, p. 558; cf. Moehring 1975, pp. 124–58.

13 Recent authors who accept the authenticity of the decrees include Tcherikover 1961, p. 306; Schalit 1971, col. 260; Schürer, Vermes and Millar 1973, 1, pp. 52–3 n19; Millar 1977, pp. 252, 321; Bickerman 1980a, pp. 4, 27 n8; Rabello 1984, pp. 1289–90; Saulnier 1981, p. 162 n2; Feldman 1984a, p. 805; cf. Alexander 1984, p. 588.

14 On the date see Hatzfeld 1907, pp. 9–10; Juster 1914, 1, p. 135. On the decree see also Ritschl 1873, pp. 609–10; Rajak 1981, pp. 78–9; Schürer, Vermes and Millar 1973, 1, pp. 204–5; 1986, 3.1, p. 18. On its authenticity see Hatzfeld 1907, pp. 9–10; Bickerman 1980a, p. 43 n41; T. Reinach 1899, p. 164.

15 See Cicero, *pro Flacco* 28.68; see also Hatzfeld 1907, pp. 11–12. On the later evidence for Jews at Pergamum see Ovadiah 1978, pp. 857–8; chapter 7, section 4.7.

16 Note that Pergamum was adopting the view of the Roman Senate; they would therefore have needed a good reason to oppose the envoy's request. The decree provides the only evidence for a friendship between the ancestors of the Jews and those of the people of Pergamum 'in the time of Abraham'. Since Pergamum was of comparatively recent foundation its people might have been happy to accept a suggestion like this in the Hellenistic or Roman periods. That such a claim was perhaps made could show the influence of the Jewish community in Pergamum. Compare the claim that Jews and Spartans were related in 1 Macc 12:21.

17 See Hatzfeld 1907, pp. 12–13; Gauger 1977, p. 175; on the name Θεόδωρος which was often used by Jews see Reynolds and Tannenbaum 1987, p. 101; and, for example, Lifshitz 1967, nos. 1, 2, 38, 53, 67, 93.

18 On the composition of these letters and their translation into Greek in Rome see Abbott and Johnson 1926, p. 239; Millar 1977, pp. 219–29. The documents are to be found in Ant 14:186–267, 306–23, 16:160–78; see also Philo, Leg. 311–16. We should recall that Josephus was writing an apologetic work and that one of his reasons for citing these decrees was to convince his readership of the friendliness of the Romans towards the Jewish people; see Ant 14:267, 14:186; Moehring 1975, pp. 155–8; S. J. D. Cohen 1979, pp. 152–6, 236–42; Attridge 1984, pp. 210–27.

19 See e.g. Juster 1914, 1, pp. 223–4; Applebaum 1979, p. 186; Smallwood 1981, p. 124.

20 Rajak 1984, pp. 107–23.

21 Rajak 1984, p. 107. Apart from Caligula's demand for Jewish participation in the Imperial cult, Jews were generally free from this obligation as an ancient right; see Schürer, Vermes and Millar 1986, 3.1, pp. 121–2; Lane Fox 1986, pp. 428–30. Perhaps *at times* Jews would be asked to take part in the cult of the city's gods; see for example Ant 12:125–6. But it was not always the case that Jews would be in the situation where they would be faced with pressure to worship these gods, and so they did not need *permanent* privileges. It is only when one assumes that bad relations existed generally that one imagines the cities constantly raising the issue of reverence for the gods or such other dilemmas as the Jews could have faced.

22 Ant 12:138–44, 147–53.

23 Rajak 1984, pp. 108–9. On Ephesus see, for example, Ant 14:228–30.

24 Rajak 1984, pp. 109–10. This is not to deny that Julius Caesar had a favourable attitude towards the Jews; see Holmes 1923, pp. 507–9; Büchler 1956, pp. 1–23; Saulnier 1981, pp. 169–80; Ant 14:143–4, 190–222; Suetonius, *Divus Iulius* 84–5.

25 See, for example, Pliny *Ep.* x, 66, 1–2.

26 See Ant 14:215, 221, 224–7, 228, 306–23, 16:162f; all limited in scope.
27 Rajak 1984, p. 112; see also Saulnier 1981, p. 192. The one area in which the Roman authorities may actually have formulated a general policy was that of the Temple tax; see Philo, Leg. 311–16, which speaks of Jews everywhere being allowed to send money to Jerusalem. That this one area was singled out may be a consequence of Julius Caesar's exemption of Jews from his general ban on collegia; see Ant 14:216; Rajak 1985b, p. 23. However, this provision would not be sufficient for us to speak of a charter. On Ant 19:283 see Rajak 1984, p. 115.
28 See Ant 19:286–91; see also Ant 19:299–311; Rajak 1984, p. 115; Millar 1966, p. 161.
29 Antiochus IV Epiphanes was of course the exception here. For what is known of the situation under the Seleucids in Asia Minor, see section 1.
30 See Juster 1914, 1, p. 214; Abbott and Johnson 1926, p. 74; Saulnier 1981, p. 187.
31 On beneficia see Safrai and Stern 1974, p. 457; Rajak 1984, p. 116; Millar 1983a, pp. 77–8, 84. On Hyrcanus II and Julius Caesar see Smallwood 1981, pp. 37–42, 135; Ant 14:127–39, 192–3, 301–22. On Marcus Agrippa and Herod see Ant 16:29, 60; Roddaz 1984, pp. 450–63; also Ant 19:286–91.
32 Juster 1914, 1, pp. 213, 221; Rabello 1980, p. 696; Saulnier 1984, pp. 194–5; Ant 16:60.
33 Juster 1914, 1, p. 220; Büchler 1956, pp. 2–5, 22–3; Rabello 1980, p. 692.
34 Some scholars overlook this point and think that there was continual enmity between the Jews and their cities; see, for example, Ramsay 1904b, pp. 142–57; Hemer 1986, p. 66.
35 Rajak 1984, pp. 122–3; see, for example, Ant 16:45. On anti-Judaism in this period see Sevenster 1975; Gager 1983; Klassen in P. Richardson 1986, pp. 1–19.
36 This is shown by the Ionians' claim that, if the Jews really belonged to their community, they should honour the gods of the city; see Ant 12:125–6; also CAp 2:65.
37 See Tcherikover 1961, p. 373; Goldenberg 1979, p. 418; Rajak 1984, p. 118; Ant 14:241–3.
38 Ant 14:244–6. See also from Ephesus Ant 14:262–4, 16:167–8; Rajak 1984, p. 119; Roddaz 1984, p. 460.
39 See Rabello 1980, p. 682; Rajak 1984, pp. 119–22. A fine was specified at Halicarnassus (Ant 14:258) for those who hindered the Jews, but was this actually imposed?
40 This aspect is often ignored; see for example the studies of Moehring 1975, pp. 134–58 and Saulnier 1981, pp. 161–98, both of whom fail to mention it.
41 On Caesar's ban on collegia see Ant 14:213–16; Suetonius, *Divus Iulius* 42; Smallwood 1970, pp. 205, 236–7. For the letter of 'Julius Gaius' (whose name is quite uncertain) see Ant 14:213–16; Paros

could be read instead of Parium. Another instance of the grant in Philo, Leg. 311−12. It is likely that the grant only needed to be made after some dispute had arisen. Whilst the Roman authorities seem to have classified synagogues as collegia, they actually differed from collegia in some significant respects; see Juster 1914, 1, pp. 413−24; La Piana 1927, pp. 348−51; Smallwood 1981, pp. 133−6.

42 Ant 14:259−61; see also 14:235; Safrai and Stern 1974, p. 450. This was probably a predecessor of the synagogue discovered at Sardis; see chapter 2.

43 Ant 16:162−5. The term used for the synagogue was 'σαββατεῖον', which means a house in which the Sabbath service was held; see Zeitlin 1964−5, pp. 161−3.

44 See Philo, Spec. 1.77−8; Leg. 156; Josephus BJ 7:218; Ant 14:110−12, 18:312−13; Matt 17:24; Mishnah Shek. *passim*; see also Safrai and Stern 1974, pp. 188−91; 1976, pp. 880−1; Liver 1963, pp. 173−98; cf. Mandell 1984, pp. 223−32.

45 For discussion of the passage see T. Reinach 1888, pp. 204−7; Stern 1974, pp. 273−4; A. J. Marshall 1975b, pp. 147−8; Smallwood 1981, p. 125. On the Jews on Cos see S. M. Sherwin-White 1976, pp. 183−8. It has been suggested that the sum involved was 80 rather than 800 talents since the latter is the huge sum of 4,800,000 drachmae. However, the gold could have included voluntary gifts for the Temple and personal funds and perhaps even the entire community funds of a number of Asian Jewish communities sent to Cos for 'safe keeping'.

46 Cicero, *Pro Flacco* 28:66−9; text in Stern 1974, no. 68; on the passage in general see Wardy 1979, pp. 596−609. On the explanation for the amount of money see A. J. Marshall 1975b, pp. 146−8; Safrai and Stern 1974, p. 143; Ramsay 1897, p. 667. Note the siege of Jerusalem by Aretas in 65−64 BCE and Pompey's capture of the city in 63 BCE, which Cicero mentions. Additional gifts for the Temple in Ant 18:312; BJ 5:205. We also know, for example, of a number of Jewish communities in the Apamean conventus; see chapters 3 and 4.

47 See A. J. Marshall 1975b, pp. 143−5, 148−54; Macdonald in Cicero vol. 10 (LCL), p. 519 note a; Pilcher 1903, p. 230. The ruling of the Senate had been most recently re-enacted in 63 BCE. See Pro Flacco 28, 67. The Jewish communities seem not to have had a formal right to send the tax at this time; their customary practice of sending the tax at this time was probably unopposed despite the Senate's ban.

48 *Ephesus* − Ant 16:167−8 (23−21 or 16−13 BCE); Ant 16:172−3 (between 9 and 2 BCE); Philo, Leg. 315−6 (18−12 BCE); *Sardis* − Ant 16:171 (18−12 BCE); *Asia* − Ant 16:162−5 (12 BCE); Ant 16:166 (18−16 BCE (?)); see also Juster 1914, 1, pp. 377−85.

49 Ant 16:171; see also Ant 16:166, 168, 173; Philo, Leg. 315. Ant 16:171 is probably to be dated between 18−12 BCE; see Atkinson 1958, pp. 319−23; Rajak 1984, p. 114 n24; see also Broughton 1952, 2, p. 390; Syme 1979, p. 267. We know that the Romans generally confirmed unobjectionable long-standing practices of conquered peoples; see Abbott and Johnson 1926, pp. 43−6.

50 Ant 16:168; Marcus Agrippa was in the Orient from 23 to 21 and 16 to 13 BCE. The letter is to be dated to one of these two periods; see Safrai and Stern 1974, p. 156; Atkinson 1958, pp. 305, 320; Roddaz 1984, pp. 459–60.

51 Ant 16:162–5. On this decree see Juster 1914, 1, pp. 151, 382–3; Bowersock 1964, pp. 207–10; Zeitlin 1964–5, p. 163; Rajak 1984, p. 113 n23. It is probably to be dated in 12 BCE and not between 2 BCE and 2 CE. It is possible that in Ionia one of the reasons the Temple tax was confiscated on occasions was due to disputes over civic status with the city claiming that the money was due as a tax owing to the city; see Ant 16:45, cf. Ant 16:169–70, 160–1; Applebaum 1964, pp. 297–301; 1979, pp. 183–5.

52 See Millar 1966, pp. 156, 166; 1977, pp. 208, 213f, 313f; Abbott and Johnson 1926, pp. 185–6, 237–9; Levick 1985, pp. 6f. Some examples of rare unsolicited communication from the Emperor in Millar 1977, pp. 319–21; Talbert 1984, p. 402.

53 Ant 16:172–3; dated between 9 and 2 BCE; see Magie 1950, p. 1581; Atkinson 1958, p. 327. Similar evidence in Ant 16:27f, 160–1. These decrees cover a fairly limited timescale with a large number of them coming from the period of the civil war and of the triumvirate. In a time of political instability in Roman politics, Jewish communities may have suspected that the local cities would take advantage of Roman preoccupation elsewhere and challenge their right to follow certain customs. The Jewish communities appealed to Rome at this time to prevent such an occurrence.

54 Liver 1963, p. 190; Safrai and Stern 1974, p. 190; see also Roth-Gerson 1972, English summary, p. 6.

55 Smallwood 1981, p. 127. The decrees reported by Josephus on this subject are in considerable confusion. We have several documents, or parts thereof (Ant 14:228–32, 234, 236–40), together with two reports from Lentulus' staff (Ant 14:229, 238–9).

56 On L. Lentulus Crus recruiting in Asia see Cichorius 1922, p. 135; Rostovtzeff 1941, pp. 989–94; also Broughton, 1952, 2, pp. 256, 276; Suolahti 1958, pp. 152–63. The edict exempting Jews from military service in Ant 14:228. That the exemption applied to Jews who were Roman citizens is stated in Ant 14:231, 234, 236, 240. The exemption of 43 BCE in Ant 14:223–7; see also Smallwood 1981, p. 128; Saulnier 1980, pp. 180–2. On Dolabella who wrote the letter see Broughton 1952, 2, pp. 317, 344; Magie 1950, pp. 419–21; Syme 1979, p. 369. These exemptions were ad hoc decisions; cf. Atkinson 1959, p. 254.

57 Ant 14:226; see also 14:228, 232, 237; cf. Ant 18:84, 13:251–3.

58 Whilst Jews in a Jewish armed unit could probably compel a commander to consider Jewish needs and hence let them observe (for example) the Sabbath (see Ant 13:251–3), individual Jews in the Roman army would have to obey orders or face punishment. This is probably the reason why Jews asked for exemption from mobilisation in the Roman army, where they would be called up as individuals, whilst Jews perhaps served in Jewish 'units' in

Seleucid and Ptolemaic armies. On Jews in Persian garrisons and in the Ptolemaic forces in Egypt and Cyrenaica see CAp 1:186–9, 2:49–52; Safrai and Stern 1974, pp. 421–30, 702; Tcherikover 1961, pp. 279–84, 300–1, 334–5; Schürer, Vermes and Millar 1986, 3.1, pp. 41–3. On Jewish mercenaries serving under the Seleucids and Jewish military settlers in that era see Ant 13:135–42; 1 Macc 11:45–51; Safrai and Stern 1974, pp. 431f. On Jews serving in the Roman army (all from outside of Asia Minor) see Applebaum 1971, pp. 181–4. See also *CIJ* 79, 640, 920.

59 *Parium or Paros* – Ant 14:213–16, 46 BCE. *Ephesus* – Ant 14:225–7, 43 BCE; Ant 14:262–4, 42 BCE (?; see Safrai and Stern 1974, p. 144); Ant 16:167–8, 23–21 or 16–13 BCE. *Laodicea* – Ant 14:241–3; the document mentions an envoy of Hyrcanus and this could be either Hyrcanus I or Hyrcanus II; see Juster 1914, 1, pp. 146–7; Syme 1979, pp. 639–40. *Miletus* – Ant 14:244–6, 46–44 BCE; see Moehring 1975, p. 135. *Halicarnassus* – Ant 14:256–8, 48–4 BCE; see Safrai and Stern 1974, pp. 145, 938. *Sardis* – Ant 14:259–61, date uncertain. General decree to the Jews in *Asia* – Ant 16:162–5, 12 BCE.

60 Ant 14:244–6; see also 14: 256–8, 262–4.

61 Ant 14:259–61; see also 14:262–4. Ant 14:213–14 may refer to community meals held on the Sabbath.

62 Ant 14:241–2. It is possible that Hyrcanus I is meant. The text shows a double involvement of the envoys from Hyrcanus. On the name of the proconsul see Homolle 1882, pp. 608–12; Ritschl 1873, p. 612; Broughton 1952, 2, p. 481.

63 See notes 56 and 57 above.

64 Ant 16:163; perhaps to be dated in 12 BCE; see also Ant 16:167–8. The 'day of preparation' is mentioned in Mt 27:62; Mk 15:42; Lk 23:54; Jn 19:31; and see Zeitlin 1951–2, pp. 252–5; 1964–5, p. 161.

65 On the Sabbath see Goldenberg 1979, pp. 422–9; Mann 1914, pp. 434–56, 498–532; Schürer, Vermes and Millar 1979, 2, pp. 424–7, 447–54, 467–75; 1986, 3.1, pp. 140–2. See *CPJ* III, pp. 46–56 for a discussion of four inscriptions from Asia Minor of interest here. *CIJ* 752 from Thyateira mentions a 'Sambatheion' which is probably another name for a synagogue; see also Ant 16:164. The synagogue community concerned was not necessarily syncretistic since, as Tcherikover (*CPJ* 3, p. 46) pointed out, the Sambatheion was not built near the sarcophagus but the sarcophagus in the vicinity of the Sambatheion. The Jewish community could not prevent Fabius Zosimos from building a grave nearby. On this inscription see Kraabel 1968, pp. 160f; Safrai and Stern 1974, p. 151; Schürer, Vermes and Millar 1986, 3.1, p. 19. Two inscriptions from Cilicia show the existence of a community of worshippers of a god called Σαββατιστής; see Hicks 1891, pp. 233–6, nos. 16, 17; Sokolowski 1955, no. 80. Another inscription from Lydia concerns a deity called Σαβαθικός. These clearly pagan inscriptions seem to come from gentile groups influenced by Jewish ideas of the Sabbath; see Johnson 1984, p. 1604; Cumont 1906, p. 65; Nilsson 1950, pp. 638–9;

Kraabel 1968, pp. 191–6. They probably therefore testify to the influence of Jewish communities in the areas concerned.

66 Ant 14:225–7; see Juster 1914, 1, p. 361.

67 The decree from Sardis in Ant 14:261; the date is uncertain; see also Hanfmann 1967a, p. 13; Kraabel 1983, p. 179; Saulnier 1981, p. 189 n 133. On the dietary laws in this period see R. M. Grant 1980, pp. 302–4. The proconsul Publius Servilius Galba wrote to Miletus saying he had heard that they were forbidding the Jews to manage their 'καρπούς' in accordance with their custom (Ant 14:244–6 to be dated after 46 BCE; see Juster 1914, 1, p. 147 n1). The decree could imply that the Jews had been unable to obtain or sell the food they required, in which case this would be another example of Jews in Asia Minor being concerned about food laws. Alternatively, καρπός could refer to the delivery of the tithes of the produce of the land to Jerusalem; see Büchler 1956, p. 5. The letter was written by the proconsul and so the wording may not reflect actual Jewish usage. καρπός, used at times in the LXX to mean first-fruits, could simply refer to Jewish money here.

68 Decree from Ephesus in Ant 14:262–4. Note also the similar wording in Ant 14:213–16, 225–7, 235, 241–3, 244–6, 256–8, 259–61, 16:162–5, 172–3. The concern to follow tradition is not confined to Judaism; see the example of the followers of the Persian Zeus at Sardis in Robert 1975a, pp. 306–330; New Docs 1976, p. 23. For Jewish communities approaching Roman authorities see e.g. Ant 14:213–16, 225–7, 241–3, 244–6, 262–4.

69 Note that permission to live in accordance with 'ancestral tradition' is not legally precise and thus its value in a judicial setting is not great; see Rajak 1984, pp. 115–16; 1985b, p. 24. The general Roman policy towards subject peoples was to confirm existing rights.

70 The only other matter upon which the documents throw some light is the observance of festivals by Jewish communities in Asia Minor. The people of Halicarnassus stated in a decree about the Jews that 'their sacred service to God and their customary festivals [ἑορταί, used in the LXX] and religious gatherings shall be carried on' (Ant 14:257–8; undated; see also Ant 14:213–16; 46 BCE). Little can be made of such general expressions, but they seem to indicate that Jewish communities in Asia Minor observed the Jewish festivals. Humann et al. 1898, no. 342 = CIJ 777, a Jewish inscription from Hierapolis, mentions the feasts of Passover and Pentecost. A number of the names of Jews at Aphrodisias refer to festivals; this suggests that the community there observed the Jewish festivals; see Reynolds and Tannenbaum 1987, p. 96. Evidence from elsewhere in this regard in CPJ III, no. 452a; Lüderitz 1983, no. 71; CIJ 725; Schürer, Vermes and Millar 1986, 3.1, p. 144 n26.

71 For example, Epictetus was born in Hierapolis, Phrygia and knows some details about Judaism, but he does not say that he is speaking about Jewish communities in particular places, and it is likely that he gained his knowledge in Rome. The first report of a Jew in Asia Minor comes from Clearchus writing around 300 BCE. He relates

that when Aristotle was in Asia Minor he met with a Jew from Coele-Syria who 'not only spoke Greek but had the soul of a Greek'; see Stern 1974, no. 15. However, the account of the meeting is probably legendary; see H. Lewy 1938, pp. 205–28; Tcherikover 1961, p. 287; Safrai and Stern 1976, pp. 1110–11. Even if the report does contain an historical reminiscence, it would only suggest that a Jew visited Asia Minor not that there were Jewish settlements there in the fourth century BCE; see Silberschlag 1933, pp. 75–7; cf. e.g. Oesterley 1935, p. 126.

72 On these three authors see Stern 1974, 1, pp. 148–56, 157–64, 165–6 respectively.

73 See Stern 1974, 1, p. 165; Schürer, Vermes and Millar 1986, 3.1, p. 599.

74 See J. T. Sanders 1987, *passim* (who has undoubtedly overstated his case); see also Cadbury 1955, pp. 91–2; Petersen 1978, pp. 81–92; Gaston in P. Richardson 1986, pp. 127–40. On Luke and the Jewish people, see most recently Brawley 1987, pp. 1f; Tyson 1988, pp. 1f; Weatherly 1989, pp. 107–17. There are large issues in the current debate about Luke–Acts which cannot be dealt with here. We can note that to recognise Luke has theological aims in view does not necessarily mean that he has misrepresented the historical realities of early Christianity. On God-worshippers in Jewish communities in Asia Minor see chapter 7.

75 See Acts 13:45, 50, 14:5, 18:12. It is possible that these floggings go back to the earliest period of Paul's mission work.

76 See E. P. Sanders in P. Richardson 1986, pp. 86–9; Mishnah Mak. See also Rom 9:1–5, 10:1.

77 Paul's letters also show that he considered the mission to the Jews to have been mainly unsuccessful; see Rom 9:30–3; 10:16–19, 21; 11:7, 11–15, 20, 25, 28; 2 Cor 3:14. That Jews did persecute Christians is confirmed by Paul's reference to his own persecution of the Church; see Gal 1:13, 23; Phil 3:6; 1 Cor 15:9.

78 The catalogue of suffering in 2 Cor 11:23–9 shows that Acts does not inform us about a number of Paul's difficult experiences. Whilst some of these were undoubtedly at the hands of Gentiles (e.g. 2 Cor 11:25–6), it is likely that Luke did not know about many of the persecutions at the hands of Jews. Would he not have told about some of these five beatings? The Aorist participle ἐκδιωξάντων in 1 Thess 2:15 suggests a definite event is in view and this favours the possibility that it is the missionaries' ejection from Thessalonica in Acts 17:5–10; see Best 1972, p. 116. The use of the plural ἡμᾶς (Paul, Silas and Timothy) also supports this.

79 See, for example, Gal 2–4; cf. Acts 21:21.

80 See E. P. Sanders in P. Richardson 1986, pp. 85–6. Note that some scholars see I Thess 2:13–16 as an interpolation, but see, for example, Hurd in P. Richardson 1986, pp. 21–36. It was his zeal for the law that led the pre-Christian Paul to persecute the Church; see Gal 1:13–14; Phil 3:6. Some scholars suggest Paul's preaching of a Messiah who had been crucified as one condemned by the Law,

a σκάνδαλον to the Jews (1 Cor 1:23; Gal 5:11; see also Gal 3:13), was also a reason for his being persecuted. However, the general freedom of the Jerusalem apostles from persecution suggests that preaching a law-free gospel was the decisive factor that caused Jews to persecute Paul.

81 See Bruce 1988, p. 265; also Roloff 1981, p. 209; cf. Acts 5:17, 17:5.
82 See Stählin 1962, p. 187; Roloff 1981, p. 210. Gentiles of high standing supporting the Jews are unusual in Acts; they generally protect and defend Paul (e.g. 18:12–17, 19:31, 35–41). This verse runs counter to Luke's presentation.
83 See Acts 14:1, 16:13, 17:2, 10, 17, 18:4, 19, 19:8. On the programmatic rejections of the Jews (13:46, 18:6, 28:28) see Dibelius 1956, pp. 149–50; Brawley 1987, pp. 68–83; Tannehill in Tyson 1988, pp. 83–101.
84 The agreement of Gal 2:9 seems to have meant that Paul was to concentrate on preaching to the Gentiles, but it did not preclude Paul also preaching to the Jews on occasions, as evidenced by 1 Cor 9:20, where Paul explicitly states that he attempted to win both Jews and Greeks. Gal 2:9 simply defined areas in which those involved would concentrate.
85 See Roloff 1981, p. 211; G. Schneider 1982, p. 112; cf. Haenchen 1971, p. 420 n10.
86 Although Antioch is over 100 miles from Lystra, an inscription has been discovered at Antioch on a statue of Concord set up by the citizens of Lystra in honour of Antioch; see Ramsay 1904a, p. 50. This shows there was some contact between the two cities.
87 See Hengel 1979, p. 109; Trocmé 1957, p. 153; that the incident of 14:19 is referred to in 2 Cor 11:25 is agreed by Haenchen 1971, p. 429 n4; Bultmann 1985, p. 216; Stählin 1962, p. 195.
88 See, for example, Haenchen 1971, pp. 417–18, 421–3, 429–39; Koester 1982, 2, p. 101.
89 For example Beroea (17:14); Corinth (18:5–17). Acts may be dependent on 2 Tim as a source, in which case a strongly attested element of Acts 13–14 is the tradition that Paul was persecuted. If Luke is drawing on the tradition independently of 2 Tim, then our case is even stronger; see G. Schneider 1982, 2, pp. 112, 156.
90 See Hengel 1979, pp. 108–10; see also Haenchen 1971, p. 433; Lüdemann 1989, pp. 157, 163–5.
91 See Gal 5:3, 6, 11; 1 Cor 7:17–20; Haenchen 1971, pp. 480–2; Conzelmann 1987, p. 125; and the review of scholarship in S. J. D. Cohen 1986, pp. 251–63. It has been suggested that the account is based on a confused memory of the story of Titus in Gal 2:3; see Loisy 1920, pp. 618–21; Walker 1981, pp. 231–5. The incident is in accord with the Lucan portrayal of Paul as a law-abiding Jew (see Acts 18:18, 21:23f, 23:6f). That Luke had a motive for recording the incident does not necessarily mean it is fictitious.
92 See Hengel 1979, p. 64; Bruce 1988, p. 304; Strack and Billerbeck 1928, 4, pp. 378–9, 383. On the children of a Jewish mother and a Gentile father being Jews see mQidd 3:12; mYebam 7:5; Qidd 68a, b;

Belkin 1935, p.46; Strack and Billerbeck 1924, 2, p.741. The rabbinic legal view found in the Mishnah can be dated to before the first century CE; see Schiffman 1981, pp.117–22; Lüdemann 1989, p.175; cf. S.J.D. Cohen 1986, pp.265–7. However, we do not know whether Jews in Asia Minor would have known or followed this rabbinic principle; see S.J.D. Cohen 1986, p.267.

93 See Foakes Jackson and Lake 1920–33, 2, p.293; Stählin 1962, p.213; Pesch 1986, 2, p.97; Lüdemann 1989, pp.176–7. There is nothing in the incident to suggest that Paul was willing to compromise the freedom of Gentile converts.

94 On Jews not marrying Gentiles see Dt 7:3; Ezra 10:2, 11; Neh 13:25; Jub 30:7–17; Ant 20:141–4; PsPhilo 9:5; TLevi 9:10, 14:6; Yebamoth 45b. See the previous paragraph for Timothy being regarded as a Jew.

95 If this was the case he may not have been a Jew. On Sceva see Mastin 1976, pp.405–12. There is no reason to think of him as high priest of the Imperial Cult.

96 On Jews, exorcism and magic see Lk 11:19; Ant 8:45–9; Simon 1986, pp.339–68; Schürer, Vermes and Millar, 1986, 3.1, pp.342–79. On Jews in Asia Minor and magic see chapter 3, n32. On Ephesus and magic see C.E. Arnold 1989, pp.14–20.

97 See, for example, Loisy 1920, pp.727–33; Dibelius 1956, p.19; Koester 1982, 2, p.114.

98 On the general historicity of the incident see A.N. Sherwin-White, 1963, pp.83–92; see also G. Schneider 1982, 2, p.273; cf. Haenchen 1971, pp.576–9. The involvement of the Jews is incidental to the whole event, and this favours the historicity of vv33–4.

99 The exact meaning of συνεβίβασαν is unclear; it probably means that some of the crowd informed Alexander about what was going on.

100 Luke does not say how the crowd recognised that Alexander was a Jew. Perhaps it was from the fact that a group known to be Jews had put him forward or that he was known to be a Jew. On the interpretation of the incident see e.g. Roloff 1981, p.293; Pesch 1986, 2, pp.181–2.

101 MS ℵ omits the word 'Jews' from v5, but the reading should not be followed; see J.T. Sanders 1987, pp.232–3. The list of nations in the passage is not Luke's creation; see Metzger 1970, pp.123–33; G. Schneider 1980, 1, pp.253–5; cf. Brinkman 1963, pp.418–27.

102 See Hengel 1979, pp.71–3; cf. Acts 9:29. Commentators discuss how many synagogues are involved in Acts 6:9; *CIJ* 1404 may be relevant.

103 Haenchen 1971, p.266; and in general Lüdemann 1989, pp.79–85; cf. J.T. Sanders 1987, pp.72–3, 245–7. On the Hellenists see Haenchen 1971, pp.264–8; Hengel 1979, pp.71–80; 1983, pp. 1–29.

104 That 6:9 may go back to a written source see Hengel 1983, p.4; Trocmé 1957, pp.166, 188; see also Pesch 1986, 1, p.235. Diaspora

Jews who returned to Jerusalem generally did so for religious reasons, such as the importance of the Temple and the law to them; see Hengel 1983, pp. 18, 20. All Jews in Asia Minor might not have held the same views of course.

105 That they are not present (legally they should have been) when Paul defended himself before Felix suggests that they had gone back to Asia; see 24:18–19. See also 26:21; cf. A. N. Sherwin-White 1963, pp. 52–3. On pilgrimage in general see Safrai 1975, pp. 53–62; Safrai and Stern 1974, pp. 191–204; 1976, pp. 898–904; *CIJ* 1404.

106 Hengel 1983, pp. 105–6 concludes that the passage has a basis in history since the event and its setting correspond closely to what is known of the conditions of the time; cf. J. T. Sanders 1987, pp. 285–6. Note too the differences in the accusations made against Stephen and Paul, despite the parallels. This suggests reliable tradition for both incidents; see Hengel 1983, pp. 21–2. For Luke the charges made against Paul are all false. See, for example, 16: 1–3, 21:20–6, 25:8, 28:17. Palestinian Jews also made trouble for Paul; see e.g. 23:12–22.

107 See Gaston in S. G. Wilson 1986, pp. 42–3; see also Schrage 1988, pp. 394–5. The so-called Jews could also be Jewish Christians.

108 See Fiorenza 1973, p. 572; see also A. Y. Collins 1985, pp. 204–10; on the Nicolaitans see Fiorenza 1973, pp. 567–71. They are John's main opponents and seem to be a Christian libertine group.

109 John is not explicit about why the Jews opposed the Christians. There are probably Jewish elements in the teaching opposed in Colossians and the Pastorals. See Col 2:8–10, 16–23; 1 Tim 1:4, 7, 4:7; 2 Tim 4:4. (Tit 1:10–14 gives evidence for Jewish Christians on Crete; see van der Horst 1988, p. 188.) However, the exact nature of the teaching is much debated, and the Jewish elements are probably mediated by Jewish Christians (or perhaps Gentile Christians influenced by Judaism and/or gnosticism). It is exceedingly difficult, then, to gain any information about Jewish communities themselves in Asia Minor from this evidence. In the case of Galatians the Judaisers definitely come from outside of Asia Minor.

110 On relationships between the Church and the synagogue see especially Simon 1986, pp. 65–97, 135–78, 202–33, 306–38; Wilken 1971, pp. 8–38.

111 It is debated whether Ignatius is writing against two separate groups or one group which combined both 'heresies'; see e.g. C. C. Richardson 1935, pp. 51–4, 79–85; Molland 1954, pp. 1–6; Barrett 1976, pp. 220–30; Donahue 1978, pp. 81–93.

112 See Schoedel 1985, pp. 209–10; see also 1978, pp. 97–106; 1985, pp. 200–9; Gaston in S. G. Wilson 1986, p. 37; also Speigl 1987, pp. 369–71; Barrett 1976, pp. 233–4. See also Phld 5:2, 9:1.

113 Lightfoot (1889, 2, ii, p. 125) suggests 'until now' means 'when two or three generations have passed since the true doctrine of grace was revealed'. The first generation of Christians might have been excused for following Jewish practices, but for those of Ignatius' time there

was no excuse. Thus the passage probably does not suggest that Jewish Christians are in view, although we cannot rule out this possibility.

114 See Schoedel 1985, pp. 118–27; Gaston in S. G. Wilson 1986, pp. 37–8.

115 Our evidence for a Jewish community in Philadelphia is Rev 3:9 and *CIJ* 754 (third century CE); note also Sardis is close to Philadelphia.

116 See Simon 1986, pp. 145, 306–38; Wilken 1971, pp. 18, 35–8; see also 1980, pp. 460–1, 466–71.

117 See Lane Fox 1986, p. 481. Text in Musurillo 1972, pp. 2–21. The account of Polycarp's death sets out to show the parallelism between Christ's death and Polycarp's martyrdom; see MPoly 1:1, 19:1, also 1:2, 6:2, 12:2, 16:1; Simon 1986, p. 122. However, the part played by the Jews does not correspond exactly with their part in the Gospel accounts. For example it is a pagan and Jewish crowd which condemns Polycarp, not just a Jewish one; see MPoly 9–12. Thus, the details of the Jews' involvement are not unreasonable. The account is generally regarded as trustworthy; see e.g. Smallwood 1981, pp. 507–8; Parkes 1934, pp. 136–7; Hemer 1986, p. 67.

118 On Justin's knowledge of Judaism see Goodenough 1923, pp. 92–6; Barnard 1964, pp. 400–6; Sigal 1978–9, pp. 82–94. On the Dialogue being set in Ephesus see Eusebius H.E. 4.18.6; Dial 1.1 simply locates it in 'the walks of the Xystus'.

119 Remus in S. G. Wilson 1986, p. 72; also Barnard 1967, pp. 23–4; Trakatellis 1986, pp. 287–97.

120 See Dial 108:2; see also 69:7, 17:1, 117:3; Stanton 1985, pp. 379–84.

121 See 8:4; see also 10:1–4. On Justin and the law see Stylianopoulos 1975, pp. 7–44. Justin also says that Jews curse Christ and his followers in their synagogues; see 16:4, 47:4, 93:4, 95:4, 133:6. This is probably a reference to the Twelfth of the Eighteen Benedictions.

122 See Stanton 1985, p. 378; see also Remus in S. G. Wilson 1986, pp. 72–4. On Sardis see chapter 2. Justin's conversion probably occurred in Ephesus; see Quasten 1950, 1, p. 197. As a Christian he taught in Rome and probably also in other cities at different times, perhaps including Ephesus; see Barnard 1967, p. 12.

123 On Apollinaris see Eusebius H.E. 4.27.1; Quasten 1950, 1, pp. 228–9; R. M. Grant 1988, pp. 85–7. On the Jewish community at Hierapolis see chapter 8, section 3; Schürer, Vermes and Millar 1986, 3.1, pp. 27–8. On Miltiades see Eusebius H.E. 5.17.5; Quasten 1950, 1, p. 228.

124 See Lane Fox 1986, pp. 460–92; cf. Eusebius H.E. 4.15.46–7; Musurillo 1972, pp. xxviii–xxx. Note, in particular, that people like Politta, Rufinus and Macedonia from Karine who play a part in the text can all be located in Smyrna in this period with the help of other evidence. The text of MPion is in Musurillo 1972, pp. 136–67. On MPoly and MPion see also Kraabel 1968, pp. 37f; Gero 1978, pp. 164–8; Hilhorst 1982, pp. 91–6; Den Boeft and Bremmer 1985, pp. 110–30.

125 Lane Fox 1986, pp. 479–80; see MPion 13:3–9; van der Horst 1989, pp. 116–17. On the legendary Martyrdom of Conon, set in Pamphylia, which also refers to Jewish polemic against Jesus, see Lane Fox 1986, p. 483. Even if it is fictional, such accusations were probably thought plausible by the author.

126 For explanations of the term see e.g. Lightfoot 1889, 2, i, pp. 710–13; Lane Fox 1986, pp. 485–7 who suggests it was the Jewish festival of Purim.

127 See also MPion 18:8; Lane Fox 1986, pp. 485–7; see also Lightfoot 1889, 2, i, pp. 713–15.

128 See Lane Fox 1986, p. 487; cf. Parkes 1934, p. 137.

129 See chapter 2, section 4 and chapter 4, section 6 respectively. Note also evidence from Cyril of Alexandria, Gregory of Nazianzus and Gregory of Nysa in chapter 7, section 4.8. Some scholars have argued that the Epistle to Diognetus belongs in Asia Minor, but this is uncertain; see Johnson 1975, p. 118. On possible Jewish elements in Montanism, see Johnson 1975, p. 141; cf. Ford 1966, pp. 145–57.

130 On the Diaspora and the revolt see Moehring 1984, pp. 870, 907; Smallwood 1981, pp. 356–7, 364. Help from Adiabene is noted in BJ 2:520, 5:474, 6:356–7. Help was hoped for from Jews across the Euphrates; see BJ 1:5, 2:388–9, 6:343, and some perhaps eventuated; see Dio Cassius lxvi. 4.3, in Stern 1980, no. 430. It is possible that more help was forthcoming than Josephus was prepared to admit. On Vespasian and Titus confirming privileges see BJ 7:100–11; Ant 12:119–24. On the tax and its subsequent history see BJ 7:218; Dio Cassius in Stern 1980, no. 430; Suetonius in Stern 1980, no. 320, pp. 129–31; Ginsburg 1930–1, pp. 281–91; Smallwood 1956, pp. 3f; 1981, pp. 371–84, 515–16; *CPJ* 1, pp. 80–8; 2, pp. 108–36, 204–8; Thompson 1982, pp. 329–42; cf. Mandell 1984, pp. 223–32. Domitian did not alter the religious liberty of the Jews (cf. his action against 'Judaisers') but exacted the tax with vigour. Nerva relaxed the application of the tax.

131 On the revolt see *CPJ* 2, pp. 225–60; Fuks 1961, pp. 98–104; Schürer, Vermes and Millar 1973, 1, pp. 529–34; Kasher 1976a, pp. 147–58; Smallwood 1981, pp. 389–421. On possible small-scale trouble in Palestine at this time see Applebaum 1976, p. 18; Smallwood 1981, pp. 421–7.

132 On the revolt and Hadrian's ban see Mildenberg 1984, pp. 13–15, 65–109; Bowersock 1980, pp. 131–41; Schürer, Vermes and Millar 1973, 1, pp. 534–57, 1986, 3.1, pp. 123–4; Applebaum 1976, pp. 1f; 1984, pp. 35–41; Smallwood 1959b, pp. 334–47; 1961, pp. 93–6; 1981, pp. 428–73. Blanchetière (1984, p. 55) and Roth-Gerson (1972, English summary, p. 2) note the lack of evidence for Jews in Asia Minor being involved in any of the Jewish revolts.

133 On the situation from Antoninus Pius to Constantine, for which our evidence is meagre, see Rabello 1980, p. 673; Gager 1973, pp. 89–101. The ban on proselytism was probably not always enforced. On the action of Christian Emperors see J. Cohen 1976, pp. 1–29; Wilken 1980, pp. 464–6; Schürer, Vermes and Millar

1986, 3.1, pp. 124–5. Examples of prohibition of proselytism, the limiting of a Jewish right whilst generally upholding existing rights in Cod. Theod 16.8.1, 3, 9 respectively; see also Linder 1987, pp. 120–32, 189–91.

134 See the instructive debate in McEleney 1973, pp. 19–42; 1978, pp. 83–8; Aune 1976, pp. 1–10; Grabbe 1977, pp. 149–53.

135 See Ant 19:279, 289–91, 300–12. On Caligula's demands that all people observe the Emperor cult see Schürer, Vermes and Millar 1973, 1, pp. 394–7; 1986, 3.1, pp. 121–2. Claudius restored the former situation.

136 See also Blanchetière 1974, p. 377; Safrai and Stern 1974, p. 443 and n9.

2 The Jewish communities at Sardis and Priene

1 See Hanfmann 1983, pp. 1–16, 109–19, 125–8, 141–8, 191f (references to the articles in this book are given under the name of the editor Hanfmann, apart from the two articles by Seager (= 1983, pp. 168–78) and Kraabel (= 1983, pp. 178–90)); Mitten 1966, pp. 38–68; Foss 1976, pp. 1–27.

2 On the Lydian–Aramaic bilingual see S. A. Cook 1917, p. 80; Torrey 1917–18, pp. 186–8; Donner and Röllig 1962, 1, no. 260; 1964, 2, pp. 305–6. A number of scholars are convinced that Sepharad in Obadiah 20 is Sardis; see, for example, Kraabel 1968, pp. 198–9; Pedley 1972, p. 85. The issue is left open by others, for example Hemer 1986, pp. 134–6, 150.

3 See Ant 12:147–53; Robert 1964, pp. 9–15; Hanfmann 1983, pp. 110–13.

4 See Juster 1914, 1, pp. 143–5; Noakes 1975, p. 244.

5 This probably refers to offerings in general, but see Bickerman 1958, p. 151.

6 On τόπος as a synagogue see Krauss 1922, pp. 24–5; Hanfmann 1983, p. 118.

7 See Noakes 1975, p. 245. See chapter 8, section 1 for a discussion of whether the Jewish community at Sardis was organised as a politeuma.

8 See Hanfmann 1972, pp. 294–5; 1983, pp. 148–61; Seager 1972, pp. 430–1. The palaestra was not completed before the mid third century CE.

9 See Seager 1972, pp. 425–35; 1983, pp. 172–3.

10 See Hanfmann 1967a, pp. 23–5; Seager 1972, p. 432; 1983, pp. 282 n30.

11 On Stage 3 see Seager 1983, pp. 172–3; Hanfmann 1971, p. 15. On the date when the building became a synagogue see also Kraabel 1983, pp. 179, 188; Foss 1976, pp. 21, 36.

12 Buckler and Robinson 1932, no. 17, line 7, pp. 37–40.

13 On the forecourt see Hanfmann 1968, pp. 29–31; 1972, p. 284, fig 212; 1983, pp. 193–4, 286; Seager 1972, pp. 425, 432–4; 1983, pp. 169, 173; Ramage 1972, p. 39.

14 See Seager 1981a, p. 184; 1983, p. 170; Shiloh 1968, pp. 54–7; cf. Hachlili 1976, pp. 43–53.

15 See Seager 1981a, pp. 182–3; Hanfmann 1968, pp. 26–8; cf. Georgi 1987, pp. 403–4. On the lack of a gallery see Seager 1983, pp. 170–1; Brooten 1982, pp. 124–5. Twelve of the dedicatory inscriptions from the synagogue mention a wife as co-donor; see Kroll forthcoming, nos. 10, 14–15, 18, 21, 25, 29, 33, 42, 48, 60, 67. This suggests that women were fully involved in the life of the community; see further in general in chapter 5.

16 The eagles and the table belong to the late Hellenistic or early Roman period; see Hanfmann and Ramage 1978, pp. 148–9. On the table see Hanfmann 1964, pp. 34–6; Seager 1975, pp. 159–60. On the lions, to be dated between 450 and 350 BCE, see Hanfmann and Ramage 1978, pp. 63–5, no. 25; Goodenough 1953–68, 7, pp. 55, 85; Nock 1972, pp. 914–15. On the menorah see Hanfmann and Ramage 1978, p. 151, no. 226; Hanfmann 1964, pp. 36–8. On the other menorahs see Seager 1983, pp. 171, 176; Waldbaum 1983, pp. 20, 103. See also the inscriptions in Kroll forthcoming, nos. 66, 69, 70; cf. van Buren 1908, pp. 195–7. On the Samoe inscription see section 4 below.

17 On the mosaics see Hanfmann 1967a, pp. 27–46; Ramage 1972, p. 39. On the wall decorations and other small finds and furnishings see Hanfmann 1967a, pp. 46–50; Ramage 1972, p. 20; Seager 1983, pp. 174–7.

18 Seager 1983, p. 177; see also Seager 1981b, pp. 39–47; E. M. Meyers in *IDB* Supplement, pp. 842–4.

19 On the lack of annexe rooms see Greenewalt 1973, p. 26; Seager 1983, p. 174. On multiple uses of the hall see Seager 1975, p. 161; Kraabel 1983, p. 188. On the shops see Hanfmann 1965, pp. 19–29; 1968, pp. 16–22; 1983, pp. 161–7, 192, 210; Greenewalt 1976, p. 67. Four Jews are known from the shops – Jacob, a presbyter in the synagogue, Sabbatios, Theoktistos and John; see Robert 1964, p. 57; Hanfmann 1983, pp. 165–6.

20 See Seager 1983, p. 174. Theodosius' ban in Linder 1987, pp. 323–37. On the later history of Jews in the area see Foss 1976, pp. 42, 156 n80, 172 n42.

21 Seager 1983, p. 171. Six of these inscriptions contain the term θεοσεβής and are discussed in chapter 7, section 4. After the manuscript of this book was completed, I received from Professor John H. Kroll a copy of his chapter entitled 'The Greek Inscriptions' to be published in the forthcoming volume *The Synagogue at Sardis*, Archaeological Exploration of Sardis Report, Cambridge, MA: Harvard University Press. I am very grateful to Professor Kroll for allowing me to see the chapter and to use it here. Unfortunately, his work arrived at too late a stage for me to interact with it substantially, but I have been able to add references to his work and to make my discussion more complete at several points.

22 See Seager 1972, pp. 426 n11, 433–4; 1983, p. 173. Robert (1964,

pp. 37–47, 53) originally dated the inscriptions between 175–250 CE, but subsequent work has shown this to be unlikely.

23 The inscription is given in Hanfmann 1963, pp. 43–4. It has only been published in English transliteration. On the inscription see Seager 1983, pp. 171, 282 n25; Kraabel 1983, p. 179; Hanfmann 1983, pp. 145, 286 n26. For what is known of Lucius' journey at this time see Barnes 1967, pp. 71–2. Direct proof of a visit exists only for Ephesus. For similar action by other Jewish communities see chapter 8, section 3. One other Hebrew inscription reads 'Shalom'; see Hanfmann 1963, p. 44; see also Kraabel 1971, p. 80 n17.

24 Robert 1964, pp. 45–6, no. 6; Lifshitz 1967, no. 19; Kroll forthcoming, no. 10.

25 On Leontioi referring to a tribe see Robert 1964, pp. 46–7; see also Safrai and Stern 1974, p. 480; Lifshitz 1967, pp. 27–8. On the name Leontios see Robert 1958b, p. 42 n7; Lifshitz 1965, pp. 526–7; Reynolds and Tannenbaum 1987, p. 6 line 21; p. 102. For the example previously found in Sardis see J. and L. Robert, *BE*, 1954, p. 102; see also Hanfmann 1964, p. 38 n12. For donors to the Sardis synagogue named Leontios see Kroll forthcoming nos. 22–3 (who is θεοσεβής), 39, 48. The ben Leho inscription is in Kraabel 1983, pp. 184–5. The large Lydian lion is in Hanfmann and Ramage 1978, p. 68, no. 31. Note also a lion-head spout and a lion on a pilaster capital in Hanfmann 1963, p. 33, fig. 34, p. 46. The lion is found in other synagogues; see Goodenough 1953–68, 7, pp. 29–37, 78–86; Chiat 1982, p. 346.

26 Robert 1964, p. 47; see Deut 33:22; Nu 23:24, 24:9; Mic 5:8; 1 Macc 3:4–5; IV Ezra 11:37–12:34.

27 Twenty-two lion statues have been catalogued; see Hanfmann and Ramage 1978, pp. 20–3, 34. On Herodotus see Pedley 1972, no. 116; see also nos. 88, 98, 99. Lions also feature on the coins of Sardis; see e.g. Head 1901, p. 240 no. 37, 265 no. 171.

28 See Kraabel 1983, p. 184.

29 Kroll forthcoming, no. 29; cf. Robert 1964, pp. 48–9, no. 7; Lifshitz 1967 no. 20. The synagogue was divided up into seven bays.

30 On the term in the LXX see Hatch and Redpath, pp. 1053–4; and, for example, see 2 Kg 7:8; Am 3:13; Zech 1:3. See also 2 Macc 1:25, 5:20; 3 Macc 2:2, 6, 18; Wis 7:25; LetAris 185; SibOr 1:66, 2:330; TSol 3:5, 6:8. It is also found in four Jewish inscriptions from Gorgippia; see chapter 6, section 4.7. See also Bousset 1926, p. 312 n2; Marcus 1931–2, pp. 100–1. It is found in the NT, for example in Rev 1:8, 4:8. The term σκούτλωσις which is common in the Sardis inscription was derived from the Latin *scutula* and came to mean marble revetments in general; see A. Cameron 1931, p. 257; Robert 1964, pp. 50–1. The paintings referred to were probably on the upper walls and ceiling.

31 Kroll forthcoming, no. 37; Robert 1964, p. 55, no. 14; Lifshitz 1967, no. 23. The inscription is from the marble wall revetments of Bay 7.

32 Text in Kroll forthcoming, no. 3; J. and L. Robert, *BE* 1968, p. 517, no. 478; on the date see Hanfmann 1967a, p. 38; 1971, p. 15.
33 See Hanfmann 1983, pp. 165–6; Waldbaum 1983, p. 20; Kraabel 1983, p. 185. For the other two goldsmiths see Kroll forthcoming, nos. 25–6, 36. Interesting comparative material is provided by the Aphrodisias inscription. It seems that in that city also the occupations of the Jews and of the θεοσεβεῖς were not much different from that of Gentiles; see Reynolds and Tannenbaum 1987, pp. 116–23, 127–8.
34 See Kroll forthcoming, nos. 3, 11, 13, 16–17, 24, 27, 30–3, 37, 41, 43, 66–7; see also chapter 8 for a discussion of Jewish citizenship and Jews holding public office.
35 See Seager 1983, p. 171; Kraabel 1983, p. 183. City councillors are mentioned in the following inscriptions: Kroll forthcoming, nos. 3, 13, 16–17, 24, 25–6, 31, 34 (the city councillor from Hypaepa), 37, 67.
36 Severus and Caracalla's enactment in Dig. L.2.3.3; text in Watson *et al.* 1985; see also Linder 1987, pp. 103–6; Reynolds and Tannenbaum 1987, pp. 66–7. Modestinus commented that Marcus Aurelius and Commodus regularised the participation by Jews in public office, but the law itself has not come down to us; see Dig. XXVII.1.15.6; see also Gager 1973, p. 93; Rabello 1980, pp. 686–7. On offices becoming burdensome see A. H. M. Jones 1940, pp. 175–6, 181–91; Abbott and Johnson 1926, pp. 101–11; Rostovtzeff 1957, pp. 483–5; Sheppard 1975, pp. 181–93; Lane Fox 1986, pp. 50, 302. On Jews and pagan cults see chapter 8, section 3.
37 A. H. M. Jones 1940, pp. 182, 189–91.
38 See Pliny Ep x, 79, 110, 112–15; A. N. Sherwin-White 1966, pp. 105, 670–3, 719–26; A. H. M. Jones 1940, pp. 170–2, 176–91; Magie 1950, pp. 603, 640–2; Chapot 1904, pp. 195–201. It is noteworthy that the Jews Euphrosynos I and his son Euphrosynos II were both city councillors in Sardis; see Kroll forthcoming, nos. 31, 16–17.
39 The inscription is in Kroll forthcoming, no. 70; it was inscribed on a pedestal. On the office see Magie 1950, pp. 446, 490, 541, 567–9, 681; Millar 1964, pp. 185–7; 1977, pp. 180–1; A. H. M. Jones 1964, pp. 435, 790–1; Brunt 1983, pp. 52–5; Levick 1985, pp. 16–18, 55–60.
40 The inscription is in Kroll forthcoming, no. 5; Ramage 1972, p. 20. On the title see Millar 1977, pp. 61, 117–19; A. H. M. Jones 1964, pp. 104–5, 526; Foss 1976, p. 30. Note that 'Lectorius the *comes*' in the early fifth century in Minorca was probably a Jew; see Hunt 1982, p. 121.
41 See Kroll forthcoming, nos. 13–14b. On the title see Magie 1950, pp. 568–9.
42 On the integration of the Sardis Jewish community in the city see Mitten 1966, p. 65; Kraabel 1968, pp. 9–10; 1983, p. 178; Seager 1974, pp. 43, 50; 1981a, p. 184. Another fragmentary inscription from the synagogue may read (ὁ ἀξιολογ)ώτατος; see Kroll forthcoming, no. 45; Robert 1964, p. 56, no. 19. Robert thinks it

involved a position in the life of the city. We know of very few Jews in other cities who held office, or other Jewish communities where this degree of involvement in city life can be documented; see chapter 8, section 3.

43 The inscription given is in Kroll forthcoming, no. 22; see also nos. 12, 16–17, 19, 20–1, 23–4, 58, 66. The only other occurrence in a synagogue inscription is *CIJ* 682, from Olbia. On Jewish usage see IV Macc 9:24, 13:19, 17:22; see also Dan 6:19; II Macc 4:6; III Macc 4:21; Wis 14:3; SibOr 5:226–7; LetAris 201; Marcus 1931–2, p. 105; Attridge 1984, pp. 218–19. On the term in pagan thought see R. T. Wallis 1972, pp. 142, 146–50; Foss 1976, pp. 22–7; C. P. Jones 1982, pp. 267–8.

44 Kraabel 1983, p. 186.

45 Text in Kroll forthcoming, no. 4. Kroll notes that the name Samoe is a transcription of the Biblical name Shamu'a (2 Kgs 5:14; 2 Es 21:17). For other inscriptions mentioning priests see *CIJ* 746, as read by Robert 1960b, pp. 381–4 (Ephesus); *CIJ* 785 (Corycus); Reynolds and Tannenbaum 1987, p. 5, inscription *a* line 27 (Aphrodisias). For those known from elsewhere see Brooten 1982, pp. 95–8, 249 n 73. On the functions of priests see Leon 1960, p. 192; Brooten 1982, pp. 90–9.

46 See Hanfmann 1967a, p. 29; Kraabel 1968, pp. 222–6; Seager 1983, p. 170; see also Hanfmann and Bloom 1987, pp. 10*–14*. It is noteworthy that of the usual designations for synagogue leaders only the title πρεσβύτερος has been found in the synagogue; see Kroll forthcoming, nos. 52, 75. Was Samoe *the* leader for a period of time? Do his Hebrew name and titles indicate a return to more traditional values, compared with those of people who were city councillors? The evidence only permits us to raise such issues.

47 See S. J. D. Cohen 1981–2, pp. 1–17; van der Horst 1987, pp. 102–6, who give fifty-nine Rabbis known from inscriptions. *CIJ* 1414 is the epitaph of a Rabbi from Phrygia buried in Jerusalem. He is the only Rabbi from Asia Minor known from inscriptions.

48 Text in Kroll forthcoming, no. 65; it was found outside the synagogue, in a secondary position. Translation from Kraabel 1983, p. 189.

49 On the inscription see Hanfmann 1967a, pp. 27–9; 1972, p. 120; Kraabel 1983, p. 189; φυλάσσω often means 'to observe the commandments' in the LXX; see, for example, Ex 12:17; 15:26; Lev 18:26; Deut 4:2.

50 Text in Kroll forthcoming, no. 63; see also Seager 1981a, p. 183; 1983, p. 171.

51 Text in Kroll forthcoming, no. 76; see also no. 71. Jews and Christians in Sardis seem to have shared this invocation; see Foss 1976, p. 41, 158 n 109. In the LXX see, for example, 1 Kg 7:12; Ps 40:4; 93:17; Prov 20:22; Isa 50:9. Similar synagogue inscriptions from elsewhere in Lifshitz 1967, no. 64, 70, 77a, 84, 89, 90; *CIJ* 864; Reynolds and Tannenbaum 1987, p. 5 inscription *a* line 1, p. 26; Robert 1964, p. 45 n2; van der Horst 1987, pp. 102–3.

52 See Hanfmann 1967a, pp. 23–5.
53 See Seager 1974, p. 43; 1975, p. 155; Kraabel 1983, p. 185. These factors suggest that contacts between individual Jews and Gentiles were generally friendly.
54 See Johnson 1975, p. 100 n63; Safrai and Stern 1974, p. 479.
55 On the Church see Hanfmann 1983, pp. 194–9; Kraabel 1983, pp. 179–80, 187. On the Ostia synagogue see Moe 1977, pp. 148–57. On the later situation see Mitten 1966, p. 65; Foss 1976, p. 31.
56 As mentioned earlier, if the fountain was a public one, then the forecourt was accessible to all.
57 Kraabel 1981a, p. 81; 1983, p. 188; he points to the comparison with the Dura synagogue which, although lavishly decorated, was not easily identifiable behind a complex of other rooms. See further in chapter 7, section 4 on the six θεοσεβής inscriptions.
58 Hanfmann and Ramage 1978, p. 64.
59 Seager 1983, p. 176; Hanfmann 1975, pp. 89–90. Such stones were available for use by both Jews and Christians; see Seager 1974, p. 52. That they were available to Christians in this post-Constantinian period is not surprising; that Jews were able to use the stones is noteworthy. For other stones re-used in the piers and walls see Hanfmann and Ramage 1978, p. 38, Index s.v. 'Synagogue'.
60 Hanfmann and Ramage 1978, pp. 58–60; Seager 1983, p. 176.
61 See text in S. G. Hall 1979, section 72–99.
62 On Melito and the Jews in Sardis see Kraabel 1971, pp. 77–85; 1983, pp. 179, 186–7; Noakes 1975, pp. 244–9; Wilken 1976, pp. 53–69; S. G. Wilson in S. G. Wilson 1986, pp. 81–102; see also Werner 1966, pp. 199–210; Norris 1986, pp. 16–24. On Christianity in Sardis see Johnson 1961, pp. 81–9; Hanfmann 1983, p. 191–204; Foss 1976, p. 30–4. The relatively small size and peripheral location of the fourth-century Church called 'EA' by the excavators indicates that the size and means of the Christian community at this time were limited compared with the Sardis Jewish community.
63 On the city see Stillwell *et al.* 1976, pp. 737–9; Bean 1966, pp. 197–219; Akurgal 1985, pp. 185–206.
64 On the synagogue see Wiegand and Schrader 1904, p. 287, Abb. 301, pp. 480–1, Abb. 582, 586; Tafel XXI, House XXIV; Goodenough 1953–68, 2, p. 77; Kleiner in *RE*, Supp IX, 1962, col. 1221; Kraabel 1968, pp. 24–5; 1979a, pp. 489–91; 1981a, p. 82; Ovadiah 1978, pp. 859–60; Levine 1981, pp. 165–6; Brooten 1982, p. 125. It was first identified as a synagogue by Schultze 1922, pp. 135–7 and Sukenik 1934, pp. 34f.
65 See Wiegand and Schrader 1904, p. 480; Kraabel 1981a, p. 79.
66 On the theatre inscription see chapter 7, section 4. On the building see von Gerkan 1921, pp. 177–81; Kleiner 1968, pp. 56–9. The following agreed with von Gerkan's identification: Sukenik 1934, pp. 40–2; Kittel 1944, col. 12–13; Robert 1958b, p. 45 n4; Ovadiah 1978, pp. 860–1; Smallwood 1981, p. 509. For the argument against it being a synagogue see Kraabel 1979a, p. 489; Brooten 1982, p. 125.
67 See Kraabel 1968, pp. 9–10; 1969, p. 87. Kraabel (1978, p. 32) also

notes: 'At Sardis at least, proximity appears to have produced clarity, and the enjoyment of a gentile culture did not automatically produce capitulation to "paganism"; the Jews are strong and self-confident, they have a firm grasp on their Judaism and they express it in their building, their inscriptions and even in their iconography. And that may have happened because there were so many pagans so very close nearby! Ancient religions may coalesce in art and literature, but that is a very different thing from what might happen between self-conscious and specific religious communities.' Some writers have thought that the Sardis Jewish community was highly hellenised; see Shanks 1979, p. 174; Mitten 1966, p. 64; Noakes 1975, p. 245; Foss 1976, p. 28. However, hellenisation is a very vague term; see Hengel 1980, pp. 51, 60–1. At Sardis there were close professional contacts between Jews and Gentiles and the Jews had adopted the Greek language and (in a discriminating way) Greek culture. Complete assimilation did not occur. We must therefore be very careful about speaking of Sardis Jews as 'hellenised'.

3 The Jewish community at Acmonia

1 Ramsay 1897, pp. 621–31; Calder 1925, pp. 8–11; A. H. M. Jones 1971, p. 71; Robert 1975b, pp. 153–5, 158. On the gold see chapter 1, section 5.
2 Text from *MAMA* 6, 264; cf. *CIJ* 766; S. Reinach 1888, p. 225, no. 13; *IGR* 4, 655.
3 Schürer 1909, p. 21; Lifshitz 1967, p. 36.
4 See Ramsay 1897, p. 639; Head 1906, pp. xxii, 6, 9–11; von Aulock 1968, 18, no. 8311; *MAMA* 6, 263; Schürer, Vermes and Millar 1986, 3.1, p. 31.
5 Ramsay 1897, pp. 639, 650–1, 673; see also Juster 1914, p. 430 n5; Blanchetière 1974, p. 379; Bruce 1984, p. 7.
6 *MAMA* 6, p. 48. On the name Tyrronius see *MAMA* 6, 264–5; Robert 1938, pp. 181–2; 1975, p. 159. Other Jews had Latin names; see, for example, Robert 1960b, p. 384; Ussishkin 1977, pp. 215–18.
7 Many scholars have come to this conclusion. See, for example, Groag 1919, col. 947–8; Walton 1929, p. 45; Lifshitz 1967, pp. 35–6; Kraabel 1968, pp. 74–9; Stern 1980, pp. 6, 382; Brooten 1982, p. 144; J. and L. Robert, *BE* 1983, p. 82; Schürer, Vermes and Millar 1986, 3.1, p. 31; cf. Kraemer 1986a, pp. 196–7. The many statements made about Jewish apostasy and syncretism on the basis of Julia Severa are therefore misguided; see, for example, R. McL. Wilson 1958, pp. 13–14; Oesterley 1935, pp. 128–9.
8 Levick 1967, pp. 106–7; see also S. Reinach 1888, pp. 225–6; Ramsay 1897, pp. 639, 648–51, 673; Walton 1929, pp. 44–5; S. Mitchell 1974, pp. 34–8.
9 On Sardis see chapter 2; on Dura-Europos see Goodenough 1953–68, vols. 9–11; Perkins 1973; Gutmann 1973; Hopkins 1979; Kraeling 1979; Levine 1981, pp. 172–7.

10 *MAMA* 6, 347; see also J. and L. Robert, *BE* 1939, p. 512. Note the similar plaques found in the Sardis synagogue; see Shiloh 1968, pp. 54-7.
11 See Lifshitz 1967, p. 36; Robert 1958b, p. 41 n1.
12 Parrot 1939, pp. 103-39; Lattimore 1942, pp. 108-18; Carrington 1976, pp. 260-81; Iluk 1979, pp. 279-86. On fines elsewhere see Liebenam 1900, pp. 43-53.
13 Lifshitz 1965, p. 535; Parrot 1939, p. 60. For other Jewish inscriptions from Asia Minor which used fines to deter violation see *CIJ* 741, 757, 775, 776, 788, 791. This participation in the general concern for the grave often makes it difficult to determine if an inscription is Jewish or not. On this problem see *CPJ* 1, pp. xvii-xx; Kraemer 1986a, pp. 187-92, 194.
14 On the gravestone see Ramsay 1914b, pp. 358-61; Robert 1955, pp. 249-51; *MAMA* 6, p. 116. Illustrations of similar grave-reliefs from Dorylaion in F. Noack 1894, pp. 315-34; Joubin 1894, pp. 181-3.
15 Text from *MAMA* 6, 335a; also in Robert 1955, p. 249; partially correct in Ramsay 1914b, p. 358 n2; *CIJ* 760.
16 Text in *MAMA* 6, 335.
17 Text in Robert 1955, p. 253. It was first published by Legrand and Chamonard 1893, pp. 263-4 n48 without comment; see also *CIJ* 770.
18 Ramsay 1914b, pp. 362-3; cf. *New Docs* 1976, p. 101; Reynolds and Tannenbaum 1987, p. 66.
19 For other Jews who held public office see chapter 8, section 3.
20 See Liebenam 1900, pp. 362-5, 539-42; Levy 1901, pp. 365-7; A. H. M. Jones 1940, pp. 215-17, 255; Magie 1950, pp. 60-1, 645-6. We know of another Jewish agoranomos at Jaffa in the time of Trajan; see Kaplan 1963-4, p. 113.
21 σειτωνεία means 'the office of σιτώνης'. On the title see Diehl and Cousin 1887, pp. 31-2 n45; Liebenam 1900, pp. 368-70; Broughton 1938b, pp. 55-7; Larsen 1938, pp. 344-8; A. H. M. Jones 1940, pp. 217-19; Magie 1950, p. 646. Titus Flavius Alexandros held the position twice. On Jewish sitologoi in the Fayum in 101/102 CE see *CPJ* no. 428. On grain in general see Rathbone 1983, pp. 45-55; Garnsey 1983, pp. 118-30.
22 παραφυλακεία means to serve as a παραφύλαξ. On the title see Anderson 1897, pp. 411-13; Levy 1899, p. 284; Robert 1938, pp. 99-104, 340; Magie 1950, p. 647.
23 See Liebenam 1900, pp. 286-8, 558-64; Chapot 1904, p. 240-3; A. H. M. Jones 1940, pp. 46, 163; Magie 1950, pp. 644, 844-6; see also chapter 5, section 2.11.
24 See A. H. M. Jones 1940, pp. 170-2, 176-81; chapter 2, section 4.
25 See Liebenam 1900, pp. 246-7; Chapot 1904, pp. 201-3; A. H. M. Jones 1940, p. 179.
26 See Levy 1899, pp. 282, 287; Chapot 1904, pp. 260-2; A. H. M. Jones 1940, p. 212-13; Magie 1950, p. 647. πάσας ἀρχὰς καὶ λειτουργίας τελέσας (3.1) covers the minor offices which Aurelios

Phrougianos fulfilled without listing them in full; cf. Robert 1938, p. 548; 1946, p. 33; Paris and Holleaux 1885, p. 76, no. 6; *SEG* 2.653. 'Archon' in 3.3 is a general name for a member of the magisterial board, the more specific designation 'strategos' is given at the end of the inscription. See Magie 1950, pp. 644, 1509 n37.

27 Compare Flavius Josephus, on whom Vespasian bestowed Roman citizenship; see Vita 422–3.
28 On the Constitutio Antoniniana see chapter 8, section 2.
29 See chapter 2, section 4.
30 Ramsay, 1914b, pp. 361–2; see also Frey *CIJ* 2, p. 25.
31 Kraabel 1968, p. 82.
32 We know that there was considerable Jewish involvement in magic in this period; see, for example, TJud 23; TJob 47:11; PrJacob; TSol; Acts 13:6–12, 19:13–20; *CIJ* 717; Simon 1986, pp. 339–68; M. Smith 1986, pp. 455–62; Schürer, Vermes and Millar 1986, 3.1, pp. 342–79; Robert 1981, pp. 5–27. On magic amongst Jews in Asia Minor see Acts 19:13–20; van Lennep 1870, p. 20; Pétridès 1905, pp. 88–90; Kraabel 1968, pp. 56–9; C. E. Arnold 1989, pp. 31–4. However, that the authors of our inscriptions were acting in accordance with Deut 27–30, as we hope to show, suggests that magic was not involved in these particular cases. We also know that the Jewish community at Acmonia used the LXX; see section 5 below.
33 On Deut 27:15–26 see particularly Buis 1967, pp. 478–9; G. Wallis 1974, pp. 47–63; Bellefontaine 1975, pp. 51–9. On blessings and curses and the treaty form see McCarthy 1981, pp. 2, 6 *passim*; Hillers 1964, pp. 6–40; Weinfeld 1972, pp. 83f; Levenson 1975, pp. 208f.
34 On the implications of this structure for the history of the text see Hillers 1964, pp. 30–40; Levenson 1975, pp. 208–12; McCarthy 1981, pp. 178–81, 194–205.
35 McCarthy 1981, p. 187.
36 See Levenson 1975, p. 208; Le Déaut 1981, p. 181; von Rad 1966; p. 183; Driver 1902, pp. 328–30; Mayes 1979, p. 368.
37 It is clear from Deut 30:1 that 'these curses' are those in Deut 27–9.
38 Philo in Praem. 127–72 follows Deut 28–30 quite closely, but includes some expansions. He interprets Deut 30:1–10 to refer to 'those who a little while ago were scattered in Greece and the outside world' (165). They will pass from exile to the land of Israel. God will turn the curses against the enemies of these people scattered throughout the world (169, with reference to Deut 30:7). We see therefore that another Diaspora Jew understood Deut 30:1–10 to be significant for his situation, and thus interpreted it in a similar way to Acmonian Jews, although without reference to grave violation. This confirms that our view is very likely. See also Praem. 115; Conf. 197; Som. 2:175.
39 1QS 2:11–18 from Qumran makes direct use of Deut 29:18–20a, consciously changing and extending it to fit the current ways of thought in the community; see Laubscher 1980, pp. 49–55.

A number of inscriptions from elsewhere either quote from Scripture or are heavily dependent on Biblical ideas and thus show the significance of Scripture for other Jewish communities in this period; see Klein-Franke 1983, pp. 80–4 (Egypt); *CIJ* 629 (Tarente); *CIJ* 821–3 (Palmyra); Lifshitz and Schiby 1968, pp. 368–74 = *CIJ* 693a (Thessalonica, Samaritan); *CIJ* 201, 370 (Rome); A. M. Schneider 1943, no. 68 (Iznik-Nicaea). Dependence on Biblical ideas in *CIJ* 725 (Delos); Lifshitz 1965, p. 535 (on Beth Shearim); *CIJ* 693b (Thessalonica); Petrie 1906, p. 124, no. 6 line 7, (Phrygia) may be Jewish. Another indication of the importance of the Scriptures for a Jewish community in Asia Minor is given by the new Aphrodisias inscription. The society responsible for initiating the building was called the 'decany of the students/disciples/sages of the law, also known as those who fervently/continually praise God.' The decany therefore was probably dedicated to the study of Scripture and to prayer, although they seem to be involved in other activities (such as the 'soup kitchen') as well. See Reynolds and Tannenbaum 1987, pp. 30–41, 125.

40 Even in inscription 3.3 the areas of action of the curse are specified but not what the curse involved. The four areas of curse specified are particularly prevalent in Deut 28; see, for example, Deut 28:25–9, 53–7. There is no indication that a Jewish cemetery existed at Acmonia and see further in chapter 4 note 71. On Jewish cemeteries elsewhere see Künzl 1981, p. 474.

41 Lattimore 1942, p. 109; see also Parrot 1939, p. 197.

42 On the title of Deut see Swete 1902, pp. 214–15; see section 5 for further evidence on the use of the LXX.

43 Robert 1955, pp. 253–5. One of the altars is also to be found in Wiegand 1911, pp. 291–4; another stone in the series in Drew-Bear 1978, pp. 84–7, no. 20; J. and L. Robert, *BE* 1979, no. 520.

44 Robert 1955, p. 248.

45 See Robert 1978a, pp. 245–52.

46 On Amphikles see C. P. Jones 1970, pp. 223–55; 1980, pp. 377–9; Robert 1978a, pp. 251–2.

47 Text from Robert 1978a, pp. 245–9; see also *New Docs* 1978, p. 124; C. P. Jones 1980, pp. 377–8.

48 Text from *MAMA* 6, 287; also in Ramsay 1897, pp. 653 n565 and incompletely in *CIG* 3861; *CIG*, vol. 3, p. 1094; *CIJ* 763.

49 γούντη is an enigmatic word only found at Acmonia. It may be Phrygian in origin; see Ramsay 1914b, p. 369 n2; Kubinska 1968, p. 154. The word, and the related γουτάριον found in *MAMA* 6, 277, evidently mean the grave or some part or accessory thereof. See Keil and Premerstein 1911, p. 137; Ramsay 1914b, p. 369 n2; *MAMA* 6, p. 101.

50 Text in Keil and Premerstein 1911, p. 137, no. 255; date in Kraabel 1968, p. 84. The text in *CIJ* 767 is incomplete.

51 Text in Paris 1884, p. 233, no. 1; *CIJ* 761. The name Onesimos, although found in the NT (Col 4:9; Phlm 10) and in Christian inscriptions in the area (*MAMA* 6, 32), is also found in pagan

inscriptions (e.g. *MAMA* 4, 257; 6, 246). The name is not an indicator of a Christian, nor of a Jew. Eumeneia, founded by Attalus II (159−138 BCE), was a leading city in the Apamean conventus and thus the Jewish population in the city probably contributed to the money seized by Flaccus' officials. On the city see Ramsay 1897, pp. 353−73; Ritterling 1927, pp. 30−1. Acmonia and Eumeneia, which were about thirty-seven miles apart, entered into a concord as is shown by Homonoia coins minted under Maximinus (235−8 CE); see Karwiese 1971, pp. 40−2; Robert 1975b, p. 155; in general Sheppard 1975, pp. 156−79. The Jewish communities in the two cities may have been in contact as is shown by their sharing this formula.

52 Text in Dörner 1940, p. 132, no. 12; see also J. and L. Robert, *BE* 1941, p. 260.

53 Ramsay 1914b, pp. 364, 369, complains of the grammar of this inscription. Kraabel notes that it is not faulty grammar 'but the familiarity of the curse formula which prompts a lapidary terseness' (Kraabel 1968, p. 84 n 1; see also Robert 1965, pp. 96−8). Note also the consistency of formulation of the curse, which suggests that the abbreviation is a standard one. The other inscriptions which contain the formula are *MAMA* 6, 277, 323 (Acmonia); *MAMA* 4, 27, 28 (Prymnessos). *MAMA* 4, 84, an inscription from Synnada to be dated in the first or second century CE, contains the phrase κατάρᾳ αὐ[τῷ γένο]ιτο εἰς ἐγ[γόνων] ἐγγόνους which is probably a variation of the children's children curse; see Kraabel 1968, p. 85; *MAMA* 4, 90 shows there was a Jewish community at Synnada in this period.

54 Kraabel 1968, p. 82.

55 On curses affecting children see, for example, Gibson 1978, p. 38, no. 15; and in general Lattimore 1942, pp. 112−14; Parrot 1939, pp. 118, 134−5. The phrase τέκνων τέκνοις occurs in a first-century BCE inscription from Triostomo, but it is not part of a curse and so is not relevant here; see Arkwright 1911, p. 273 n 29; Parrot 1939, p. 111.

56 See especially Ramsay 1914b, p. 364; J. and L. Robert, *BE* 1939, p. 511; Kraabel 1968, pp. 85−6.

57 See Ex 10:2; Joel 1:3; Jos 22:24, 27; Prov 17:6. Gen 45:10 in the LXX reads οἱ υἱοὶ τῶν υἱῶν σου, and thus is not relevant here.

58 On the passage see Freedman 1960, p. 154; Dentan 1963, pp. 36−51; Beyerlin 1965, pp. 137−8; Moberly 1983, pp. 86−8, 128−31. On Ex 34, see Childs 1974, pp. 601−20.

59 *SIG* Indexes, s.v. ἔνοχος. For ἀνομία in the LXX see e.g. Ps 31:1; Isa 5:7; Hos 6:9.

60 At least part of the passage is quoted in Nu 14:18; Neh 9:17, 31; Ps 86:15, 103:8; 111:4, 145:8; Jonah 4:2; Joel 2:13; Nah 1:3. It is echoed in Ex 20:5 (= Dt 5:9f); Dt 7:9f; 2 Chr 30:9b; Ps 116:5; Jer 30:11b, 32:18, 46:28b. On this see Scharbert 1957, pp. 130f; Dentan 1964, pp. 34−9; Fishbane 1985, pp. 335−50. The passage (or part of it) was quoted or alluded to in the Pseudepigrapha; see

JosAsen 11:10; HelSynPr 2:3, 4:2–3; see also 4 Ezra 7:132–8. TIsaac 1:8, 2:1, 26. On its use as a liturgical formula see Beyerlin 1965, p. 138; Stoebe 1952, pp. 249–50.

61 P. D. Miller 1981, p. 330.

62 On Jewish liturgy and prayer see Schürer, Vermes and Millar 1979, 2, pp. 447–63; Charlesworth 1985, 2, pp. 671–97; 1986, pp. 411–36. In the new inscription from Aphrodisias we learn of a ψαλμο(λόγος); see Reynolds and Tannenbaum 1987, pp. 9, 46. Another psalm-singer is known in a recently discovered inscription from Rome; see Schürer, Vermes and Millar 1986, 3.1, p. 81. The holder of this office presumably had a part in the general liturgical activity of the synagogue community. The extant Hellenistic Synagogue Prayers do not quote Ex 34:6–7, but Prayer 4:2–3 (see Funk 1905, 1, p. 428) seems to echo Ex 34:6 strongly. There were probably many variations in the liturgy of different Diaspora communities.

63 P. D. Miller (1981, pp. 330–1) has analysed inscriptions found at Khirbet el Qom and Khirbet Beit Lei which show that in the time of the Divided Monarchy another Jewish community utilised Ex 34:6–7 in its praise and worship. Those responsible for the prayer of Inscription B have re-used the traditional material in Ex 34:6–7 so that it serves a new purpose. We note the parallel with our present series of inscriptions. It is most likely that the process of inner-Biblical re-interpretation shown, for example, in the re-use of Ex 34:6–7 in Scripture itself has played a part in inspiring Jewish communities to utilise Scripture in their liturgy and inscriptions. On this re-use of authoritative teaching see also Fishbane 1977, pp. 281–6.

64 See the inscriptions given in 5.2 below.

65 This supplements our findings in 3.3 above.

66 Text in Herrmann 1962, p. 59, no. 54.

67 Kraabel 1968, p. 86.

68 There are other inscriptions which are perhaps to be related to this curse formula. One inscription which mentions a curse on the τέκνα τέκνων from Oenoanda in Lycia is clearly pagan (text in Heberdey and Kalinka 1896, no. 74). Three other inscriptions are similar but do not refer to a curse. They are from Cabalide in Lycaonia (in Heberdey and Kalinka 1896, no. 22), the plain of Karayuk in Southern Phrygia and Isbarta in Pisidia (both inscriptions in Robert 1978a, pp. 280–3). They are probably not related to the series given above because of the distance of these sites from Acmonia. It seems best to regard them as independent occurences of the formula.

69 Text from *MAMA* 6, 316; those in Legrand and Chamonard 1893, p. 271, no. 60; Ramsay 1897, p. 565, no. 465–6; *CIJ* 768 are incomplete. Side A was inscribed while Amerimnos was alive, side B after his murder.

70 Text in Ramsay 1897, p. 652, no. 563; *CIJ* 769.

71 *MAMA* 6, p. 111; Kittel 1944, col. 15–17; Robert 1960b, pp. 399–400; Lifshitz 1961, p. 404; Kraabel 1968, pp. 62, 87–8;

Drew-Bear 1976, p. 248; cf. Sheppard 1979, p. 173–4; Schepelern 1929, p. 87 n359.

72 Thus both Zech 5:1–5 and the inscription concern theft; see Kittel 1944, col. 15; cf. Kraabel 1968, p. 87.

73 Kittel 1944, col. 15; *MAMA* 6, p. 111. On the use of the LXX see section 3 above; note that Hebrew was perhaps used in part of the liturgy; see 6.3 below.

74 See H. G. Mitchell *et al.* 1912, p. 171; Björck 1938, p. 43 n1; Kittel 1944, col. 15. In Joel 3:13 (MT; LXX Joel 4:13) the δρέπανον is an instrument of judgement. It is possible that this verse in Joel inspired the translation of the Hebrew 'scroll' by the Greek 'sickle' in the LXX of Zech 5:1. The LXX of Zech 5:1 also considerably intensifies the penalty meted out.

75 Lifshitz (1965, pp. 532f) shows how widespread was the familiarity with Greek even in Beth Shearim. Use of Greek does not necessarily imply the renunciation of Jewish religious belief and tradition. In general see Lieberman 1965, pp. 1f; Solin 1983, pp. 702f; Safrai and Stern 1976, pp. 1040–60.

76 For the reading in Aquila and Theodotion see Reider 1966, p. 59. On Aquila's translation see Jellicoe 1968, pp. 74–83; Schürer, Vermes and Millar 1986, 3.1, pp. 493–9. It was in use until the seventh century.

77 The word is a synonym for house. Zingerle (1923, pp. 63–5; see also *SEG* 6.171) suggests that the word is ξενῶνα, a Phrygian correlative of οἶκος.

78 Text in Ramsay 1897, p. 654, no. 567; Zingerle 1923, p. 63, no. 3; *SEG* 6.171; *CIJ* 762.

79 See Ramsay 1914b, p. 364; Robert 1960b, p. 400 n3; Lattimore 1942, p. 115; cf. *CIJ* 762; Kraabel 1968, p. 89.

80 Kraabel 1968, p. 90; cf. Lifshitz 1965, pp. 535–6.

81 Text from G. Weber 1900, p. 467 corrected by *SEG* 6.172. It is considered as Jewish by J. and L. Robert, *BE* 1954, p. 103.

82 Kraabel 1968, p. 90.

83 Text in *MAMA* 6, 325; Robert 1960b, p. 407. Legrand and Chamonard 1893, p. 273, no. 63; and Ramsay 1897, p. 615, no. 526 are incomplete.

84 See Moulton, Geden and Moulton 1978, p. 703; Hatch and Redpath 1897, pp. 1008–10. The 'anger of God' (or 'of the Lord') is often referred to in the Pseudepigrapha; see ApZeph 12; Sib Or 3:632; 4:159–70; TIsaac 4:54; TLevi 6:11; TReub 4:4; LAE (Vita) 15–6, 49; PrMan 5, 13; 1 En 89:33, 99:16; Jub 15:34; cf. Ign. Eph 11:2; Shep. Hermas Vis. 1.3.1. For references to judgement in Jewish and Christian inscriptions see Robert 1960b, pp. 401–7.

85 The Christian inscription from Acmonia is ˙*MAMA* 6, 336, but it contains the Eumeneian formula which is also used by Jews. *MAMA* 6, 340 is ninth century; the inscriptions in Ramsay 1897, pp. 562–8 are either late or only possibly Christian. On this scarcity of Christian inscriptions in Acmonia, see Robert 1960b, pp. 409–10; Sheppard 1979, p. 174. The following think this inscription is Jewish: *MAMA*

6, 325; J. and L. Robert *BE* 1939, p. 511; Robert 1960b, p. 407; Kraabel 1968, p. 91; N. G. Cohen 1976, p. 120.
86 Text in Ramsay 1897, p. 520, no. 361; *CIG* 3891; Robert 1960b, p. 436.
87 Scourging in the LXX in III Ki 12:11, 14; II Chr 10:11, 14; Ps 72:4, 88:33; Jer 6:7; Isa 50:6; Sir 23:11, 28:17; II Macc 7:1, 37; IV Macc 6:3, 6; Job 21:9; see also Juster 1914, 2, pp. 161–2. In the Mishnah see Makk 1:1–3, 3:1–15; also San 1:2; and see Kraabel 1968, p. 69. Apollinarius of Hierapolis, in a tractate against Montanism preserved by Eusebius in *HE* 5.16.12, writes that Orthodox Christians but not Montanists were scourged in the synagogues of the Jews in the late second century CE in Phrygia.
88 See Matt 20:19; Mk 10:34; Lk 18:32; Acts 22:24–5; Heb 11:36 cf. 12:6.
89 See section 3 above, and chapter 8, section 3.
90 Robert 1960b, pp. 436–9; Kraabel 1968, p. 69 think the inscription is Jewish; see also Sheppard 1979, p. 175. Cumont 1895, p. 276; no. 146; Schultze 1922, p. 467; Parrot 1939, p. 133; Lattimore 1942, p. 111; Ramsay 1897, pp. 520–1 think the inscription Christian.
91 Text from Ramsay 1897, pp. 562–4, nos. 455–7 with date.
92 Ramsay 1883, p. 400; 1888, p. 406 thought it was Christian because of its use of the Eumeneian formula which he thought was always Christian. The following authors agreed with Ramsay: Cumont 1895, p. 277, no. 164; Perdrizet 1900, p. 302; Schepelern 1929, pp. 84, 87; Nilsson 1920, col. 1114.
93 The literature on δικαιοσύνη is large; note the following: Dodd 1935, pp. 45–59; Bultmann 1964, pp. 12–16; Hill 1967, pp. 82–162; Käsemann 1969, pp. 168–82; Ziesler 1972, pp. 1f; Soards 1985, pp. 104–9. In the LXX see, for example, Dt 33:21; Ps 49:6, 118:7, 62, 75, 142; Isa 5:19. In the NT see Acts 17:31; James 1:20. δικαιοσύνη is also frequently found in the intertestamental literature; see PssSol 2:15, 4:24, 8:24–6, 9:4, 5; Wis 5:18, 12:16; 1En 13:10, 14:1; Fiedler 1970, pp. 120–43.
94 Robert 1960b, pp. 409–12; see also J. and L. Robert *BE* 1954, p. 103.
95 See Calder 1939a, pp. 15–26; 1955, pp. 25–7; Robert 1960b, pp. 399–406, 412–13; see also Cumont 1895, pp. 252–6; Ramsay 1897, pp. 496–8, 514–16, 653. Pagans could use expansions of the formula as examples from Kabalide, Lycia (see Schepelern 1929, p. 87) and Termessos, Pisidia (see *TAM* 3, 331, 345, 365 etc.) show. However, in Asia Minor there is a strong individuality in style of inscriptions in each small district. The lack of pagan examples from Phrygia shows that the formula is limited to Jews and Christians in this area. Schepelern 1929, p. 87 and Waelkens 1979, pp. 126–7 overlook this. Other inscriptions using the formula could be Jewish or Christian; see *MAMA* 6, 225, 231; Sterrett 1888, pp. 153–4, no. 138; Legrand and Chamonard 1893, p. 248, no. 19; Ramsay 1897, no. 353–4, 369, 388. The common use of the formula suggests some contacts between Jews and Christians in this period.

96 See note 85 above.
97 Robert 1960b, p. 411 nn 1–3; 1963b, Index; Zgusta 1964, p. 279 and n 20; see also *CIJ* 1275 (Jerusalem); Μαθάς in *CIJ* 1061 (Beth Shearim).
98 On γειτοσύνη see Robert 1960b, p. 410 n 1. The emendation suggested by Vattioni 1977, pp. 28–9 is unlikely.
99 On burial societies see Dill 1905, pp. 256–63; MacMullen 1974, pp. 78–9.
100 Ramsay 1888, pp. 407–8.
101 Societies were generally united by the worship of a deity; see Dill 1905, p. 263. The inscription is evidence for some sort of Jewish area in the city near the 'First Gate'; see Seston 1967, p. 289 n 2. This does not mean that Jews were forced to live there, nor that only Jews lived in this area. The following think the inscription is Jewish: Robert 1960b, pp. 409–12; Kraabel 1968, pp. 109–14; Safrai and Stern 1974, p. 484.
102 Kraabel 1968, p. 114. The society may have dealt with matters other than those concerned with burial. We know very little about Jewish burial societies in this period; see the discussion in Reynolds and Tannenbaum 1987, pp. 29–30 who note the probable example from Beth Shearim. Another possible example is *CPJ* 138. The rarity of Jewish burial societies highlights the notable position of the Jewish community at Acmonia.
103 Robert 1950, p. 92; Nilsson 1920, col. 1111; Collart 1931, p. 58.
104 R.O. Fink *et al.* 1940, p. 119; Robert 1950, p. 92; 1975b, p. 158. The custom was adopted by local people and is not evidence for the dispersion of Italians; cf. Perdrizet 1900, p. 303; Nilsson 1951a, p. 121; Collart 1931, p. 58.
105 Lattimore 1942, pp. 137–40; Fränkel 1890, pp. 264–6; Perdrizet 1900, pp. 300–2; Nilsson 1920, col. 1111–15; 1951b, pp. 312–19; Seyrig 1928, pp. 275–7; cf. Picard and Avezou 1914, pp. 47–62 refuted in Collart 1931, pp. 60–9; Lemerle 1936, pp. 341–2. On the 'Rosalia Signorum' celebrated by the garrison at Dura-Europos, see Hoey 1937, pp. 15–35; R.O. Fink *et al.* 1940, pp. 115–20.
106 ἀπόκαυσις or παράκαυσις are used in the inscriptions when a sacrifice of some sort is involved; see Lemerle 1936, pp. 341–2 and n 3. In Thrace where the festival was originally linked to the Dionysios cult it survived the decline of the cult, because it was a general celebration which had lost any distinctively religious character. See Nilsson 1920, cols. 1112–14; 1951a, pp. 121–2; Robert 1960b, p. 412. Mishnah Ohol. 2:4 states that grave stones convey uncleanness; see also Ohol. 17:1–18:6 on grave areas. However, we cannot use rabbinic evidence to prescribe what Jews could or could not do in Asia Minor.
107 See Collart 1930, p. 387 and n 3; Laum 1914, 1, p. 87. A bequest in Laum 1914, 2, no. 202; land or vineyard in *SEG* 31, 1679; Collart 1930, p. 388.
108 Text in Laum 1914, 2, no. 173; see also Cumont 1913, p. 155; Broughton 1938a, p. 771; Laum 1914, 1, p. 86.

109 Kraabel 1968, p. 113.
110 Robert 1960b, p. 412.
111 Text in Ramsay 1897, p. 651, no. 561; *CIJ* 771.
112 This stone is probably to be dated after 135 CE and so it is unlikely that πατρίς refers to the Jews of Palestine as a 'fatherland'.
113 See, for example, *CIJ* 754; Lifshitz 1967, nos. 31, 32, 100.
114 For Josephus see Rengstorf 1968f, 3, p. 360. Philo in Flacc. 46.
115 See *MAMA* 6, 40, 41, 73, 79, 98, etc; SEG 2, 653; *IGR* 4, 1230; Ramsay 1897, pp. 722–3 (the epitaph of Avircus, bishop of Hierapolis, on which see Wischmeyer 1980, pp. 22f).
116 This is the meaning favoured by Ramsay 1897, p. 652; Oehler 1909, p. 534; Kittel 1944, col. 13; cf. Krauss 1922, p. 233; Lifshitz 1967, p. 36.
117 For other Jews in Asia Minor who made donations to their city see chapter 8, section 3.
118 Text in *MAMA* 6, 334. No date has been given for this inscription. See the similar Hebrew inscriptions in *CIJ* 973–4; cf. also *CIJ* 1175, 1391, which suggest that Sukenik's reading is likely.
119 Sardis and Smyrna are the only other Jewish communities in Asia Minor where Hebrew has been discovered in inscriptions; see Robert 1964, p. 57; chapter 2, section 4; *CIJ* 739, cf. 756a. 'Shalom' is common, on which see Dinkler 1974, pp. 121–44; more generally see Lifshitz 1965, pp. 520–38; Lieberman 1965, pp. 1f; Klein-Franke 1983, pp. 80–4; Schwartz 1984, pp. 141–2. The rarity of Hebrew inscriptions in Asia Minor is not unusual.
120 See *MAMA* 6, 334; cf. *SEG* 32.1485. Prayers were probably normally in Greek; see Lieberman 1965, pp. 29–37; Schürer, Vermes and Millar 1986, 3.1, pp. 142–4. This does not preclude prayer in Hebrew also.
121 Lifshitz 1965, pp. 537–8; see also Dinkler 1974, p. 135. The suggested reconstruction of the Greek phrase as 'Undertake prayers' would fit in well with the stone being part of the door frame of the synagogue.
122 For other inscriptions from Acmonia see chapter 6, no. 4.6, 5.1. Other Jewish evidence from the area is given in Ramsay 1897, no. 691 (Dokimion); no. 562 = *CIJ* 764 (Diokleia); *MAMA* 6, 339 (Acmonia, Christian or Jewish).
123 Some of the undated inscriptions may belong to the second century.

4 The Jewish community at Apamea

1 On the city see Ramsay 1897, pp. 396–450; Leclercq 1924, cols. 2500–7; Tcherikover 1927, pp. 32, 155; Magie 1950, pp. 125f; G. M. Cohen 1978, pp. 38, 88. Celaenae's history goes back at least to the Lydian period.
2 See Hogarth 1888, pp. 343–9; Hirschfeld 1894, cols. 2664–5; Imhoof-Blumer 1901, p. 211; Strabo xii, 8, 15 wrote that Apamea was 'A great emporium of Asia ... and ranks second only to Ephesus'.

3 Ramsay 1897, p. 422; Leclercq 1924, col. 2501; Magie 1950, pp. 19, 126.
4 Dio Chrysostom *Orat.* xxxv; Ramsay 1897, pp. 427–31, 445–50.
5 On settlement by Seleucid kings see Ant 12:119, 16:160–1; CAp 2:39, on which see chapter 8, section 1. On Zeuxis see Ant 12:147–53; Robert 1962, p. 282 n1; and chapter 1, section 1.
6 The uniqueness of the coins is noted by Calder 1922, p. 209; Meshorer 1981, p. 38. Scholars who see them as the result of 'Jewish influence' include Babelon 1891, p. 176; Schürer 1904, p. 94; 1909, p. 18; Juster 1914, 1, p191 n19; Schalit in *EJ* 3, 747; Lietzmann 1938, p. 143; Malten 1939, p. 188; Schmidtke 1950, col. 601; Klauser 1961, p. 143; Meeks 1983, p. 210 n228; J. P. Lewis 1984, p. 231; Den Boeft and Bremmer 1985, p. 117. See also the longer treatments in Madden 1866; A. Reinach 1913; Kindler 1971. It is unlikely that the coins are the result of Christian influence as Madden 1866, pp. 207–13 argued; see Schürer 1892, p. 54; 1909, p. 19.
7 In depictions of Danae and Perseus, and of Auge and Telephus, Danae and Auge both floated across the sea in a box; see Ramsay 1897, p. 670; J. Fink 1955, p. 4 and plates 1–3. In the Mosaic of the Church or Synagogue at Mopsuestia, Cilicia, the Ark is also depicted as a box; see Levine 1981, pp. 186–7; Ovadiah 1978, pp. 846–8.
8 Grabar 1951, p. 11; J. Fink 1955, p. 4, plates 10f; Toynbee 1967, p. 316.
9 Babelon 1891, p. 181; Goodenough 1953–68, 2, p. 120. For the debate about the coins as evidence for Jewish figurative art see Grabar 1951, pp. 10–14; Dinkler 1953, p. 324; J. Fink 1955, pp. 4, 9, 14, 104; Hooyman 1958, pp. 113f; Klauser 1961, pp. 142–5; Strauß 1966, pp. 134–6 n28; Franke 1973, pp. 171f.
10 Grabar 1951, p. 11.
11 Babelon 1891, p. 181; Svoronos and Head 1976, p. 49.
12 Pilcher 1903, p. 226.
13 von Aulock 1964, 9, no. 3506.
14 Kindler 1971, pp. 24–5, who lists the five known specimens. That Alexander was a Jew (as argued by Ramsay 1897, p. 672; Pilcher 1903, pp. 250–3; Grabar 1951, p. 12) is highly unlikely, since he was high priest of the city. Although some Jews did apostasise, we can only postulate that this occurred in cases where there is explicit evidence, which is lacking in this case.
15 von Aulock 1964, 9, no. 3513.
16 Schultze, 1922, p. 455; Ramsay 1897, pp. 431–6 and plates 1 and 5. The coins of Apamea bear a wide range of deities; for example, Dionysos, Athena and Artemis. On 'local types' on coinage see Carrington 1976, pp. 287–90.
17 Ramsay 1897, p. 432; Grabar 1951, p. 11. The coins show sufficient variations to suggest that they are not all struck from the same die; see Ramsay 1897, p. 669. The last coin in the series reverses the two scenes.
18 Ramsay 1897, pp. 432–3. He has been followed by Head 1906,

p. xxxix; Grabar 1951, p. 13; Dinkler 1953, p. 324; Kindler 1971, p. 29; Kraabel 1983, p. 181. Ramsay also noted that such painted Stoas were common in the Roman period, for example, at Thyateira and suggested that since statues often influenced coin types, it is probable that paintings could have likewise influenced coinage.

19 See, for example, Ovid, *Metam* i 125–415; Apollodorus, *Biblio* I, 7, 2. See Frazer 1919, pp. 146–59.

20 See Suidas s.v. Νάνvακος; Zenobius *Cent*, vi, 10 in Leutsch and Schneidewin 1839, 1, p. 164; Stephanus Byzantium s.v. Ἰκόνιον. Nannakos is also mentioned by Apostolius *Cent*, xv, 100; and Macarius *Cent*, ii, 23; viii, 4.

21 On original Phrygian charactes see Fontenrose 1945, pp. 110, 113. On the *Mimes* of Herondas see Nairn 1904, p. 31; *Mimes* III 1.10; see also Dossin 1963, p. 336.

22 Scholars who think that Nannakos was the Biblical Enoch include Madden 1866, pp. 211–2; Babelon 1891, p. 180; Schürer 1904, p. 94; 1909, pp. 19–20; Frazer 1919, p. 156 n1; Bousset 1926, p. 493 n1; Kittel 1944, cols. 15–16. Nannakos lived for 300 years, Enoch for 365 years. For Enoch's prophecies see 1 En 106:13–19; 2 En 33:12, 34:2–3. Both Nannakos and Annakos are good Greek names; see Paton and Hicks 1891, no. 10 c51; no. 160. Thus Annakos is not necessarily a Grecising of the Semitic Enoch.

23 Calder 1924a, pp. 31–2; 1924b, p. 113; Scherling 1935, col. 1681; Stern 1974, pp. 452–3.

24 Ovid *Metam* viii, 618–724. This is the only source for the story except for the summary in Lactantius. For a detailed analysis see Malten 1939, pp. 176–206; Fontenrose 1945, pp. 93–119; Calder 1922, pp. 207–11; Hollis 1970, pp. 106–27. Calder notes that in only one other story in the *Metamorphoses* does Ovid emphasise the veracity of the story to such an extent.

25 Fontenrose 1945, p. 118; Calder 1922, pp. 208–11; 1930, p. 88.

26 Nonnos, *Dionysiaca* 13, 522–45; 37, 649; see Malten 1939, p. 187 n5; Fontenrose 1945, p. 105.

27 Plutarch, *Parall*, 5; it is also found in Stobaeus. On the story see Ramsay 1897, pp. 415, 672; A. Reinach 1913, pp. 10–14; 1915, pp. 326–8.

28 Babelon 1891, pp. 176–83 has argued that the Phrygian flood legend was derived from the Jews. He has been followed by Schürer 1909, p. 19; and Leclercq 1924, col. 2510; Schürer, Vermes and Millar 1986, 3.1, pp. 29–30. His argument that Nannakos was the Biblical Enoch does not stand and he ignores the other three indigenous flood legends which were not created by the Jews.

29 Fontenrose 1945, p. 105.

30 Strabo xii, 8, 13; Pliny (23–79 CE) N.H.V, 106; Ptolemy (fl. 127–148 CE) v, 2, 17. LSJ, p. 950 record no instance in which κιβωτός means 'ark' except in Jewish and Christian writings.

31 Coins with five chests in Head 1906, p. 96, no. 155 and pl. xi, 10; Imhoof-Blumer 1901, p. 211, no. 19; von Aulock 1964, 9, no. 3492.

With one or two chests von Aulock 1964, 9, no. 3493; and Imhoof-Blumer 1901, p. 212, no. 20.

32 See Hatch and Redpath 1897, pp. 763–4; J. P. Lewis 1968, p. 87. It is also used for the ark of the covenant and for the Torah shrine. An inscription from the Ostia synagogue mentions the 'κειβωτός for the holy law'; see *AE* 1967, no. 77.

33 Ramsay 1897, p. 671; A. Reinach 1913, pp. 17–19.

34 See Babelon 1891, pp. 174–5; Leclercq 1924, col. 2509.

35 See for instance Nonnos, *Dionysiaca* iii, 209f; vi, 367f; Apollodorus, *Bibliotheca* 1, vii, 2; Lucian, *De Dea Syria* 12; Plutarch, *De Sollertia Animalium* 13; *Hellanikos* fr 117 in Jacoby 1957, I, p. 135. Lucian in *Timon* iii does, however, use κιβωτός. Josephus uses λάρναξ for the Ark of Noah (see Ant 1:77, 78, 90, 92) and not the κιβωτός of the Septuagint (cf. Philo Plant. 43), which he does use for the Ark of the Covenant (see Ant 3:134). This is probably under the influence of the story of Deucalion in classical authors, which Josephus clearly knew; see J. P. Lewis 1968, p. 78 n4; and in general Feldman 1984a, pp. 794–5. It is possible that the translators of the Septuagint used the unusual word for the Ark – κιβωτός – precisely to distinguish the story from the Greek myth of Deucalion.

36 Head 1911, p. 666; see also Madden 1866, p. 210; Hirschfeld 1894, cols. 2664–5; Imhoof-Blumer 1901, p. 211; A. Reinach 1913, p. 18; Magie 1950, p. 984 n20; Goodenough 1953–68, 2, p. 120.

37 Ramsay 1897, pp. 671f; Tcherikover 1927, p. 32; see also Pilcher 1903, pp. 255–8.

38 Magie 1950, p. 984 n20; also Schürer, Vermes and Millar 1986, 3.1, p. 29.

39 Ramsay 1897, p. 671. This became clear to me on a visit to the site in April 1986.

40 Magie 1950, p. 984 n20; Goodenough 1953–68, 2, p. 120. Gen 8:4 describes the Ark as landing on Mt Ararat but does not locate this mountain.

41 See Malten 1939, p. 188.

42 The localisation of the Nannakos legend at Iconium in Stephanus of Byzantium had this sort of significance for that city. For a similar example from Aizani, Phrygia, see Lane Fox, 1986, pp. 68–9.

43 On coins not naming the figure portrayed see Head 1906, pp. 75f; 1911, pp. 666–7. The fact that we have a series of coins strongly suggests that the Noah story was officially accepted by the city as a whole, rather than that some of the mint-masters (none of whom seem to have been Jews) were sympathetic towards the Jews; cf. Baron 1952, 2, p. 24.

44 This point has generally been overlooked. For Noah alone see Gen 5:30–10:1; Ez 14:14, 20; Is 54:9; I Chr 1:4; Matt 24:38; Lk 17:27; Heb 11:7. For the whole group see Gen 7:13; I Peter 3:20, 21; II Peter 2:5. Geffcken 1902b, p. 49 thought the coins depicted Noah and the Sibyl, and he is followed by J. J. Collins 1983a, p. 331; 1984b, p. 377. The Sibyl is regarded as Noah's daughter-in-law in SibOr Prol 33; SibOr 1,287–90, 3,827 cf.

1,205,277; see Nikiprowetzky 1970, pp. 44f. However, the coins seem to follow the Biblical account (for example, in the matter of the two birds) whilst SibOr I/II is more closely related to Babylonian traditions; see Rzach 1923, col. 2148. It seems more likely that the coins are inspired directly by the Biblical text rather than by Sib Or I/II and that the woman is Noah's wife.

45 Philo, Quaest Gen ii, 49. She is named in Jub 4:33; the story continues in Jub 5 and 7. This trend is also found in Tobit 4:12; I Enoch 67:1–3; Sir 44:17; II Esdras 3:11; Ant 1:75–112, where she is not named. See J. P. Lewis 1968, pp. 10–81. She is similarly unimportant in Rabbinic literature; see J. P. Lewis 1968, p. 124.

46 On the flood in Christian art see Hooyman 1958, pp. 113–14; Franke 1973, p. 172; Kötzsche-Breitenbruch 1976, pp. 51–4; J. P. Lewis 1984, p. 224; J. Fink 1955, pl. 6–52. On the Trier sarcophagus see J. Fink 1955, pl. 53. On the catacomb in Rome (Chamber B of the newly discovered catacomb on the Via Latina) see Kötzsche-Breitenbruch 1976, pp. 51–4, pl. 4a; Stichel 1979, p. 87.

47 J. P. Lewis 1984, p. 238.

48 See note 45. She is also named as Naamah in one passage in Rabbinic literature; see J. P. Lewis 1968, p. 124. In the late Christian *Book of Adam and Eve* 3, i, she is called Haikal; see further Stichel 1979, pp. 54–88.

49 Fontenrose 1945, p. 104; cf. A. Reinach 1913, p. 19.

50 The identity of a group is connected with the 'hero figures' they revere. Perhaps the group identity of both the Jewish community and the city were to some extent connected with the same two figures – Noah and his wife.

51 It is significant that the Roman Christian community seems to have resisted embarking on this sort of re-interpretative process. Although the Deucalion and Pyrrha story was probably known to them, their representation of the flood story generally shows Noah alone; in only one case do we see Noah and his wife by themselves. This suggests a difference between the Roman Christians and the Jewish community of Apamea with regard to their relationship to their environment.

52 Geffcken 1902b, p. 50; Rzach 1923, col. 2152; J. J. Collins 1983a, p. 332; 1984b, p. 378. It is generally agreed that Books 1 and 2 constitute a unit; see Geffcken 1902b, p. 47. Ararat was generally identified with a mountain in Armenia; see Ant 1:90; Julius Africanus (*c*. 190–250 CE) records that some people located Ararat in Phrygia, although he himself placed it in Parthia; see A. Reinach 1913, pp. 179–80.

53 J. J. Collins assigns as Jewish 2, 154–76, 214–37; as Christian 2, 34–55, 149–53, 177–86, 190–2, 238–51, 264, 311; whilst the remainder can only be classified as 'probably Jewish'. See J. J. Collins 1984b, pp. 376–9; also Geffcken 1902b, pp. 47–8, 51–2; Kurfess 1941, pp. 160f. 2, 56–148 is a direct extract from the Jewish Pseudo-Phocylides l.5–69, 76–9 and was probably interpolated by the Christian redactor; see van der Horst 1978, pp. 64, 84.

54 J.J. Collins 1987, p.442. He refutes the third century dating proposed by Geffcken 1902b, p.49; see also Kurfess 1941, pp. 151–65; 1956, p.152; Bousset 1911, p.398. The Christian redaction should probably be dated no later than 150 CE; see J.J. Collins 1983a, p.332; Kurfess 1941, pp.162, 165. There is nothing to indicate the provenance of this redaction. The fact that Book I/II is not cited by Christian authors of the first three centuries (see Harnack 1896, 2 i, p.582; Schürer, Vermes and Millar 1986, 3.1, p.645), is not of critical significance with regard to the date of the Jewish substratum. That it was probably used by Book 8 (perhaps from Egypt, written between 175–95) shows that it did circulate to some extent.

55 Rzach 1923, cols.2148f; Kurfess 1956, pp.147–53.

56 J.P. Lewis 1968, pp.7, 21–2, 46; VanderKam 1980, pp.13–32. See, for example, Ez 14:14, 20; Sir 44:17; Wis 10:4–6.

57 Briefly noted by Rzach 1923, col.2147; Nikiprowetzky 1970, p.46; and others.

58 Jos Ant 1:74, 99. In Rabbinic writings see also *Genesis Rabbah* xxx, 7; BT Sanhedrin 108 a-b; on these passages see Ginzberg 1909f, 1, p.153; J.P. Lewis 1968, p.135. See another late text in Nikiprowetzky 1970, p.46 n5. For references to Noah as a preacher of repentance see J.P. Lewis 1968, p.37 n6; Ginzberg 1909f, 5, p.174 n19.

59 On 2 Peter 2:5 see especially Dalton 1965, p.154. See also 1 Pet 3:20, which may imply that Noah preached to his contemporaries. Noah as a preacher of repentance in *Apocalypse of Paul* 50, in Hennecke 2, p.794; see also the late Christian *Book of Adam and Eve* 3, ii, iv. Patristic references in Theophilus *ad. Autol.* iii, 19; Hippolytus, *Fragments from commentaries* 2/3; Methodius, *Conv decem virg.* 10, 3; Chrysostom, *Ep I Thess* c.4 hom 8.2; Augustine, *De catechesis*, 32.

60 Circumcision, food laws, etc. are therefore not in view. This is a 'pre-mission document', as is appropriate for the genre. To 'propitiate God' probably involved prayer, since sacrifice is not explicitly mentioned as it is in SibOr 3, 624–9. On ἱλάσκομαι see especially Dodd 1935, pp.82–95.

61 See Schürer, Vermes and Millar 1986, 3.1, pp.617–18, 627–8. The ethics encouraged by Noah's exhortation differ from the later Noachian laws, on which see J.J. Collins 1983b, p.144; on ethics in Diaspora Judaism see J.J. Collins 1983b, pp.137–74.

62 J.J. Collins 1984a, p.192; 1984b, pp.378–9.

63 A comparison with Jub 7:20–39, appealed to by commentators on 2 Pet 2:5 as a parallel to Sib Or 1, 125f (see, for example, Windisch 1930, p.94; Schelkle 1970, p.208 n1.) is helpful here. In Jubilees, after the flood Noah exhorts his grandsons to be righteous in order to avoid a judgement similar to the flood. This exhortation is therefore addressed to the Jewish community. By contrast, the addressees in SibOr 1 are Noah's contemporaries; the sermon is thus aimed at 'outsiders'.

64 See J. P. Lewis 1968, p. 34.

65 We may note here the parallel with Nannakos, who wept because his people were to perish in the flood.

66 On the Jewish and Christian origin of the formula see chapter 3 note 95. The three inscriptions from Apamea are Legrand and Chamonard 1893, p. 248, no. 19 = *CIJ* 773; Ramsay 1897, p. 534, no. 388; *MAMA* 6, 231.

67 Text in *CIJ* 774; Ramsay 1897, no. 399 bis; 1914b, p. 364 nix.

68 Ramsay 1897, p. 668; see also Pilcher 1903, p. 232; date in Juster 1914, p. 191 n19.

69 Ramsay 1914b, p. 365.

70 Ramsay 1914b, p. 361; Lifshitz 1961, p. 404 n25. For the inscription from Acmonia see *MAMA* 6, 335a, given in chapter 3, section 3.

71 There is no evidence to suggest that the inscriptions containing these grave curses were from 'Jewish cemeteries' or other places where it could be thought that the inscriptions would address only Jews. The only indication we have from Asia Minor of anything like a Jewish cemetery is the inscription from Tlos in which Ptolemaeus built a burial place for the Jews in the city; see Hula 1893, pp. 99–102; *CIJ* 757, revised in *TAM* 2.2, no. 612.

72 It is interesting to note that Den Boeft and Bremmer (1985, p. 117) suggest that the Martyrdom of Pionius implies that pagan listeners to Pionius in Smyrna would have known who Noah was and would have had a considerable knowledge of Judaism.

73 Hefele 1876, p. 299; for the date see Hefele 1876, p. 296; Labriolle 1952, p. 528.

74 Text in Hefele 1876, pp. 302–19.

75 Labriolle 1952, pp. 531–2; Kraabel 1968, p. 138; Simon 1986, pp. 323–5, 329–30.

76 Kraabel's view (1985, pp. 232–41) that the references in these canons to 'the Jews' are really to Christian groups which followed Jewish practices is unlikely. In the third century CE Martyrdom of Pionius 13:1, Pionius says 'I understand also that the Jews have been inviting some of you to their synagogues.' The context suggests that Pionius is referring to Christians, as Den Boeft and Bremmer (1985, p. 117) note; see also Hilhorst 1982, pp. 93–4. This suggests that the problem addressed by the Council of Laodicea in the fourth century was not a new one, and that it was quite widespread.

77 See Simon 1986, pp. 326–8; Meeks and Wilken 1978, pp. 19–36, 83f; Parkes 1934, pp. 163–6; Wilken 1983, pp. 66f. Other canons against judaising in the Apostolic Canons from Syria (nos. 64–5, 70–1); the Canons of the Council of Elvira in Spain (nos. 16, 49, 50, 78) show close contacts between Christians and Jews. Note also the evidence discussed in chapter 1, section 7.

78 Lightstone 1984, p. 131; see also Kraabel 1968, p. 139.

79 Wilken 1976, p. 74; Kittel 1944, col. 16.

5 The prominence of women in Asia Minor

1 Text in S. Reinach 1883, p.161; *CIJ* 741; *IGR* 4.1452. Brooten 1982 has made major advances in the study of these inscriptions.
2 On the date of the inscription see S. Reinach 1883, p.162; Brooten 1982, p.5. On the Jewish community at Smyrna see Goodenough 1953–68, 2, pp.79–81; Schürer, Vermes and Millar 1986, 3.1, pp.19–20; chapter 8, section 3. On the title see Brooten 1982, pp.5–33; Juster 1914, pp.450–3; Safrai and Stern 1974, p.492; Schürer, Vermes and Millar 1979, 2, p.435; S.J.D. Cohen 1980, p.25. More than one archisynagogos could serve at a given time. People seem to have undertaken the office through appointment, election or inheritance. The fact that it could be inherited (see *CIJ* 584, 1404) probably explains the unique occurrence of an archisynagogos aged three at Venosa; see *CIJ* 587. The child would probably become active at a specified age. The inscription does not mean that the title was generally symbolic. The title does occur in a pagan context, although this is rare; see *New Docs* 1976, no.5.
3 See Krauss 1922, p.118; Frey *CIJ*, 1, p.xcix; Bandy 1963, pp. 227–8.
4 The other two examples are section 1.2 and *CIJ* 731c.
5 *CIJ* 166, 619d; Kraemer 1985b, pp.431–8; see also Brooten 1982, pp.9–10; Irvin 1980, p.79.
6 See *CIJ* 265, 553, 744.
7 See Brooten 1982, p.7; Kraemer 1986a, p.196.
8 S. Reinach 1883; p.165; 1886, p.241; T. Reinach 1901, p.2.
9 See S. Reinach 1883, p.165.
10 See Brooten 1982, pp.30–1. Others accepted their views; see, for example, Ramsay 1897, p.650; Petzl 1982, p.134.
11 Baron 1942, 1, p.97; 3, p.17; see also Schechter 1896, p.317; Ginzberg 1902, p.86; Oehler 1909, p.531; Juster 1914, p.453; Cadoux 1938, p.402; Rappaport 1971, 3, cols.335–6; Swidler 1976, p.93; Schürer, Vermes and Millar 1979, 2, p.435.
12 Inscriptions in Brooten 1982, pp.157–61; the one exception is given in section 1.2. There, if Theopempte had received the title as a result of her donation, her son Eusebios would probably also share the title, but he does not. In one case, a woman built a whole synagogue for the community and although she was honoured by them, she did not receive a title; see section 1.4.
13 See Brooten 1982, pp.7–10; Kraemer 1985b, pp.437–8. On *clarissima femina* see Raepsaet-Charlier 1981, pp.189–212. On πρώτη γυναικῶν see *New Docs* 1976, no.25 bis.
14 We know that women exercised control over slaves; see Pomeroy 1975, p.130. That a Jewish woman had some wealth was not unusual. *CIJ* 740, 762–3 record women building tombs for their families or doing other work out of their own means. Women were often donors to the synagogue; see Brooten 1982, pp.157–64; also S.J.D. Cohen 1980, p.24. The archive of Babata from the Judaean

desert shows that a woman could amass wealth; see Nathanson 1987, p. 263. In addition, numerous women in the ancient world acted on their own initiative in financial transactions, as is shown by inscriptions and papyri; see *New Docs* 1977, p. 28.

15 See Kraabel 1968, p. 43; S. J. D. Cohen 1980, p. 26; Irvin 1980, p. 78; Brooten 1982, pp. 30–3; Fiorenza 1983, p. 250; Kant 1987, p. 698; van der Horst 1988, pp. 198–9.

16 Text in T. Reinach 1901, p. 1; *CIJ* 756. On the Jewish community in Myndos see *CIJ* 756a; 1 Macc 15:23.

17 T. Reinach 1901, p. 2. On the date see T. Reinach 1901, p. 1; Brooten 1982, p. 13.

18 See S. J. D. Cohen 1980, p. 26; Brooten 1982, pp. 32–3.

19 Reynolds and Tannenbaum 1987, p. 5; dating on pp. 19–22. A late fourth or fifth century CE date is possible but seems unlikely. The inscription will be also discussed in chapter 7, section 4.

20 Reynolds and Tannenbaum 1987, p. 101. Prior to publication see Brooten 1982, p. 151; Rajak 1985a, p. 255; Schürer, Vermes and Millar 1986, 3.1, pp. 25–6.

21 Reynolds and Tannenbaum 1987, p. 41.

22 See Moore 1927, 2, pp. 128–9; Goodblatt 1975, pp. 68–85.

23 See Reynolds and Tannenbaum 1987, pp. 93–105. On the use of Biblical names elsewhere see Applebaum 1961, pp. 35–6; *CIJ*², pp. 98–9; Lifshitz 1967, pp. 85–7; N. G. Cohen 1976, pp. 97–128. At Aphrodisias other names were favoured as the equivalent of, or having a resemblance to, well-known Jewish names; for example Θεόδοτος and Θεόδωρος as the equivalents of Jonathan and Nathaniel.

24 On the woman Jael see J. G. Williams 1982, pp. 72–5; Gottlieb 1981, pp. 197–200; Brenner 1985, pp. 118–21; see also Ant 5:208–9; Ps-Philo 31:3–9, 32:12.

25 See Brooke et al. 1935, p. 628. Rahlfs' edition favours 'Ιηλ.

26 Reynolds and Tannenbaum 1987, p. 101 also compare the name to the masculine name in IV Ezra 10:26. This reads יְחִיאֵל and is translated as 'Ιαηλ in the majority of the manuscripts, with 'Ιαειηλ, 'Ιειηλ, 'Αιειηλ and 'Ιαιηλ also being found; see Brooke et al. 1935, pp. 626–7. Again, it is very unlikely that 'Ιαηλ is original. We should also note that the fact that προστάτης is the masculine form of the title (cf. προστάτις in Rom 16:2) does not point definitively towards Jael being a man. The masculine form of a title is given a number of times to women about whose gender there can be no question. See, for example, section 1.1, 1.2 above, cf. *CIJ*² 731c.

27 See note 20 for those who have thought Jael was a woman.

28 On the meaning of προστάτης see *LSJ*, pp. 1526–7; Montevecchi 1981, pp. 103–6; *New Docs* 1979, pp. 241–4. The inscriptions are *CPJ* 3, 1441 (Xenephyris); *CPJ* 2, 149 (Alexandria, the prostates of a loan society); *CPJ* 1, pp. 101–2 n26, (Oxyrhynchos); *CIJ* 100 and 365 (Rome); *SEG* 29.969 (Naples). In the LXX it translates שׂר ruler (1 Chr 27:31, 29:6; 2 Chr 8:10), פְּקֻדָּה – overseer (2 Chr 24:11) and פָּקִיד – commissioner (2 Chr 24:11). See also

1 Esdras 2:12 (cf. 6:18); Sir 45:24; 2 Macc 3:4. In Josephus προστάτης means patron nine times (e.g. Ant 14:157, 444), leader nine times (e.g. BJ 1:633; Ant 7:376), and champion once (BJ 2:135). Philo uses the term three times with each meaning, e.g. Virt. 155; Abr. 221; Spec. I, 337 respectively. In the fourth century CE, John Chrysostom in *Adversus Judaeos* Homily 6 (*PG* XLVIII, Section V , 887) refers to archons and prostatai of the Jewish community of Antioch. He gives no information about either group but he does mention the archons first; see also Grissom 1978, p. 185. On the term in Asia Minor see Magie 1950, p. 59; on πρυτάνεις see section 2.5. On προστάτης as a patron see Reynolds and Tannenbaum 1987, p. 41.

29 See Safrai and Stern 1974, pp. 496–7; Reynolds and Tannenbaum 1987, p. 41; cf. Juster 1914, 1, pp. 442–3; Krauss 1922, pp. 145, 245; Frey *CIJ*, 1, pp. xciv–xcv. That Samouel was ἀρχιδ(έκανος?) (president of the decany, found here for the first time) does not help solve the issue, since he could be either a patron or a leader.

30 See *CIJ*, 1, pp. xciv–xcv.

31 Note that in Rom 16:2, Phoebe is described as being a προστάτις, the rare feminine form of προστάτης. In view of the fact that προστάτης involved an office in the synagogue, it is likely that Paul used the feminine form in Romans as a title. Translations such as 'helper' (RSV) are inadequate; it is better translated as 'patron' or 'leader'. Cf. *BAG*, p. 718.

32 Text in S. Reinach 1886, pp. 236f; *CIJ* 738; *IGR* 4.1327.

33 J. and L. Robert (*BE* 1960, no. 216) note that a genitive following the name of a woman is normally her father, not her husband; see also Kraemer 1986a, p. 197.

34 For the site see S. Reinach 1886, p. 238; date in Lifshitz 1967, p. 22. Donation of (part of) a building in *CIJ* 694 (Stobi; see Hengel 1975b, pp. 110–48); *CIJ* 766 (Acmonia); Lk 7:5 (Capernaum). P. Rutilius Ioses and his wife Visinnia Demo rebuilt the synagogue at Teos; see Robert 1940, pp. 27–8; Lifshitz 1967, no. 16. For women donors see Brooten 1982, pp. 157–64. Kraemer 1986a, p. 197 suggested that Tation might have been a non-Jew. However, if this inscription was mounted on the outside of the synagogue (which seems likely given its contents) then the phrases mentioning 'the Jews' are understandable and do not suggest that Tation was not Jewish.

35 The προεδρία is probably the equivalent of the πρωτοκαθεδρία mentioned in the NT; see Mk 12:39; Lk 11:43; Jas 2:2, 3. On Dura-Europos see chapter 3, note 9; on Delos see chapter 6, section 4.3; on Ostia see Shanks 1979, p. 168; Kraabel 1979a, p. 498; cf. Floriani Squarciapino 1963, p. 198. Similar seats elsewhere in Sukenik 1934, pp. 58–61; Chiat 1982, p. 336. The Qumran community had a hierarchical seating order in their assembly; see IQS 6:8–9, IQSa 2:17–22; Philo Prob. 81 (note that Philo is here discussing the Essenes). On pagan decrees see S. Reinach 1886, pp. 239–40; also Bieber 1961, pp. 70, 108–10, 172–4.

36 On crowns in the ancient world see Danker 1982, pp. 467f; Reynolds

1982, no. 4.12; 5.26, 29.11–12; Ant 14:304, 313. In Jewish inscriptions see Lüderitz 1983, no. 70, 1.17; no. 71, 1.23; *CIJ* 777, 1450; Bruneau 1982, pp. 469–75 (Samaritan inscriptions). In Jewish art see Goodenough 1953–68, 2, p. 17; 7, pp. 148–71. In OT see 2 Sam 12:30; SongSol 3:11; Ps 8:5. In intertestamental literature see 3 Enoch 12:3–13:2, 18:1–25; TBen 4:1; JosAsen 5:5, 21:5. In NT see Heb 2:7; Rev 4:4, 10, 14:14.

37 On wealthy women as benefactors see, for example, *New Docs* 1976, no. 25 bis, p. 111; *New Docs* 1977, nos. 16, 61.

38 The distinguished Julia Severa, a 'Gentile sympathiser', built a synagogue for the Jewish community in Acmonia; see chapter 3, section 2. Clearly, this Jewish community was willing to accept her as their patroness. A comparable case may be Pisidian Antioch where, according to Acts 13:50, the Jews had some influence over the women of high standing.

39 See Brooten 1982, Index; Eulogia from Malta in Kraemer 1985b, pp. 431–8.

40 See Brooten 1982, p. 44. Venosan inscriptions in *CIJ* 569–619, 619a–619e.

41 Archisynagogoi in Brooten 1982, p. 229 n 87. For Asia Minor three women title-bearers out of around 135 inscriptions (*CIJ* 738–800; J. and L. Robert, *BE* 1954, pp. 102–4; Kroll forthcoming (excluding very fragmentary inscriptions); the Aphrodisias inscription). For Rome, five women in 532 inscriptions (*CIJ* 1–523, 35a, 732a, 733a–733g).

42 See Brooten 1982, pp. 157–62 for thirty-eight of the inscriptions concerning women donors. The Sardis synagogue has yielded twelve inscriptions in which wives are co-donors; see chapter 2 note 15. This gives nineteen women donors from Asia Minor out of a total of forty-seven women donors. 135 inscriptions out of a total of 1,614 (using *CIJ* and *CIJ*^{2}, vol. I as a rough guide) come from Asia Minor. Pagan women were often donors to their cities in Asia Minor, either alone or with their husband; see Chapot 1904, pp. 159–60; Hicks 1890a, p. 126; Radet 1887, pp. 478–9; *SEG* 28.869.

43 The donor inscriptions from Asia Minor, excluding Sardis, are given in Lifshitz 1967, nos. 12–37; see also Brooten 1982, pp. 157–62 nos. 3–6, 24–9. Thirty-eight of the Sardis inscriptions are well enough preserved for us to judge exactly who had made the donation (see Kroll forthcoming). Twelve of these inscriptions mention wives as co-donors (see note 42). Only in the fourth century CE synagogue at Apamea, Syria do we find a higher percentage of women donors – sixteen out of nineteen inscriptions; see Lifshitz 1967, nos. 38–56.

44 Jewish inscriptions from Asia Minor also show that some women played active roles in the public lives of their families. For example, in Acmonia, Ammia prepared a tomb for her husband and paid for it out of her own dowry; see *CIJ* 763; also *CIJ* 762. Two married women were the owners of burial sites at Hierapolis (see *CIJ* 775–6; cf. *SEG* 33.492); it was husbands who generally owned burial sites

in the city. This suggests that women had independent financial resources; see Kraemer 1986a, pp. 194–5. With the close link between wealth and leadership in the ancient world, this evidence also suggests that some women had leadership roles in the Jewish communities in Asia Minor. Note also that no Diaspora synagogue known to us had a women's gallery or a separate women's section and there is no unambiguous literary evidence which requires or refers to separate seating as a regular practice in the synagogue. It is most likely then that women leaders would have been able to take an active part in the synagogue; see Brooten 1982, pp. 103–38.

45 Sophia on Crete; see Bandy 1963, pp. 227–8; van der Horst 1988, pp. 188–9.

46 Some scholars have noted this prominence of women in Judaism in Asia Minor; see Ramsay 1897, p. 673; Kraabel 1968, pp. 43f; Saltman 1971, pp. 47–52; Johnson 1978, p. 99; Kraemer 1986a, pp. 198–9. Saltman's suggested explanation (1971, pp. 47f) that there were two different waves of Jewish immigration into Asia Minor is unconvincing and does not fit the evidence; see Johnson 1975, pp. 98–100.

47 On Ben Sira see Trenchard 1982; and e.g. Sira 25:13–26, 26:5–12. On Philo, see e.g. Quaest Exod 1:7; Wegner 1982, pp. 551–63. On Josephus see e.g. CAp 2:201; Amaru 1988, pp. 143–70; Stagg and Stagg 1978, pp. 45–8. On the Rabbis see T.Ber 7.18; pBer 13b; Neusner 1979a, pp. 138–53; 1979b, pp. 79–100; 1980, pp. 3–13; Moore 1927, 2, pp. 119–35; Montefiore and Loewe 1938, pp. xviii, 502, 507–15; Loewe 1966, pp. 30–2, 49–50; Archer 1983, pp. 277–84. Note that Rabbinic Judaism was not a monolithic entity and there are positive statements about women. See also ApMos 32:1–2; LAE 9–11; 2 Enoch 30:17–18; TReu 4:8–5:6. In the OT a woman's primary role was as wife and mother, although there were a number of women who entered the male domain of political and social life; for example Deborah, Huldah, Miriam, Athaliah; see Bird 1974, pp. 41–88; C. Meyers 1978, pp. 91–103; Murray 1979, pp. 155–89; Camp 1981, pp. 14–29; Gottlieb 1981, pp. 194–203; J. G. Williams 1982, pp. 1f; Exum 1985, pp. 72–85; Brenner 1985, pp. 1f.

48 See Judith 8:9–34, 16:4–25; Skehan 1963, pp. 94–110; Craghan 1982, pp. 13–17; Craven 1983, pp. 49–61. On TJob see TJob 21–6, 39–40, 46–53; J. J. Collins 1974b, pp. 37f; Kee 1974, pp. 54–63; Charlesworth 1983, 1, pp. 829–34; van der Horst 1986, pp. 273–89. On Pseudo-Philo see LAB 9:5–6, 30–33, 38:2, 40, 50–51; Bogaert 1972, pp. 339–43; Nickelsburg 1980, pp. 55–60. The treatment of Rebecca in Jubilees 19–35 is considerably more positive than in the Genesis account. Note also the position of women at Elephantine among the Therapeutae and women such as Alexandra and Queen Helena of Adiabene. More generally see also Segal 1979, p. 135; Brooten 1981b, p. 284.

49 P. Paris *Quatenus Feminae Res Publicas in Asia Minore, Romanis Imperantibus, Attigerint*. Paris: Burdigale 1891; see also Paris 1883,

pp. 452–6; 1885, p. 339. Other authors have commented upon the prominence of women in Asia Minor; see, for example, Ramsay 1897, p. 673; 1906a, pp. 186–8; Levy 1901, pp. 369–71; Chapot 1904, pp. 158–63; Delling 1931, p. 10; Cadoux 1938, pp. 28, 403; J. and L. Robert, *BE* 1972, pp. 427–8; Kraabel 1968, pp. 42–50; Casarico 1982, p. 123; Fiorenza 1983, p. 249. There has been no detailed treatment since Braunstein.

50 On this see Lattimore 1942, pp. 299–300; Lefkowitz and Fant 1982, pp. 157–60; for an example from Pisidia see J. and L. Robert, *BE* 1973, no. 475. The present investigation is conducted on narrow lines. I do not investigate the question of the legal status of women in Asia Minor, nor do I seek to explain in detail how it was that the women discussed here were able to have an increased role in their cities; on this see van Bremen 1983, pp. 223–42.

51 On priestesses see Hardy 1970, pp. 265–7; Pomeroy 1975, pp. 75–8. The priestesses in the widespread cult of Isis, however, performed a role subsidiary to the male priests. See Kraemer 1983, p. 132; Pomeroy 1975, pp. 219–23. The study of women in Greece and Rome is a growing area which need not be dealt with in detail here. Some recent work has emphasised our lack of knowledge (see Walcot 1984, pp. 38–9) and the importance of avoiding generalisations (see Averil Cameron 1980, pp. 60–8; Harvey 1984, p. 46). Other helpful treatments with regard to the general area discussed here are found in A. J. Marshall 1975a, pp. 109–27; Averil Cameron 1980, pp. 60–8; Gould 1980, pp. 38–59; MacMullen 1980, pp. 208–18; Cabanes 1983, pp. 201–9; Kraemer 1983, pp. 127–39; Pomeroy 1984a, pp. 1f.

52 See Pomeroy 1973, pp. 133, 226; Kraemer 1983, p. 131.

53 Juster 1914, 1, pp. 457–8; Kraabel 1983, p. 188.

54 See the discussion in Smallwood 1981, pp. 133–6.

55 See Chapot 1904, pp. 161, 237; on his view see A. J. Marshall 1975a, p. 124.

56 See, for example, Levy 1895, p. 242; Abbott and Johnson 1926, p. 79; Gardner 1986, p. 264.

57 Magie 1950, p. 649.

58 Magie 1950, p. 653; cf. A. H. M. Jones 1940, p. 175. See on Magie's view A. J. Marshall 1975a, pp. 124–5. Note the parallel with the scholarly discussions of women ἀρχισυνάγωγοι noted in section 1.1.

59 Brooten 1982, pp. 8–9.

60 See Kearsley 1986, pp. 183–92.

61 Office holding by an Emperor in Magie 1950, pp. 470, 515, 1508 n34; by a deity or deceased person in Magie 1950, pp. 650, 839 n24; A. H. M. Jones 1940, pp. 167–8.

62 Magie (1950, p. 649) clearly sees the holding of office by a deity and by a woman as comparable.

63 *IGR* 3, 802; (see also 3, 801). Dating in Turner 1936, p. 13 n16. On Menodora see also van Bremen 1983, p. 223.

64 We should note that city life in Asia Minor developed spontaneously as various tribal confederations adopted an urban way of life, rather

than under the influence of central governments. Thus we do not find uniformity in the titles used for civic officials. See A. H. M. Jones 1940, pp. 46–7; Abbott and Johnson 1926, pp. 56–7, 72–4, 77.

65 See Turner 1936, pp. 7–19; Braunstein 1911, p. 58; Magie 1950, p. 648; Abbott and Johnson 1926, pp. 94–5; Chapot 1904, pp. 272–3.

66 A detailed search was made (in the case of this and all other titles dealt with here) of L'Institut Fernand Courby 1972–5; Marcillet-Jaubert and Vérilhac 1979; 1983; and *SEG* 26–34. Turner 1936, p. 17 n5 notes that there may perhaps have been δεκάπρωται in the Fayum in Egypt. Note van Bremen's comment (1983, p. 225) which applies to all the titles investigated here: 'Women appear to have rendered the same social, political and financial services to their cities as their male fellow citizens and they were honoured for these services in much the same way. Women thus seem to have encroached upon the traditionally sacrosanct, male dominated sphere of public life and city politics.'

67 Braunstein 1911, p. 56 lists eight; two more in *IGR* 3.794; *SEG* 1.393.

68 See *SEG* 1.393; *IGR* 4.984. On the eponymous demiourgos see Schoeffer 1901, col. 2860. The honour of the eponymous title is shown by it being given to Emperors; see Magie 1950, pp. 1508 n34. On the title in the earlier period see Murakawa 1957, pp. 385–415.

69 See A. H. M. Jones 1940, p. 311 n62; Schoeffer 1901, col. 2862. For the Mallus inscription see Ramsay 1882a, p. 143.

70 See A. H. M. Jones 1940, p. 220; Magie 1950, pp. 61–2. The gymnasium was a very elaborate centre and included not only places for exercise but also baths, lecture halls, rooms for general conversation and sometimes even a library. See A. H. M. Jones 1940, pp. 220–4; G. M. Cohen 1978, pp. 36–7.

71 See A. H. M. Jones 1940, pp. 221–5; Levy 1901, pp. 368–71; *New Docs* 1977, no. 82; Harris 1976, pp. 75, 78–9, 86; Magie 1950, p. 852 n36.

72 Braunstein (1911, pp. 29–30) lists twenty-nine women gymnasiarchs and Magie (1950, p. 1522 n55) a further six. The following may now be added: Keil 1939, p. 120, no. 3; Robert 1954, nos. 64, 67, 68; 1960b, p. 598, no. 3; p. 599, no. 4; J. and L. Robert, *BE* 1956, p. 152, no. 213 (gymnasiarch four times); *BE* 1967, p. 552, no. 623; *SEG* 17.575; *SEG* 31.958–9; Keil and Maresch 1960, cols. 91–2 nos. 17; Knibbe and Iplikcioglu 1984, p. 123. Casarico (1982, pp. 117–23) recently listed the women gymnasiarchs known to him; unfortunately he overlooked a number of inscriptions; see J. and L. Robert, *BE* 1983, no. 84. Robert (1960a, pp. 285–98) has shown that in three inscriptions from Mytilene, Lesbos, Julia Agrippina, the wife of Germanicus, was given the title γυμνασίαρχον εἰς τὸν αἰῶνα. This means that she had made a foundation, the interest from which was to pay for the expenses of the gymnasium. This is therefore a special case of a woman gymnasiarch; see also J. and L. Robert, *BE* 1983, no. 84.

73 Cyrene – *CIG* 5132 = *SEG* 9.58; Hermopolis – see Frank 1938, 2, pp. 684–5. The status of women in Egypt and Cyrene was probably somewhat higher than elsewhere; see Préaux 1959, pp. 127–75; Pomeroy 1984a, pp. 1f.

74 Woman gymnasiarch but not her husband in J. and L. Robert, *BE* 1955, p. 263 n202; but not her father in T. Reinach 1906, pp. 241–3, no. 141; *CIG* 2714, 3953c; Keil and Maresch 1960, no. 17; see also Braunstein 1911, p. 28. Both husband and wife with the title in Paris 1885, pp. 338–40, no. 21, 22; Robert 1960b, p. 598, no. 3.

75 On wealth see Pomeroy 1975, pp. 162–3, 198; on education see A. H. M. Jones 1940 pp. 222–3; Pomeroy 1975, pp. 137, 170–4; 1977, pp. 51–68; *New Docs* 1977, p. 56, no. 16; on sport see Harris 1972, pp. 40–1, 178; on earlier work see Lämmer 1981, pp. 16–23.

76 See J. and L. Robert, *BE* 1948, p. 201 n229.

77 See Levy 1901, pp. 370–1; see also Forbes 1933, pp. 22, 31.

78 See Braunstein 1911, p. 35. For the use of εὐεργεσία, for example, in this way see *SEG* 30.1640. See also εὐεργέτις used of a woman who was also a 'demiourgos' in *IGR* 4.984.

79 Robert 1960b, p. 599, no. 4; see also p. 598, no. 3. In two inscriptions from Attaleia a woman is described as γυμνασιαρχήσασαν γεραιῶν καὶ νέων καὶ παίδων ἀρετῆς ἕνεκεν; see J. and L. Robert, *BE* 1948, n229; *SEG* 2.696. This suggests that the woman involved actively fulfilled the office.

80 *IGR* 4.1325.

81 *IGR* 4.1323.

82 See Gschnitzer 1973, cols. 738–46 for a discussion of those cities in which it was eponymous; on the title see also Liebenam 1900, p. 291; Chapot 1904, pp. 209, 236–9; Braunstein 1911, pp. 49–50; A. H. M. Jones 1940, pp. 46–7.

83 See Gschnitzer 1973, col. 743; *IGR* 4.1167; Robert 1937b, p. 19 n1.

84 Braunstein (1911, pp. 47–9) did not distinguish between the eponymous and non-eponymous prytanis in his list. In thirteen of the inscriptions he lists the position is eponymous. To these may be added *IGR* 4.1687; Hepding 1910, p. 450, no. 31; Heberdey 1915, cols. 85–86; Keil 1939, p. 120, no. 3; Robert 1954, p. 117, no. 27, p. 173, no. 66; Keil and Maresch 1960, cols. 91–2, no. 17 (three women); Knibbe 1968–70, cols. 64–5, no. 6; J. and L. Robert, *BE* 1976, no. 585; *SEG* 27.743; *SEG* 28.857; *SEG* 29.1112 (and see *SEG* 16.721); *SEG* 33.936 = Knibbe and Iplikçioglu 1981–2, p. 146, no. 160.

85 Woman prytanis but not her father or husband in Clerc 1886, pp. 404–6; Knibbe 1968–70, cols. 64–5, no. 6; Keil and Maresch 1960, cols. 91–2, no. 17; 'πρυτανεύσασαν καλῶς' in Hepding 1910, p. 450, no. 31. Woman prytanis along with her husband or other relatives, for example, in Paris 1885, pp. 338–9; Robert 1954, p. 173, no. 66.

86 See Kearsley 1986, p. 191 n32; see also Levy 1899, p. 265.

87 On the πρυτάνεις as non-eponymous see A. H. M. Jones 1940, pp. 46–7; Magie 1950, p. 643; Gschnitzer 1973, cols. 783–90.

On Phocaea see Hiller von Gaertringen 1906, no. 64. In Phocaea in the Imperial period it became the title for members of the non-eponymous board of magistrates; see Gschnitzer 1973, cols. 733, 780, 786. For the three women in Thyateira see Braunstein 1911, p. 49; Keil and Premerstein 1911, no. 47 = *IGR* 4.1232. On the title there see Gschnitzer 1973, col. 736.

88 On the wide use of the title see Gschnitzer 1973, cols. 730–816. That it was never given to a woman outside of Asia Minor see Braunstein 1911, p. 50; Gschnitzer 1973, col. 745.

89 On the title see A. H. M. Jones 1940, pp. 46–7, 234–5; Hiller von Gaertringen 1906, no. 208; Robert 1938, p. 134; MacMullen 1980, p. 213. MacMullen notes (p. 215): 'It was the deference secured forever from one's fellow citizens through one's being, for only a day, or for only a few days in a year, at the head of the parade or in front of crowds and thereafter known by a new title and memorialized in stone in the forum. Rewards of this sort were had ... quite as much through titular elevation as through the direct responsibility for executive decisions and quite as fully (though nowhere near so often) by women as by men.'

90 Braunstein (1911, pp. 53–4) lists twenty-six inscriptions, seven of which concern one woman from Aphrodisias who held the title sixteen times in all; see T. Reinach 1906, pp. 241f. Magie (1950, pp. 1507 n34, 1518 n50) lists nine further women. Now add Keil and Premerstein 1911, no. 165; Ins Magnesia 158 (see Casarico 1982, pp. 117f); Robert 1938, pp. 128–34; *SEG* 30.1349, 1354; 31.939; 33.851; Petzl 1982, pp. 65–6, no. 201.

91 Buckler and Robinson 1932, pp. 108–9, no. 111.

92 Hiller von Gaertringen 1906, no. 208.

93 Father: *LBW* 1630, 1634; T. Reinach 1906, p. 273 n168; Robert 1938, p. 128–35; Husband: J. and L. Robert, *BE* 1955, p. 263, no. 202 (non-eponymous stephanephorate); Husband and wife: *LBW* 1592, 1612; Paris 1885, pp. 338–40, nos. 21–2; Hicks 1890a, p. 126; Keil and Premerstein 1911, no. 165; Father and daughter: *CIG* 2714. See also Foucart 1887, pp. 101–4.

94 Ten are given in Braunstein 1911, pp. 54–5; add Keil and Premerstein 1911, no. 58; Robert 1954, pp. 172–3, no. 64, p. 173, no. 66, p. 174, no. 67 (a new reading of *CIG* 3953c), p. 175, no. 68.

95 Robert 1954, p. 174–5, no. 67.

96 It was held by men in Rome (*IG* 14.1020) and Athens (*IG* 3.1280a).

97 Magie 1950, pp. 653–4; Harris 1976, pp. 75–6; Liebenam 1900, pp. 373–4.

98 Twelve in Braunstein 1911, pp. 35–6; three in Magie 1950, p. 1523 n57; see also J. and L. Robert, *BE* 1956, p. 152, no. 213; *BE* 1972, p. 498, no. 522; Robert 1960b, p. 598, no. 3.

99 Women on their own: *IGR* 4.1183.1542; with other family members: Paris 1885, pp. 338–9; Foucart 1887, pp. 101–4; Radet 1887, pp. 478–9; *CIG* 3489. The inscription from Thyateira in Clerc 1886, pp. 410–11; see also *CIG* 3508. Also note that Pomeroy (1982, pp. 118–19) argues that the involvement of nude male athletes in

an event would not necessarily have been a deterrent to women being present at competitions and, by implication, to a woman being active as an agonothete; see also van Bremen 1983, p. 241 n63.

100 On its widespread use see Braunstein 1911, p. 37; Liebenam 1900, pp. 542–5. The Spartan inscription is in *CIG* 1444; on which see Braunstein 1911, pp. 36–7.

101 On the title see Magie 1950, p. 653; Chapot 1904, pp. 275–6. The panegyriarch was probably the director of the whole festival whereas the agonothete directed particular contests, although in some cities they may have been alternative titles. The inscription from Cnidus in *CIG* 2653.

102 On the title see Braunstein 1911, p. 57; Liebenam 1900, p. 554; Sève 1981, p. 193 and n12; J. and L. Robert, *BE* 1972, pp. 427–8 note that the title was eponymous only in Cyzicus. Women title-holders in Braunstein 1911, p. 57; J. and L. Robert, *BE* 1972, pp. 427–8, no. 287. Father who does not hold the title in *CIG* 3665 = *IGR* 4.154; no man mentioned in Mordtmann 1881, nos. 4, 10; J. and L. Robert, *BE* 1972, no. 287.

103 On the gerousia see A. H. M. Jones 1940, p. 266; Levy 1895, pp. 231–50; Ramsay 1895a, p. 110–14; Liebenam 1900, pp. 565–6. The inscription from Sebaste in Paris 1883, pp. 452–6; *IGR* 4.690; from Heracleia Salbace in Robert 1954, p. 174 n67; from Thessalonica in Robert 1954, p. 175 and n3.

104 On the title see chapter 3, section 3. The inscription from Aegiale in Braunstein 1911, p. 57; *IG* 12, 7.409.

105 On the Federations and the title of Lyciarch see Abbott and Johnson 1926, pp. 162–76; Magie 1950, pp. 1388–9; Jameson 1980, pp. 843–4. For the women Lyciarchs see *TAM* 3.1, 277, 485; *IGR* 3, 583–4; see also Jameson 1980, pp. 847–8. For the woman with the title of Asiarch see *IGR* 4, 1481; cf. Chapot 1904, p. 470 n4. On the title see Magie 1950, pp. 449–50. On the title of archiereia of Asia, see Kearsley 1986, pp. 183–92. For the two Pontarchs see *IGR* 3.97; Braunstein 1911, pp. 46–7.

106 I have not included the title ἄρχων in the text because it occurs only in the coastal islands and once in Histria. In nine inscriptions we find women with the title ἄρχων or its feminine equivalent of ἀρχίς; see Braunstein 1911, p. 42; *IG* 12.5.688; J. and L. Robert, *BE* 1960, p. 189 n322; Pleket 1969, no. 2. A woman may have held the influential position of γραμματεύς at Tralles; see Sterrett 1888, no. 390; Magie 1950, p. 1519 n50. I have not examined here the evidence about women in Asia Minor which comes from coins, on which see MacMullen 1980, p. 213.

107 We have found one gymnasiarch in Egypt and another in Cyrene, one agonothete in Sparta, one archon in Histria and another on Thasos; one woman was president (?) of the gerousia in Thessalonica.

108 See MacMullen 1980, p. 216; Abbot and Johnson 1926, pp. 86–7, 142–3; Sheppard 1975, p. 58; van Bremen 1983, p. 233.

109 On the general economic activity of women see van Bremen 1983, pp. 223–43; Mohler 1932, pp. 114, 116; Pomeroy 1975, pp. 130–1,

162–3, 198–9. Since a number of women held civic office well before it became a burden to be avoided in the third century CE (see chapter 2, section 4), we cannot discount this evidence by saying that women were able to hold office simply because they were willing to spend money in difficult times; cf. A. H. M. Jones 1940, p. 175; see also van Bremen 1983, pp. 226, 233f.

110 See a similar explanation in Ramsay 1906a, p. 187; Kraabel 1968, pp. 49–50.

111 Inscriptions from Smyrna in *CIG* 3150; *CIG* 2173 = *IGR* 4.1393b (the same woman is mentioned as stephanephoros in 83 CE in a coin given in Head 1892, p. 250, no. 132); Petzl 1982, pp. 65–6, no. 201; *LBW* 5 respectively. Inscription from Phocaea in *CIG* 3415. Inscriptions from Aphrodisias in T. Reinach 1906, pp. 241f; and see Braunstein 1911, p. 53. We have no record of women leaders in Myndos, the home of Theopempte.

112 Gold: chapter 1, section 4; inscriptions: chapter 4, section 5.

113 See further in chapter 8, section 3. The Jewish communities in Asia Minor had probably been established long enough for them to have been influenced by the local positive attitude towards women; on the founding see chapter 1, section 1. Various Christian communities in Asia Minor accorded a prominent place to women; note particularly the leading role played by women in Montanism and the importance of Thecla in *The Acts of Paul and Thecla*. See more generally Fiorenza 1983, pp. 245–50. Although this area is beyond the confines of our study, we can note that it seems likely that the practice of the environment affected Christian communities in this regard as it had the synagogues before them. This suggestion seems to be confirmed by the fact that women did not play a significant role in Montanism in North Africa.

6 Theos Hypsistos and Sabazios – syncretism in Judaism in Asia Minor?

1 Cumont 1906, p. 73; 1913, pp. 67–8; 1929, p. 99.

2 Cumont 1897, pp. 6–7; 1916, cols. 446–8; 1929, pp. 99–103. See also, for example, Weinreich 1912, pp. 43–4; Nilsson 1950, pp. 636–40; Widengren 1961, p. 64; Hengel 1974, 1, p. 263.

3 A. B. Cook 1925, 2, ii, p. 889; Robert 1958a, pp. 118–19; Nilsson 1963, pp. 106–15.

4 A. B. Cook 1925, 2, ii, pp. 868–90; Nock et al. 1936, pp. 56–9; Bickerman 1958, pp. 154–8; Robert 1958a, pp. 112–21.

5 See Nock et al. 1936, p. 59. For inscriptions mentioning Zeus Hypsistos or Theos Hypsistos see A. B. Cook 1925, 2, ii, pp. 876–90; 1940, 3, ii, pp. 1162–4; see also Kraabel 1969, pp. 88–91; Cormack 1974, pp. 51–5; Tatscheva-Hitova 1977, pp. 274–90; 1983, pp. 190–215; Peppers 1980, pp. 173–5. In keeping with the process of identification of indigenous deities with gods of the Greek pantheon, many local deities were given the name Zeus, and thus 'Zeus Hypsistos', along with other local epithets; see Nock et al.

1936, pp. 71–2; Simon 1981a, p. 495. Literary references to Zeus Hypsistos in Schürer 1897, p. 209; *TDNT* 8, pp. 614–15.
6 Nock et al. 1936, pp. 55–6; Schürer 1897, pp. 212–14. 'Theos Hypsistos' in dedications is sometimes identified as Zeus by the depiction of an eagle, one of the common symbols for Zeus.
7 Nock et al. 1936, p. 61.
8 For the inscriptions see A. B. Cook 1925, 2, ii, pp. 885–6; Seyrig 1933, pp. 248–52 (Syria); Nock et al. 1936, pp. 62–3 (Lydia); *New Docs* 1976, p. 28 (Egypt). Other deities who received the epithet include Sabazios, Men, Attis, Poseidon, Eshmun, Eshmun-Melkart and perhaps Helios; see A. B. Cook 1925, 2, ii, p. 889; Gressmann 1925, pp. 18–19; A. S. Hall 1978, p. 265; Tatscheva-Hitova 1983, pp. 212–15. Often it is impossible to tell which pagan deity is meant; see, for example, Robert 1937b, pp. 287–8; 1958a, pp. 112–19.
9 See Schürer 1897, pp. 214–15; Simon 1981a, pp. 496–502.
10 Text from De Jonge 1978, p. 140; See also, e.g. TSim 2:5, 6:7; TLevi 3:10, 4:1, 2, 16:3, 18:7; TGad 3:1, 5:4; TAsh 2:6; TJos 1:4, 6, 9:3; TBenj 4:5, 9:2.
11 Used by Jews see also 8:10, 14:7, 15:7 (twice), 23:10; cf. 9:1. Used by pagans speaking to Jews, see also 21:3, 4. Other instances of its use in the Pseudepigrapha include SibOr 2:177, 245 (which show the use of the title in Judaism in Asia Minor) 3:519, 574, 719; LAE 15:3, 28:1; TAb 9:2, 3, 8, 14:9; PhEPoet in Eusebius PE 9, 24, 1; EzekTrag in Eusebius PE 9, 29.14; 1 Enoch in 9:3, 10:1, 98:7, 100:4, 101:1, 6.
12 Quoting LXX in e.g. L.A. III, 24; Ebr. 105; Cong. 58; Mut. 202. Orders of Emperors in Leg. 157, 317. Schürer (1897, p. 216) thought that the term ὁ ὕψιστος Θεός served the Roman authorities as a way to describe the Jewish God. However, Philo does not profess to quote the Emperors verbally and it is probable that he is merely using language which he thought was acceptable. It is not therefore evidence that the Roman authorities used the term as an official designation for Yahweh; no other evidence from the period suggests this. See Nock et al. 1936, p. 67 n74. Celsus and Julian both used 'Theos Hypsistos' to refer to the Jewish God; see Cumont 1916, col. 446. Both of these authors were familiar with biblical usage and are thus not evidence that 'Theos Hypsistos' was an official Roman designation for Yahweh.
13 See Gen 14:18.
14 Jewish context in Lk 1:32, 35, 76, 6:35; Acts 7:48. Gentile context in Mk 5:7; Lk 8:28; Acts 16:17; cf. Heb 7:1; see Foakes Jackson and Lake 1920–33, 4, p. 193; Trebilco 1989, pp. 51–73.
15 The title ὕψιστος by itself (without Θεός, Ζεύς etc.) is rare in pagan inscriptions; it occurs at times (e.g. in Athens) along with other inscriptions from the same centre which make it clear which 'Most High' god is meant; see A. B. Cook, 1925, vol 2, ii, pp. 876–7.
16 See Simon, 1981a, pp. 496–502. On the very limited use of Hypsistos in Early Christian writings see Simon 1981a, pp. 503–8; and, for example, 1 Clem 29:2, 45:7, 52:3. Christian inscriptions occasionally

use Hypsistos of God; see, for example, *New Docs* 1978, no. 76 and p. 89; improved by J. and L. Robert, *BE* 1979, no. 363.

17 Cumont 1911, p. 227 n30; see also 1912, p. 165. Others have accepted his view; see Keil 1923, p. 263; Laumonier 1934, p. 337; Pouilloux 1976, p. 151; Fellmann 1981, p. 319.

18 Nilsson 1950, p. 637; see also 1960a, p. 180.

19 Such a relationship would be very unlikely in any case. Whilst we know that Yahweh was identified with other gods by some Jews (for example, with Zeus Olympius by the 'Hellenists' in 167 BCE (2 Macc 6:2) and with Zeus or Jove in the LetAris 16) this occurred very rarely, as far as we know. We need positive evidence from Asia Minor to suggest that Jews worshipped a pagan god, and this is lacking. See Kraabel 1978, pp. 13–33; Johnson 1984, p. 1607.

20 Anderson 1906, p. 211; note the apologetic motive. On Jewish influence as the main cause for the popularity of 'Theos Hypsistos' as a title see Cumont 1906, p. 73; Keil 1923, p. 263; Clemen 1924, p. 60; A. B. Cook 1925, 2, ii, p. 889; Kittel 1944, col. 16; R. McL. Wilson 1958, p. 13; Safrai and Stern 1974, p. 157; 1976, p. 712; Sanie 1978, pp. 1108, 1111–12; cf. Tatscheva-Hitova 1977, pp. 271–4; Sheppard 1980–1, p. 94.

21 A number of scholars have thought that the epithet 'Hypsistos' did not necessarily imply Jewish influence. See Nock et al. 1936, pp. 64–9; Robert 1958a, p. 119; Kraabel 1968, pp. 87–93; Pippidi 1974, p. 265; Drew-Bear 1976, p. 248; 1978, p. 42; S. M. Sherwin-White 1976, p. 187; *New Docs* 1976, p. 26; Lane 1976, 3, p. 94; Tatscheva-Hitova 1977, pp. 292, 295–300; 1983, pp. 203–4, 211–15; Bernand 1983, p. 111; Johnson 1984, pp. 1606–7.

22 Robert 1958a, pp. 118–19; see also 1969, 2, p. 1359. For a pagan dedication which shows that the title 'Theos Hypsistos' was part of the trend involving the popularity of abstract divine titles, see Robert 1958a, p. 111–20. On 'Hosios and Dikaios' see Körte 1900, pp. 431–4; Robert 1955, pp. 95–6, 106–7; 1978a, pp. 268–9; Drew-Bear 1976, pp. 249, 262–4 n68; Petzl 1978b, p. 268, no. 14. Note also the series of 'confession inscriptions' in which the dedicator confesses to some deed done against the deity; see Drew-Bear 1976, pp. 260–5. This is one aspect of what has been called 'the Lydian–Phrygian mentality', which involved remote deities and a strict piety and ethics; see Kraabel 1968, pp. 82–4; Pleket 1981, pp. 156, 178–81.

23 See Pleket 1981, pp. 188–9; cf. Robert 1978a, p. 268; Sheppard 1980–1, p. 98.

24 See Robert 1958a, pp. 120–2; 1971, pp. 613–14; Sokolowski 1960, p. 226; Johnson 1968, pp. 548–9; Kraabel 1969, pp. 83–4; Sheppard 1980–1, pp. 77–101. Some of the inscriptions are dedications to Zeus Hypsistos.

25 It is noticeable that this local trend was not recognised by early scholars in this field such as Cumont. They sought a local factor to explain the frequency of the occurrence of the epithet Hypsistos

and fastened upon Jewish influence. The popularity of abstract divine titles is a far more convincing explanation.

26 On Jewish provenance see Plassart 1914, pp. 529–30; Kraabel 1968, p. 97. A sufficient indication that a 'Theos Hypsistos' inscription is pagan would be the occurrence of a dedication to Zeus Hypsistos in the area. In this case 'Theos Hypsistos' would probably be another name for Zeus.

27 *CPJ* 3, 1433; 1443; Bernand 1983, pp. 107–11; now in *SEG* 33.1326.

28 Deissmann 1927, pp. 413–24; Plassart 1914, pp. 532–3; Cumont 1916, cols. 446–7; *New Docs* 1976, p. 29; Schürer, Vermes and Millar 1986, 3.1, p. 70.

29 See Plassart 1914, p. 532; on the dating of the building see Bruneau 1970, pp. 491–3; 1982, pp. 495–9.

30 (a) *CIJ* 727; first–second century CE; see also Plassart 1914, pp. 526–8; Lifshitz 1967, nos. 3–7; Bruneau 1970, p. 484 (where the dates given above can be found). (b) *CIJ* 728; first century BCE. (c) *CIJ* 729; first century BCE. (d) *CIJ* 730; first–second century CE. (e) *CIJ* 726; first century BCE. This inscription was found in a nearby building, but probably came originally from the synagogue; see Bruneau 1982, pp. 499–502.

31 Bruneau 1970, pp. 480–93; see Plassart 1914, pp. 523–34, for the case put forward originally that the building was a synagogue. This was challenged by Mazur 1935, pp. 15–24, whose objections have been fully answered in the ensuing debate.

32 Sukenik 1949, pp. 21–2 and Shanks 1979, p. 44 do not mention the Rheneia inscriptions in deciding that the building was not a synagogue, yet they are a vital part of the evidence. On Zeus Hypsistos on Delos see Bruneau 1970, pp. 240–1; A. B. Cook 1940, 3, ii, p. 1162. On the sanctuary on Mt Cynthus see Bruneau and Ducat 1965, pp. 150–2. The sanctuary is dated not before the first century BCE; even if it was built after the synagogue, it is unlikely that both sanctuaries were for 'Zeus Hypsistos', who was probably a local Baal rather than the Greek Zeus.

33 Mazur 1935, p. 21; Wischnitzer 1964, p. 11. Plassart 1914, pp. 529–30, thought it meant 'in the synagogue'. On προσευχή as a Jewish term see Robert 1958b, p. 44 n7; Nock et al. 1936, p. 65; Bruneau 1970, pp. 475, 488; *SEG* 32.810; cf. Sukenik 1949, pp. 21–2. See note 42 below on the rare pagan usage of the term, generally under Jewish influence.

34 This view has gained considerable recent support; see e.g. Hengel 1974, 2, p. 201 n265; Aupert and Masson 1979, p. 381; Künzl 1981, p. 464; Levine 1981, p. 166; Kraabel 1979a, pp. 491–4; 1984, pp. 44–6; Schürer, Vermes and Millar 1986, 3.1, pp. 70–1; Kant 1987, pp. 707–8; White 1987, pp. 133–60. There is nothing in the architecture of the building which would make it exceptional as a synagogue; the orientation towards the east, the three entrances, the seat for the synagogue leader and the well are all important features of synagogue buildings, although there was no standard synagogue 'type' in this period; see Bruneau 1982, pp. 490–1.

We would not expect any Jewish symbols at this early date; see Goodenough 1953–68, 2, p. 73. Two Samaritan inscriptions have been discovered recently 100 yards from the synagogue. However, the evidence from Josephus (Ant 14:213–6; 231–2; cf. 1 Macc 15:15–24) and the care taken to define the Samaritan group in the inscriptions make it likely that the synagogue is Jewish rather than Samaritan. On these inscriptions see Bruneau 1982, pp. 465–88; Kraabel 1984, pp. 44–6; White 1987, pp. 141–7.

35 Paton and Hicks 1891, no. 63; S. M. Sherwin-White 1976, p. 187; to be dated in the first or second century CE. The other inscriptions in Paton and Hicks 1891, nos. 278, 303, 323.

36 S. M. Sherwin-White 1976, p. 188; see also J. and L. Robert, *BE* 1977, no. 332; *SEG* 26, no. 949; Horsley in *New Docs* 1976, pp. 25–6; 1 Macc 15:16–24; Ant 14:112–13.

37 *CIJ* 769; chapter 3, section 5; it is probably to be dated in the third century CE.

38 Text in Drew-Bear 1976, p. 248; *New Docs* 1976, p. 25.

39 Drew-Bear 1976, p. 248.

40 Text in *IOSPE* 2 no. 400; *CIJ* 690; *CIRB* 1123.

41 See Schürer 1897, pp. 204–6; Lifshitz 1964, pp. 160–1. παντοκ-ράτωρ Θεός is found in a Sardis synagogue inscription; see Kroll forthcoming, no. 29. However, it is also used of pagan deities such as Hermes and Isis; see Kraabel 1978, p. 25; Goodenough 1956–7, p. 221. Nock et al. (1936, p. 65) write that εὐλογητός 'has no chance of being Greek'.

42 Schürer, Vermes and Millar 1986, 3.1, p. 37. The following also think this is a Jewish inscription: Lifshitz 1964, pp. 159–61; Safrai and Stern 1974, p. 156; J. and L. Robert, *BE* 1965, no. 283; Kant 1987, p. 684 n 81; cf. Siegert 1973, p. 145 n 5; *New Docs* 1976, p. 27; Rajak 1985a, p. 259 who are uncertain. Plassart 1914, p. 530 n 2; Deissmann 1927, pp. 321–2; Foakes Jackson and Lake 1920–33, 5, pp. 90–4 do not think it is Jewish. There are rare and isolated cases of pagan use of προσευχή to refer to a pagan place of prayer, although Jewish influence is generally the most likely explanation of these instances; see Robert 1969, 3, p. 1611; *IOSPE* I^2, 176; Sheppard 1980–1, p. 96; Schürer, Vermes and Millar 1979, 2, p. 440 n 61; Rajak 1985a, p. 259. *IG* 4^2, 1, 106 line 27 from Epidaurus (IV BCE) is an exception.

43 The three other inscriptions from Gorgippia in CIJ^2, no., 690a = *CIRB* 1126 (67 CE); *IOSPE* 2, no. 401 = *CIJ* 1, no. 78* = *CIRB* 1125 (end of second or beginning of the third century CE) and see now *SEG* 32.790. The inscription from Panticapaeum in *IGR* 1, no. 873 = Weinreich 1912, no. 117.

44 Text in Bean 1960, no. 122; improved by J. and L. Robert, *BE* 1961, no. 750; *SEG* 19.852.

45 J. and L. Robert, *BE* 1965, no. 412; cf. Lifshitz 1964, p. 160 n6. For καταφυγή in the LXX see, for example, Ex 17:15; Ps 9:10, 17:3, 143:2; Jer 16:19 II Macc 10:28.

46 For ἅγιος in the LXX see Hatch and Redpath 1897, pp. 12–15.

47 Text in S. Mitchell 1982, no. 209B; translation from Sheppard 1980–1, p. 94, no. 11.
48 On the article see Hatch and Redpath 1897, pp. 1420–1. For Ἐπουράνιος see Ps 67:15; II Macc 3:39; III Macc 6:28, 7:6; IV Macc 4:11. On ἅγιοι ἄγγελοι see C. P. Jones 1982, p. 268; *SEG* 31, no. 1080; Job 5:1; Tobit 11:14; Mk 8:38; Lk 9:26; Acts 10:22; Sheppard 1980–1, p. 96. On προσευχή see note 33.
49 See J. and L. Robert, *BE* 1983, no. 434; Lane Fox 1986, p. 686 n 27; S. Mitchell 1982, p. 178; cf. Sheppard 1980–1, pp. 96–7. S. Mitchell 1982 also provides further evidence for Jews in North Galatia; see nos. 133, 246, 509–12; see also Bittel 1975, pp. 108–13. These inscriptions increase the likelihood that 4.9 and 4.10 are also Jewish.
50 Text in S. Mitchell 1982, no. 141.
51 S. Mitchell 1982, p. 45. For δύναμις in the LXX see Hatch and Redpath 1897, pp. 350–3; *TDNT* 2, pp. 290–9; and for example III Kings 18:15; IV Kings 3:14; Ps 67:29; Wis 6:3; III Macc 7:9; Lk 1:35. The epithet δύναμις was applied to pagan deities, for example to Men; see Lane 1971, 1, no. 83; 1976, 3, p. 79 and n62. It is possible that Men was also called Θεὸς Ὕψιστος in one inscription; see Lane 1976, 3, pp. 94–5. On the epithet used of pagan deities see Pleket 1981, pp. 178–83. Thus we cannot be certain that the inscription is Jewish, although this remains the most likely possibility; cf. Schürer, Vermes and Millar 1986, 3.1, p. 35; *SEG* 32.1263. There are a number of other inscriptions which use the term Θεὸς Ὕψιστος but it cannot be determined if they are Jewish or pagan. See (a) *SEG* 26.1697 (Sinai). (b) A. B. Cook 1940, 3, ii, p. 1163; Nock et al. 1936, p. 65; Colpe 1967, col. 1292 (Thessalonica). (c) Reynolds and Tannenbaum 1987, pp. 138–9, nos. 11–12 (Aphrodisias). (d) Aupert and Masson 1979, pp. 380–1; Mitford 1946, pp. 34–6 (Cyprus).
52 This difficulty is often admitted (see Cumont 1897, p. 3; Hengel 1974, 2, p. 200 n264) and is the root of the problem which led to the (in our view, incorrect) attempts to find Jewish influence in the majority of the Hypsistos inscriptions. For discussion of possible Jewish influence on Gentile piety see Robert 1978a, p. 249 n47, 268; Pleket 1981, pp. 184–9; Sheppard 1980–1, pp. 77–101.
53 On God-worshippers see chapter 7. We are not arguing against the authors cited above (note 21) who denied that Jewish influence was generally involved in the usage of Hypsistos. They were not arguing that Jewish influence was *never* a factor in the use of the term. Kraabel (1969, pp. 81–93), who has rightly rejected the idea of Jewish influence in most cases, has gone too far and rejected Jewish influence completely. He discussed only the inscription given in 4.5 above and thus did not give a balanced picture of the Jewish use of the title; see also J. and L. Robert, *BE* 1970, no. 153.
54 Text in Drew-Bear 1976, p. 249.
55 There is clearly no legal necessity to use it here, in contrast to 4.7 above.
56 See Kraemer 1986a, p. 198; cf. Drew-Bear 1976, p. 249. No Jewish

usage of 'Αγαθῇ Τύχῃ is known. It is possible that 'Theos Hypsistos' is used in *SEG* 6.266 from Apamea because of the influence of the local Jewish community; cf. Kraabel 1968, pp. 102–3.

57 *IOSPE* 2, no. 449, 450, 452, 456; see Schürer 1897, pp. 200–25.
58 *IOSPE* 2, no. 445–8, 453, etc.
59 Schürer 1897, pp. 217–19, 221, 225. On these points see Brooten 1982, pp. 95–8, 249 n73; Goodenough 1956–7, pp. 226–44.
60 Goodenough 1956–7, pp. 225–6, 232–3.
61 Schürer 1897, pp. 221, 225 had originally suggested this, although his reasoning was incorrect as we have noted. His conclusion was accepted by Cumont 1897, pp. 1–3; Nock et al. 1936, p. 63.
62 Bertram cites these inscriptions as 'the clearest instance of the use of the Hypsistos title in syncretistic Judaism' (*TDNT* 8, p. 619). However, these groups, whilst influenced by Judaism, seem not to belong inside the Jewish fold. They are autonomous units which appear to have been independent of any synagogue community and to have been some distance from Jewish faith and practice. These inscriptions cannot rightly be called an example of syncretistic Judaism; see also Safrai and Stern 1974, p. 157.
63 On the characteristics of Sabazios, his worship, the iconography of the cult and its geographical extent see Dodds 1940, pp. 172–6; Johnson 1968, pp. 542–50; 1978, pp. 98–100; 1984, pp. 1583–1602; Widengren 1961, pp. 62–4; Picard 1961, pp. 129–76; Carrington 1976, pp. 158–220, 309–14; Tatscheva-Hitova 1978, pp. 1217–30; 1983, pp. 162–89; Lane 1980, pp. 9–33; 1985, pp. 1f; Fellmann 1981, pp. 316–40; Vermaseren 1983, pp. 1f. Sabazios was also associated with a number of other deities; see A. B. Cook 1914, 1, pp. 390–403; and for example Herrmann 1962, p. 50, no. 45.
64 Cumont 1897, pp. 5–7; 1906, pp. 63–79; 1910, pp. 55–60. Cumont (1911, p. 226 n24) described Sabazios as 'as much Jewish as Phrygian'. Scholars who have accepted Cumont's view include Weinreich 1912, pp. 43–4; Keil 1923, pp. 263–4; Oesterley 1935, pp. 119–58; Nock et al. 1936, p. 63; Janne 1937, pp. 40–3; R. McL. Wilson 1958, pp. 11–13; Picard 1961, p. 146; Widengren 1961, p. 64; Blanchetière 1974, pp. 380–1; cf. 1984, p. 57; Sanie 1978, p. 1109; Fellmann 1981, p. 318; Simon 1981a, pp. 634–8. The connection with Asia Minor was made because (a) Sabazios was thought to be a Phrygian god in origin and was known to be very popular in Asia Minor. (b) There was a considerable Jewish population in Asia Minor at an early date. (c) The Noah coins from Apamea were (rightly) interpreted as evidence that, in places, the Jewish communities in Asia Minor were influential and in contact with their pagan neighbours. (d) This was an explanation for the early and rapid success of Christianity in Asia Minor. If Jews there were 'syncretistic' it was thought this would make them more receptive to Christian preaching.
65 Valerius Maximus, *Facta et Dicta Memorabilia* I, 3, 2; texts in Stern 1974, p. 358, no. 147a, 147b; Lane 1985, p. 47, no. 12. Sabazios'

identification with Jupiter explains the suggestion that Jews were expelled for the worship of 'Jupiter Sabazios'.
66 See Cumont 1906, pp. 66f; Nilsson 1950, pp. 636–40.
67 Lane 1979, pp. 35–7; see also Jamar 1909, pp. 227f; Johnson 1978, pp. 98–9; 1984, pp. 1602–3; Schürer, Vermes and Millar 3.1, pp. 74–5. Cf. Cumont 1906, pp. 66–7; 1910, pp. 55–60. Note that in Plutarch (Stern 1974, no. 258) Yahweh is identified with Dionysus. Since Dionysus was identified with Sabazios, pagans could have equated Sabazios and Yahweh in this way. However, Plutarch reflects the understanding of one Gentile observer rather than what Jews themselves believed and practised; see Kraabel 1978, p. 29; Jamar 1909, p. 229.
68 See Cumont 1906, p. 66; Nilsson 1950, p. 636; 1960a, pp. 178–9. Cf. Bickerman 1958, p. 149; Schürer 1909, 3, pp. 58–9; Stern 1974, p. 359.
69 See Johnson 1984, pp. 1603–4. Cumont's only literary evidence for the identification is from Plutarch (see note 67), that Tacitus (Hist v. 5) also knew of the identification of Yahweh and Dionysus, but dismissed it, and that Lydus identified the Chaldean Θεὸς 'Ιαώ, Sabazios and Sabaoth, see Cumont 1897, p. 6. However, this is not evidence that *Jews* identified Yahweh and Sabazios.
70 See Goodenough 1953–65, 2, pp. 45–50, 3, figs. 839–43; Nilsson 1960a, pp. 176–81; Johnson 1984, pp. 1604–6; Lane 1985, pp. 31–2, no. 65 and pl. 27.
71 Cumont 1897, pp. 4–5; 1906, pp. 72–9; 1929, pp. 102–3; Oesterley 1935, pp. 155–7; Widengren 1961, p. 64; Gressmann 1925, pp. 17–18.
72 On angels see Sokolowski 1960, pp. 225–9; Sheppard 1980–1, pp. 77–101. On banquets see Johnson 1978, pp. 102–3; Jamar 1906, pp. 248–50.
73 Text in Lane 1985, p. 3, no. 6; on which see Cumont 1897, pp. 3–4; 1906, p. 67; Oesterley 1935, pp. 148–9; Fellmann 1981, p. 319.
74 Johnson 1984, pp. 1597, 1602, 1606; Carrington 1976, p. 186.
75 The amulet in Goodenough 1953–68, 2, p. 267, 3, fig. 1139. On Jews and pagan symbols see Johnson 1984, p. 1606; and in general Goodenough 1953–68.
76 For further comments on Cumont's work see Jamar 1906, pp. 236–43; Kraabel 1978, pp. 27–33; Carrington 1976, pp. 184–9; Schwertheim and Sahin 1977, pp. 260–1; Robert 1978b, pp. 432–7. Note that there is no link between the Sambatheion (see *CIJ* 752) and Sabazios; see Kraabel 1968, pp. 168–81.
77 Kraabel 1978, pp. 29–33.
78 Texts in Johnson 1968, pp. 542f; Robert 1975a, pp. 306–30. The second inscription suggests that the cult of Sabazios had invited syncretism for a very long time, yet the Jewish community appears to have had no connection with it.
79 This is not to deny that some individual Jews probably apostasised; see, for example, Tiberius Julius Alexander in Smallwood 1981, pp. 257–9; Goodenough 1962, pp. 3–4; and perhaps Μόσχος

Μοσχίωνος Ἰουδαῖος from Oropos, Boetia, on whom see J. and L. Robert, *BE* 1956, no. 121. Perhaps also the man from Jerusalem who made a contribution to Dionysus at Iasus; see Robert 1946, p. 101. Theories of syncretism have also been based on *CIJ* 752, but these are unconvincing.

80 Nock et al. 1936, p. 65.
81 Nock et al. 1936, p. 66.
82 Burchard in Charlesworth, 1985, 2, p. 211 n 8f; see also *TDNT* 8, p. 618; Colpe 1967, col. 1291.
83 Dodd 1935, p. 13.
84 Date of majority of occurrences in Hengel 1974, 2, p. 201 n265; Kraabel 1979a, p. 492. Inscription 4.9 is also later, but note that Hypsistos is not found at all in the Jewish inscriptions from Rome.
85 See Tatscheva-Hitova 1977, p. 300; Kraabel 1979a, p. 492.
86 A systematic investigation of the dating of the many pagan occurrences of the term has never been undertaken as far as I am aware.

7 'God-worshippers' in Asia Minor

1 'God-worshipper', a translation of θεοσεβής, which is used by Jews in Asia Minor, is a more appropriate term than 'God-fearer', a translation of φοβούμενοι τὸν θεόν, which occurs only in Acts; see Rajak 1985a, p. 255. I will use the term 'sympathiser' for those who were favourably disposed towards Judaism and/or Jewish communities and perhaps followed some Jewish customs but did not adopt a regular relationship with the synagogue community; see Siegert 1973, p. 110 n1, 147–51.
2 Bernays 1885 (reprint of 1877), pp. 71–80. Other scholars who adopted his view include Schürer 1897, pp. 218–20; Lévi 1905, pp. 1–2; Juster 1914, 1, p. 274 n6; Strack and Billerbeck 1924, 2, pp. 715–20; Safrai and Stern 1976, pp. 1158–9.
3 Foakes Jackson and Lake 1920–33, 5, pp. 84–8; Feldman 1950, pp. 200–8.
4 For example, Robert 1964, pp. 40–5 argued that θεοσεβής referred to Jews and always meant 'pious'.
5 See Kraabel 1982, pp. 453–4; and see the Conclusion here.
6 Herodotus 2.37; see also 1.86; Sophocles *Oedipus at Colonus* 260; Plato *Cratylus* 394d; Aristophanes *Aves* 897. On the term see Feldman 1950, p. 204; Robert 1964, p. 42 n4, p. 44.
7 See Pfuhl and Möbius 1979, 2, no. 1697, with photo; it is now in the Bursa Museum and probably from Asia Minor; see also *SEG* 29.1697. This new inscription now undermines Robert's argument (1964, p. 44 and n5, p. 45) that θεοσεβής only occurs in Jewish inscriptions. Even if θεοσεβής was only found in the Jewish sphere, this would not mean that Jews never used it to refer to God-worshippers as Robert (1964, pp. 44–5) and after him Wilcox (1981, p. 113) want to argue. Terms related to θεοσεβής also occur in pagan inscriptions. An inscription from Istropolis (around 100 BCE) shows that θεοσεβεῖν does not reveal whether the 'θεός' in question is to

be thought of as singular or, as in this case, plural. See *SIG*³ 2, no. 708 lines 19–20; see also Kenyon and Bell 1893, p. 38, no. 23a line 20; Wilcken 1927, p. 159; *IG* 7, 2712 lines 66–8; Eger *et al.*, 1910–12, 1, p. 94, no. 55 line 1.

8 See Siegert 1973, p. 155 and n3 for a list of those who have thought θεοσεβής was a Jewish technical term. On εὐσεβής see Robert 1946, p. 81; 1964, p. 44; Gauger 1977, pp. 70–5; see in general Tod 1951, pp. 182–90. It occurs in only one known Jewish inscription – *CIJ* 683 from Stobi.

9 Job 1:1, 8, 2:3; see also Ex 18:21; Jud 11:17; IV Macc 15:28, 16:12. See also Romaniuk 1964, p. 69. The related term θεοσέβεια – 'reverence for God' – occurs only seven times in the LXX. Philo uses θεοσεβής only in Mut. 197. He uses θεοσέβεια nine times.

10 See also Ant 7:130, 153 and the variant reading of Ant 9:260.

11 Many scholars have thought that Poppaea was a 'God-worshipper'. Smallwood (1959a, pp. 329–35) argued that θεοσεβής here meant Poppaea was 'religious' and so convinced Nero that other people's religious scruples should be respected. However, M. H. Williams (1988, pp. 97–111) has convincingly refuted Smallwood and also shown that the linguistic usage of Josephus is against understanding θεοσεβής as 'God-worshipper'. Rather, Josephus indicates that Poppaea's attachment to the Jewish religion was 'very unspecific indeed'.

12 See JosAsen 4:9, 8:5–7, 20:8, 22:8, 23:9, 10, 28:4, 29:3; see Philonenko 1968, pp. 142–3; Charlesworth 1985, 2, p. 206 n. m. See also, for example, TJos 6:7; TNaph 1:10; TAbram 4:6; LetAris 179. In the NT θεοσεβής is only found in Jn 9:31 and is rare in the usage of the Early Church; see *TDNT* 3, pp. 126–8; also Eusebius HE 4.26.5, quoting Melito.

13 Marcus in Josephus vol. 7, p. 505; Foakes Jackson and Lake 1920–33, 5, p. 85 respectively.

14 Marcus 1952, p. 249. On the grammatical issue see Blass, Debrunner and Funk 1961, section 276; Moulton 1963, 3, p. 181. Marcus gives examples from Xenophon, e.g. *Anab* I, 7, 2. His grammatical view has been accepted by Lifshitz 1970, pp. 78–9; Siegert 1973, p. 127 n4; Wilcox 1981, p. 121 n46; Kant 1987, p. 688 n106.

15 Those who follow Marcus include Bellen 1965–6, p. 173 n19; Zeitlin 1974, p. 416; Stern 1980, p. 105; Simon 1981a, p. 470; Finn 1985, p. 81 n33; Schürer, Vermes and Millar 1986, 3.1, p. 162. On involvement in the synagogue see Marcus 1952, p. 249; in Josephus, vol. 7, p. 505 n. a. In this one passage then σεβόμενοι τὸν θεόν *does* mean Gentiles who worship God, but this does not make it a technical term. Its meaning in each occurrence must be determined from the context.

16 Finn 1985, p. 82; see also Siegert 1973, p. 139; Reynolds and Tannenbaum 1987, p. 49. On μοῖρα see BJ 4:86, Ant 17:303.

17 For Josephus on proselytes see for example BJ 2:560; Ant 18:82. Other passages may refer to God-worshippers; see Ant 20:34–5

(see Reynolds and Tannenbaum 1987, p. 50); BJ 2:462 (see Smallwood 1981, p. 206 n15).
18 Finn 1985, p. 83; Wolfson 1948, 2, pp. 369–71; cf. Nolland 1981,
pp. 173–9. Philo calls these Gentiles proselytes, not because they
were converted but because the passage in Ex 22 used this term. Philo
elsewhere distinguishes between proselytes and others. These
Gentiles are allegorically proselytes; see Finn 1985, pp. 82–3. In
Mos. II, 41–5 Philo may speak of God-worshippers or perhaps
'sympathisers'.
19 Text in Stern 1980, no. 301, pp. 102–3. See Bernays 1885, p. 73;
Kuhn and Stegemann 1962, col. 1260; Leon 1960, p. 251; Finn 1985,
p. 81. The Satire was written between the two Jewish wars (70–135
CE) and thus shows that 'God-worshippers' continued to exist after
the first Jewish War.
20 Siegert 1973, p. 154; Simon 1986, p. 281. The inscription from
Aphrodisias (see below) may reveal just the sort of father–son pair
Juvenal describes; see Reynolds and Tannenbaum 1987, p. 46. This
interpretation does not depend on the incorrect view that 'metuens'
is a technical term for a God-worshipper but depends rather on the
meaning of the text as a whole. The actual inscriptions in which
metuens occurs, none of which were found in Jewish catacombs,
are all ambiguous and could refer to Jews, pagans or God-
worshippers; see *CIJ* 5, 285, 524, 529, 642; Le Bohec 1981a, p. 191,
no. 72. Metuens does occur in pagan inscriptions; see *CIL* 6.390a
which is clearly addressed to Jupiter.
21 See Stern 1974, no. 254, pp. 542–4; see also Siegert 1973, p. 161;
Reynolds and Tannenbaum 1987, pp. 44–5, 62. It is difficult to
know how much is involved in someone 'acting the part' –
ὑποκρίνεται – of a Jew. It must involve some association with a
Jewish community and adoption of Jewish customs for the person
to be identifiable. A possible reference to God-worshippers is given
by Suetonius in *Domitianus* 12:1. The first group prosecuted for
not paying the Jewish tax is thought to have been those who 'lived
as Jews' but were neither Jews by birth (as the second group were)
nor converts, in other words 'God-worshippers'. See Keil and
Premerstein 1914, p. 33; Smallwood 1981, pp. 376–7; Reynolds and
Tannenbaum 1987, p. 52; cf. Thompson 1982, pp. 336–40.
22 See note 3 above. σεβόμενοι is found in a pagan inscription
from Magnesia ad Maeander which reads ... τοῖς σεβομένοις
Απ[όλλωνα]; see *SIG*³ 2, no. 557 line 7; see also Plutarch, *Isis and
Osiris* 44. The term is a general one for a 'worshipper' and not a
technical expression restricted to Judaism.
23 Haenchen 1971, p. 419 n2.
24 See Wilcox 1981, p. 113. On προσήλυτος in this period see Lévi
1905, pp. 1–9; 1906, pp. 1–31; 1907, pp. 56–61; Juster 1914, 1,
pp. 253–74; Braude 1940, pp. 3–135; Levison 1957, pp. 45–56;
Moore 1927, I, pp. 327–53; Nolland 1979b, pp. 347–55; Simon
1986, pp. 271–305, 390–95. For proselytes in Asia Minor see
Reynolds and Tannenbaum 1987, pp. 5, 43–5.

25 Even if we follow ℵ and omit 'Ιουδαῖοι in v5 (which is unlikely), Gentiles are hardly in view here. Commentators are agreed that 'Ιουδαῖοί τε καὶ προσήλυτοι is a general statement applicable to all the people in the list and not just those from Rome; see, for example, Haenchen 1971, p. 171.

26 Confirmation of this is provided by Luke's usage of "Ελληνες in Acts. He clearly always means non-Jews and non-proselytes by the term; see 16:1, 3, 18:4, 19:10, 17, 20:21, 21:28; also 11:20, in addition to the four passages under consideration here; see also *TDNT* 2, pp. 503–16. Philo also knows the technical meaning of προσήλυτος; see, for example, Spec. I, 51–2; see also Spec. IV, 178; Virt. 102–4, 178–82; Wolfson 1948, 2, pp. 355–64. Overman 1988, pp. 18–20 is unconvincing.

27 See e.g. G. Schneider 1982, 2, p. 150; Pesch 1986, 2, p. 51. Josephus notes in BJ 7:45 that at Antioch many Gentiles attended the Jewish 'religious ceremonies'. This is helpful confirmatory evidence at this point. Foakes Jackson and Lake (1920–33, 5, p. 87) and Wilcox (1981, p. 112) note that some synagogues were clearly 'mixed'.

28 See Foakes Jackson and Lake 1920–33, 5, p. 87; on the textual problems see Wilcox 1981, pp. 111–12.

29 See Foakes Jackson and Lake 1920–33, 5, p. 87; *New Docs* 1978, p. 54; Reynolds and Tannenbaum 1987, p. 51.

30 Cornelius (10:2, 22, 35), described as φοβούμενος τὸν θεόν, is clearly a Gentile whose piety is noteworthy, but we have no proof that he actually attended the synagogue. We cannot decide if 13:16, 26 refer to God-worshippers, although the probability is stronger in the latter case. In 13:50a the 'σεβομένας γυναῖκας' are difficult to define. They seem to be distinguished from 'the Jews', although this is not necessarily the case. Even if they are Gentiles, they could simply be 'devout' in the same sense as Cornelius, that is, they could be pious without having any regular involvement in the synagogue. In 16:14 Lydia is clearly a part of the προσευχή, but is she a devout Jew, a proselyte or a God-worshipper? Titius Justus (18:7) could simply be a devout Jew. On these passages see Foakes Jackson and Lake 1920–33, 5, pp. 84–8; Wilcox 1981, pp. 104–15; cf. Esler 1987, pp. 36–45; Sanders 1987, pp. 137–40, 151–3; see also Romaniuk 1964, pp. 67–84; Lifshitz 1970, pp. 79–80; Siegert 1973, pp. 129–40; Simon 1981b, cols. 1060–4. However, in view of the probability that Luke does refer to God-worshippers elsewhere, the likelihood that he also does so in (some of) these passages is increased.

31 Kraabel 1981, pp. 118–21; 1985, pp. 224–32; 1986, pp. 150–7; in general Petersen 1978, pp. 81–92. According to Kraabel, Luke uses the 'God-fearers' in part to show how Christianity has legitimately become a Gentile religion. For further discussion of Kraabel's work see Finn 1985, pp. 75–84; Gager 1986, pp. 91–9; Overman 1988, pp. 17–26.

32 It has been methodologically important to deal with Acts last, rather than to start with Acts and add other references to this, as has often been done.

33 For the first opinion see, for example, Bellen 1965–6, pp. 171–6; for the second see Robert 1964, pp. 41–5; Kraabel 1981b, p. 116. φοβούμενοι / σεβόμενοι τὸν θεόν do not occur in inscriptions.
34 Reynolds and Tannenbaum 1987, pp. 1–131; see also the debate in Kraabel and MacLennan 1986, pp. 47–53; Tannenbaum 1986, pp. 55–7; Feldman 1986, pp. 58–69. As Goodman (1988, pp. 261–2) points out in a review, Reynolds and Tannenbaum are too quick to use rabbinic evidence to understand the inscription; e.g. Reynolds and Tannenbaum 1987, pp. 26–8, 78–86.
35 On the date and purpose of the inscription see Reynolds and Tannenbaum 1987, pp. 19–23; a late fourth or fifth century date is possible but unlikely. The full name of the decany was probably 'the decany of the students/disciples/sages of the law, also known as those who fervently/continually praise God'; see Reynolds and Tannenbaum 1987, p. 41. This seems to be more than just a pious name; it was probably a society for the study of the law and for prayer, but it may also have been a general-purpose benevolent society. If its activities included study and prayer (as seems very likely), then it is another indication of the importance of the Torah and of education in the Torah in Judaism in Asia Minor. See further in chapter 3, sections 3 and 4. We can also note the enthusiasm in the group of Jews as a whole for names which refer to festivals – the Sabbath and probably the Feast of Tabernacles – indicated, for example, by the name Ἑορτάσιος. Reynolds and Tannenbaum (1987, p. 96) go on to note that a degree of 'pietism' is involved in this, as it is in names derived from θεός and in the name Εὐσέβιος. Thus, the inscription reveals some significant aspects of the group's faith.
36 See Reynolds and Tannenbaum 1987, p. 6. θεοσεβῖς is a common spelling of the case ending; see Reynolds and Tannenbaum 1987, p. 12.
37 Reynolds and Tannenbaum 1987, pp. 54–6, 93–115; see also Meeks 1983, p. 208 n175; Rajak 1985a, p. 256; Schürer, Vermes and Millar 1986, 3.1, pp. 26, 166; Gager 1986, pp. 97–8. Εὐσαββάθιος and Ὁρτάσιος are the two names with Jewish connections. The few with names favoured by the Jews could be sons of fathers who were θεοσεβεῖς themselves and thus gave their children names used by the Jews. Εὐσαββάθιος is related to names like Σαμβάθιος which were often given to children in Egypt by Gentile parents who were interested in Judaism, specifically in the Sabbath; on 'the Sambathions' see *CPJ* III, pp. 43–87.
38 This inscription therefore undermines Kraabel's argument (see Kraabel 1981b, pp. 113–26; Kraabel and MacLennan 1986, pp. 47–53), that, for the Roman Diaspora, the evidence for Gentile God-worshippers is far from convincing. See Rajak 1985a, pp. 255–6; Schürer, Vermes and Millar 1986, 3.1, p. 166. However, Kraabel has sought to interpret this inscription in a way that would support his contentions about the 'God-fearers'. He wishes to translate καὶ ὅσοι θεοσεβῖς as 'and (the following) who (are) pious'.

(Kraabel 1985, pp. 231–2.) Rather than being sympathetic to the Jewish religion, these Gentiles were simply friendly towards Jews as fellow-townspeople and the local Jews honoured them as such. However, it is difficult to understand why Jews would call 'good neighbours' who were not positive towards their religion 'pious'. This is completely beyond the known Jewish meaning of θεοσεβής. It is very hard to avoid the implication that here the term does have a religious meaning, one that implies an approval of the Gentiles' belief and actions in the eyes of the Jews and thus that involves these Gentiles being 'God-worshippers'.

39 Reynolds and Tannenbaum 1987, p. 55.

40 *Ibid.* p. 57.

41 *Ibid.* pp. 43–5, 125.

42 Note that eleven to thirteen of the θεοσεβεῖς were craftsmen; see Reynolds and Tannenbaum 1987, pp. 119–22. In addition there were probably θεοσεβεῖς who were too poor to have made a donation to the building. It is therefore likely that the θεοσεβεῖς included people from a wide social spectrum.

43 See Reynolds and Tannenbaum 1987, p. 126; Rajak 1985a, p. 256. We note that no Jews seem to have been city councillors. The inscription may date to before Severus and Caracalla passed the edict which allowed cities to recruit Jews into their councils; see Reynolds and Tannenbaum 1987, pp. 66–7; chapter 2, section 4. That they attracted nine Gentile city councillors suggests that the Jewish community included some men of comparably high status and income; see Reynolds and Tannenbaum 1987, pp. 127–30. As a group the Jews seem to span a large range of status positions.

44 This inscription is from outside our geographical area, but Panticapaeum is close to Asia Minor and the evidence the inscription provides is related to the Aphrodisias inscription.

45 Text from *CIJ*² no. 683a. See also *CIRB* 71; cf. Bellen 1965–6, pp. 172–3.

46 On the date see Lifshitz 1969, p. 96; Rajak 1985a, p. 259. *CIJ*² p. 66 dates it to the second century CE. The other inscriptions are *CIJ* 683 = *CIRB* 70 (dated in 81 CE); *CIJ* 684 = *CIRB* 73; *CIJ*² no. 683b = *CIRB* 72. On the Jews of Panticapaeum see Schürer, Vermes and Millar 1986, 3.1, pp. 36–7.

47 On the possibility of linking with the previous phrase and leaving the text as it stands, see Bellen 1965–6, p. 173; Lifshitz 1969, pp. 95–6; *CIJ*², p. 65.

48 Bellen 1965–6, p. 173; the emendation is accepted by Siegert 1973, pp. 158–9; Hommel 1975, p. 175 n 38; Hengel 1975a, pp. 43–4. In addition, the end of the line occurs at ν, which probably led the mason to complete a familiar word.

49 See Bellen 1965–6, pp. 173–4; Lifshitz 1969, p. 96.

50 This point is made in part by Bellen 1965–6, p. 175; see also Hommel 1975, p. 175 n 38.

51 See Bellen 1965–6, p. 175; Couroyer 1969, p. 149; Simon 1981a, pp. 474–5; Rajak 1985a, p. 259; Schürer, Vermes and Millar 1986,

3.1, pp. 166, 168; Reynolds and Tannenbaum 1987, p. 54; cf. Siegert 1973, p. 159. Note that no ancient synagogue known to us had a 'pious' name; see Reynolds and Tannenbaum 1987, p. 32.

52 Reading from Schürer, Vermes and Millar 1986, 3.1, p. 167 also given as a possibility in Robert 1964, p. 44; cf. Lifshitz 1967, p. 32; who reads ἀξιολογ(ωτάτη) καὶ θεοσεβ(εστάτη).

53 Text from Lifshitz 1967, no. 30; see also *CIG* 2924. The βάθρον could be a platform for the Torah or for a menorah, similar to the two discovered at Sardis; see Robert 1964, p. 50 n4. Alternatively, it could be another name for a bema, used by the reader of Scripture or by a speaker. On the term's use see Kubinska 1968, pp. 86, 126. On σκούτλωσις see Robert 1964, pp. 50–2; A. Cameron 1931, p. 257.

54 For the date see Lifshitz 1967, p. 33. On this as a Jewish inscription see Robert 1937b, pp. 409–12; cf. Groag 1907, p. 283. For Εὐλογία in Jewish inscriptions see e.g. Lifshitz 1967 nos. 2, 38, 69, 81a; *CIJ* 25, 327, 693a, 776, 798, 1537–8; *TAM* 4.1, 375; Robert 1960b, pp. 392, 395; Pleket 1981, pp. 183–9. For the Jewish community in Tralles see Ant 14:242. Robert (1964, p. 54 n1) notes that the expression ὑπὲρ εὐχῆς is very rare in pagan inscriptions, which reinforces the view that Capitolina is connected with the Jewish community.

55 See Groag 1907, pp. 282–90; *IGR* 4.1340; Robert 1937b, p. 410.

56 Robert (1937b, p. 411; see also Kittel 1944, col. 12) argued that she was a proselyte, but if this was the case the Jewish community in a synagogue inscription would surely have proudly proclaimed the fact when such an important person was involved.

57 Bellen 1965–6, p. 175 n33 and Bickerman 1958, p. 158 n58 regard her as a 'God-worshipper'; Lifshitz 1967, p. 32 as 'très pieuse'; Schürer, Vermes and Millar 1986, 3.1, pp. 24, 167 are uncertain.

58 We recall the city councillors among the God-worshippers at Aphrodisias.

59 Texts in Kroll forthcoming, nos. 9, 8; Robert 1964, p. 39, nos. 4, 5; Lifshitz 1967, nos. 17, 18. Original positions given in Hanfmann 1983, fig. 254; Seager 1974, p. 45.

60 The other four inscriptions are in Kroll forthcoming, nos. 22, 57, 59, 66. They read respectively: (a) Λεόντιος θεοσεβὴς ἐκ τῶν τῆς Προνοίας δομάτων τὸ διαχώρον ὑπὲρ εὐχῆς ἐσκούτλωσα. (b) Εὐχὴ Εὐτυχ[ίδο]υ θεοσ[εβοῦς.] (c) [Εὐχὴ --- θ]εοσεβοῦς.] (d) Αὐρ. Ἑρμογένης Σαρδ. θεοσεβὴς ἐκ τῶν τῆς Προνοίας εὐξάμενος τὸ ἐπταμύξιον ἐποίησα. For the dating of the synagogue see chapter 2, section 3.

61 See Robert 1964, pp. 40–5 (he calls God-worshippers 'sympathisers'); see also Seager 1983, p. 169. Robert placed weight on the Miletus inscription (see 4.5 below) but this is so difficult to interpret that it cannot be used as a guide to the interpretation of θεοσεβής in other contexts.

62 See chapter 3, section 2.

63 On involvement in the city's life see chapter 2, especially sections 4 and 5. On the fountain see chapter 2, section 3. On the building

as a 'show piece' see chapter 2, section 5. It is surprising therefore that Kraabel (1981b, pp. 113–26; 1985, pp. 224–32) has denied (or at least doubted) that any Gentiles were sufficiently interested or attracted to become regularly involved in the synagogue as God-worshippers. He does not examine these inscriptions in either article referred to above.
64 See Schürer, Vermes and Millar 1986, 3.1, p. 167; Robert 1964, p. 40; and compare for example *CIJ* 22. It could also be the sort of name a God-worshipping father would give his son. Leontios (see Kroll forthcoming, no. 22) can similarly be understood in this way.
65 Schürer, Vermes and Millar 1986, 3.1, p. 167 think there is no proof either way; as does Lifshitz 1966, p. 62; 1967, p. 25. Simon 1981b, col. 1068; Bellen (1965–6, p. 175) and Hommel (1975, pp. 174–5) think the donors are God-worshippers, but their methodology is questionable. Reynolds and Tannenbaum 1987, p. 126 and Kroll forthcoming, Introduction, think that θεοσεβής at Sardis refers to Gentile God-worshippers.
66 Text in Hommel 1975, p. 167; *SEG* 4.441. For its position in the theatre see Deissmann 1927, p. 451; corrected in Schwank 1969, pp. 262–3. On the Roman theatre at Miletus see Kleiner 1968, pp. 69–76; 1970, pp. 18–21.
67 The date of the inscription in Deissmann 1927 p. 451; Hommel 1975, pp. 168–9; Rajak 1985a, p. 258. For θεοσεβής as a personal name see Crosby 1941, pp. 14–20. On θεοσεβίον as a group name see Robert 1964, pp. 46–7; cf. Lifshitz 1966, p. 62. On the Jewish community at Miletus see Ant 14:244–6.
68 See, for example, Deissmann 1927, pp. 451–2; Sukenik 1934, p. 42; Feldman 1950, p. 204; *CIJ* 748; Robert 1964, p. 41; Siegert 1973, pp. 159–60; Wilcox 1981, pp. 112–13. τῶν καί would then be a form of the stereotyped formula ὁ καί which is used for double names.
69 See Schürer 1909, 3, p. 174 n70; Lifshitz 1966, pp. 62–3; 1970, pp. 81–2. See also Romaniuk 1964 p. 81 n2, Bellen 1965–6, pp. 172, 175; Simon 1981a, pp. 474–5; Rajak 1985a, p. 258. It is also likely that the theatre management would have used εὐσεβής had they wished to designate the Jews as pious, this being the normal Greek term for the concept; see Robert 1964, p. 44.
70 See, for example, Deissmann 1927, p. 452; Robert 1964, p. 41; Siegert 1973, p. 160.
71 Hommel 1975, pp. 177–87; see also Kleiner 1970, p. 20.
72 Cassius Dio, Stern 1980, no. 406, *Historia Romana* xxxvii 16.5–17.1. Hommel did not cite this passage but relied on the evidence that the Rabbis were favourable to those interested in Judaism to argue that the Jews in Miletus would have been prepared to give God-worshippers the title of 'Jews' (Hommel 1975, pp. 185–7). This is highly unlikely. It is possible that Cassius Dio refers to proselytes, in which case the passage does not support Hommel's thesis at all.
73 Hommel states this but he does not argue the point.
74 Rajak 1985a, p. 258; see also Schürer, Vermes and Millar 1986, 3.1, p. 167.

75 See Schürer, Vermes and Millar 1986, 3.1, p. 168; Reynolds and Tannenbaum 1987, p. 54.
76 See von Gerkan 1921, p. 181; Sheppard 1980–1, p. 82; Rajak 1985a, p. 258. There were different seats for different ranks of society in the Roman theatre; see Bieber 1961, p. 189.
77 Text in Keil and Premerstein 1941, p. 32–4, no. 42; see also *CIJ* 754. That Jews lived in Philadelphia is confirmed by Rev 3:9. The base was attached to the column; see Kohl and Watzinger 1916, p. 144.
78 This indication given by the inscription has been overlooked by others in the past. Deissmann 1927, p. 452 n2; Frey *CIJ* 2, p. 19; Kittel 1944, col. 17 thought Eustathios was a proselyte. The following thought he was a God-worshipper: Krauss 1922, p. 239; Bickerman 1958, p. 158 n58; Bellen 1965–6, p. 175; Wilcox 1981, p. 118 n1. Lifshitz (1967, p. 31) translated the term as 'le pieux'. Schürer, Vermes and Millar (1986, 3.1, p. 167) note that the inscription implies a possible contrast between Eustathios and the 'Hebraioi', but the word could simply be part of the title of the synagogue as it is elsewhere; see *CIJ* 718, 510, also 291, 317, 535.
79 Text in Delling 1964–5, p. 74; Nilsson 1960b, pp. 297–8. Dating in Bickerman 1958, p. 158.
80 For Jewish usage see Delling 1964–5, pp. 74–6. Pagan parallels in Hengel 1974, 2, p. 177 n61; Cumont 1906, p. 68; Nock et al. 1936, p. 67 n75.
81 See Nilsson 1960b, pp. 298–9; Delling 1964–5, pp. 74–7. Most of the parallels to ὁ ὤν are from Hellenistic Judaism; see e.g. Ex 3:14; Wis 13:1; cf. Sir 18:1; Dan 6:27, 12:7. For the word order Θεὸς Κύριος see e.g. Jos 22:22; Ps 117:27. Some parallels exist in paganism for the emphasis on the deity's eternity; see Bickerman 1958, p. 155 n51. In addition, syncretistic groups (probably influenced by Judaism) did address the god Ἰαω with the formula ὁ ὤν; see Preisendanz 1973, 1, 4, line 1564; Winter 1936, 3, no. 155 line 2; Goodenough 1953–68, 2, p. 259.
82 See Delling 1964–5, p. 80; Tatscheva-Hitova 1983, pp. 194, 213. For the use of lamps in Judaism see CAp 2:118, 282; Ant 12:325; Seneca (Stern 1974, no. 188); Persius (Stern 1974, no. 190).
83 Bickerman's view (1958, pp. 137–64) is based on an incorrect understanding of Ant 14:227, 260 and the questionable use of Rabbinic literature to decide on the use of the Pergamum altar. On sacrificial worship in Jerusalem see e.g. Ant 5:112, CAp 2:193. Note, however, the existence of temples at Elephantine, Araq el-Emir and Leontopolis in an earlier period. On the bomos as a base for the lantern stand see Delling 1964–5, pp. 79–80. Alternatively, it is possible that the base was used for burning incense (on which see Goodenough 1953–68, 4, pp. 195–208) or that it may simply have carried the inscription.
84 Bickerman 1958, p. 158; Delling 1964–5, p. 79; Nilsson 1960b, pp. 298–301; J. and L. Robert, *BE* 1958, no. 413; Siegert 1973, pp. 142–4 think Zopyros was probably a God-worshipper. Kraabel (1969, p. 90 n40) thought he was probably a Gentile convert; Nock

(1972, p. 895 n1) thought he was a Jew and used the altar to burn incense. Other relevant inscriptions from outside Asia Minor cannot be dealt with in detail here. However, the evidence is insufficient to decide if the people referred to in *CIJ* 202, 228, 500, 619a, 731e, Paton and Hicks 1891, no. 278 are Jews or God-worshippers. *IG* 14, 2259 may well refer to a Jew.

85 See Cyril of Alexandria, *De Adoratione in Spiritu et Veritate* 3, 92 in Migne *PG* 68.281 BC. On this group see Schürer 1897, pp. 222–3; Bickerman 1958, p. 157; Simon 1981b, col. 1069.

86 *PG* 35.990f and *PG* 45.482–4 respectively. See on this group (which Gregory of Nazianzus calls 'Υψιστάριοι), Schürer 1897, pp. 221–5; Ramsay 1906b, pp. 35–6; Foakes Jackson and Lake 1920–33, 5, p. 95; Simon 1981b, cols. 1068–70.

87 We have identified other probable God-worshippers elsewhere; see, for example, Aurelia Tatis at Acmonia, in chapter 6, section 5.1.

88 Bellen 1965–6, pp. 171–2; Rajak 1985a, p. 258; Schürer, Vermes and Millar 1986, 3.1, p. 168; Kant 1987, pp. 689–90; Reynolds and Tannenbaum 1987, p. 22. Kraabel (1981b, pp. 113–26; 1985, pp. 224–32), who has questioned the existence of the 'God-fearers', believes that they should have left some trace in excavated synagogues. However, the Aphrodisias inscription is precisely the sort of evidence he required. Secondly, in his 1981 article, Kraabel does not discuss the inscriptional evidence from Panticapaeum, Tralles or Miletus. Finally, he does not deal with literary references in Juvenal, Epictetus, Josephus and Philo which, at the least, suggest that the phenomenon of the 'God-fearer' was well-known.

89 See Simon 1981b, col. 1067; Reynolds and Tannenbaum 1987, pp. 56–66.

90 The only inscriptional evidence from the first century is from Panticapaeum. The earliest inscription from Asia Minor is the inscription from Miletus, probably to be dated in the second century.

91 Cf. Reynolds and Tannenbaum 1987, pp. 88–9. Note how much our inscriptional evidence for Jewish communities increases in the later period, making the argument from silence difficult.

8 Jewish community and Greek city in Asia Minor

1 On citizenship in the Greek city see A. H. M. Jones 1940, pp. 157–62, 172–3; Safrai and Stern 1974, p. 434. Citizenship was determined by birth but could also be granted to foreigners who were, for example, benefactors of the city.

2 Tcherikover 1961, pp. 328–9; see also Gauger 1977, pp. 46–8; Schürer, Vermes and Millar 1986, 3.1, p. 127; Marcus in Josephus, vol. 7, pp. 737–41. Josephus states that citizenship was at least in part a reward for serving in the army of Seleucus Nicator. However, we have no independent evidence that Jews served in his army; see Gauger 1977, pp. 42–3. Note also the difference between BJ 7:44 and Ant 12:119–20/CAp 2:39 as regards which king gave the Jews citizenship in Antioch. The difficulty of reconciling Claudius' letter

(see CPJ 153) with the Edict given in Ant 19:280–5 also casts doubt
on Josephus' general usage of legal terminology and thus on these
passages. A number of scholars understand these passages to mean
that the Jewish community at Antioch had its own politeuma. This
could be suggested by BJ 7:110 and the use of δικαιώματα; see also
Ant 12:121; BJ 7:43–4; Safrai and Stern 1974, p. 138; Smallwood
1981, pp. 358–60. πολιτεία could then mean citizenship of the
Jewish politeuma; see Smallwood 1981, pp. 229–30, 359 and note
11 below. This does not necessarily mean that the Jews in Ionia were
organised in politeumata, however. Some scholars accept the claims
of Ant 12:119; see, for example, Ramsay 1897, p. 668; Kittel 1944,
col. 11; Blanchetière 1974, p. 374.

3 See Safrai and Stern 1974, pp. 436, 445–6; *LSJ*, p. 840.
4 To the Greeks' accusation that 'by merely spreading over their
 country the Jews were now doing them all kinds of harm', Josephus
 writes: 'But the Jews proved that they were natives (ἐγγενεῖς) ...'
 (Ant 16:59; a variant reads εὐγενεῖς). This would seem to be an
 opportunity for the Jews to assert their citizenship, if they did in
 fact possess it. Josephus' use of ἐγγενής is therefore revealing.
5 See the discussions of these two passages in Tcherikover 1961,
 pp. 329–30; Schürer, Vermes and Millar 1986, 3.1, pp. 129–30;
 Safrai and Stern 1974, pp. 441–2; Marcus in Josephus, vol. 7,
 pp. 741–2; cf. Ramsay 1902a, pp. 92–4; Hemer 1986, pp. 38, 224
 n 10. On Ant 16:27–61 see also Schalit 1969, pp. 426–34; Roddaz
 1984, pp. 451–63. Smallwood 1981, pp. 140–1 reads the text too
 much in the light of the Alexandrian situation.
6 See Schürer, Vermes and Millar 1986, 3.1, p. 120 n 52; Safrai and
 Stern 1974, p. 442. The inscriptions from the synagogue are from
 a much later period.
7 On the term see Ziebarth in *RE* 21, 2, 1952, cols. 1401–2; Tarn 1952,
 p. 147; Tcherikover 1961, p. 299; Fraser 1962, pp. 147–52; Smallwood 1981, pp. 139, 225–6. Politeumata were a regular feature of
 Hellenistic cities, and a number of non-Jewish examples are known.
8 See *CPJ* 153. It seems that at least part of the Jewish community
 sought to gain Alexandrian citizenship through such means as
 entering the ephebate, but Claudius' letter put an end to these
 aspirations. The literature on Alexandria is extensive. See Bell 1924,
 pp. 1–37; H. S. Jones 1926, pp. 17–35; *CPJ* 2, pp. 25–107;
 Tcherikover 1961, pp. 311–26; Safrai and Stern 1974, pp. 125–33,
 421–30, 435–40, 473–7; Smallwood 1970, pp. 6–14; 1981, pp.
 224–55; Kasher 1985, pp. 29f.
9 See Lüderitz 1983, nos. 70–1; Schürer, Vermes and Millar 1986,
 3.1, pp. 88–9, 94–5; Applebaum 1979, p. 183; Baldwin Bowsky
 1987, pp. 495–510; cf. Lüderitz 1983 no. 72.
10 See Schürer, Vermes and Millar 1986, 3.1, p. 90. The term also
 occurs in an inscription from Nysa (see later in this section) and in
 Lüderitz 1983, no. 71.
11 A number of scholars think the Sardis community was organised
 as a politeuma; see Smallwood 1970, p. 8; 1981, p. 139; Safrai and

Stern 1974, pp. 477–8; Rajak 1979, p. 193. The range of meaning of πολιτεύω is quite wide.

12 That πολῖται was an interpolation see Tarn and Griffith 1952, p. 221 n9; Schürer, Vermes and Millar 1986, 3.1, p. 130 n17. That members of a politeuma may have been called πολῖται see Marcus, Josephus, vol. 7, p. 587 n. f; Smallwood 1970, p. 8; 1981, pp. 229–30, 359; see also Kasher 1985, pp. 234f.

13 The suggestion that Jews used πολίτης to designate a member of their politeuma seems to explain the use of πολίτης by Philo and Josephus with reference to Jews in Alexandria. They would then be claiming membership of the politeuma not citizenship of the city. (See, for example, Ant 12:121; 14:188; Philo, Flacc. 47, Leg. 193, 349.) This sort of technically incorrect usage of legal terms is similar to Josephus describing Jews as Alexandrians and Antiochians in CAp 2:38–9 and Ant 19:281. However, it is another matter to claim that a *city* used πολίτης of Jewish members of a politeuma; see H. S. Jones 1926, p. 28.

14 On Antioch see Meeks and Wilken 1978, p. 2 and note 2 above. There was perhaps a Jewish politeuma at Caesarea; see Kasher 1977–8, pp. 16–27. That this was the general constitutional form of organisation see e.g. Tcherikover 1961, pp. 299–305; Hengel 1974, 1, p. 38; Smallwood 1981, pp. 139, 226.

15 See Rajak 1979, pp. 192–3; Schürer, Vermes and Millar 1986, 3.1, p. 113.

16 Text in Humann et al. 1898, no. 212 = *CIJ* 775. On κατοικία see Oertel in *RE* 11, 1922, cols. 1–13; Schürer, Vermes and Millar 1986, 3.1, p. 89; Kraabel 1968, pp. 130–4. It perhaps indicates that the community began as a military settlement, see Bar-Kochva 1976, pp. 22–6. The Jewish community at Hierapolis also possessed an archive; see *CIJ* 775–6, 778; Solin 1983, p. 698 n239a. This suggests they had a significant measure of independence. In another inscription from Hierapolis a fine is to be paid τῷ λαῷ τῶν 'Ιουδαί[ω]ν; see Humann et al. 1898, no. 69. Thus at Hierapolis the Jewish community's constitutional position was probably that of a κατοικία, whilst the community also called itself 'the people of the Jews'. Other terms which were used as a designation by Jewish communities in Asia Minor are: οἱ 'Ιουδαῖοι (Ephesus) see Robert 1960b, pp. 381–4; λαός (Smyrna) see Robert 1960b, pp. 259–62; ἔθνος (Smyrna) see *CIJ* 741; συναγωγή was common, e.g. at Phocaea, Deliler, Hyllarima. No conclusions concerning the legal or political position of the Jewish communities can be drawn from these general terms.

17 Text in Robert 1960b, p. 261; Lifshitz 1967, no. 31. See also Schürer, Vermes and Millar 1986, 3.1, pp. 89–90. σύνοδος is also found with regard to Sardis in Ant 14:235, as noted above.

18 Ramsay's view (1902a, pp. 22–33) that Jews were enrolled as citizens of a special Jewish tribe within the Greek city is unlikely; see Welles 1962, p. 59.

19 On Paul's citizenship of Tarsus see in particular Cadbury 1955,

pp. 80–1; Welles 1962, pp. 61–2; A. N. Sherwin-White 1963, pp. 178–9. On Sardis see chapter 2, section 4. For the inscription from Corycus see *CIJ* 788. None of the seventy-one Jews listed in the new Aphrodisias inscription can be said to have had local citizenship (see Reynolds and Tannenbaum 1987, pp. 124–5), which suggests that very few Jews had local citizenship in the period from which the inscription comes. The Jewish ἀρχίατρος at Ephesus (see section 3) may well have been a citizen of the city and perhaps a Roman citizen as well. We know of a few Jews who were citizens of their cities elsewhere, most notably in Alexandria and Cyrene.

20 The later exemption by Dolabella seems to exempt all Jews and not just Roman citizens; see Ant 14:225–7. Roman citizenship could be gained through an individual grant, through discharge after serving as an auxiliary and through formal manumission. See A. N. Sherwin-White 1973, pp. 245–50, 322f; Balsdon 1979, pp. 82–96; see also Bell 1942, pp. 47–8. It could not officially be purchased. The cost mentioned in Acts 22:26–8 would be to bribe officials.

21 Smallwood 1981, pp. 127–8; see also Saulnier 1981, pp. 168–9, 194. For the view that a significant number of Jews possessed Roman citizenship see Safrai and Stern 1974, p. 152; Tcherikover 1961, p. 330; Schürer, Vermes and Millar 1986, 3.1, p. 120. Some Jews could have gained citizenship through emancipation by Roman masters.

22 (a) See Acts 16:37, 22:25–9, 23:27; see also Cadbury 1955, pp. 65–82; A. N. Sherwin-White 1963, pp. 145–62, 172–85; Welles 1962, p. 62. (b) See chapter 3, section 2; the inscription is to be dated in the 80s–90s. (c) See Robert 1960b, pp. 381–4, to be dated towards the end of the second century CE. (d) See *CIJ* 770, improved in Robert 1955, p. 253. (e) See Robert 1960b, pp. 259–62; Petzl 1982, no. 296. This could be before or after 212 CE. Other inscriptions concern people who are citizens but the inscriptions cannot be dated accurately enough; see, for example, *CIJ* 762. No Jewish Roman citizens are found in the new list of Jews at Aphrodisias, but the inscription was probably dated to before 212 CE; see Reynolds and Tannenbaum 1987, p. 126. We know of Jewish Roman citizens prior to 212 CE elsewhere; Lüderitz 1983 no. 70, 71 (Berenice); *CPJ* 162, 174 (Alexandria); Le Bohec 1981b, pp. 215–17 (Carthage and Roman Africa, some before 212). On the situation at Rome see Philo, *Leg.* 155–8; Smallwood 1970, pp. 233–5, 242.

23 On the Constitutio Antoniniana see A. H. M. Jones 1936, pp. 223–35; Bell 1942, pp. 39–49; Millar 1962, pp. 124–31; A. N. Sherwin-White 1973, pp. 280–7, 380–94. Some inscriptions from Asia Minor are difficult to date and thus we do not know if they are before or after 212. For example in a third-century inscription we learn of Π(όπλιος) 'Ρουτ(ίλιος) 'Ιωσῆς, archisynagogos at Teos; see Robert 1940, pp. 27–8; cf. *CIJ* 744; Pottier and Hauvette-Besnault 1880, p. 181, no. 44. But was this before 212? See also *CIJ* 776.

24 The issue of the attitude of Jews who were involved in the city to pagan cults will be dealt with at the end of this section.

25 On Sardis see chapter 2, section 4. On Acmonia see chapter 3, section 3. On Corycus see *MAMA* 3, 262; *CIJ* 788; Robert 1964, p. 56. The Side inscription is in Bean et al. 1956, no. 69; reinterpreted by Robert 1958b, pp. 36–47. On ζυγοστάτης see also Theodosian Code 12.7.2 in Pharr 1969, p. 378; cf. Brooten 1982, p. 229 n93.

26 Text in Hicks 1890b, no. 677. On these doctors see Wellmann, *RE* 2, 1896, cols. 464–6; Liebenam 1900, pp. 100–4; Keil 1905, pp. 128–38 (the series of inscriptions from Ephesus); Wolters 1906, pp. 295–7; *New Docs* 1977, pp. 10–25; Nutton 1977, pp. 198–226; Dig. XXVII.1.6, 2–4; L.9.4, 2. Another Jewish doctor is known at Venosa; see *CIJ* 600; cf. *CIJ* 1, 5*; 1100. On the Jews in Ephesus see Schürer, Vermes and Millar 1986, pp. 22–3; Kraabel 1968, pp. 51–60.

27 It has been thought that two magistrates, Melito and Andronicus, whose names appear on second-century coins in Sala were Jews by birth because their father's name was Σαλαμῶνος. Melito was also a pagan high priest or an archon. See the coins in Head 1901, pp. 227–30, 232; and for this view see Ramsay 1902a, pp. 102–3; Kraabel 1968, p. 74 n2. However, it seems likely that the name Σαλαμῶνος is Lydian; see Zgusta 1964, p. 451; Schürer, Vermes and Millar 1986, p. 3.1, p. 26. In *MAMA* 3, 607 = *CIJ* 793 from Corycus, the Jew [M]ωσῖ is described as προταυράριος. But was this a position in a city organisation or a Jewish group? One of the members of the Jewish decany in the new Aphrodisias inscription is called Θεόδοτος Παλατῖν(ος?). Reynolds and Tannenbaum (1987, pp. 42–3) suggest he was a former employee of the court. This is not a magistracy but a position which could give someone in a small provincial town tremendous social prestige. The parents of Debborah, probably from Antioch on the Maeander in the late second or third century CE (see *MAMA* 4.202; cf. *CIJ* 722), had won many honours in their city and may have held office, but this is not definite; see Robert 1963b, pp. 401–6; *MAMA* 7, p. x n1; cf. Ramsay 1907, pp. 255–9.

28 On Jews holding significant positions before 200 CE in Egypt see CAp 2:49–53, 64; Ant 13:284–7, 348–55; *CIJ* 1450, 1531; *CPJ* 1, pp. 18–19, 49 n4, 194–226; *CPJ* 25, 132, 137, 428, 677; Kasher 1978, pp. 65–7. Other evidence in Lüderitz 1983, no. 8; Applebaum 1964, pp. 292–303 (Cyrene); Malalas in *PG* 97, col. 440, lines 9–10; Nock 1972, p. 961 (Antioch); Kaplan 1963–4, p. 113 (Jaffa). For possible office holders after 200 CE outside Asia Minor see Le Bohec 1981a, no. 79 (Volubilis, Mauretania); Rahmani 1972, p. 114 (near Hebron); Lifshitz in *CIJ*², pp. 47–8 (Venosa); see also A. H. M. Jones 1964, pp. 947–8, 1392–3; Hunt 1982, pp. 106–23.

29 See Smallwood 1981, p. 514; Reynolds and Tannenbaum 1987, p. 126.

30 Inscription in *IGR* 4, 1431; *CIJ* 742. Translated as 'the former Jews' by e.g. Smallwood 1981, pp. 234 n59, 507; Frend 1965, p. 148 n47; Safrai and Stern 1974, p. 57. That the phrase means 'those of the former Jewish nation' (see Ziebarth 1896, p. 129; Ramsay 1904c,

pp. 323–4) is unlikely. Translated as 'the former Judaeans' by Kraabel 1968, pp. 30–2; 1982, p. 455; Brooten 1982, p. 11; Lane Fox 1986, p. 481; see also Solin 1983, pp. 647–9. These Jews had perhaps arrived after the Jewish War.

31 See chapter 3, section 6. The inscription is undated. *MAMA* 4.202 may be comparable; see Robert 1963b, pp. 401–6.

32 Inscription in chapter 7, section 4.5. On the theatre see Bieber 1961, pp. 1f; *OCD* pp. 1051–2. Philo probably attended the theatre and athletic competitions; see Prob. 26, 110–13, 141; Agr. 111–17, 119–21; Deissmann 1927, p. 452; Goodenough 1929, pp. 2–3; Harris 1976, pp. 51–95; see also Poliakoff 1984, pp. 59–65. Ant 19:332–4 suggests that there was controversy about theatre going amongst Jews in Josephus' time.

33 Inscriptions in Reynolds and Tannenbaum 1987, p. 132; see also Alan Cameron 1976, p. 315. On the odeum in general see Bieber 1961, pp. 174–7, 220–1. The Jewish community at Berenice set up two inscriptions in an 'amphitheatre'; see Lüderitz, 1983, nos. 70–1. This was probably the city's amphitheatre which suggests that the Jews attended games there along with their Greek neighbours; see Reynolds 1981, p. 247; Schürer, Vermes and Millar 1986, 3.1, p. 104.

34 Ant 16:165; on this decree and its date see chapter 1, note 51.

35 A comparable example from Alexandria in Philo, Flacc. 97–103. A third century CE inscription from Hyllarima, Caria might begin 'For the health ... of the King ...' but the inscription is fragmentary; see Lifshitz 1967, no. 32.

36 See chapter 2, section 4.1.

37 See chapter 4, section 3.

38 There is some similar evidence from elsewhere; see *CPJ* 1532A, *CIJ* 1432, 1440–4 (Egypt); Lüderitz 1983, no. 71; Baldwin Bowsky 1987, pp. 495–510 (Berenice); *CIJ* 972 (Palestine); *CIJ*^{2} 677 (Intercisa in the Balkans); *CIJ*^{2} 678a (Mursa); *AE* 1967, no. 77 (Ostia); Philo, Leg. 133, 280; Fl. 48 (Alexandria). Often these concern dedications by a Jewish community to a ruler.

39 See Magie 1950, p. 62; Sheppard 1975, pp. 36–8, 44–6. On the high value placed upon education in the Hellenistic world see Marrou 1956, pp. 95f; Hengel 1974, 1, pp. 65–70; Feldman 1960, p. 224.

40 Inscription in Robert 1937a, pp. 85–6. The name 'Ioudas' occurs frequently among Jews at Rome, see *CIJ* 1, p. 610; also Robert 1940, pp. 28–9; 1946, p. 101 n2. On others in the list being Jewish see Tcherikover 1971, p. 350; Kraabel 1968, p. 16.

41 Inscription in S. Reinach 1885a, pp. 74–5; *CIJ* 755; it is complete. On the association of young men see Forbes 1933, pp. 1–69; Sheppard 1975, pp. 51–5. On the interpretation of the inscription see S. Reinach 1885a, pp. 75–6; *CIJ* 2, p. 20; Kraabel 1968, p. 181; Poliakoff 1984, p. 63. One of the donors to the Sardis synagogue was a citizen and council member of Hypaepa; see chapter 2, section 4. This suggests that some Jews were involved in the life of the city which adds weight to the interpretation given in the text. Krauss (1922, p. 231, no. 60, p. 395) thought the inscription designated the

place where the younger Jews sat in the synagogue, whilst the older Jews sat elsewhere; see also Achelis 1900, pp. 95–6. However, we have no convincing evidence for segregation of this sort; cf. Reynolds and Tannenbaum 1987, p. 132. It has been suggested that the inscription shows that some young Jews were organised in their own gymnasium; see Safrai and Stern 1974, p. 478; Kasher 1976b, pp. 155, 161 n64, but this is unlikely in view of the other Jewish ephebes known to us and the situation at Sardis.

42 Note the difference in attitude to the gymnasium compared with that in 2 Macc 4:9–17. However, Judaism in the Diaspora was not shaped by the events of the Maccabean period to anything like the same degree as the Judaism of Palestine, and so different attitudes probably emerged; see Kraabel 1987, pp. 55–6. We know of Jewish ephebes elsewhere; see Applebaum 1979, pp. 167–8, 177–8, 185; Lüderitz 1983, nos. 6, 7 (Cyrenaica); *CIJ*^{2} 721c (Coronea in the Peloponnese). Claudius' letter implies that some Jews in Alexandria had joined the ephebate; see *CPJ*, vol. 1, pp. 38–9. vol. 2, no. 153. Note also that one of the God-worshippers at Aphrodisias was probably an athlete and another a boxer; see Reynolds and Tannenbaum 1987, pp. 119, 121. On Jewish involvement in the gymnasium see in general Safrai and Stern 1974, pp. 447–9; Hengel 1974, 1, pp. 67–8.

43 On names used by Jews in Asia Minor see Ramsay 1902a, pp. 103–4; Kittel 1944, col. 14; Kraabel 1983, p. 184; Reynolds and Tannenbaum 1987, pp. 93–105; in general see Juster 1914, 2, pp. 221–34.

44 Text in Humann *et al.* 1898, no. 342; *CIJ* 777. On the Jews in the city see Kraabel 1968, pp. 125–35; J. and L. Robert, *BE* 1971, no. 645.

45 That they were Jewish guilds see Ziebarth 1896, p. 129; Ramsay 1902a, pp. 98–101; Krauss 1922, p. 234; Safrai and Stern 1974, pp. 480–3. Other clearly pagan inscriptions from Hierapolis mention the guild of the purple dyers by the same name; see Humann *et al.* 1898, nos. 41–2, 133, 227, pp. 50–1. Could a Jewish guild and a different pagan guild be called by exactly the same name in the one city? This is possible, but Aelius Glykon could be expected to indicate that he meant the *Jewish* purple dyers' guild. That the guilds had both Gentile and Jewish members see Cichorius in Humann *et al.* 1898, pp. 46, 51; Kraabel 1983, p. 181.

46 Judeich's view in Humann *et al.* 1898, p. 174.

47 See Humann *et al.* 1898, pp. 129–30; Ramsay 1895a, pp. 105–7; see also Broughton 1938a, pp. 819f, 841–6.

48 On decorating a grave with a wreath see Humann *et al.* 1898, nos. 133, 195. On the arrangements for this see Humann *et al.* 1898, pp. 129–130; K. M. Miller 1985, p. 47.

49 On Julia Severa see chapter 3, section 2. On Capitolina see chapter 7, section 4.3. On Aphrodisias see chapter 7, section 4.1. Augustus and his adviser M. Agrippa may have been patrons of two synagogues in Rome; see e.g. *CIJ* 284, 301, 365, 503.

50 See Lane Fox 1986, pp. 64–101; Price 1984, pp. 101–32; A. H. M. Jones 1940, pp. 227–35. Note that Jews were not compelled to participate in the Imperial cult, apart from under Caligula; see Lane Fox 1986, pp. 428–30.

51 See chapter 1, section 7. What the Jews in Smyrna actually did when faced with pagan worship at close range is not revealed by the incident.

52 See mAbod.Zar. 1:1–2. MAbod.Zar. 4:7 suggests that Roman Jews did not follow Rabbinic ideas on idolatry; see Rajak 1985a, p. 253. This line of action is also urged for Christians by Tertullian; see e.g. *De Idolatria* 13–16.

53 CAp 2:65 suggests that in Apion's time the Jews in Alexandria followed the same course.

54 On the exemption see chapter 2, section 4.

55 See Nock 1972, pp. 960–1; also Meeks 1983, pp. 37–8; Smallwood 1981, pp. 234–5; cf. Ramsay 1904b, pp. 148–9. The author of Acts clearly thought it credible that Paul was a citizen of Tarsus and a Roman citizen and a practising Jew. The Sardianoi in the Sardis synagogue in a later period seem to be practising Jews.

56 See bAbod.Zar. 51b, 52a; cf. mAbod.Zar. 4:4; Urbach 1959, pp. 157–65; Reynolds and Tannenbaum 1987, p. 57; contrary opinions in bAbod.Zar. 52a; note also mAbod.Zar. 3:4. The rabbinic legislation on this subject is not uniform, some rulings demonstrate severity, others leniency, which indicates how difficult the problem was in concrete situations and the debate it created; see Urbach 1959, p. 158.

57 Urbach 1959, p. 233.

58 See chapter 6, section 4.7. Another example in Rajak 1985a, pp. 259–60 from Cyrene. Perhaps Jews could cite the Biblical precedent of Naaman who had to make a compromise between his beliefs and necessity and thus 'bowed down in the house of Rimmon'; see 2 Kgs 5:18.

59 See *CIJ* 749; see also Tcherikover 1961, p. 352; Kraabel 1968, p. 17; Hengel 1976, pp. 104–5.

60 See Reynolds and Tannenbaum 1987, pp. 56–7. Note also that nine of the God-worshippers were city councillors and thus would have been expected to be present at pagan sacrifices, whilst none of the Jews seem to have been city councillors. This is probably before the ruling of Severus and Caracalla.

61 See Acts 13:50, 14:2, 5, 19; chapter 1, section 6. Note also that in chapter 2, section 5 I suggested there was continuity of good relations between the Jewish community and the city of Sardis from the mid first century BCE onwards until the destruction of the synagogue in 616 CE. However, there is no evidence from the first century CE itself.

Conclusions

1 See e.g. Askowith 1915, p. 69; M. Weber 1952, pp. 417—18; Bickerman 1958, pp. 150—1; Tcherikover 1961, p. 296; Frend 1965, p. 130; Meeks 1983, p. 36; Smallwood 1981, p. 123.

2 Scholars have often thought or implied that Jewish communities had to remain insular in order to remain Jewish. If the communities were involved in the life of the city or had adopted local practices it was thought to be a sign of syncretism. See e.g. Levy 1900, pp. 187—8; Bousset 1926, p. 473; Cumont 1929, p. 100; Oesterley 1935, pp. 119—24; Nilsson 1950, p. 639. We do know of some individual Jews who abandoned Judaism; see Hengel 1974, 1, p. 31; 2, p. 25 n224.

3 Modern authors include Smallwood 1981, p. 123; Frend 1965, p. 130; Malherbe 1977, pp. 51—2; Balsdon 1979, p. 67. They cite such authors as Diodorus (in Stern 1974, no. 63); Juvenal (in Stern 1980, no. 301); Philostratus (in Stern 1980, no. 403); Tacitus (*Historiae* V, 5; in Stern 1980, no. 281); see Smallwood 1981, p. 123 n15.

4 An example which shows how distorted the general pagan view of Judaism could be is the fact that a number of classical authors thought the Sabbath was a day of gloom and fasting; see, for example, Pompeius Trogus (Stern 1974, no. 137); Martial (Stern 1974, no. 239); and in general Goldenberg 1979, pp. 435—42. It seems that although classical authors knew of the Sabbath, they knew very little about it.

5 See Hengel 1980, pp. 55—6; in general see Balsdon 1979, pp. 18—29, 64—70.

6 Our appreciation of the variety and diversity within Judaism in Palestine and the Diaspora in this period has greatly increased in recent years; see e.g. M. Smith 1956, pp. 67—81; Kraabel 1982, pp. 457—8; Porton 1986, pp. 57—80; Georgi 1987, pp. 366—71.

7 A third-century CE inscription from Deliler, Lydia, contains the word μασκαύλης, a transliteration of a Talmudic Hebrew term which means washbasin; see Keil and Premerstein 1914, no. 42; Lifshitz 1967, no. 28. However, we do not know if the word came directly from a rabbinic source in the third century or if it had been used in Deliler for a very long time, perhaps since ancestors of Jews living in Deliler had lived in Babylon or Palestine. Reynolds and Tannenbaum 1987, p. 27 (see also pp. 78—86) propose that the word πάτελλα in the Aphrodisias inscription is evidence for the spread of rabbinic authority in the Diaspora, but see the review in Goodman 1988, p. 262. On bShab. 147b, often thought to refer negatively to Jews in Phrygia, see Kraabel 1968, pp. 148—9; 1982, p. 450; cf. Ramsay 1897, p. 674; Kittel 1944, col. 15.

8 The expression is from Wilken 1980, p. 467.

9 In all of this the problem of dating, namely that a good deal of our evidence comes from after the period of the NT, must not be overlooked.

REFERENCES

Abbott, F.F., & Johnson, A.C. 1926. *Municipal Administration in the Roman Empire.* Princeton University Press.

Achelis, H. 1900. 'Spuren des Urchristentums auf den griechischen Inseln?' *ZNW* 1, pp. 87–100.

Akurgal, E. 1985. *Ancient Civilisations and Ruins of Turkey.* Eighth edn. Istanbul: Haset Kitabevi.

Alexander, P.S. 1984. 'Epistolary Literature.' In *Jewish Writings of the Second Temple Period*, ed. M.E. Stone, pp. 579–96. Compendia Rerum Iudaicarum ad Novum Testamentum 2, ii. Assen: Van Gorcum.

Amaru, B.H. 1988. 'Portraits of Biblical Women in Josephus' Antiquities.' *JJS* 39, pp. 143–70.

Anderson, J.G.C. 1897. 'A Summer in Phrygia I.' *JHS* 17, pp. 396–424.

1906. 'Paganism and Christianity in the Upper Tembris Valley.' In *Studies in the History and Art of the Eastern Provinces of the Roman Empire*, ed. W.M. Ramsay, pp. 183–227. Aberdeen University Press.

Applebaum, S. 1961. 'The Jewish Community of Hellenistic and Roman Teucheira in Cyrenaica.' *Scripta Hierosolymitana* 7, pp. 27–52.

1964. 'Jewish Status at Cyrene in the Roman Period.' *La Parola Del Passato* 19, pp. 291–303.

1971. 'Jews and Service in the Roman Army.' In *Roman Frontier Studies 1967. The Proceedings of the Seventh International Congress held at Tel Aviv*, ed. M. Gichon, pp. 181–4. Tel Aviv: Students' Organisation of Tel Aviv University.

1976. *Prolegomena to the Study of the Second Jewish Revolt. (A.D. 132–135).* Oxford: British Archaeological Reports Supplementary Series 7.

1979. *Jews and Christians in Ancient Cyrene.* SJLA 28. Leiden: Brill.

1984. 'The Second Jewish Revolt (AD 131–35).' *PEQ* 116, pp. 35–41.

Archer, L.J. 1983. 'The Role of Jewish Women in the Religion, Ritual and Cult of Graeco-Roman Palestine.' In *Images of Women in Antiquity*, eds. A. Cameron & A. Kuhrt, pp. 273–87. London: Croom Helm.

Arkwright, W. 1911. 'Penalties in Lycian Epitaphs of Hellenistic and Roman Times.' *JHS* 31, pp. 269–75.

Arnold, C.E. 1989. *Ephesians: Power and Magic. The Concept of Power in Ephesians in Light of its Historical Setting.* SNTSMS 63. Cambridge University Press.

Askowith, D. 1915. *The Toleration of Jews under Julius Caesar and Augustus*. Ph.D. Thesis, Faculty of Political Science, Columbia University, New York.

Atkinson, K.M.T. 1958. 'The Governors of the Province Asia in the Reign of Augustus.' *Historia* 7, pp. 300–30.

1959. 'The Historical Setting of the Habakkuk Commentary.' *JSS* 4, pp. 238–63.

Attridge, H.W. 1984. 'Josephus and His Works.' In *Jewish Writings of the Second Temple Period*, ed. M.E. Stone, pp. 185–232. Compendia Rerum Iudaicarum ad Novum Testamentum 2, ii. Assen: Van Gorcum.

Aune, D.E. 1976. 'Orthodoxy in First Century Judaism? A Response to N.J. McEleney.' *JSJ* 7, pp. 1–10.

Aupert, P., & Masson, O. 1979. 'Inscriptions d'Amathonte I.' *BCH* 103, pp. 361–89.

Babelon, E. 1891. 'La tradition phrygienne du déluge.' *RHR* 23, pp. 174–83.

Baldwin Bowsky, M.W. 1987. 'M. Tittius Sex. F. Aem. and the Jews of Berenice.' *AJPh* 108, pp. 495–510.

Balsdon, J.P.V.D. 1979. *Romans and Aliens*. London: Duckworth.

Bandy, A.C. 1963. 'Early Christian Inscriptions of Crete.' *Hesperia* 32, pp. 227–47.

Bar-Kochva, B. 1976. *The Seleucid Army. Organization and Tactics in the Great Campaigns*. Cambridge University Press.

Barnard, L.W. 1964. 'The Old Testament and Judaism in the Writings of Justin Martyr.' *VT* 14, pp. 395–406.

1967. *Justin Martyr His Life and Thought*. Cambridge University Press.

Barnes, T.D. 1967. 'Hadrian and Lucius Verus.' *JRS* 57, pp. 65–79.

Baron, S.W. 1942. *The Jewish Community. Its History and Structure to the American Revolution*. 3 vols. Philadelphia: Jewish Publication Society of America.

1952. *A Social and Religious History of the Jews*. Second edn. Vols. 1 and 2. New York: Columbia University Press.

Barrett, C.K. 1976. 'Jews and Judaizers in the Epistles of Ignatius.' In *Jews, Greeks and Christians, Religious Cultures in Late Antiquity. Essays in Honor of William David Davies*, eds. R. Hamerton-Kelly & R. Scroggs, pp. 220–44. SJLA 21. Leiden: Brill.

Bean, G.E. 1960. 'Notes and Inscriptions from Pisidia Part II.' *AS* 10, pp. 43–82.

1966. *Aegean Turkey. An Archaeological Guide*. London: Ernest Benn.

1979. *Turkey's Southern Shore*. Second edn. London: Ernest Benn.

1980. *Turkey Beyond the Maeander*. Second edn. London: Ernest Benn.

Bean, G.E., Mansel, A.M., & Inan, J. 1956. *Die Agora von Side und die benachbarten Bauten. Bericht über die Ausgrabungen im Jahre 1948*. Ankara: Turk Tarih Kurumu Basineui.

Belkin, S. 1935. 'The Problem of Paul's Background.' *JBL* 54, pp. 41–60.

Bell, H.I. 1924. *Jews and Christians in Egypt. The Jewish Troubles in Alexandria and the Athanasian Controversy, Illustrated by Texts from Greek Papyri in the British Museum*. London: British Museum.

1942. 'P. Giss. 40 and the *Constitutio Antoniniana*.' *JEA* 28, pp. 39–49.

Bellefontaine, E. 1975. 'The Curses of Deuteronomy 27: Their Relationship to the Prohibitives.' In *No Famine in the Land. Studies in honor of John L. McKenzie*, eds. J. W. Flanagan & A. W. Robinson, pp. 49–61. University of Montana, Missoula: Scholars Press.

Bellen, H. 1965–6. 'Συναγωγὴ τῶν 'Ιουδαίων καὶ Θεοσεβῶν. Die Aussage einer bosporanischen Freilassungsinschrift (*CIRB* 71) zum Problem der "Gottfürchtigen".' *JAC* 8/9, pp. 171–6.

Bernand, E. 1983. 'Au Dieu Très Haut.' In *Hommages à Jean Cousin. Rencontres avec l'Antiquité Classique*, Institut Felix Gaffiot, vol. 1, pp. 107–11. Paris: Les Belles Lettres.

Bernays, J. 1885. 'Die Gottesfürchtigen bei Juvenal.' In *Gesammelte Abhandlungen* 2, ed. H. Usener, pp. 71–80. Reprint 1971, Hildesheim: Georg Olms.

Best, E. 1972. *A Commentary on the First and Second Epistles to the Thessalonians*. London: A. & C. Black.

Beyerlin, W. 1965. *Origins and History of the Oldest Sinaitic Traditions*. Oxford: Blackwell.

Bickerman, E. J. 1947. 'Apocryphal Correspondence of Pyrrhus.' *CPh* 42, pp. 137–46.

   1958. 'The Altars of Gentiles. A Note on the Jewish "ius sacrum".' *RIDA* 5, pp. 137–64.

   1980a. 'Une question d'authenticité: les privilèges juifs.' In *Studies in Jewish and Christian History*, Part 2, pp. 24–43. AGJU 9. Leiden: Brill.

   1980b. 'La charte séleucide de Jérusalem.' In *Studies in Jewish and Christian History*, Part 2, pp. 44–85. AGJU 9. Leiden: Brill.

Bieber, M. 1961. *The History of the Greek and Roman Theater*. Second edn. Princeton University Press.

Bird, P. 1974. 'Images of Women in the Old Testament.' In *Religion and Sexism. Images of Women in the Jewish and Christian Traditions*, ed. R. R. Ruether, pp. 41–88. New York: Simon an=Schuster.

Bittel, K. 1975. 'Christliche und jüdische Grabsteine.' *Bogazköy* 5 (Abhandlungen der Deutschen Orient-Gesellschaft 18), pp. 108–13. Berlin: Mann.

Björck, G. 1938. *Der Fluch des Christen Sabinus. Papyrus Upsaliensis 8*. Arbeter Utgivna Med Understöd Av. Vilhelm Ekmans Universitetsfond, Uppsala 47. Uppsala: Almquist & Wiksells.

Blanchetière, F. 1974. 'Juifs et non juifs. Essai sur la diaspora en Asie Mineure.' *RHPhR* 54, pp. 367–82.

   1984. 'Le juif et l'autre: la diaspora Asiate.' In *Etudes sur le judaïsme hellénistique*, eds. R. Kuntzmann & J. Schlosser, pp. 41–59. LD 119. Paris: Les Editions du Cerf.

Blass, F. Debrunner, A., & Funk, R. W. 1961. *A Greek Grammar of the New Testament and Other Early Christian Literature*. Cambridge University Press.

Bogaert, P-M. 1972. 'Les "Antiquités Bibliques" du Pseudo-Philo. Quelques observations sur les chapitres 39 et 40 à l'occasion d'une réimpression.' *RTL* 3, pp. 334–44.

Bousset, W. 1911. 'Sibyl, Sibylline Books.' *The New Schaff–Herzog Encyclopedia of Religious Knowledge* X, pp. 396–400. New York: Funk & Wagnalls.

1926. *Die Religion des Judentums im späthellenistischen Zeitalter.* Third edn rev. by H. Gressmann. HNT 21. Tübingen: J. C. B. Mohr (Paul Siebeck).

Bowersock, G. W. 1964. 'C. Marcius Censorinus, Legatus Caesaris.' *HSCPh* 68, pp. 207–10.

1980. 'A Roman Perspective on the Bar Kochba War.' In *Approaches to Ancient Judaism, vol. 2,* ed. W. S. Green, pp. 131–41. BJS 9. Chico, California: Scholars Press.

Braude, W. G. 1940. *Jewish Proselytising in the First Five Centuries of the Common Era. The Age of the Tannaim and Amoraim.* Providence RI: Brown University.

Braunstein, O. 1911. *Die politische Wirksamkeit der griechischen Frau. Eine Nachwirkung vorgriechischen Mutterrechtes.* Leipzig: August Hoffmarin.

Brawley, R. L. 1987. *Luke–Acts and the Jews. Conflict, Apology and Conciliation.* SBLMS 33. Atlanta, Georgia: Scholars Press.

Brenner, A. 1985. *The Israelite Woman. Social Role and Literary Type in Biblical Narrative.* The Biblical Seminar 2. Sheffield: JSOT Press.

Brinkman, J. A. 1963. 'The Literary Background of the "Catalogue of the Nations" (Acts 2.9–11).' *CBQ* 25, pp. 418–27.

Brooke, A. E., McLean, N., & Thackeray, H. St. J. 1935. *The Old Testament in Greek, vol. 2, The Later Historical Books.* Cambridge University Press.

Brooten, B. J. 1981a. 'Inscriptional Evidence for Women as Leaders in the Ancient Synagogue.' In *SBL 1981 Seminar Papers,* ed. K. H. Richards, pp. 1–17. Chico, California: Scholars Press.

1981b. 'Jüdinnen zur Zeit Jesu. Ein Plädoyer für Differenzierung.' *ThQ* 161, pp. 281–5.

1982. *Women Leaders in the Ancient Synagogue. Inscriptional Evidence and Background Issues.* BJS 36. Chico, California: Scholars Press.

Broughton, T. R. S. 1938a. 'Roman Asia Minor.' In *An Economic Survey of Ancient Rome,* ed. T. Frank, vol. 4, pp. 499–916. Baltimore: Johns Hopkins Press.

1938b. 'A Greek Inscription from Tarsus.' *AJA* 42, pp. 55–7.

1951, 1952, 1960, 1986. *The Magistrates of the Roman Republic.* 4 vols. New York: American Philological Association.

Bruce, F. F. 1984. 'Colossian Problems Part I: Jews and Christians in the Lycus Valley.' *BSac* 141, pp. 3–15.

1988. *The Book of the Acts.* Revised ed. NICNT. Grand Rapids: Eerdmans.

Bruneau, P. 1970. *Recherches sur les cultes de Délos à l'époque hellénistique et à l'époque impériale.* BEFAR 217. Paris: de Boccard.

1982. ' "Les Israélites de Délos" et la juiverie délienne.' *BCH* 106, pp. 465–504.

Bruneau, P., & Ducat, J. 1965. *Guide de Délos.* Paris: Ecole française d'Athènes.

Brunt, P. A. 1983. 'Princeps and Equites.' *JRS* 73, pp. 42–75.

Büchler, A. 1956. *Studies in Jewish History. The Adolph Büchler Memorial Volume.* eds. I. Brodie & J. Rabbinowitz. Jews' College Publications New Series 1. Oxford University Press.

Buckler, W. H., & Robinson, D. M. 1932. *Sardis. Publications of the American Society for the Excavation of Sardis, vol. 7, Greek and Latin Inscriptions.* Part 1. Leyden: Brill.

Buis, P. 1967. 'Deuteronome XXVII 15–26: Malédictions ou exigences de l'alliance?' *VT* 17, pp. 478–9.

Bultmann, R. 1964. 'ΔΙΚΑΙΟΣΥΝΗ ΘΕΟΥ.' *JBL* 83, pp. 12–16.

1985. *The Second Letter to the Corinthians.* Minneapolis: Augsburg.

Cabanes, P. 1983. 'La place de la femme dans l'Epire antique.' *Iliria* 13, pp. 201–9.

Cadbury, H. J. 1955. *The Book of Acts in History.* London: A. & C. Black.

Cadoux, C. J. 1938. *Ancient Smyrna. A History of the City from the Earliest Time to 324 AD.* Oxford: Blackwell.

Calder, W. M. 1922. 'New Light on Ovid's Story of Philemon and Baucis.' *Discovery* 3, pp. 207–11.

1924a. 'Notes on Anatolian Religion. II. Nannakos and Enoch.' *Journal of the Manchester Egyptian and Oriental Society* 11, pp. 30–2.

1924b. 'The Tears of Nannakos.' *CR* 38, p. 113.

1924c. 'Studies in Early Christian Epigraphy II.' *JRS* 14, pp. 85–92.

1925. 'The Royal Road in Herodotus.' *CR* 39, pp. 7–11.

1930. 'Lake Trogitis.' *Klio* 23, pp. 88–91.

1939a. 'The Eumeneian Formula.' In *Anatolian Studies Presented to William Hepburn Buckler,* eds. W. M. Calder & J. Keil, pp. 15–26. Manchester University Press.

1939b. 'The Epitaph of Avircius Marcellus.' *JRS* 29, pp. 1–4.

1955. 'Early Christian Epitaphs from Phrygia.' *AS* 5, pp. 25–38.

Cameron, A. 1931. 'Latin Words in the Greek Inscriptions of Asia Minor.' *AJPh* 52, pp. 232–62.

Cameron, Alan. 1976. *Circus Factions. Blues and Greens at Rome and Byzantium.* Oxford: Clarendon Press.

Cameron, Averil. 1980. 'Neither Male Nor Female.' *G & R* 27, pp. 60–8.

Camp, C. V. 1981. 'The Wise Woman of 2 Samuel: A Role Model for Women in Early Israel?' *CBQ* 43, pp. 14–29.

Carrington, P. 1976. *The Distribution and History of Elements of the Native Culture of Roman Phrygia with Reference to their Ethnic Origin.* Thesis submitted to the Faculty of Arts of the University of Newcastle-upon-Tyne for the Degree of Doctor of Philosophy.

Casarico, L. 1982. 'Donne Ginnasiarco (a proposito di P. Med. inv. 69.01).' *ZPE* 48, pp. 117–23.

Chapot, V. 1904. *La province romaine proconsulaire d'Asie.* Paris: Librairie Emile Bouillon.

Charlesworth, J. H. 1981. *The Pseudepigrapha and Modern Research with a Supplement.* SBLSCS 7S. Chico, California: Scholars Press for SBL.

ed., 1983, 1985. *The Old Testament Pseudepigrapha.* 2 vols. London: Darton, Longman & Todd.

1986. 'Jewish Hymns, Odes, and Prayers (ca. 167 BCE–135 CE).' In *Early Judaism and its Modern Interpreters,* eds. R. A. Kraft & G. W. E. Nickelsburg, pp. 411–36. Atlanta, Georgia: Scholars Press.

Chiat, M. J. S. 1982. *Handbook of Synagogue Architecture* BJS 29. Chico, California: Scholars Press.

Childs, B. S. 1974. *Exodus*. OT Library. London: SCM.

Cichorius, C. 1922. *Römische Studien. Historisches, Epigraphisches, Literargeschichtliches aus vier Jahrhunderten Roms*. Leipzig: B. G. Teubner.

Clemen, C. 1924. *Religionsgeschichtliche Erklärung des Neuen Testaments*. Second edn. Berlin: Alfred Töpelmann.

Clerc, M. 1886. 'Inscriptions de Thyatire et des environs.' *BCH* 10, pp. 398–423.

Cohen, G. M. 1978. *The Seleucid Colonies. Studies in Founding, Administration and Organization*. Historia Einzelschriften Heft 30. Wiesbaden: Franz Steiner.

Cohen, J. 1976. 'Roman Imperial Policy Toward the Jews from Constantine Until the End of the Palestinian Patrarchate (ca. 429).' *Byzantine Studies* 3, pp. 1–29.

Cohen, N. G. 1969. *Jewish Names and their Significance in the Hellenistic and Roman Periods in Asia Minor*. 2 vols. Thesis submitted to the Hebrew University of Jerusalem for the degree of Doctor of Philosophy. Hebrew with English summary.

1976. 'Jewish Names as Cultural Indicators in Antiquity.' *JSJ* 7, pp. 97–128.

Cohen, S. J. D. 1979. *Josephus in Galilee and Rome. His Vita and Development as a Historian*. Columbia Studies in the Classical Tradition 8. Leiden: Brill.

1980. 'Women in the Synagogues of Antiquity.' *Conservative Judaism* 34, pp. 23–9.

1981–2. 'Epigraphical Rabbis.' *JQR* 72, pp. 1–17.

1986. 'Was Timothy Jewish (Acts 16:1–3)? Patristic Exegesis, Rabbinic Law, and Matrilineal Descent.' *JBL* 105, pp. 251–68.

Collart, P. 1930. 'Inscription de Sélian-Mésoréma.' *BCH* 54, pp. 376–91.

1931. 'ΠΑΡΑΚΑΥΣΟΥΣΙΝ ΜΟΙ ΡΟΔΟΙΣ.' *BCH* 55, pp. 58–69.

Collins, A. Y. 1985. 'Insiders and Outsiders in the Book of Revelation and its Social Context.' In *'To See Ourselves As Others See Us.' Christians, Jews, 'Others' in Late Antiquity*, eds. J. Neusner & E. S. Frierichs, pp. 187–218. Chico, California: Scholars Press.

Collins, J. J. 1974a. *The Sibylline Oracles of Egyptian Judaism*. SBLDS 13. University of Montana, Missoula: Scholars Press.

1974b. 'Structure and Meaning in the Testament of Job.' In *SBL 1974 Seminar Papers*, ed. G. MacRae, vol. 1, pp. 35–52. Cambridge, Massachusetts: SBL.

1983a. 'Sibylline Oracles.' In *The Old Testament Pseudepigrapha*, ed. J. H. Charlesworth, vol. 1, pp. 317–472. London: Darton, Longman & Todd.

1983b. *Between Athens and Jerusalem. Jewish Identity in the Hellenistic Diaspora*. New York: Crossroad.

1984a. *The Apocalyptic Imagination. An Introduction to the Jewish Matrix of Christianity*. New York: Crossroad.

1984b. 'The Sibylline Oracles.' In *Jewish Writings of the Second Temple Period*, ed. M. E. Stone, pp. 357–81. Compendia Rerum Iudaicarum ad Novum Testamentum 2, ii, Assen: Van Gorcum.

1987. 'The Development of the Sibylline Tradition.' *ANRW* II, 20.1, pp. 421–59.

Colpe, C. 1967. 'Hypsistos.' *Der Kleine Pauly* 2, cols. 1291–2.

Conzelmann, H. 1987. *A Commentary on the Acts of the Apostles.* Hermeneia. Philadelphia: Fortress Press.

Cook, A. B. 1914, 1925, 1940. *Zeus. A Study in Ancient Religion.* 3 vols. Cambridge University Press.

Cook, S. A. 1917. 'A Lydian–Aramaic Bilingual.' *JHS* 37, pp. 77–87, 219–31.

Cormack, J. M. R. 1974. 'Zeus Hypsistos at Pydna.' In *Mélanges helléniques offerts à Georges Daux,* pp. 51–5. Paris: de Boccard.

Couroyer, B. 1969. 'Antiquités chrétiennes.' *RB* 76, pp. 148–9.

Craghan, J. F. 1982. 'Esther, Judith and Ruth: Paradigms for Human Liberation.' *BTB* 12, pp. 11–19.

Craven, T. 1983. 'Tradition and Convention in the Book of Judith.' *Semeia* 28, pp. 49–61.

Crosby, M. 1941. 'Greek Inscriptions: A Poletai Record of the Year 367/6 BC.' *Hesperia* 10, pp. 14–27.

Cumont, F. 1895. 'Les inscriptions chrétiennes de l'Asie Mineure.' *Mélanges d'archéologie et d'histoire de l'école française de Rome* 15, pp. 245–99.

1897. *Hypsistos.* Supplément à la Revue de l'instruction publique en Belgique.

1906. 'Les mystères de Sabazius et le judaïsme.' *CRAIBL*, pp. 63–79.

1910. 'A propos de Sabazius et du judaïsme.' *MB* 14, pp. 55–60.

1911. *The Oriental Religions in Roman Paganism.* Chicago: The Open Court Publishing Co.

1912. 'Un ex-voto au Théos Hypsistos.' *RHR* 66, p. 165.

1913. *Catalogue des sculptures et inscriptions antiques (monuments lapidaires) des musées royaux du cinquantenaire.* Brussels: Vromant.

1916. '"Υψιστος.' *RE* 9, cols. 444–50.

1929. *Les religions orientales dans le paganisme romain.* Troisième edn Paris: Librairie Leroux.

Dalton, W. J. 1965. *Christ's Proclamation to the Spirits. A Study of 1 Peter 3:18–4:6.* AnBib 23. Rome: Pontifical Biblical Institute.

Danker, F. W. 1982. *Benefactor: Epigraphic Study of a Graeco-Roman and New Testament Semantic Field.* St Louis, Missouri: Clayton Publishing House.

Daux, G. 1971. 'Réflexions sur l'épigraphie.' In *Acta of the Fifth International Congress of Greek and Latin Epigraphy, Cambridge 1967,* pp. 1–8. Oxford: Blackwell.

Deissmann, A. 1927. *Light from the Ancient East. The New Testament Illustrated by Recently Discovered Texts of the Graeco-Roman World.* Fourth edn. London: Hodder and Stoughton.

De Jonge, M. 1978. *The Testaments of the Twelve Patriarchs. A Critical Edition of the Greek Text.* PVTG 1. Leiden: Brill.

Delling, G. 1931. *Paulus' Stellung zu Frau und Ehe.* Stuttgart: Kohlhammer.

1964–5. 'Die Altarinschrift eines Gottesfürchtigen in Pergamon.' *NovT* 7, pp. 73–80.

1975. *Bibliographie zur jüdisch-hellenistischen und intertestamentarischen Literatur 1900–1970.* Second edn. TU 106.2. Berlin: Akademie.

Den Boeft, J., & Bremmer, J. 1985. '"Notiunculae Martyrologicae"

III. Some Observations on the Martyria of Polycarp and Pionius.'
VC 39, pp. 110–30.

Dentan, R. C. 1963. 'The Literary Affinities of Exodus xxxiv 6f.' *VT* 13,
pp. 34–51.

Dibelius, M. 1956. *Studies in the Acts of the Apostles*. London: SCM.

Diehl, C., & Cousin, G. 1887. 'Inscriptions de Lagina.' *BCH* 11, pp. 5–39,
145–63.

Dill, S. 1905. *Roman Society from Nero to Marcus Aurelius*. Second edn.
London: Macmillan and Co.

Dinkler, E. 1953. 'Literaturbericht zur christlichen Archäologie, 1938–1953.'
TRu 21, pp. 318–40.

1974. 'Schalom–Eirene–Pax. Jüdische Sepulkralinschriften und ihr
Verhältnis zum frühen Christentum.' *RDAC* 50, pp. 121–44.

Dodd, C. H. 1935. *The Bible and the Greeks*. London. Hodder and Stoughton.

Dodds, E. R. 1940. 'Maenadism in the Bacchae.' *HTR* 33, pp. 155–76.

Donahue, P. J. 1978. 'Jewish Christianity in the Letters of Ignatius of
Antioch.' *VC* 32, pp. 81–93.

Donner, H., & Röllig, W. 1962–4. *Kanaanäische und Aramäische Inschriften*.
3 vols. Wiesbaden: Otto Harrassowitz.

Dörner, F. K. 1940. 'Außerbithynische Inschriften im Museum von Bursa
und neue Funde aus Eskischehir (Dorylaion).' *JÖAI* 32, Beiblatt,
cols. 107–36.

Dossin, G. 1963. 'La légende phrygienne de Nannakos.' *Bulletin de la classe
des lettres de l'Académie Royale de Belgique* 49, pp. 336.

Drew-Bear, T. 1976. 'Local Cults in Graeco-Roman Phrygia.' *GRBS* 17,
pp. 247–68.

1978. *Nouvelles inscriptions de Phrygie*. Studia Amstelodamensia 16.
Zutphen: Terra.

Driver, S. R. 1902. *A Critical and Exegetical Commentary on Deuteronomy*.
Third edn. ICC. Edinburgh: T. & T. Clark.

Eger, O., Kornemann, E., & Meyer, P. M. 1910–12. *Griechische Papyri im
Museum des Oberhessischen Geschichtsvereins zu Giessen*. 1. Reprint
1973, Milano: Cisalpino.

Elbogen, I. 1931. *Der jüdische Gottesdienst in seiner geschichtlichen
Entwicklung*. Third edn. Frankfurt am Main: Kauffmann.

Esler, P. F. 1987. *Community and Gospel in Luke–Acts. The Social and
Political Motivations of Lucan Theology*. SNTSMS 57. Cambridge
University Press.

Exum, J. C. 1985. '"Mother in Israel": A Familiar Figure Reconsidered.'
In *Feminist Interpretation of the Bible*, ed. L. M. Russell, pp. 72–85.
Oxford: Blackwell.

Feldman, L. H. 1950. 'Jewish "Sympathizers" in Classical Literature and
Inscriptions.' *TAPA* 81, pp. 200–8.

1960. 'The Orthodoxy of the Jews in Hellenistic Egypt.' *Jewish Social
Studies* 22, pp. 215–37.

1984a. *Josephus and Modern Scholarship (1937–1980)*. Berlin: Walter
de Gruyter.

1984b. 'Flavius Josephus Revisited: The Man, His Writings and His
Significance.' *ANRW* II, 21.2, pp. 763–862.

1986. 'The Omnipresence of the God-Fearers.' *BAR* 12.5, pp. 58–69.

Fellmann, R. 1981. 'Der Sabazios-Kult.' In *Die orientalischen Religionen im Römerreich*, ed. M. J. Vermaseren, pp. 316–40. EPRO 93. Leiden: Brill.

Fiedler, M. J. 1970. 'Δικαιοσύνη in der diaspora-jüdischen und intertestamentarischen Literatur.' *JSJ* 1, pp. 120–43.

Fink, J. 1955. *Noe der Gerechte in der frühchristlichen Kunst*. Beihefte zum Archiv für Kulturgeschichte Heft 4. Münster/Cologne: Bohlau.

Fink, R. O., Hoey, A. S., & Snyder, W. F. 1940. 'The Feriale Duranum.' *YCS* 7, pp. 1–222.

Finn, T. M. 1985. 'The God-Fearers Reconsidered.' *CBQ* 47, pp. 75–84.

Fiorenza, E. 1973. 'Apocalyptic and Gnosis in the Book of Revelation.' *JBL* 92, pp. 565–81.

1983. *In Memory of Her*. New York: Crossroad.

Fishbane, M. 1977. 'Torah and Tradition.' In *Tradition and Theology in the Old Testament*, ed. D. A. Knight, pp. 275–300. London: SPCK.

1985. *Biblical Interpretation in Ancient Israel*. Oxford: Clarendon Press.

Floriani Squarciapino, M. 1963. 'The Synagogue at Ostia.' *Archaeology* 16, pp. 194–203.

Foakes Jackson, F. J., & Lake, K. 1920–33. *The Beginnings of Christianity. Part 1. The Acts of the Apostles*. 5 vols. London: Macmillan and Co.

Fontenrose, J. 1945. 'Philemon, Lot and Lycaon.' *University of California Publications in Classical Philology* 13, 1944–1950, pp. 93–119.

Forbes, C. A. 1933. *Neoi. A Contribution to the Study of Greek Associations*. Middletown, Connecticut: American Philological Association.

Ford, J. M. 1966. 'Was Montanism a Jewish–Christian Heresy?' *JEH* 17, pp. 145–58.

Foss, C. 1976. *Byzantine and Turkish Sardis*. Archaeological Exploration of Sardis Monograph 4. Cambridge, Massachusetts: Harvard University Press.

1979. *Ephesus after Antiquity: A Late Antique, Byzantine and Turkish City*. Cambridge University Press.

Foucart, P. 1887. 'Exploration de la plaine de l'Hermus par M. Aristotle Fontrier.' *BCH* 11, pp. 79–107.

Frank, T. 1938. *An Economic Survey of Ancient Rome*. Baltimore: John Hopkins Press.

Franke, P. 1973. 'Bemerkungen zur frühchristlichen Noe-Ikonographie.' *RDAC* 49, pp. 171–82.

Franke, P. R., Leschhorn, W., & Stylow, A. U., eds. 1981. *Sylloge Nummorum Graecorum Deutschland Sammlung v. Aulock Index*. Berlin: Mann.

Fränkel, M. 1890. *Die Inschriften von Pergamon*. Altertümer von Pergamon Band VIII.2. Königliche Museen zu Berlin. Berlin: Spemann.

Fraser, P. M. 1962. 'Inscriptions from Ptolemaic Egypt.' *Berytos* 13, pp. 123–61.

Frazer, J. G. 1919. *Folk-Lore in the OT. Studies in Comparative Religion, Legend and Law*. London: Macmillan and Co.

Freedman, D. N. 1960. 'The Name of the God of Moses.' *JBL* 79, pp. 151–6.

Frend, W. H. C. 1965. *Martyrdom and Persecution in the Early Church. A Study of a Conflict from the Maccabees to Donatus*. Oxford: Blackwell.

Fuks, A. 1961. 'Aspects of the Jewish Revolt in AD 115–117.' *JRS* 51, pp. 98–104.

Funk, F. X. 1905. *Didascalia et Constitutiones Apostolorum*, vol. 1. Paderborn: Ferdinandi Schoeningh.

Furnish, V. P. 1984. *II Corinthians*. AB. New York: Doubleday.

Gager, J. G. 1973. 'The Dialogue of Paganism with Judaism: Bar Cochba to Julian.' *HUCA* 44, pp. 89–118.

1983. *The Origins of Anti-Semitism. Attitudes Toward Judaism in Pagan and Christian Antiquity.* Oxford University Press.

1986. 'Jews, Gentiles, and Synagogues in the Book of Acts.' In *Christians Among Jews and Gentiles. Essays in Honor of Krister Stendal on his Sixty-Fifth Birthday*, eds. G. W. E. Nickelsburg, G. W. MacRae, pp. 91–9. Philadelphia: Fortress Press.

Galanté, A. 1937, 1939. *Histoire des juifs d'Anatolie*. 2 vols. Istanbul: M. Babok.

Gardner, J. F. 1986. *Women in Roman Law and Society.* London: Croom Helm.

Garnsey, P. 1983. 'Grain for Rome.' In *Trade in the Ancient Economy*, eds. P. Garnsey, K. Hopkins & C. R. Whittaker, pp. 118–30. London: Hogarth Press.

Gauger, J-D. 1977. *Beiträge zur jüdischen Apologetik. Untersuchungen zur Authentizität von Urkunden bei Flavius Josephus und im I. Makkabäerbuch.* BBB 49. Cologne–Bonn: Peter Hanstein.

Geffcken, J. 1902a. *Die Oracula Sibyllina*. GCS. Leipzig: J. C. Hinrichs.

1902b. *Komposition und Entstehungszeit der Oracula Sibyllina.* TU 23.1. Leipzig: J. C. Hinrichs.

Georgi, D. 1987. *The Opponents of Paul in Second Corinthians.* Edinburgh: T. & T. Clark.

Gero, S. 1978. 'Jewish Polemic in the Martyrium Pionii and a "Jesus" Passage from the Talmud.' *JJS* 29, pp. 164–8.

Gibson, E. P. 1978. *The 'Christians for Christians' Inscriptions of Phrygia. Greek Texts, Translations and Commentary.* HTS 32. University of Montana, Missoula: Scholars Press.

Ginsburg, M. S. 1930–1. 'Fiscus Judaicus.' *JQR* 21, pp. 281–91.

Ginzberg, L. 1902. 'Archisynagogue.' *JE* 2, p. 86.

1909f. *The Legends of the Jews.* 7 vols. Philadelphia: Jewish Publication Society of America.

Goldenberg, R. 1979. 'The Jewish Sabbath in the Roman World up to the Time of Constantine the Great.' *ANRW* II, 19.1, pp. 414–47.

Goldstein, J. A. 1976. *I Maccabees*. AB. New York: Doubleday.

Goodblatt, D. 1975. 'The Beruriah Traditions.' *JJS* 26, pp. 68–85.

Goodenough, E. R. 1923. *The Theology of Justin Martyr. An Investigation into the Conceptions of Early Christian Literature and its Hellenistic and Judaistic Influences.* Reprint 1968, Amsterdam: Philo Press.

1929. *The Jurisprudence of the Jewish Courts in Egypt. Legal Administration by the Jews under the Early Roman Empire as described by Philo Judaeus.* New Haven: Yale University Press.

1953–68. *Jewish Symbols in the Greco-Roman Period.* 13 vols. New York: Pantheon Books.

1956–7. 'The Bosporus Inscription to the Most High God.' *JQR* 47, pp. 221–44.

1962. *An Introduction to Philo Judaeus*. Second edn. Oxford: Blackwell.

Goodman, M. 1988. 'Review of J. Reynolds and R. Tannenbaum, *Jews and God-Fearers at Aphrodisias: Greek Inscriptions with Commentary*, Cambridge: Philological Society.' *JRS* 78, pp. 261–2.

Gordon, A. E. 1983. *Illustrated Introduction to Latin Epigraphy*. Berkeley: University of California Press.

Gottlieb, F. 1981. 'Three Mothers.' *Judaism* 30, pp. 194–203.

Gould, J. 1980. 'Law, Custom and Myth: Aspects of the Social Position of Women in Classical Athens.' *JHS* 100, pp. 38–59.

Grabar, A. 1951. 'Images bibliques d'Apamée et fresques de la synagogue de Doura.' *Cahiers Archéologiques* 5, pp. 9–14.

Grabbe, L. L. 1977. 'Orthodoxy in First Century Judaism. What Are The Issues?' *JSJ* 8, pp. 149–53.

Graetz, H. 1886. 'Die Stellung der kleinasiatischen Juden unter der Römerherrschaft.' *MGWJ* 30, pp. 329–46.

Grant, M. 1973. *The Jews in the Roman World*. London: Weidenfeld and Nicolson.

Grant, R. M. 1980. 'Dietary Laws among Pythagoreans, Jews and Christians.' *HTR* 73, pp. 299–310.

1988. *Greek Apologists of the Second Century*. London: SCM.

Greenewalt, C. H. 1973. 'The Fifteenth Campaign at Sardis (1972).' *BASOR* 211, pp. 14–36.

1976. 'The Seventeenth Campaign At Sardis 1974.' *AASOR* 43, pp. 61–71.

Gressmann, H. 1925. 'Die Aufgaben der Wissenschaft des nachbiblischen Judentums.' *ZAW* 43, pp. 1–32.

Grissom, F. A. 1978. *Chrysostom and the Jews: Studies in Jewish–Christian Relations in Fourth-Century Antioch*. Ph.D. Thesis, Southern Baptist Theological Seminary.

Groag, E. 1907. 'Notizen zur Geschichte kleinasiatischer Familien.' *JÖAI* 10, pp. 282–99.

1919. 'Iulia Severa.' *RE* X, cols. 946–8.

Gschnitzer, F. 1973. 'Prytanis.' *RE* Supplement XIII, cols. 730–816.

Gutmann, J., ed. 1973. *The Dura–Europos Synagogue: A Re-evaluation. (1932–1972)*. University of Montana, Missoula: AAR and SBL.

Hachlili, R. 1976. 'The Niche and the Ark in Ancient Synagogues.' *BASOR* 223, pp. 43–53.

Haenchen, E. 1971. *The Acts of the Apostles. A Commentary*. Oxford: Blackwell.

Hall, A. S. 1978. 'The Klarian Oracle at Oenoanda.' *ZPE* 32, pp. 263–8.

Hall, S. G., ed. 1979. *Melito of Sardis. On Pascha and Fragments. Texts and Translations*. Oxford: Clarendon Press.

Hanfmann, G. M. A. 1963. 'The Fifth Campaign at Sardis (1962).' *BASOR* 170, pp. 1–65.

1964. 'The Sixth Campaign at Sardis (1963).' *BASOR* 174, pp. 3–58.

1965. 'The Seventh Campaign at Sardis (1964).' *BASOR* 177, pp. 2–37.

1966. 'The Eighth Campaign at Sardis (1965).' *BASOR* 182, pp. 2–54.

1967a. 'The Ninth Campaign at Sardis (1966).' *BASOR* 187, pp. 9–62.

1967b. 'The Ancient Synagogue of Sardis.' In *Fourth World Congress of Jewish Studies Papers*, vol. 1, pp. 37–42. Jerusalem.

1968. 'The Tenth Campaign at Sardis (1967).' *BASOR* 191, pp. 2–41.

1970. With J. C. Waldbaum. 'The Eleventh and Twelfth Campaigns at Sardis.' *BASOR* 199, pp. 7–58.

1971. With R. S. Thomas. 'The Thirteenth Campaign at Sardis (1970).' *BASOR* 203, pp. 5–22.

1972. *Letters from Sardis*. Cambridge, Massachusetts: Harvard University Press.

1974. 'The Sixteenth Campaign at Sardis (1973).' *BASOR* 215, pp. 31–60.

1975. *From Croesus to Constantine. The Cities of Western Asia Minor and their Arts in Greek and Roman Times*. Ann Arbor: University of Michigan Press.

1983. *Sardis from Prehistoric to Roman Times. Results of the Archaeological Exploration of Sardis 1958–1975*. Cambridge, Massachusetts: Harvard University Press.

Hanfmann, G. M. A., & Bloom, J. B. 1987. 'Samoe, Priest and Teacher of Wisdom.' *Eretz Israel* 19 (M. Avi-Yonah Memorial Volume), pp. 10*–14*.

Hanfmann, G. M. A., & Ramage, N. H. 1978. *Sculpture from Sardis: The Finds Through 1975*. Archaeological Exploration of Sardis Report 2. Cambridge, Massachusetts: Harvard University Press.

Hanfmann, G. M. A., & Waldbaum, J. C. 1975. *A Survey of Sardis and the Major Monuments Outside the City Walls*. Archaeological Exploration of Sardis Report 1. Cambridge, Massachusetts: Harvard University Press.

Hardy, E. R. 1970. 'The Priestess in the Greco-Roman World.' *Churchman* 84, pp. 264–70.

Harnack, A. 1896. *Geschichte der altchristlichen Literatur bis Eusebius*. Part 2. Reprint 1958, Leipzig: J. C. Hinrichs.

Harris, H. A. 1972. *Sport in Greece and Rome*. New York: Cornell University Press.

1976. *Greek Athletics and the Jews*, eds. I. M. Barton, A. J. Brothers. Trivium Special Publications 3. Cardiff: University of Wales Press.

Harvey, D. 1984. 'Women in Ancient Greece.' *History Today* 34, 8, pp. 45–7.

Hatch, E., & Redpath, H. A. 1897. *A Concordance to the Septuagint*. 3 vols. Oxford: Clarendon Press.

Hatzfeld, J. 1907. 'Une ambassade juive à Pergame.' *REJ* 53, pp. 1–13.

Head, B. V. 1892. *Catalogue of the Greek Coins of Ionia*. London: British Museum.

1901. *Catalogue of the Greek Coins of Lydia*. London: British Museum.

1906. *Catalogue of the Greek Coins of Phrygia*. London: British Museum.

1911. *Historia Numorum. A Manual of Greek Numismatics*. Second edn. Oxford: Clarendon Press.

Heberdey, R. 1915. 'Vorläufiger Bericht über die Grabungen in Ephesos 1913.' *JÖAI* 18, Beiblatt, cols. 77–88.

Heberdey, R., & Kalinka, E. 1896. *Bericht über zwei Reisen im südwestlichen Kleinasien*. DAW, philosophisch-historische Klasse Band 45.1. Vienna: Carl Gerolds Sohn.

Hefele, C.J. 1876. *A History of the Councils of the Church from the Original Documents*, vol. 2. Edinburgh: T. & T. Clark.

Hemer, C.J. 1986. *The Letters to the Seven Churches of Asia in their Local Setting.* JSNTSS 11. Sheffield: JSOT Press.

Hengel, M. 1974. *Judaism and Hellenism. Studies in their Encounter in Palestine during the Early Hellenistic Period.* 2 vols. London: SCM.

— 1975a. 'Proseuche und Synagoge: Jüdische Gemeinde, Gotteshaus und Gottesdienst in der Diaspora und in Palästina.' In *The Synagogue: Studies in Origins, Archaeology and Architecture,* ed. J. Gutmann, pp. 27–54. New York: Ktav.

— 1975b. 'Die Synagogeninschrift von Stobi.' In *The Synagogue: Studies in Origins, Archaeology and Architecture,* ed. J. Gutman, pp. 110–48. New York: Ktav.

— 1979. *Acts and the History of Earliest Christianity.* London: SCM.

— 1980. *Jews, Greeks and Barbarians. Aspects of the Hellenization of Judaism in the pre-Christian Period.* London: SCM.

— 1983. *Between Jesus and Paul. Studies in the Earliest History of Christianity.* London: SCM.

Hennecke, E., ed. 1963, 1965. *New Testament Apocrypha.* English translation ed. by R. McL. Wilson, 2 vols. London: SCM.

Hepding, H. 1910. 'Die Arbeiten zu Pergamon 1908–1909.' *AM* 35, pp. 345–523.

Herrmann, P. 1962. *Ergebnisse einer Reise in Nordostlydien.* Denkschriften der österreichischen Akademie der Wissenschaften, philosophisch-historische Klasse Band 80. Vienna: Hermann Böhlau.

Hicks, E.L. 1890a. 'Ceramus and its Inscriptions.' *JHS* 11, pp. 109–28.

— 1890b. *The Collection of Ancient Greek Inscriptions in the British Museum. Part 3, Priene, Iasos and Ephesus.* Oxford: Clarendon Press. Reprint 1978, Milan: Cisalpino.

— 1891. 'Inscriptions from Western Cilicia.' *JHS* 12, pp. 225–73.

Hilhorst, A. 1982. 'L'Ancien Testament dans la polémique du martyr Pionius.' *Augustinianum* 22, pp. 91–6.

Hill, D. 1967. *Greek Words and Hebrew Meanings: Studies in the Semantics of Soteriological Terms.* SNTSMS 5. Cambridge University Press.

Hiller von Gaertringen, F.F., ed. 1906. *Inschriften von Priene.* Königliche Museen zu Berlin. Berlin: Georg Reimer.

Hillers, D.R. 1964. *Treaty-Curses and the Old Testament Prophets.* BibOr 16. Rome: Pontifical Biblical Institute.

Hirschfeld, G. 1894. 'Apameia Kibotos.' *RE* 1, cols. 2664–5.

Hoey, A.S. 1937. 'Rosaliae Signorum.' *HTR* 30, pp. 15–35.

Hogarth, D.G. 1888. 'Notes upon a visit to Celaenae-Apamea.' *JHS* 9, pp. 343–9.

Holleaux, M. 1920. 'Décret des auxiliaires crétois de Ptolémée Philométor trouvé à Délos.' *APF* 6, pp. 9–23.

Hollis, A.S. 1970. *Ovid Metamorphoses Book VIII. Edited with an Introduction and Commentary.* Oxford: Clarendon Press.

Holmes, T.R. 1923. *The Roman Republic and the Founder of the Empire,* vol. 3. Oxford; Clarendon Press.

Hommel, H. 1975. 'Juden und Christen im kaiserzeitlichen Milet.' *IM* 25, pp. 167–95.

Homolle, T. 1882. 'Le proconsul Rabirius. Correction au texte de Josèphe.' *BCH* 6, pp. 608–12.

Hooyman, R. P. J. 1958. 'Die Noe-Darstellung in der frühchristlichen Kunst. Eine christlich-archäologische Abhandlung zu J. Fink: Noe der Gerechte in der frühchristlichen Kunst.' *VC* 12, pp. 113–35.

Hopkins, C. 1979. *The Discovery of Dura-Europos*, ed. B. Goldman. New Haven: Yale University Press.

Hula, E. 1893. 'Eine Judengemeinde in Tlos.' *Eranos Vindobonensis* 1893, pp. 99–102.

Hulen, A. B. 1932. 'The "Dialogues with the Jews" as sources for the Early Jewish Argument against Christianity.' *JBL* 51, pp. 58–70.

Humann, C., Cichorius, C., Judeich, W., & Winter, F. 1898. *Altertümer von Hierapolis*. Jahrbuch des Kaiserlich Deutschen Archaeologischen Instituts Ergänzungsheft IV. Berlin: Georg Reimer.

Hunt, E. D. 1982. 'St Stephen in Minorca. An Episode in Jewish–Christian Relations in the Early 5th Century A.D.' *JTS* 33, pp. 106–23.

Iluk, J. 1979. 'Drachmae in the Sepulchral–Penal System of Asia Minor in the Period of the Early Roman Empire.' *Eos* 67, pp. 279–86.

Imhoof-Blumer, F. 1901. *Kleinasiatische Münzen*. Sonderschriften des Österreichischen Archäologischen Institutes in Wien Band I. Vienna: Alfred Hölder.

L'Institut Fernand Courby. 1972–5. *Index du Bulletin Epigraphique de J. et L. Robert 1938–1965*. 3 vols. Paris: Les Belles Lettres.

Irvin, D. 1980. 'The Ministry of Women in the Early Church: The Archaelogical Evidence.' *Duke Divinity School Review*, 45, pp. 76–86.

Jacoby, F. 1957. *Die Fragmente der griechischen Historiker*. Teil 1. Leiden: Brill.

Jamar, A. 1909. 'Les mystères de Sabazius et le judaïsme.' *MB* 13, pp. 227–52.

Jameson, S. 1980. 'The Lycian League: Some Problems in its Administration.' *ANRW* II, 7.2, pp. 832–55.

Janne, H. 1937. 'Magiciens et religions nouvelles dans l'ordre romain.' *Latomus* 1, pp. 37–56.

Jellicoe, S. 1968. *The Septuagint and Modern Study*. Oxford: Clarendon Press.

Johnson, S. E. 1961. 'Christianity in Sardis.' In *Early Christian Origins. Studies in honor of Harold R. Willoughby*, ed. A. Wikgren, pp. 81–90. Chicago: Quadrangle Books.

  1968. 'A Sabazios Inscription from Sardis.' In *Religions in Antiquity. Essays in Memory of Erwin Ramsdell Goodenough*, ed. J. Neusner, pp. 542–50. Leiden: Brill.

  1975. 'Asia Minor and Early Christianity.' In *Christianity, Judaism and Other Greco-Roman Cults. Studies for Morton Smith at Sixty*, ed. J. Neusner, Part 2, pp. 77–145. SJLA 12. Leiden: Brill.

  1978. 'Sabaoth/Sabazios: A Curiosity in Ancient Religion.' *Lexington Theological Quarterly* 13, pp. 97–103.

  1984. 'The Present State of Sabazios Research.' *ANRW* II, 17.3, pp. 1583–1613.

Jones, A. H. M. 1936. 'Another Interpretation of the Constitutio Antoniniana.' *JRS* 26, pp. 223–35.
1940. *The Greek City from Alexander to Justinian*. Oxford: Clarendon
Press.
1964. *The Later Roman Empire, 284–602. A Social, Economic and
Administrative Survey*. 2 vols. Oxford: Blackwell.
1971. *The Cities of the Eastern Roman Provinces*. Second edn. Oxford:
Clarendon Press.
Jones, C. P. 1970. 'A Leading Family of Roman Thespiae.' *HSCPh* 74,
pp. 223–55.
1980. 'Prosopographical Notes on the Second Sophistic.' *GRBS* 21,
pp. 373–80.
1982. 'A Family of Pisidian Antioch.' *Phoenix* 36, pp. 264–71.
Jones, H. S. 1926. 'Claudius and the Jewish Question at Alexandria.' *JRS*
16, pp. 17–35.
Joubin, A. 1894. 'Stèles funéraires de Phrygie.' *RArch* Third Series, 24,
pp. 181–3.
Juster, J. 1914. *Les juifs dans l'Empire romain. Leur condition juridique,
économique et sociale*. 2 vols. Paris: Librairie Paul Geuthner.
Kant, L. H. 1987. 'Jewish Inscriptions in Greek and Latin.' *ANRW* II,
20.2, pp. 671–713.
Kaplan, J. 1963–4. 'The Fifth Season of Excavation at Jaffa.' *JQR* 54,
pp. 110–14.
Karwiese, S. 1971. 'Der Caesar Maximus und die Homonoia Akmoneia-
Eumeneia.' *Numismatische Zeitschrift* 86, pp. 40–2.
Käsemann, E. 1969. *New Testament Questions of Today*. London: SCM.
Kasher, A. 1976a. 'Some Comments on the Jewish Uprising in Egypt in the
Time of Trajan.' *JJS* 27, pp. 147–58.
1976b. 'The Jewish Attitude to the Alexandrian Gymnasium in the First
Century A.D.' *AJAH* 1, pp. 148–61.
1977–8. 'The Isopoliteia Question in Caesarea Maritima.' *JQR* 68,
pp. 16–27.
1978. 'First Jewish Military Units in Ptolemaic Egypt.' *JSJ* 9, pp. 57–67.
1985. *The Jews in Hellenistic and Roman Egypt. The Struggle for Equal
Rights*. Tübingen: J. C. B. Mohr (Paul Siebeck).
Kearsley, R. A. 1986. 'Asiarchs, *Archiereis* and the *Archiereiai* of Asia.'
GRBS 27, pp. 183–92.
Kee, H. C. 1974. 'Satan, Magic and Salvation in the Testament of Job.'
In *SBL 1974 Seminar Papers*, ed. G. MacRae, vol. 1, pp. 53–76.
Cambridge, Massachusetts: SBL.
Keil, J. 1905. 'Ärzteinschriften aus Ephesos.' *JÖAI* 8, pp. 128–38.
1923. 'Die Kulte Lydiens.' In *Anatolian Studies Presented to Sir William
Mitchell Ramsay*, eds. W. H. Buckler & W. M. Calder, pp. 239–66.
Manchester University Press.
1939. 'Kulte im Prytaneion von Ephesos.' In *Anatolian Studies presented
to William Hepburn Buckler*, eds. W. M. Calder & J. Keil, pp. 119–28.
Manchester University Press.
Keil, J., & Maresch, G. 1960. 'Epigraphische Nachlese zu Miltners Ausgra-
bungsberichten aus Ephesos.' *JÖAI* 45, Beiblatt, cols. 75–100.

Keil, J., & Premerstein, A. von. 1911. *Bericht über eine zweite Reise in Lydien.* DAW, philosophisch-historische Klasse Band 54.2. Vienna: Alfred Hölder.

1914. *Bericht über eine dritte Reise in Lydien und den angrenzenden Gebieten Ioniens.* DAW, philosophisch-historische Klasse Band 57.1. Vienna: Alfred Hölder.

Kellett, E. E. 1928. *The Story of Myth.* London: Kegan Paul, Trench & Trubner.

Kenyon, F. G., & Bell, H. I. 1893, 1907. *Greek Papyri in the British Museum.* vol. 1, 3. Reprint 1973, Milan: Cisalpino.

Kindler, A. 1971. 'A Coin-type from Apameia in Phrygia (Asia Minor) depicting the Narrative of Noah.' *Museum Haaretz Bulletin* 13, pp. 24–32.

Kittel, G. 1944. 'Das kleinasiatische Judentum in der hellenistisch-römischen Zeit. Ein Bericht zur Epigraphik Kleinasiens.' *TLZ* 69, cols. 9–20.

Klauser, T. 1961. 'Studien zur Entstehungsgeschichte der christlichen Kunst IV.' *JAC* 4, pp. 128–45.

Kleiner, G. 1968. *Die Ruinen von Milet.* Deutsches Archäologisches Institut Abteilung Istanbul. Berlin: Walter de Gruyter.

1970. *Das römische Milet. Bilder aus der griechischen Stadt in römischer Zeit.* Sitzungsberichte der Wissenschaftlichen Gesellschaft Frankfurt/Main Band 8, Nr 5. Wiesbaden: Franz Steiner.

Klein-Franke, F. 1983. 'A Hebrew Lamentation from Roman Egypt.' *ZPE* 51, pp. 80–4.

Knibbe, D. 1968–70. 'Neue Inschriften aus Ephesos III.' *JÖAI* 49, Beiblatt, cols. 57–88.

Knibbe, D., & Iplikçioglu, B. 1981–2. 'Neue Inschriften aus Ephesos VIII.' *JÖAI* 53, pp. 87–150.

1984. 'Neue Inschriften aus Ephesos IX.' *JÖAI* 55, pp. 107–35.

Koester, H. 1982. *Introduction to the New Testament.* 2 vols. Berlin: Walter de Gruyter.

Kohl, H., & Watzinger, C. 1916. *Antike Synagogen in Galilaea.* Leipzig: J. C. Hinrichs.

Körte, A. 1900. 'Kleinasiatische Studien VI. Inschriften aus Phrygien.' *AM* 25, pp. 398–444.

Kötzsche-Breitenbruch, L. 1976. *Die neue Katakombe an der Via Latina in Rom. Untersuchungen zur Ikonographie der alttestamentlichen Wandmalereien.* JAC Ergänzungsband 4. Münster: Aschendorff.

Kraabel, A. T. 1968. *Judaism in Western Asia Minor under the Roman Empire with a Preliminary Study of the Jewish Community at Sardis, Lydia.* D. Th. Thesis, Harvard University, Cambridge, Massachusetts.

1969. 'Hypsistos and the Synagogue at Sardis.' *GRBS* 10, pp. 81–93.

1971. 'Melito the Bishop and the Synagogue at Sardis: Text and Context.' In *Studies Presented to George M. A. Hanfmann,* eds. D. G. Mitten, J. G. Pedley & J. A. Scott, pp. 77–85. Fogg Art Museum, Harvard University, Monographs in Art and Archaeology II. Mainz: Philipp von Zabern.

1974. 'Synagogues, Ancient.' *New Catholic Encyclopedia: Supplement (1967–1974)* 16, pp. 436–9.

1978. 'Paganism and Judaism: The Sardis Evidence.' In *Paganisme, Judaïsme, Christianisme. Influences et affrontements dans le monde antique. Mélanges offerts à Marcel Simon*, eds. A. Benoit, M. Philonenko & C. Vogel, pp. 13–33; Paris: de Boccard.

1979a. 'The Diaspora Synagogue: Archaeological and Epigraphic Evidence since Sukenik.' *ANRW* II, 19.1, pp. 477–510.

1979b. 'Jews in Imperial Rome: More Archaeological Evidence from an Oxford Collection.' *JJS* 30, pp. 41–58.

1981a. 'Social Systems of Six Diaspora Synagogues.' In *Ancient Synagogues. The State of Research*, ed. J. Gutmann, pp. 79–91. BJS 22. Chico, California: Scholars Press.

1981b. 'The Disappearance of the "God-fearers".' *Numen* 28, pp. 113–26.

1981c. 'The Excavated Synagogues of Late Antiquity From Asia Minor to Italy.' *JÖB* 32, pp. 227–36.

1982. 'The Roman Diaspora: Six Questionable Assumptions.' *JJS* 33, pp. 445–64.

1983. 'Impact of the Discovery of the Sardis Synagogue.' In *Sardis from Prehistoric to Roman Times. Results of the Archaeological Exploration of Sardis 1958–1975*, ed. G. M. A. Hanfmann, pp. 178–90. Cambridge, Massachusetts: Harvard University Press.

1984. 'New Evidence of the Samaritan Diaspora Has Been Found on Delos.' *BA* 47, pp. 44–6.

1985. 'Synagoga Caeca: Systematic Distortion in Gentile Interpretations of Evidence for Judaism in the Early Christian Period.' In *'To See Ourselves As Others See Us.' Christians, Jews, 'Others' in Late Antiquity*, eds. J. Neusner & E. S. Frierichs, pp. 219–46. Chico, California: Scholars Press.

1986. 'Greeks, Jews and Lutherans in the Middle Half of Acts.' In *Christians Among Jews and Gentiles. Essays in Honor of Krister Stendahl on His Sixty-Fifth Birthday*, eds. G. W. E. Nickelsburg & G. W. MacRae, pp. 147–57. Philadelphia: Fortress Press.

1987. 'Unity and Diversity among Diaspora Synagogues.' In *The Synagogue in Late Antiquity*, ed. L. I. Levine, pp. 49–60. Philadelphia: ASOR.

Kraabel, A. T., & MacLennan, R. S. 1986. 'The God-Fearers – A Literary and Theological Invention.' *BAR* 12.5, pp. 47–53.

Kraabel, A. T., & Meyers, E. M. 1986. 'Archaeology, Iconography and Nonliterary Written Remains.' In *Early Judaism and its Modern Interpreters*, eds. R. A. Kraft & G. W. E. Nickelsburg, pp. 175–210. Atlanta, Georgia: Scholars Press.

Kraeling, C. H. 1979. *The Excavations at Dura-Europos. Final Report VIII.I. The Synagogue*. Reprint with new foreword and indices. New York: Ktav. First published 1956.

Kraemer, R. S. 1983. 'Women in the Religions of the Greco-Roman World.' *RelSRev* 9, pp. 127–39.

1985. 'Review of *In Memory of Her: A Feminist Theological Reconstruction of Christian Origins*, by E. Schüssler Fiorenza.' *RelSRev* 11, pp. 6–9.

1985b. 'A New Inscription from Malta and the Question of Women Elders in the Diaspora Jewish Communities.' *HTR* 78, pp. 431–8.

1986a. 'Hellenistic Jewish Women: The Epigraphical Evidence.' In *SBL 1986 Seminar Papers*, ed. K. H. Richards, pp. 183–200. Atlanta, Georgia: Scholars Press.

1986b. 'Non-Literary Evidence for Jewish Women in Rome and Egypt.' *Helios* 13, pp. 85–101.

Kraft, R. A., & Nickelsburg, G. W. E. 1986. *Early Judaism and its Modern Interpreters*. Atlanta, Georgia: Scholars Press.

Krauss, S. 1922. *Synagogale Altertümer*. Berlin–Vienna: Benjamin Harz.

Kroll, J. H. Forthcoming. 'The Greek Inscriptions.' In *The Synagogue at Sardis*, Archaeological Exploration of Sardis Report. Cambridge, Massachusetts: Harvard University Press.

Kubinska, J. 1968. *Les monuments funéraires dans les inscriptions grecques de l'Asie Mineure*. Warsaw: PWN Editions scientifiques de Pologne.

Kuhn, K. G., & Stegemann, H. 1962. 'Proselyten.' *RE* Supp IX, cols. 1248–83.

Künzl, H. 1981. 'Das Judentum.' In *Die orientalischen Religionen im Römerreich*, ed. M. J. Vermaseren, pp. 459–84. EPRO 93. Leiden: Brill.

Kurfess, A. 1941. 'Oracula Sibyllina I/II.' *ZNW* 40, pp. 151–65.

1956. 'Homer und Hesiod im 1. Buch der Oracula Sibyllina.' *Philologus* 100, pp. 147–53.

Labriolle, P. de. 1952. *The Church in the Christian Roman Empire*. London: Burns, Oates and Washbourne.

Lämmer, M. 1981. 'Women and Sport in Ancient Greece. A Plea for a Critical and Objective Approach.' *Medicine Sport* 14, pp. 16–23.

Lane, E. N. 1971, 1976. *Corpus monumentorum religionis dei Menis (CMRDM), vols. I, III*. EPRO 19. Leiden: Brill.

1979. 'Sabazius and the Jews in Valerius Maximus: A Re-examination.' *JRS* 69, pp. 35–8.

1980. 'Towards a Definition of the Iconography of Sabazius.' *Numen* 27, pp. 9–33.

1985. *Corpus Cultus Iovis Sabazii (CCIS) II. The Other Monuments and Literary Evidence*. EPRO 100. Leiden: Brill.

Lane Fox, R. 1986. *Pagans and Christians*. Harmondsworth: Viking.

La Piana, G. 1927. 'Foreign Groups in Rome during the First Centuries of the Empire.' *HTR* 20, pp. 183–403.

Larsen, J. A. O. 1938. 'Roman Greece.' In *An Economic Survey of Ancient Rome*, ed. T. Frank, vol. 4, pp. 259–498. Baltimore: John Hopkins Press.

Lattimore, R. 1942. *Themes in Greek and Latin Epitaphs*. Illinois Studies in Language and Literature 28, no. 1–2. Urbana, Illinois: University of Illinois.

Laubscher, F. Du T. 1980. 'Notes on the Literary Structure of IQS 2:11–18 and its Biblical Parallel in Deut 29.' *JNSL* 8, pp. 49–55.

Laum, B. 1914. *Stiftungen in der griechischen und römischen Antike. Ein Beitrag zur antiken Kulturgeschichte*. Reprint 1964. Aalen: Scientia.

Laumonier, A. 1934. 'Inscriptions de Carie.' *BCH* 58, pp. 291–380.

Le Bohec, Y. 1981a. 'Inscriptions juives et judaïsantes de l'Afrique romaine.' *Antiquités Africaines* 17, pp. 165–207.

1981b. 'Juifs et judaïsants dans l'Afrique romaine. Remarques onomastiques.' *Antiquités Africaines* 17, pp. 209–29.

Leclercq, H. 1924. 'Apamée.' *DACL* I.2, cols. 2500–23.

Le Déaut, R. 1981. 'Le thème de la circoncision du coeur (Dt xxx 6; Jér iv 4) dans les versions anciennes (LXX et Targum) et à Qumran.' In *Congress Volume Vienna 1980*, ed. J. A. Emerton, pp. 178–205. VTSup 32. Leiden: Brill.

Lefkowitz, M. R., & Fant, M. B. 1982. *Women's Life in Greece and Rome. A Sourcebook in Translation*. London: Duckworth.

Legrand, E., & Chamonard, J. 1893. 'Inscriptions de Phrygie.' *BCH* 17, pp. 241–93.

Lemerle, P. 1936. 'Le testament d'un Thrace à Philippes.' *BCH* 60, pp. 336–43.

Leon, H. J. 1960. *The Jews of Ancient Rome*. Philadelphia: Jewish Publication Society of America.

Leutsch, E. L., & Schneidewin, F. G. 1839. *Corpus Paroemiographorum Graecorum*. Reprint 1965. Hildesheim: George Olms.

Levenson, J. D. 1975. 'Who Inserted the Book of the Torah?' *HTR* 68, pp. 203–33.

Lévi, I. 1905, 1906, 1907. 'Le prosélytisme juifs.' *REJ* 50, pp. 1–9; 51, pp. 1–31; 53, pp. 56–61.

Levick, B. 1967. *Roman Colonies in Southern Asia Minor*. Oxford: Clarendon Press.

1971. 'Greek and Latin Epigraphy in Anatolia: Progress and Problems.' In *Acta of the Fifth International Congress of Greek and Latin Epigraphy, Cambridge 1967*, pp. 371–6. Oxford: Blackwell.

1985. *The Government of the Roman Empire. A Sourcebook*. London: Croom Helm.

Levine, L. I., ed. 1981. *Ancient Synagogues Revealed*. Jerusalem: Israel Exploration Society.

Levison, N. 1957. 'The Proselyte in Biblical and Early Post-Biblical Times.' *SJT* 10, pp. 45–56.

Levy, I. 1895. 'Etudes sur la vie municipale de l'Asie Mineure sous les Antonins. Première série. L'ecclesia, la boulé, la gerousia.' *REG* 8, pp. 203–50.

1899. 'Etudes sur la vie municipale de l'Asie Mineure sous les Antonins. Seconde série. Les offices publics.' *REG* 12, pp. 255–89.

1900. 'Notes d'histoire et d'épigraphie.' *REJ* 41, pp. 174–95.

1901. 'Etudes sur la vie municipale de l'Asie Mineure sous les Antonins. Troisième série.' *REG* 14, pp. 350–71.

Lewis, D. M. 1957. 'The First Greek Jew.' *JSS* 2, pp. 264–6.

Lewis, J. P. 1968. *A Study of the Interpretation of Noah and the Flood in Jewish and Christian Literature*. Leiden: Brill.

1984. 'Noah and the Flood in Jewish, Christian and Muslim Tradition.' *BA* 47, pp. 224–39.

Lewy, H. 1938. 'Aristotle and the Jewish Sage according to Clearchus of Soli.' *HTR* 31, pp. 205–35.

Liebenam, W. 1900. *Städteverwaltung im römischen Kaiserreiche*. Reprint 1967. Amsterdam: Hakkert.

References   283

Lieberman, S. 1965. *Greek in Jewish Palestine. Studies in the Life and Manners of Jewish Palestine in the II–IV Centuries CE.* Second edn New York: Philipp Feldheim.
Lietzmann, H. 1938. *The Founding of the Church Universal.* London: Lutterworth.
Lifshitz, B. 1961. 'La vie de l'au-delà dans les conceptions juives.' *RB* 68, pp. 401–11.
1962. 'Les juifs à Venosa.' *RF* 90, pp. 367–71.
1964. 'Le culte du Dieu Très Haut à Gorgippia.' *RF* 92, pp. 157–61.
1965. 'L'hellénisation des juifs de Palestine. A propos des inscriptions de Besara (Beth-Shearim).' *RB* 72, pp. 520–38.
1966. 'Beiträge zur griechisch–jüdischen Epigraphik.' *ZDPV* 82, pp. 57–63.
1967. *Donateurs et fondateurs dans les synagogues juives.* Cahiers de la Revue Biblique 7. Paris: Gabalda.
1969. 'Notes d'épigraphie grecque.' *RB* 76, pp. 92–8.
1970. 'Du nouveau sur les "Sympathisants."' *JSJ* I, pp. 77–84.
1975. *Corpus of Jewish Inscriptions* by Frey, J-B. Second edn, vol. 1, with Prolegomenon by B. Lifshitz. New York: Ktav.
Lifshitz, B., & Schiby, J. 1968. 'Une Synagogue samaritaine à Thessalonique.' *RB* 75, pp. 368–78.
Lightfoot, J. B. 1889. *The Apostolic Fathers. Part II.* Second edn. 3 vols. London: Macmillan and Co.
Lightstone, J. N. 1984. *The Commerce of the Sacred. Mediation of the Divine among Jews in The Graeco-Roman Diaspora.* BJS 59. Chico, California: Scholars Press.
Linder, A. 1987. *The Jews in Roman Imperial Legislation, edited with Introductions, Translations and Commentary.* Detroit: Wayne State University Press.
Liver, J. 1963. 'The Half-Shekel Offering in Biblical and Post-Biblical Literature.' *HTR* 66, pp. 173–98.
Loewe, R. 1966. *The Position of Women in Judaism.* London: SPCK.
Loisy, A. 1920. *Les Actes des Apôtres.* Paris: Emile Nourry.
Lüdemann, G. 1989. *Early Christianity According to the Traditions in Acts. A Commentary.* London: SCM.
Lüderitz, G. 1983. *Corpus jüdischer Zeugnisse aus der Cyrenaika, mit einem Anhang von Joyce M. Reynolds.* Beihefte zum Tübinger Atlas des vorderen Orients Reihe B, nr 53. Wiesbaden: Dr Ludwig Reichert.
McCarthy, D. J. 1981. *Treaty and Covenant. A Study in Form in the Ancient Oriental Documents and in the Old Testament.* Second edn. AnBib 21A. Rome: Biblical Institute Press.
McEleney, N. J. 1973. 'Orthodoxy in Judaism of the First Christian Century.' *JSJ* 4, pp. 19–43.
1978. 'Orthodoxy in Judaism of the First Christian Century. Replies to David E. Aune and Lester L. Grabbe.' *JSJ* 9, pp. 83–8.
MacMullen, R. 1974. *Roman Social Relations. 50 B.C. to A.D. 284.* New Haven: Yale University Press.
1980. 'Women in Public in the Roman Empire.' *Historia* 29, pp. 208–18.
1981. *Paganism in the Roman Empire.* New Haven: Yale University Press.

Madden, F. W. 1866. 'On Some Coins of Septimius Severus, Macrinus, and Philip I, Struck at Apameia in Phrygia with the Legend ΝΩΕ.' *NC* New Series, 6, pp. 173–219.

Magie, D. 1950. *Roman Rule in Asia Minor to the End of the Third Century after Christ.* 2 vols. Princeton University Press.

Malherbe, A. J. 1977. *Social Aspects of Early Christianity.* Baton Rouge: Louisiana State University Press.

Malten, L. 1939. 'Motivgeschichtliche Untersuchungen zur Sagenforschung.' *Hermes* 74, pp. 176–206.

Mandell, S. 1984. 'Who Paid the Temple Tax when the Jews were under Roman Rule?' *HTR* 77, pp. 223–32.

Mann, J. 1914. 'The Observance of the Sabbath and the Festivals in the First Two Centuries of the Common Era according to Philo, Josephus, the New Testament and the Rabbinic Sources.' *Jewish Review* 4, pp. 433–56, 498–532.

Marcillet-Jaubert, J., & Vérilhac, A-M. 1979. *Index du Bulletin Epigraphique de J. et L. Robert, vols. 1966–1973.* Paris: Les Belles Lettres.

1983. *Index du Bulletin Epigraphique de J. et L. Robert. 1974–1977.* Paris: Les Belles Lettres.

Marcus, R. 1931–2. 'Divine Names and Attributes in Hellenistic Jewish Literature.' *PAAJR* 3, pp. 43–120.

1952. 'The Sebomenoi in Josephus.' *Jewish Social Studies* 14, pp. 247–50.

Marrou, H. I. 1956. *A History of Education in Antiquity.* London: Sheed and Ward.

Marshall, A. J. 1975a. 'Roman Women and the Provinces.' *Ancient Society* 6, pp. 109–27.

1975b. 'Flaccus and the Jews of Asia (Cicero Pro Flacco 28.67–69).' *Phoenix* 29, pp. 139–54.

Marshall, I. H. 1980. *The Acts of the Apostles. An Introduction and Commentary.* Tyndale NT Commentaries. Leicester: IVP.

Mastin, B. A. 1976. 'Scaeva the Chief Priest.' *JTS* 27, pp. 405–12.

Mayes, A. D. M. 1979. *Deuteronomy.* NCB. London: Oliphants.

Mazur, B. D. 1935. *Studies on Jewry in Greece I.* Athens: Hestia.

Meeks, W. A. 1983. *The First Urban Christians. The Social World of the Apostle Paul.* New Haven: Yale University Press.

Meeks, W. A., & Wilken, R. L. 1978. *Jews and Christians in Antioch in the first Four Centuries of the Common Era.* SBLSBS 13. University of Montana, Missoula: Scholars Press.

Meshorer, Y. 1981. 'An Ancient Coin Depicts Noah's Ark.' *BAR* 7.5, pp. 38–9.

Metzger, B. M. 1970. 'Ancient Astrological Geography and Acts 2:9–11.' In *Apostolic History and the Gospel: Biblical and Historical Essays presented to F. F. Bruce on his 60th Birthday,* eds. W. W. Gasque, R. P. Martin, pp. 123–33. Exeter: Paternoster.

Meyer, E. 1925. *Ursprung und Anfänge des Christentums. Zweiter Band. Die Entwicklung des Judentums und Jesus von Nazaret.* Stuttgart and Berlin: J. G. Cotta.

Meyers, C. 1978. 'The Roots of Restriction: Women in Early Israel.' *BA* 41, pp. 91–103.

Mildenberg, L. 1984. *The Coinage of the Bar Kokhba War.* ed. P.E. Mottahedek. Typos Band VI. Frankfurt am Main: Aarau.

Millar, F.G.B. 1962. 'The Date of the *Constitutio Antoniniana.*' *JEA* 48, pp.124–31.

1964. 'Some Evidence on the Meaning of Tacitus Annals XII.60.' *Historia* 13, pp.180–7.

1966. 'The Emperor, the Senate and the Province.' *JRS* 56, pp.156–66.

1977. *The Emperor in the Roman World (31BC–AD337).* London: Duckworth.

1983a. 'Empire and City, Augustus to Julian: Obligations, Excuses and Status.' *JRS* 73, pp.76–96.

1983b. 'Epigraphy.' In *Sources for Ancient History*, ed. M. Crawford, pp.80–136. Cambridge University Press.

Miller, K.M. 1985. 'Apollo Lairbenos.' *Numen* 32, pp.46–70.

Miller, P.D. 1981. 'Psalms and Inscriptions.' In *Congress Volume Vienna 1980*, ed. J.A. Emerton, pp.311–32. VTSup 32. Leiden: Brill.

Mitchell, H.G., Smith, J.M.P., & Bewer, J.A. 1912. *Haggai, Zechariah, Malachi and Jonah.* ICC. Edinburgh: T. & T. Clark.

Mitchell, S. 1974. 'The Plancii in Asia Minor.' *JRS* 64, pp.27–39.

1982. *Regional Epigraphic Catalogues of Asia Minor II. The Ankara District. The Inscriptions of North Galatia.* British Institute of Archaeology at Ankara Monograph 4. Oxford: British Archaeological Reports International Series 135.

Mitford, T.B. 1946. 'Religious Documents from Roman Cyprus.' *JHS* 66, pp.24–42.

Mitten, D.G. 1966. 'A New Look at Ancient Sardis.' *BA* 29, pp.38–68.

Moberly, R.W.L. 1983. *At the Mountain of God. Story and Theology in Exodus 32–34.* JSOTSS 22. Sheffield: JSOT Press.

Moe, D.L. 1977. 'The Cross and the Menorah.' *Archaeology* 30, pp.148–57.

Moehring, H.R. 1975. 'The *Acta pro Judaeis* in the *Antiquities* of Flavius Josephus: A Study in Hellenistic and Modern Apologetic Historiography.' In *Christianity, Judaism and Other Greco-Roman Cults. Studies for Morton Smith at Sixty*, ed. J. Neusner, Part 3, pp.124–58. SJLA 12. Leiden: Brill.

1984. 'Joseph Ben Matthia and Flavius Josephus: The Jewish Prophet and Roman Historian.' *ANRW* II, 21.2, pp.864–944.

Mohler, S.L. 1932. 'Feminism in the Corpus Inscriptionum Latinarum.' *The Classical Weekly* 25, 15 February 1932, pp.113–17.

Molland, E. 1954. 'The Heretics Combatted by Ignatius of Antioch.' *JEH* 5, pp.1–6.

Montefiore, C.G., & Loewe, H. 1938. *A Rabbinic Anthology. Selected and Arranged with Comments and Introductions.* London: Macmillan and Co.

Montevecchi, O. 1981. 'Una donna "prostatis" del figlio minorenne in un papiro del IIª.' *Aegyptus* 61, pp.103–15.

Moore, G.F. 1927–30. *Judaism in the First Centuries of the Christian Era. The Age of the Tannaim.* 3 vols. Cambridge, Massachusetts: Harvard University Press.

Mordtmann, J.J. 1881. 'Zur Epigraphik von Kyzikos.' *AM* 6, pp.121–31.

Moulton, J. H. 1908, 1963. *A Grammar of New Testament Greek*, vols. 1, 3. Edinburgh: T. & T. Clark.

Moulton, W. F., Geden, A. S., & Moulton, H. K. 1978. *A Concordance to the Greek Testament*. Fifth revised edn. Edinburgh: T. & T. Clark.

Murakawa, K. 1957. 'Demiurgos.' *Historia* 6, pp. 385–415.

Murray, D. F. 1979. 'Narrative Structure and Technique in the Deborah–Barak Story (Judges IV 4–22).' In *Studies in the Historical Books of the Old Testament*, ed. J. A. Emerton, pp. 155–89. VTSup 30. Leiden: Brill.

Musurillo, H. 1972. *The Acts of the Christian Martyrs. Introduction, Texts and Translations*. Oxford: Clarendon Press.

Nairn, J. N. 1904. *The Mimes of Herondas*. Oxford: Clarendon Press.

Nathanson, B. H. G. 1987. 'Reflections on the Silent Woman of Ancient Judaism and her Pagan Roman Counterpart.' In *The Listening Heart. Essays in Wisdom and the Psalms in Honor of Roland E. Murphy O Carm*, eds. K. G. Hoglund, E. F. Huwiler, J. T. Glass & R. W. Lee, pp. 259–79. JSOTSS 58. Sheffield: JSOT Press.

Neusner, J. 1973. *The Idea of Purity in Ancient Judaism*. SJLA 1. Leiden: Brill.

1975. *Early Rabbinic Judaism. Historical Studies in Religion, Literature and Art*. SJLA 13. Leiden: Brill.

1978. 'Comparing Judaisms.' *HR* 18, pp. 177–91.

1979a. 'From Scripture to Mishnah. The Origins of Mishnah's Division of Women.' *JJS* 30, pp. 138–53.

1979b. 'Thematic or Systematic Description: The case of Mishnah's Division of Women.' In *Method and Meaning in Ancient Judaism*, pp. 79–100. BJS 10. University of Montana, Missoula: Scholars Press.

1980. 'Women in the System of Mishnah.' *Conservative Judaism* 32.3, pp. 3–13.

1981. 'The Symbolism of Ancient Judaism: The Evidence of the Synagogue.' In *Ancient Synagogues. The State of Research*, ed. J. Gutmann, pp. 7–17. BJS 22. Chico, California: Scholars Press.

1984. 'Review of *Paul, The Law and the Jewish People*, by E. P. Sanders.' In *Ancient Judaism: Debates and Disputes*, pp. 195–203. BJS 64. Chico, California: Scholars Press.

Nickelsburg, G. W. E. 1980. 'Good and Bad Leaders in Pseudo-Philo's *Liber Antiquitatum Biblicarum*.' In *Ideal Figures in Ancient Judaism. Profiles and Paradigms*, eds. J. J. Collins & G. W. E. Nickelsburg, pp. 49–65. SBLSCS 12. Ann Arbor, Michigan: Scholars Press.

Niese, B. 1914. 'Josephus.' In *Encyclopaedia of Religion and Ethics*, ed. J. Hastings, vol. 7, pp. 569–79. Edinburgh: T. & T. Clark.

Nikiprowetzky, V. 1970. *La troisième sibylle*. Paris: Mouton.

Nilsson, M. P. 1920. 'Rosalia.' *RE* Zweiter Reiher I, cols. 1111–15.

1950. *Geschichte der griechischen Religion. Zweiter Band. Die hellenistische und römische Zeit*. Handbuch der Altertumswissenschaft 5.2. Munich: C. H. Beck.

1951a. 'Der Ursprung der Tragödie.' In *Opuscula Selecta* 1, pp. 61–145. Lund: CWK Gleerup.

1951b. 'Das Rosenfest.' In *Opuscula Selecta* 1, pp. 311–29. Lund: CWK Gleerup.

1960a. 'A propos du tombeau de Vincentius.' In *Opuscula Selecta* 3, pp. 176–81. Lund: GWK Gleerup.

1960b. 'Zwei Altäre aus Pergamon.' In *Opuscula Selecta* 3, pp. 297–303. Lund: GWK Gleerup.

1963. 'The High God and the Mediator.' *HTR* 56, pp. 101–20.

Noack, F. 1894. 'Dorylaion. II Grabreliefs.' *AM* 19, pp. 315–34.

Noakes, K. W. 1975. 'Melito of Sardis and the Jews.' In *Studia Patristica, vol. 13. Papers presented to the Sixth International Conference on Patristic Studies, Oxford 1971*, ed. E. A. Livingstone, Part 2, pp. 244–9. TU 116. Berlin: Akademie.

Nock, A. D. 1972. *Essays on Religion and the Ancient World*, ed. Z. Stewart, 2 vols. Oxford University Press.

Nock, A. D., Roberts, C. & Skeat, T. C. 1936. 'The Guild of Zeus Hypsistos.' *HTR* 29, pp. 39–88.

Nolland, J. 1979a. 'Do Romans Observe Jewish Customs (Tertullian, *Ad. Nat.* 1.13; *Apol.* 16)?' *VC* 33, pp. 1–11.

1979b. 'Proselytism or Politics in Horace *Satires* I, 4, 138–43.' *VC* 33, pp. 347–55.

1981. 'Uncircumcised Proselytes?' *JSJ* 12, pp. 173–94.

Norris, F. W. 1986. 'Melito's Motivation.' *ATR* 68, pp. 16–24.

Nutton, V. 1977. 'Archiatri and the Medical Profession in Antiquity.' *Papers of the British School at Rome*, 45, pp. 191–226.

Oehler, J. 1909. 'Epigraphische Beiträge zur Geschichte des Judentums.' *MGWJ* 53, pp. 292–302, 443–52, 525–38.

Oesterley, W. O. E. 1935. 'The Cult of Sabazios: A Study in Religious Syncretism.' In *The Labyrinth. Further Studies in the Relation between Myth and Ritual in the Ancient World*, ed. S. H. Hooke, pp. 113–58. London: SPCK.

Ovadiah, A. 1978. 'Ancient Synagogues in Asia-Minor.' In *Proceedings of the Tenth International Congress of Classical Archaeology 1973*, vol. 2, pp. 857–66. Ankara: Türk Tarih Kurumu.

Overman, J. A. 1988. 'The God-fearers: Some Neglected Features.' *JSNT* 32, pp. 17–26.

Paris, P. 1883. 'Inscriptions de Sebaste.' *BCH* 7, pp. 448–57.

1884. 'Inscriptions d'Eumenia.' *BCH* 8, pp. 233–54.

1885. With M. Holleaux. 'Inscriptions de Carie.' *BCH* 9, pp. 68–84, 324–48.

Parkes, J. 1934. *The Conflict of the Church and the Synagogue. A Study in the Origins of Antisemitism*. Reprint 1974. New York: Atheneum.

Parrot, A. 1939. *Malédictions et violations des tombes*. Paris: Librairie Orientaliste Paul Geuthner.

Paton, W. R., & Hicks, E. L. 1891. *The Inscriptions of Cos*. Oxford: Clarendon Press.

Pedley, J. G. 1972. *Ancient Literary Sources on Sardis. Archaeological Exploration of Sardis Monograph 2*. Cambridge, Massachusetts: Harvard University Press.

Peppers, J. 1980. 'Four Roman Votive Bronzes in the Getty Museum.' *Journal of the Paul Getty Museum* 8, pp. 173–80.

Perdrizet, P. 1900. 'Inscriptions de Philippes. Les Rosalies.' *BCH* 24, pp. 299–323.

Perkins, A. 1973. *The Art of Dura-Europos*. Oxford: Clarendon Press.

Pesch, R. 1986. *Die Apostelgeschichte*. 2 vols. EKKNT V/1, 2. Zurich, Einsiedeln, Cologne: Benziger, Neukirchener.

Petersen, N. R. 1978. *Literary Criticism for New Testament Critics*. Philadelphia: Fortress Press.

Pétridès, S. 1905. 'Amulette judéo-grecque.' *Echos d'Orient* 8, pp. 88–90.

Petrie, A. 1906. 'Epitaphs in Phrygian Greek.' In *Studies in the History and Art of the Eastern Provinces of the Roman Empire*, ed. W. M. Ramsay, pp. 119–34. Aberdeen University Press.

Petzl, G. 1978a. 'Vier Inschriften aus Lydien.' In *Studien zur Religion und Kultur Kleinasiens. Festschrift für Friedrich Karl Dörner*, eds. S. Sahin, E. Schwertheim & J. Wagner, pp. 745–61. EPRO 76. Leiden: Brill.

   1978b. 'Inschriften aus der Umgebung von Saittai.' *ZPE* 30, pp. 249–76.

   1982. *Die Inschriften von Smyrna. Teil 1: Grabschriften, postume Ehrungen, Grabepigramme*. IGSK Band 23. Österreichische Akademie der Wissenschaften, Rheinisch–westfälische Akademie der Wissenschaften. Bonn: Dr Rudolf Habelt.

Pfuhl, E., & Möbius, H. 1979. *Die ostgriechischen Grabreliefs II*. Mainz: von Zabern.

Pharr, C. 1969. *The Theodosian Code and Novels and the Sirmondian Constitutions. A Translation with Commentary, Glossary and Bibliography*. New York: Greenwood Press.

Philonenko, M. 1968. *Joseph et Aséneth. Introduction, texte critique, traduction et notes*. SPB 13. Leiden: Brill.

Picard, C. 1961. 'Sabazios, Dieu thraco-phrygien: Expansion et aspects nouveaux de son culte.' *RArch* 2, pp. 129–76.

Picard, C., & Avezou, C. 1914. 'Le Testament de la prêtresse thessalonicienne rites et cultes de la Macédonie.' *BCH* 38, pp. 38–62.

Pilcher, E. J. 1903. 'The Jews of the Dispersion in Roman Galatia.' *Proceedings of the Society of Biblical Archaeology* 25, pp. 225–33, 250–8.

Pippidi, D. M. 1974. 'Note de lectura.' *Studii Clasice* 16, pp. 249–65.

Plassart, A. 1914. 'La synagogue juive de Délos.' *RB* 11, pp. 523–34.

Pleket, H. W. 1969. *Epigraphica, vol. 2. Texts on the Social History of the Greek World*. Textus Minores 41. Leiden: Brill.

   1981. 'Religious History as the History of Mentality: 'The "Believer" as Servant of the Deity in the Greek World.' In *Faith, Hope and Worship. Aspects of Religious Mentality in the Ancient World*, ed. H. S. Versnel, pp. 152–92. Studies in Greek and Roman Religion 2. Leiden: Brill.

Poliakoff, M. 1984. 'Jacob, Job, and Other Wrestlers: Reception of Greek Athletics by Jews and Christians in Antiquity.' *Journal of Sport History* 11, pp. 48–85.

Pomeroy, S. B. 1973. 'Selected Bibliography on Women in Antiquity.' *Arethusa* 6, pp. 125–57.

   1975. *Goddesses, Whores, Wives and Slaves. Women in Classical Antiquity*. London: Robert Hale.

   1977. 'Technikai kai Mousikai. The Education of Women in the Fourth Century and in the Hellenistic World.' *AJAH* 2, pp. 51–68.

1982. 'Charities for Greek Women.' *Mnemosyne* 35, pp.115–35.
1984a. *Women in Hellenistic Egypt from Alexander to Cleopatra.* New York: Schocken Books.
1984b. 'Selected Bibliography on Women in Classical Antiquity.' In *Women in the Ancient World. The Arethusa Papers*, eds. J. Peradotto & J.P. Sullivan, pp.315–72. Albany: State University of New York Press.
Porton, G.G. 1986. 'Diversity in Post Biblical Judaism.' In *Early Judaism and its Modern Interpreters*, eds. R.A. Kraft & G.W.E. Nickelsburg, pp.57–80. Atlanta, Georgia: Scholars Press.
Pottier, E., & Hauvette-Besnault, A.M. 1880. 'Inscriptions d'Erythrées et de Téos.' *BCH* 4, pp.153–82.
Pouilloux, J. 1976. *Fouilles de Delphes. Tome III. Epigraphie fascicule IV. Les inscriptions de la terrasse du temple et de la région nord du sanctuaire.* Paris: de Boccard.
Préaux, C. 1959. 'Le statut de la femme à l'époque hellénistique principalement en Egypte.' In *La Femme. Recueils de la société Jean Bodin*, Part 1, pp.127–75. Brussels: Editions de la librairie encyclopédique.
Preisendanz, K. 1973. *Papyri graecae magicae. Die griechischen Zauberpapyri*, vol.1, Second revised edn by A. Heinrichs. Teubner: Stuttgart.
Price, S.R.F. 1984. *Rituals and Power. The Roman Imperial Cult in Asia Minor.* Cambridge University Press.
Quasten, J. 1950. *Patrology*, vol.1. Utrecht: Spectrum.
Rabello, A.M. 1980. 'The Legal Condition of the Jews in the Roman Empire.' *ANRW* II, 13, pp.662–762.
1984. 'L'observance des fêtes juives dans l'Empire romain.' *ANRW* II, 21.2, pp.1288–1312.
Radet, G. 1887. 'Inscriptions de Lydie.' *BCH* 11, pp.445–84.
Raepsaet-Charlier, M-T. 1981. 'Clarissima femina.' *RIDA* 28, pp.189–212.
Rahmani, L.Y. 1972. 'A Bilingual Ossuary Inscription from Khirbet Zif.' *IEJ* 22, pp.113–16.
Rajak, T. 1979. 'Review of Smallwood, E.M., *The Jews Under Roman Rule: From Pompey to Diocletian*; Applebaum, S., *Prolegomena to the Study of the Second Revolt (AD 132–135)*; Aziza, C., *Tertullien et le judaïsme.*' *JRS* 69, pp.192–4.
1981. 'Roman Intervention in a Seleucid Siege of Jerusalem?' *GRBS* 22, pp.65–81.
1983. *Josephus, The Historian and his Society.* London: Duckworth.
1984. 'Was there a Roman Charter for the Jews?' *JRS* 74, pp.107–23.
1985a. 'Jews and Christians as Groups in a Pagan World.' In *'To See Ourselves As Others See Us.' Christians, Jews, 'Others' in Late Antiquity*, eds. J. Neusner & E.S. Frierichs, pp.247–62. Chico, California: Scholars Press.
1985a. 'Jewish Rights in the Greek Cities Under Roman Rule: A New Approach.' In *Approaches to Ancient Judaism, vol.5, Studies in Judaism and its Greco-Roman Context*, ed. W.S. Green, pp.19–35. BJS 32. Atlanta, Georgia: Scholars Press.
Ramage, A. 1972. 'The Fourteenth Campaign At Sardis (1971).' *BASOR* 206, pp.9–39.

Ramsay, W.M. 1882a. 'Inscriptions of Cilicia, Cappadocia and Pontus.' *JPh* 11, pp. 142–60.
1882b. 'The Tale of Saint Abercius.' *JHS* 3, pp. 339–53.
1883. 'The Cities and Bishoprics of Phrygia.' *JHS* 4, pp. 370–436.
1888. 'Early Christian Monuments in Phrygia. A Study in the Early History of the Church.' *The Expositor*, Third Series, vol. 8, pp. 241–67, 401–27; vol. 9, pp. 141–60, 253–72, 392–400.
1895a, 1897. *The Cities and Bishoprics of Phrygia*, vol. 1, Parts 1 and 2. Oxford: Clarendon Press.
1895b. 'The Rulers of the Synagogue.' *The Expositor*, Fifth Series, vol. 1, pp. 272–7.
1902a. 'The Jews in the Graeco-Asiatic Cities.' *The Expositor*, Sixth Series, vol. 5, pp. 19–33, 92–109.
1902b. 'Nouvelles remarques sur les textes d'Acmonia.' *REA* 4, pp. 267–70.
1904a. *The Church in the Roman Empire Before AD 170*. Eighth edn. London: Hodder and Stoughton.
1904b. *The Letters to the Seven Churches of Asia and their Place in the Plan of the Apocalypse*. London: Hodder and Stoughton.
1904c. 'The Letters To The Seven Churches. The Letter to the Church in Smyrna.' *The Expositor*, Sixth Series, vol. 9, pp. 321–31.
1906a. *Pauline and Other Studies in Early Christian History*. London: Hodder and Stoughton.
1906b. 'The Christian Inscriptions of Lycaonia.' *The Expositor*, Seventh Series, vol. 1, pp. 32–51.
1907. *The Cities of St. Paul. Their Influence on His Life and Thought*. London: Hodder and Stoughton.
1914a. 'The Old Testament in Roman Phrygia.' *ET* 26, pp. 168–74.
1914b. *The Bearing of Recent Discoveries on the Trustworthiness of the New Testament*. London: Hodder and Stoughton.
Rappaport, U. 1971. 'Archisynagogos.' *EJ* 3, cols. 335–6.
Rathbone, D. 1983. 'The Grain Trade and Grain Shortages in the Hellenistic East.' In *Trade and Famine in Classical Antiquity*, eds. P. Garnsey & C.R. Whittaker, pp. 45–55. PCPhS Supplementary vol. 8. Cambridge Philological Society.
Reider, J. 1966. *An Index to Aquila*. Completed and revised by N. Turner. NovTSup 12. Leiden: Brill.
Reinach, A. 1913. 'Noé Sangariou. Etude sur le déluge phrygien et le syncrétisme judéo-phrygien.' *REJ* 65, pp. 161–80; 66, pp. 1–43, 213–44.
1915. 'L'origine du Marsyas du forum.' *Klio* 14, pp. 321–37.
Reinach, S. 1883. 'Inscription grecque de Smyrne. La juive Rufina.' *REJ* 7, pp. 161–6.
1885a. 'Les juifs d'Hypaepa.' *REJ* 10, pp. 74–8.
1885b. 'Saint Polycarpe et les juifs de Smyrne.' *REJ* 11, pp. 235–8.
1886. 'Une nouvelle synagogue grecque à Phocée.' *REJ* 12, pp. 236–43.
1888. 'Chronique d'orient.' *RArch* Third Series, 12, pp. 214–26.
Reinach, T. 1888. 'Mithridate et les juifs.' *REJ* 16, pp. 204–10.
1899. 'Antiochus Cyzicène et les juifs.' *REJ* 38, pp. 161–71.
1901. 'La pierre de Myndos.' *REJ* 42, pp. 1–6.
1906. 'Inscriptions d'Aphrodisias.' *REG* 19, pp. 205–98.

Rengstorf, K. H., ed. 1968. *A Complete Concordance to Flavius Josephus.* 4 vols. and Supplement. Leiden: Brill.

Reynolds, J. M. 1981. 'Inscriptions.' In *Excavations at Sidi Khrebish Benghazi (Berenice), vol. 1. Buildings, Coins, Inscriptions, Architectural Decoration*, ed. J. A. Lloyd, pp. 233–54. Supplements to Libya Antiqua V. People's Socialist Libyan Arab Jamahiriya: The Department of Antiquities Ministry of Teaching and Education.

1982. *Aphrodisias and Rome. Documents from the Excavation of the Theatre at Aphrodisias conducted by Professor Kenan T. Erim, together with some related texts.* JRS Monograph 1. London: Society for the Promotion of Roman Studies.

Reynolds, J. M., & Tannenbaum, R. 1987. *Jews and God-Fearers at Aphrodisias. Greek Inscriptions with Commentary.* PCPhS Supplementary vol. 12. Cambridge Philological Society.

Richardson, C. C. 1935. *The Christianity of Ignatius of Antioch.* New York: Columbia University Press.

1953. *Early Christian Fathers.* London: SCM.

Richardson, P. 1986. With D. Granskou. *Anti-Judaism in Early Christianity. Vol. 1. Paul and the Gospels.* Studies in Christianity and Judaism 2. Waterloo: Wilfrid Laurier University Press.

Ritschl, F. 1873. 'Eine Berichtigung der republikanischen Consularfasten.' *RhM* 28, pp. 586–614.

Ritterling, E. 1927. 'Military Forces in the Senatorial Provinces.' *JRS* 17, pp. 28–32.

Robert, L. 1937a. 'Un corpus des inscriptions juives.' *REJ* 101, pp. 73–86.

1937b. *Etudes anatoliennes: recherches sur les inscriptions grecques de l'Asie Mineure.* Reprint 1970, Amsterdam: Hakkert.

1938. *Etudes épigraphiques et philologiques.* Paris: Librairie ancienne Honoré Champion.

1940. *Hellenica. Recueil d'épigraphie de numismatique et d'antiquités grecques*, vol. 1. Paris: Librairie d'Amérique et d'Orient.

1946. *Hellenica. Recueil d'épigraphie de numismatique et d'antiquités grecques*, vol. 3. Paris: Librairie d'Amérique et d'Orient.

1950. *Hellenica. Recueil d'épigraphie de numismatique et d'antiquités grecques*, vol. 9. Paris: Librairie d'Amérique et d'Orient.

1954. *La Carie. Histoire et géographie historique avec le recueil des inscriptions antiques. 2. La plateau de Tabai et ses environs.* Paris: Librairie d'Amérique et d'Orient.

1955. *Hellenica. Recueil d'épigraphie de numismatique et d'antiquités grecques*, vol. 10. Paris: Librairie d'Amérique et d'Orient.

1958a. 'Reliefs votifs et cultes d'Anatolie.' *Anatolia* 3, pp. 103–36.

1958b. 'Inscriptions grecques de Sidè en Pamphylie (époque impériale et Bas-Empire).' *RPh* Third Series, 32, pp. 15–53.

1960a. 'Recherches épigraphiques.' *REA* 62, pp. 276–361.

1960b. *Hellenica. Recueil d'épigraphie de numismatique et d'antiquités grecques*, vols. 11–12. Paris: Librairie d'Amérique et d'Orient.

1962. *Villes d'Asie Mineure. Etudes de géographie ancienne.* Second edn. Paris: de Boccard.

1963a. 'Nouvelles inscriptions d'Iasos.' *REA* 65, pp. 298–329.

1963b. *Noms indigènes dans l'Asie Mineure gréco-romaine 1.* Paris: Librairie Adrien Maisonneuve.

1964. *Nouvelles inscriptions de Sardes. Ier fascicule. Décret hellénistique de Sardes, dédicaces aux dieux indigènes, inscriptions de la synagogue.* Paris: Librairie d'Amérique et d'Orient.

1965. *Hellenica. Recueil d'épigraphie de numismatique et d'antiquités grecques,* vol. 13. Paris: Librairie d'Amérique et d'Orient.

1968. 'Trois oracles de la Théosophie et un prophète d'Apollon.' *CRAIBL* 1968, pp. 568–99.

1969, 1974. *Opera Minora Selecta, épigraphie et antiquités grecques,* 4 vols. Amsterdam: Hakkert.

1971. 'Un oracle gravé à Oinoanda.' *CRAIBL* 1971, pp. 597–619.

1975a. 'Une nouvelle inscription grecque de Sardes. Règlement de l'autorité perse relatif à un culte de Zeus.' *CRAIBL* 1975, pp. 306–30.

1975b. 'Nonnos et les monnaies d'Akmonia de Phrygie.' *JS* 1975, pp. 153–92.

1978a. 'Malédictions funéraires grecques.' *CRAIBL* 1978, pp. 241–89.

1978b. 'Documents d'Asie Mineure.' *BCH* 102, pp. 395–543.

1981. 'Amulettes grecques.' *JS* 1981, pp. 3–44.

Roddaz, J. M. 1984. *Marcus Agrippa.* BEFAR 253. Paris: Ecole française de Rome, Palais Farnése.

Roloff, J. 1981. *Die Apostelgeschichte.* NTD 5. Göttingen: Vandenhoeck und Ruprecht.

Romaniuk, K. 1964. 'Die "Gottesfürchtigen" im Neuen Testament. Beitrag zur neutestamentlichen Theologie der Gottesfurcht.' *Aegyptus* 44, pp. 66–91.

Rostovtzeff, M. 1941. *The Social and Economic History of the Hellenistic World.* 3 vols. Oxford: Clarendon Press.

1957. *The Social and Economic History of the Roman Empire.* 2 vols. Second edn, revised by P. M. Fraser, Oxford: Clarendon Press.

Roth-Gerson, L. 1972. *The Civil and the Religious Status of the Jews in Asia Minor from Alexander the Great to Constantine, BC 336–AD 337.* Thesis submitted for the Degree of Doctor of Philosophy, Hebrew University.

Rzach, A. 1923. 'Sibyllinische Orakel (Buch I. [II]).' *RE* 2A, cols. 2146–52.

Safrai, S. 1975. 'Pilgrimage to Jerusalem at the Time of the Second Temple.' *Immanuel* 5, pp. 51–62.

Safrai, S., & Stern, M., eds. 1974, 1976. *Compendia Rerum Iudaicarum ad Novum Testamentum. Section One: The Jewish People in the First Century. Historical Geography, Political History, Social, Cultural and Religious Life and Institutions.* 2 vols. Assen: Van Gorcum.

Saltman, E. S. 1971. *The Jews of Asia Minor in the Greco-Roman Period: A Religious and Social Study.* M.A. Thesis, Smith College, Northampton, Massachusetts.

Sanders, E. P. 1980. 'Puzzling Out Rabbinic Judaism.' In *Approaches to Ancient Judaism, vol. 2,* ed. W. S. Green, pp. 65–79. BJS 9. Chico, California: Scholars Press.

Sanders, J. T. 1987. *The Jews in Luke–Acts.* London: SCM.

Sanie, S. 1978. 'Deus Aeternus et Theos Hypsistos en Dacie romaine.'

In *Hommages à Maarten J. Vermaseren*, eds. M.B. de Boer & T.A. Edridge, vol.3, pp.1092–1115. EPRO 68. Leiden: Brill.

Saulnier, C. 1981. 'Lois romaines sur les juifs selon Flavius Josèphe.' *RB* 87, pp.161–98.

Schalit, A. 1960. 'The Letter of Antiochus III to Zeuxis Regarding the Establishment of Jewish Military Colonies in Phrygia and Lydia.' *JQR* 50, pp.289–318.

1969. *König Herodes der Mann und sein Werk.* Studia Judaica Forschungen zur Wissenschaft des Judentums Band IV. Berlin: Walter de Gruyter.

1971. 'Archon.' *EJ* 3, cols.397–8.

Scharbert, J. 1957. 'Formgeschichte und Exegisis von Ex 34.6f und seiner Parallelen.' *Bib* 38, pp.130–50.

Schechter, S. 1896. 'Women in Temple and Synagogue.' In *Studies in Judaism.* First Series, pp.313–25. Reprint 1945. Philadelphia: Jewish Publication Society of America.

Schelkle, K.H. 1970. *Die Petrusbriefe, Der Judasbrief.* Third edn. HTKNT 13, 2. Freiburg: Herder.

Schepelern, W. 1929. *Der Montanismus und die phrygischen Kulte.* Tübingen: J.C.B. Mohr (Paul Siebeck).

Scherling. 1935. 'Nannakios.' *RE* 16, cols.1680–1.

Schiffman, L.H. 1981. 'At the Crossroads: Tannaitic Perspectives on the Jewish–Christian Schism.' In *Jewish and Christian Self-Definition. Vol.2. Aspects of Judaism in the Graeco-Roman Period*, ed. E.P. Sanders with A.I. Baumgarten & A. Mendelson, pp.115–56. London: SCM.

Schmidtke, F. 1950. 'Arche.' *RAC* I, cols.597–602.

Schneider, A.M. 1943. *Die römischen und byzantischen Denkmäler von Iznik-Nicaea.* Berlin: Istanbuler Forschungen, vol.16.

Schneider, G. 1980, 1982. *Die Apostelgeschichte.* 2 vols. HTKNT 5. Freiburg, Basle, Vienna: Herder.

Schoedel, W.R. 1978. 'Ignatius and the Archives.' *HTR* 71, pp.97–106.

1985. *Ignatius of Antioch.* Hermeneia. Philadelphia: Fortress Press.

Schoeffer, V. 1901. 'Demiurgoi.' *RE* 4, cols.2856–62.

Schrage, W. 1988. 'Meditation zu Offenbarung 2, 8–11.' *EvT* 48, pp.388–403.

Schubart, W. 1920. 'Bemerkungen zum Stile hellenistischer Königsbriefe.' *APF* 6, pp.324–47.

Schultze, V. 1922. *Altchristliche Städte und Landschaften II. Kleinasien 1.* Gütersloh: Bertelsmann.

Schürer, E. 1892. 'Die Prophetin Isabel in Thyatira. Offenb. Joh. 2.20.' In *Theologische Abhandlungen. Carl von Weizäcker zu seinem siebzigsten Geburtstage*, pp.37–58. Freiburg: J.C.B. Mohr (Paul Siebeck).

1897. 'Die Juden im bosphoranischen Reiche und die Genossenschaften der σεβόμενοι θεὸν ὕψιστον ebendaselbst.' *Sitzungsberichte der Akademie der Wissenschaften Berlin*, 1897, pp.200–25.

1901, 1907, 1909. *Geschichte des jüdischen Volkes im Zeitalter Jesu Christi.* 3 vols. 3rd and 4th edns. Leipzig: J.C. Hinrich.

1904. 'Diaspora.' *Dictionary of the Bible*, ed. J. Hastings, vol.5, pp.91–109. Edinburgh: T. & T. Clark.

Schürer, E., Vermes, G., & Millar, F. 1973, 1979, 1986, 1987. *The History of the Jewish People in the Age of Jesus Christ*, vols. 1, 2, 3.1, 3.2. Edinburgh: T. & T. Clark.

Schwank, B. 1969. 'Theaterplätze für "Gottesfürchtige" in Milet.' *BZ* 13, pp. 262–3.

Schwartz, J. 1984. 'Note sur un article de la ZPE 51 (A Hebrew lamentation from Roman Egypt).' *ZPE* 55, pp. 141–2.

Schwertheim, E., & Sahin, S. 1977. 'Neue Inschriften aus Nikomedeia und Umgebung.' *ZPE* 24, pp. 259–64.

Seager, A. R. 1972. 'The Building History of the Sardis Synagogue.' *AJAH* 76, pp. 425–35.

    1974. *Archaeology at the Ancient Synagogue of Sardis, Turkey: Judaism in a Major Roman City*. Ball State University Faculty Lecture Series 3, pp. 41–64.

    1975. 'The Architecture of the Dura and Sardis Synagogues.' In *The Synagogue: Studies in Origins, Archaeology and Architecture*, ed. J. Gutmann, pp. 149–93. New York: Ktav.

    1981a. 'The Synagogue at Sardis.' In *Ancient Synagogues Revealed*, ed. L. I. Levine, pp. 178–84. Hebrew University of Jerusalem, The Israel Exploration Society.

    1981b. 'Ancient Synagogue Architecture: An Overview.' In *Ancient Synagogues. The State of Research*, ed. J. Gutmann, pp. 39–47. BJS 22. Chico, California: Scholars Press.

    1983. 'The Synagogue and the Jewish Community: The Building.' In *Sardis from Prehistoric to Roman Times. Results of the Archaeological Exploration of Sardis 1958–1975*, ed. G. M. A. Hanfmann, pp. 169–78. Cambridge, Massachusetts: Harvard University Press.

Segal, J. B. 1979. 'The Jewish Attitude towards Women.' *JJS* 30, pp. 121–37.

Seston, W. 1967. 'Des "portes" de Thugga à la "Constitution" de Carthage.' *Revue Historique*, 237, pp. 277–94.

Sève, M. 1981. 'Inscriptions de Thasos.' *BCH* 105, pp. 183–98.

Sevenster, J. N. 1975. *The Roots of Pagan Anti-Semitism in the Ancient World*. NovTSup 41. Leiden: Brill.

Seyrig, H. 1928. 'Note sur un texte relatif aux Rosalies.' *RHR* 97, pp. 275–7.

    1933. 'Antiquités syriennes.' *Syria* 14, pp. 238–82.

Shanks, H. 1979. *Judaism in Stone. The Archaeology of Ancient Synagogues*. Co-published Washington: The Biblical Archaeology Society; New York: Harper and Row.

Sheppard, A. R. R. 1975. *Characteristics of Political Life in the Greek Cities ca. 70–120 AD, with Reference to Later Developments*. Thesis submitted for the degree of Bachelor of Letters in the University of Oxford.

    1979. 'Jews, Christians and Heretics in Acmonia and Eumeneia.' *AS* 29, pp. 169–80.

    1980–1. 'Pagan Cults of Angels in Roman Asia Minor.' *Talanta* 12–13, pp. 77–101.

Sherwin-White, A. N. 1963. *Roman Society and Roman Law in the New Testament*. Oxford: Clarendon Press.

    1966. *The Letters of Pliny. A Historical and Social Commentary*. Oxford: Clarendon Press.

1973. *The Roman Citizenship.* Second edn. Oxford: Clarendon Press.
Sherwin-White, S. M. 1976. 'A Note on Three Coan Inscriptions.' *ZPE* 21, pp. 183–8.
1978. *Ancient Cos. An Historical Study from the Dorian Settlement to the Imperial Period.* Hypomnemata 51. Göttingen: Vandenhoeck und Ruprecht.
Shiloh, Y. 1968. 'Torah Scrolls and the Menorah Plaque from Sardis.' *IEJ* 18, pp. 54–7.
Siegert, F. 1973. 'Gottesfürchtige und Sympathisanten.' *JSJ* 4, pp. 109–64.
Sigal, P. 1978–9. 'An Inquiry into Aspects of Judaism in Justin's Dialogue with Trypho.' *AbrN* 18, pp. 74–100.
Silberschlag, E. 1933. 'The Earliest Record of Jews in Asia Minor.' *JBL* 52, pp. 66–77.
Simon, M. 1981a. *Le Christianisme antique et son contexte religieux. Scripta Varia.* 2 vols. WUNT 23. Tübingen: J. C. B. Mohr (Paul Siebeck).
1981b. 'Gottesfürchtiger.' *RAC* 11, cols. 1060–70.
1986. *Verus Israel. A Study of the Relations between Christians and Jews in the Roman Empire (135–425).* Oxford University Press.
Skehan, P. W. 1963. 'The Hand of Judith.' *CBQ* 25, pp. 94–110.
Smallwood, E. M. 1956. 'Domitian's Attitude Toward the Jews and Judaism.' *CPh* 51, pp. 1–13.
1959a. 'The Alleged Jewish Tendencies of Poppaea Sabina.' *JTS* 10, pp. 329–35.
1959b. 'The Legislation of Hadrian and Antoninus Pius against Circumcision.' *Latomus* 18, pp. 334–47.
1961. 'The Legislation of Hadrian and Antoninus Pius against Circumcision: Addendum.' *Latomus* 20, pp. 93–6.
1970. *Philonis Alexandrini Legatio Ad Gaium. Edited with an Introduction, Translation and Commentary.* Second edn. Leiden: Brill.
1981. *The Jews Under Roman Rule from Pompey to Diocletian.* SJLA 20. Leiden: Brill.
Smith, J. Z. 1980. 'Fences and Neighbors: Some Contours of Early Judaism.' In *Approaches to Ancient Judaism, vol. 2*, ed. W. S. Green, pp. 1–25. BJS 9. Chico, California: Scholars Press.
Smith, M. 1956. 'Palestinian Judaism in the First Century.' In *Israel, its Role in Civilisation*, ed. M. Davis, pp. 67–81. New York: Institute of the Jewish Theological Society.
1986. 'The Jewish Elements in the Magical Papyri.' In *SBL 1986 Seminar Papers*, ed. K. H. Richards, pp. 455–62. Atlanta, Georgia: Scholars Press.
Snodgrass, A. 1983. 'Archaeology.' In *Sources for Ancient History*, ed. M. Crawford, pp. 137–84. Cambridge University Press.
Soards, M. L. 1985. 'The Righteousness of God in the Writings of the Apostle Paul.' *BTB* 15, pp. 104–9.
Sokolowski, F. 1955. *Lois sacrées de l'Asie Mineure.* Paris: de Boccard.
1960. 'Sur le culte d'angelos dans le paganisme grec et romain.' *HTR* 53, pp. 225–9.
Solin, H. 1982. *Die griechischen Personennamen in Rom. Ein Namenbuch.* 3 vols. Berlin: de Gruyter.

1983. 'Juden und Syrer im westlichen Teil der römischen Welt. Eine ethnisch-demographische Studie mit besonderer Berücksichtigung der sprachlichen Zustände.' *ANRW* II, 29.2, pp. 587–789, 1222–49.

Speigl, J. 1987. 'Ignatius in Philadelphia. Ereignisse und Anliegen in den Ignatiusbriefen.' *VC* 41, pp. 360–76.

Stagg, E., & Stagg, F. 1978. *Women in the World of Jesus.* Edinburgh: Saint Andrews Press.

Stählin, G. 1962. *Die Apostelgeschichte.* Tenth edn. NTD 5. Göttingen: Vandenhoeck und Ruprecht.

Stanton, G. N. 1985. 'Aspects of Early Christian–Jewish Polemic and Apologetic.' *NTS* 31, pp. 377–92.

Stern, M. 1973. 'Die Urkunden.' In *Literatur und Religion des Frühjudentums. Eine Einführung,* eds. J. Maier, J. Schreiner, pp. 181–99. Würzburg: Echter.

1974, 1980, 1984. *Greek and Latin Authors on Jews and Judaism.* 3 vols. Jerusalem Academic Press.

Sterrett, J. R. S. 1888. *An Epigraphical Journey in Asia Minor.* Papers of the American School of Classical Studies at Athens, vol. 2. Boston: Damrell and Upham.

Stichel, R. 1979. *Die Namen Noes, seines Bruders und seiner Frau. Ein Beitrag zum Nachleben jüdischer Überlieferungen in der außerkanonischen und gnostischen Literatur und in Denkmälern der Kunst.* Abhandlungen der Akademie der Wissenschaften in Göttingen, philologische-historische Klasse Dritte Folge, Nr 112. Göttingen: Vandenhoeck und Ruprecht.

Stillwell, R., MacDonald, W. L., & McAllister, M. H. 1976. *The Princeton Encyclopaedia of Classical Sites.* Princeton University Press.

Stoebe, H. J. 1952. 'Die Bedeutung des Wortes HÄSÄD im Alten Testament.' *VT* 2, pp. 244–54.

Strack, H. L., & Billerbeck, P. 1922, 1924, 1928. *Kommentar zum Neuen Testament aus Talmud und Midrasch.* 4 vols. Munich: C. H. Beck.

Strauß, H. 1966. 'Jüdische Quellen frühchristlicher Kunst: Optische oder literarische Anregung?' *ZNW* 57, pp. 114–36.

Stylianopoulos, T. 1975. *Justin Martyr and the Mosaic Law.* SBLDS 20. University of Montana, Missoula: Scholars Press.

Sukenik, E. L. 1934. *Ancient Synagogues in Palestine and Greece.* The Schweich Lectures of the British Academy 1930. Oxford University Press.

1949. 'The Present State of Ancient Synagogue Studies.' *Bulletin of the Louis M. Rabinowitz Fund for the Exploration of Ancient Synagogues* 1, pp. 1–23.

Suolahti, J. 1958. 'The Council of L. Cornelius P. f. Crus in the Year 49 B.C.' *Arctos* 2, pp. 152–63.

Svoronos, J. N., & Head, B. V. 1976. *The Illustrations of the Historia Numorum. An Atlas of Greek Numismatics.* Chicago: Ares.

Swete, H. B. 1902. *An Introduction to the Old Testament in Greek.* Second edn. Cambridge University Press.

Swidler, L. 1976. *Women in Judaism. The Status of Women in Formative Judaism.* Metuchen: Scarecrow Press.

Syme, R. 1979. *Roman Papers*, eds. E. Badian & A. R. Birley. 3 vols. Oxford: Clarendon Press.

Talbert, R. J. A. 1984. *The Senate of Imperial Rome*. Princeton University Press.

Tannenbaum, R. F. 1986. 'Jews and God-Fearers in the Holy City of Aphrodite.' *BAR* 12.5, pp. 55–7.

Tarn, W., & Griffith, G. T. 1952. *Hellenistic Civilisation*. Third edn. London: Edward Arnold.

Tatscheva-Hitova, M. 1977. 'Dem Hypsistos geweihte Denkmäler in Thrakien. Untersuchungen zur Geschichte der Antiken Religionen III.' *Thracia* 4, pp. 271–301.

—— 1978. 'Wesenszüge des Sabazioskultes in Moesia Inferior und Thracia.' In *Hommages à Maarten J. Vermaseren*, eds. M. B. de Boer & T. A. Edridge, vol. 3, pp. 1217–30. EPRO 68. Leiden: Brill.

—— 1983. *Eastern Cults in Moesia Inferior and Thracia (5th Century BC – 4th Century AD)*. EPRO 95. Leiden: Brill.

Tcherikover, V. 1927. *Die Hellenistischen Städtegründungen von Alexander dem Grossen bis auf die Römerzeit*. Philologus, Supplementband XIX, Heft I. Leipzig: Dieterich.

—— 1961. *Hellenistic Civilisation and the Jews*. Philadelphia: Jewish Publication Society of America.

Thompson, L. A. 1982. 'Domitian and the Jewish Tax.' *Historia* 31, pp. 329–42.

Tod, M. N. 1951. 'Laudatory Epithets in Greek Epitaphs.' *Annual of the British School of Athens* 46, pp. 182–90.

Torrey, C. C. 1917–18. 'The Bilingual Inscription from Sardis.' *AJSL* 34, pp. 185–98.

Toynbee, J. M. C. 1967. 'A Fragment of an Early Christian Sarcophagus.' *RDAC* 43, pp. 315–8.

Trakatellis, D. 1986. 'Justin Martyr's Trypho.' In *Christians Among Jews and Gentiles. Essays in Honor of Krister Stendahl on His Sixty-Fifth Birthday*, eds. G. W. E. Nickelsburg & G. W. MacRae, pp. 287–97. Philadelphia: Fortress Press.

Trebilco, P. R. 1989. 'Paul and Silas – "Servants of the Most High God" (Acts 16:16–18).' *JSNT* 36, pp. 51–73.

Trenchard, W. C. 1982. *Ben Sira's View of Women. A Literary Analysis*. BJS 38. Chico, California: Scholars Press.

Trigger, B. 1978. *Time and Traditions. Essays in Archaeological Interpretation*. Edinburgh University Press.

Trocmé, E. 1957. *Le 'livre des Actes' et l'histoire*. Paris: Presses Universitaires de France.

Turner, E. G. 1936. 'Egypt and the Roman Empire: The ΔΕΚΑΠΡΩΤΟΙ.' *JEA* 32, pp. 7–19.

Tyson, J. B., ed. 1988. *Luke–Acts and the Jewish People. Eight Critical Perspectives*. Minneapolis: Augsburg.

Urbach, E. E. 1959. 'The Rabbinical Laws of Idolatry in the Second and Third Centuries in the Light of Archaeological and Historical Facts.' *IEJ* 9, pp. 149–65, 229–45.

Ussishkin, D. 1977. 'Two Lead Coffins from Cilicia.' *IEJ* 27, pp. 215–18.

van Bremen, R. 1983. 'Women and Wealth.' In *Images of Women in Antiquity*, eds. A. Cameron, A. Kuhrt, pp. 223–42. London: Croom Helm.

van Buren, A. W. 1908. 'Inscriptions from Asia Minor, Cyprus and the Cyrenaica.' *JHS* 28, pp. 180–201.

van der Horst, P. W. 1978. *The Sentences of Pseudo-Phocylides with Introduction and Commentary*. SVTP 4. Leiden: Brill.

1986. 'The Role of Women in the Testament of Job.' *NedTTs* 40, pp. 273–89.

1987. '"Lord, Help the Rabbi"': The Interpretation of SEG XXXI 1578b.' *JJS* 38, pp. 102–6.

1988. 'The Jews of Ancient Crete.' *JJS* 39, pp. 183–200.

1989. 'Jews and Christians in Aphrodisias in the Light of their Relations in Other Cities of Asia Minor.' *NedTTs* 43, pp. 106–21.

VanderKam, J. C. 1980. 'The Righteousness of Noah.' In *Ideal Figures in Ancient Judaism. Profiles and Paradigms*, eds. J. J. Collins, G. W. E. Nickelsburg, pp. 13–32. SBLSCS 12. Ann Arbor, Michigan: Scholars Press.

van Lennep, H. J. 1870. *Travels in Little Known Parts of Asia Minor*, vol. 1. London: John Murray.

Vattioni, F. 1977. 'A proposito di πρωτοπολίτης'. *SPap* 16, pp. 23–9.

Vermaseren, M. J. 1983. *Corpus Cultus Iovis Sabazii (CCIS), I. The Hands*. EPRO 100. Leiden: Brill.

von Aulock, H. S. 1964, 1968. *Sylloge Nummorum Graecorum, Deutschland, Sammlung von Aulock*. Heft 9, 18. Berlin: Mann.

von Gerkan, A. 1921. 'Eine Synagogue in Milet.' *ZNW* 20, pp. 177–81.

von Rad, G. 1966. *Deuteronomy*. OT Library. London: SCM.

Waelkens, M. 1979. 'Ateliers lapidaires en Phrygie.' In *Actes du VIIe congrès international d'épigraphie grecque et latine*, ed. D. M. Pippidi, pp. 105–28. Bucharest: Editura Academiei.

Walcot, P. 1984. 'Greek Attitudes Towards Women: The Mythological Evidence.' *G & R* 31, pp. 37–47.

Waldbaum. J. C. 1983. *Metalwork from Sardis: The Finds Through 1974*. Archaeological Exploration of Sardis Monograph 8. Cambridge, Massachusetts: Harvard University Press.

Walker, W. O. 1981. 'The Timothy–Titus Problem Reconsidered.' *ET* 92, pp. 231–5.

Wallis, G. 1974. 'Der Vollbürgereid in Deuteronomium 27, 15–26.' *HUCA* 45, pp. 47–63.

Wallis, R. T. 1972. *Neo-Platonism*. London: Duckworth.

Walton, C. S. 1929. 'Oriental Senators in the Service of Rome.' JRS 19, pp. 38–66.

Wardy, B. 1979. 'Jewish Religion in Pagan Literature during the Late Republic and Early Empire.' *ANRW* II, 19.1, pp. 592–644.

Watson, A., Mommsen, T., & Krueger, P. 1985. *The Digest of Justinian*. 4 vols. Philadelphia: University of Pennsylvania Press.

Weatherly, J. A. 1989. 'The Jews in Luke–Acts.' *Tyndale Bulletin* 40, pp. 107–17.

Weber, G. 1900. 'Funde.' *AM* 25, pp. 452–70.

References 299

Weber, M. 1952. *Ancient Judaism*. New York: Free Press.
Wegner, J. R. 1982. 'The Image of Woman in Philo.' In *SBL 1982 Seminar Papers*, ed. K. H. Richards, pp. 551–63. Chico, California: Scholars Press.
Weinfeld, M. 1972. *Deuteronomy and the Deuteronomic School*. Oxford: Clarendon Press.
Weinreich, O. 1912. 'ΘΕΟΙ ΕΠΗΚΟΟΙ.' *AM* 37, pp. 1–68.
Welles, C. B. 1934. *Royal Correspondence in the Hellenistic Period. A Study in Greek Epigraphy*. New Haven: Yale University Press.
1962. 'Hellenistic Tarsus.' *MUSJ* 38, pp. 43–75.
Werner, E. 1966. 'Melito of Sardis, The First Poet of Deicide.' *HUCA* 37, pp. 191–210.
White, M. L. 1987. 'The Delos Synagogue Revisited. Recent Fieldwork in the Graeco-Roman Diaspora.' *HTR* 80, pp. 133–60.
Whittaker, M. 1984. *Jews and Christians: Graeco-Roman Views*. Cambridge Commentaries on Writings of the Jewish and Christian World 200BC to AD 200, 6. Cambridge University Press.
Widengren, G. 1961. 'Synkretistische Religionen.' In *Religionsgeschichte des Orients in der Zeit der Weltreligionen*, ed. B. Spuler, pp. 43–82. Handbuch der Orientalistik I.8.2. Leiden: Brill.
Wiegand, T. 1911. 'Inschriften aus der Levante II.' *AM* 36, pp. 287–301.
Wiegand, T., & Schrader, H. 1904. *Priene. Ergebnisse der Ausgrabungen und Untersuchungen in den Jahren 1895–1898*. Königliche Museen zu Berlin. Berlin: Georg Reimer.
Wilcken, U. 1927. *Urkunden der Ptolemäerzeit I*. Berlin und Leipzig: Walter de Gruyter.
Wilcox, M. 1981. 'The "God-Fearers" in Acts – A Reconsideration.' *JSNT* 13, pp. 102–22.
Wilhelm, A. 1974. 'Ein Brief Antiochus III.' In *Kleine Schriften, Abteilung I: Akademieschriften zur griechischen Inschriftenkunde (1895–1951)*, Teil 2, pp. 39–56. Leipzig: Zentralantiquariat der Deutschen Demokratischen Republik.
Wilken, R. L. 1971. *Judaism and the Early Christian Mind. A Study of Cyril of Alexandria's Exegesis and Theology*. New Haven: Yale University Press.
1976. 'Melito, the Jewish Community at Sardis and the Sacrifice of Isaac.' *TS* 37, pp. 53–69.
1980. 'The Jews and Christian Apologetics after Theodosius I *Cunctos Populos*'. *HTR* 73, pp. 451–71.
1983. *John Chrysostom and the Jews. Rhetoric and Reality in the late 4th Century*. Berkeley: University of California Press.
Williams, J. G. 1982. *Women Recounted: Narrative Thinking and the God of Israel*. Bible and Literature Series 6. Sheffield: Almond Press.
Williams, M. H. 1988. '"Θεοσεβὴς γὰρ ἦν" – The Jewish Tendencies of Poppaea Sabina.' *JTS* 39, pp. 97–111.
Willrich, H. 1924. *Urkundenfälschung in der hellenistisch-jüdischen Literatur*. Göttingen: Vandenhoeck und Ruprecht.
Wilson, R. McL. 1958. *The Gnostic Problem. A Study of the Relations between Hellenistic Judaism and the Gnostic Heresy*. London: Mowbray.

Wilson, S. G. 1986. *Anti-Judaism in Early Christianity. Vol. 2. Separation and Polemic.* Studies in Christianity and Judaism 2. Waterloo: Wilfrid Laurier University Press.

Windisch, H. 1930. *Die Katholischen Briefe.* Second edn. HNT 15. Tübingen: J. C. B. Mohr (Paul Siebeck).

Winter, J. G., ed. 1936. *Papyri in the University of Michigan Collection, Vol. III, Miscellaneous Papyri.* Ann Arbor: University of Michigan Press.

Wischmeyer, W. 1980. 'Die Aberkiosinschrift als Grabepigramm.' *JAC* 23, pp. 22–47.

Wischnitzer, R. 1964. *The Architecture of the European Synagogue.* Philadelphia: Jewish Publication Society of America.

Wolfson, H. A. 1948. *Philo.* 2 vols. Revised edn. Cambridge, Massachusetts: Harvard University Press.

Wolters, P. 1906. '' Ἀρχιατρὸς τὸ δ'.' *JÖAI* 9, pp. 295–7.

Woodhead, A.G. 1981. *The Study of Greek Inscriptions.* Second edn. Cambridge University Press.

Wright, G. E. 1971. 'What Archaeology Can and Cannot Do.' *BA* 34, pp. 70–6.

Zeitlin, S. 1951–2. 'The Last Supper as an Ordinary Meal in the Fourth Gospel.' *JQR* 42, pp. 251–60.

1964–5. 'The Edict of Augustus Caesar in Relation to the Judaeans of Asia.' *JQR* 55, pp. 160–3.

1974. 'Proselytes and Proselytism during the Second Commonwealth and the Early Tannaitic Period.' In *Solomon Zeitlin's Studies in the Early History of Judaism,* vol. 2, pp. 407–17. New York: Ktav.

Zgusta, L. 1964. *Kleinasiatische Personennamen.* Prague: Tschechoslowakischen Akademie der Wissenschaften.

Ziebarth, E. 1896. *Das griechische Vereinswesen.* Leipzig: Hirzel.

Ziesler, J. A. 1972. *The Meaning of Righteousness in Paul. A Linguistic and Theological Enquiry.* SNTSMS 20. Cambridge University Press.

Zingerle, J. 1923. 'Phrygisches Griechisch.' *Akademie der Wissenschaften in Wien, philosophisch-historische Klasse, Anzeiger* 1923, pp. 47–68.

AUTHOR INDEX

INDEX OF MAJOR SUBJECTS AND PLACES

Jesus, 30–2, 35
Jewish
 ablutions, 41, 55–7, 162
 associations, 44–5, 79–81, 171,
  175, 177–8, 261
 burial society, 79–81, 177–8, 220
 cemeteries, 215, 227
 'charter', 8–10, 171
 Christian relations, 43, 53–4,
  101–3, 189, 210, 219
 Christians, 21, 25, 28–9, 203–4
 festivals, 13, 30–1, 101–2, 178–80,
  199, 250
 food laws, 17–18, 34, 39, 164, 187,
  199
 identity, 12–19, 25, 27, 31, 34–5,
  39, 45, 50, 56–7, 84, 86, 94,
  102–3, 144, 177–8, 182–3, 186–9
 inscriptions, criteria for determining
  religious provenance, 133, 146,
  213
 law, 6, 18–19, 21, 23, 25–7, 30, 35,
  42, 51, 66, 100–1, 107–8, 148–9,
  153–4, 187, 200, 203, 250
 liturgy, 49, 51, 72–3, 82, 84, 187,
  217
 opposition to Christians, 20–2, 24,
  26–7, 29–32, 35, 150, 184,
  200–1, 205
 privileges, 7–19, 32–4, 38–9, 57,
  168–9, 183–5, 194, 205–6
 War (66–70 CE), 32–3, 165–6, 205
Jewish communities
 continuity in, 34–5, 52–3, 165–6
 honouring Gentiles, 44, 176, 260
 hostility towards, 11–12, 25, 27, 31,
  36, 54, 183–4, 189, 195
 importance of local factors, 43, 50,
  56–7, 126, 188
 influenced by environment, 44–5,
  49–50, 60–1, 68, 78–81, 83–4,
  87, 94–5, 110, 125–6, 144, 165,
  177–9, 185–6, 238
 influence with Gentiles, 22, 27–9,
  31–2, 35–6, 39, 49, 52–3, 57,
  61–5, 69, 73–4, 84, 87, 91, 94,
  103, 131–3, 137–40, 142, 164,
  176, 179, 194, 198–9, 222, 240–4
 introverted?, 186–8

 involved in city life, 32, 46–8, 57,
  61–5, 78, 81–3, 93–4, 159, 165,
  173–83, 186, 209–10, 251, 259, 263
 significant element in city, 31–2,
 35–6, 47, 49, 52–4, 65, 80, 83, 93–4,
  100–1, 103, 154, 158–9, 162, 165,
  174–6, 179–80, 184, 186
 vitality of, 53–4, 57, 102, 182, 189
Jews
 and apostasy, 23, 59, 175, 212, 222,
  245–6, 263
 and local citizenship, 46, 167–75,
  180–1, 184, 255–8
 and military service, 16–18, 169,
  172, 187
 and pagans sharing terms and
  images, 44–5, 49–50, 57, 143–4,
  176
 and pagan worship, 31, 47, 172,
  174, 180–3, 185–7, 194–5, 240, 262
 and pilgrimage, 25–7, 35, 203
 and Roman citizenship, 64–5, 83,
  169, 172–3, 184, 258
 and the gymnasium, 172, 176–7,
  180, 183, 261
 and the Imperial cult, 194, 206, 262
 and the odeum, 175, 260
 and the theatre, 24, 159–62, 175,
  180–1, 253–4, 260
 as city councillors and office
  holders, 46–8, 61–5, 78, 173–4,
  180, 209–10, 251, 259
 as soldiers, 6, 193, 197–8
 'at home' in the city, 45, 50, 81–4,
  175
 attracting others, 29, 31, 36, 53, 60,
  98, 101–3, 145–66, 179–80, 186,
  189
 economic position of, 42, 46–8,
  52–3, 55, 61–8, 83, 106–8,
  110–11, 174, 181
 in Imperial provincial administration,
  48–9, 173
 integrated into city, 43, 49, 52, 57,
  84, 162, 173, 176–8, 180, 186–8
 making contribution to city, 81–3,
  93–4, 174–6, 184, 213, *see also*
  Jews as city councillors and office
  holders

diversity of attitudes towards in
  Jewish literary sources, 112–13,
  125
leaders in the synagogue, 104–13,
  126
wealth, 106–8, 110–11, 125, 229,
  231

Women's gallery in synagogue, 41,
  207, 232

Zeus Hypsistos, 127–8, 131, 134,
  142–3, 238–41
Zeuxis, 5, 38, 58, 86, 192–3, 222

INDEX OF BIBLICAL AND OTHER
ANCIENT SOURCES

DATE DUE
